THE GLORY DAYS OF CRICKET

THE GLORY DAYS OF CRICKET

The Extraordinary Story of Broadhalfpenny Down

Ashley Mote

Robson Books

First published in Great Britain in 1997 by Robson
Books Ltd, Bolsover House, 5–6 Clipstone Street,
London W1P 8LE

**British Library Cataloguing in Publication
Data**
A catalogue record for this title is available from the
British Library

ISBN 1 86105 111 5

Set in Century Schoolbook by FSH, Ltd., London
Printed in Great Britain by St Edmundsbury Press,
Bury St Edmunds

Contents

Dedication

Cricket demands more of team captains than almost any other sport. A captain can have the most profound influence on the course of a game, and directly determine the outcome, almost regardless of his resources and the strength of his side. It is the one sport where it is possible for a captain to fashion a win simply by out-thinking his opposite number.

Few cricketers completely understand the art of captaincy. Fewer still achieve its full potential on the field.

Three of these rare men have graced Broadhalfpenny Down over the last 250 years, and all of them were captains of Hambledon.

Richard Nyren
who made Broadhalfpenny Down what it was

Edward Whalley-Tooker
who rescued it from what it had become

Colin Barrett
who loved it for what it is now

This book is dedicated to their memory.

Acknowledgements

A great many people have contributed to this book. Many have given far more of their time than I had any right to expect, and they have sometimes gone to extraordinary lengths to check even the smallest of details.

I set out to write a book and became a detective. Throughout the research, and during the piecing together of hundreds of fragments of information spread over time and distance, I often felt involved more in the construction of a giant three-dimensional jigsaw than in authorship. Sometimes I was not even sure all the pieces existed. The support and practical help I received from so many people has been invaluable, and their encouragement and interest throughout has often made the difference between stopping and going on. I hope they can now feel that their efforts and help have been rewarded, at least in part. They will, I hope, also take comfort from my frank admission that this self-imposed labour of love would never have been completed without their reinforcements. I gladly acknowledge their invaluable contributions both to the contents and to the accuracy of this record of events on Broadhalfpenny Down over the last 250 years. This book is as much theirs as mine.

A number of individuals must be singled out for contributions far beyond the call of duty. I am particularly indebted to the MCC's curator, Stephen Green, who has given me the run of the library at Lord's over many months, answered countless questions, pointed me towards sources I might have missed, and been a thoroughly hospitable host to boot. Neil Jenkinson, archivist at the Hampshire County Cricket Club, has spent many hours dredging through files, old papers of the Hambledon club, and his own collection of books and records. He has also made numerous enquiries on my behalf, and offered suggestions and encouragement throughout. Cheryl Parry has been an indefatigable assistant, and has to be credited with the thoroughness and accuracy of the match information in chapter four. She has not only brought her years of experience as the Brigands scorer to bear on Hambledon's great matches, but has also undertaken many hours of painstaking research in the county records and archives at Winchester. Philip Yetmen freely applied his legal mind to the issue of property rights on and ownership of Broadhalfpenny Down with a thoroughness which would, I suspect, have cost a normal client a small fortune.

Much of the detail about the formation and development of the Brigands came from the tireless investigations of Bryan Burns, then secretary of the club. And two men who made themselves known to me following my appeal for information in the cricket press must also be singled out. Stephen Saunders and Podge Brodhurst – who modestly omitted to mention initially that he was Harry Altham's son-in-law – kept up a running supply of information, made a great many suggestions, and answered questions galore.

At one stage I found myself in the middle of what seemed like a distinguished Wykehamist mafia, with each of the following pointing in the direction of some or all of the others. In addition to Podge Brodhurst, Patrick Maclure, Hubert Doggart, Dr Roger Custance, the archivist at Winchester College, and Robin Chute, the estates bursar, all give considerable help from their different perspectives. And Sir Patrick Kingsley tried desperately hard to cast his mind back to a match played over sixty years ago.

Meanwhile the present master in charge of cricket at Winchester College, Chris Good, was horrified to learn that he had charge of the second-oldest cricket bat known still to exist. I apologise for shocking him.

The contribution from Hambledon was equally formidable. Bob Beagley, his sister Marion and Ida Barrett all spent many hours answering questions and supplying information. Both ladies helped generously in what were, for different reasons, less than easy circumstances, and to them I say a special thank-you. I gladly acknowledge that both their contributions took courage as well as time.

My unqualified thanks also go to a substantial number of other people who have helped in a variety of ways. I hope they will accept that their inclusion in a long list in no way diminishes my appreciation of their assistance. They are, in no particular order: Olivia Collet, whose knowledge of horses was invaluable; Norma Pearce and Patrick Shervington of the Lord's Taverners; Lorraine Delatour and David Neech of Sotheby's; Dr PC Millett, Ronald Taylor and Frank Laughton of Downing College; Richard Altham, John Goldsmith, Hugh Butler, Lord Saye and Sele, Mike Wren, Charles Fry, Peter Wadham and Peter Wheble, all of whom had relations involved with Broadhalfpenny Down one way or another; Peter Tomkins, Adrian Magrath, Robert Turner and John Barrett, all one-time playing members of the Hambledon Cricket Club; Maureen Wingham, for giving me access to Colin Barrett's voluminous collection of cricket memorabilia; George Bowyer of George Gale & Co; Louise Hodgkins, Steve Burridge and Dick Orders of the Bat and Ball Inn, and Phil Harris of the New Inn, Hambledon; Sir Roy Newman, Patrick Glennie, Peter Tuke, Bernard Marshall, Anthony Banes-Walker, Steve Sims, Richard Fortin and Andrew Forsyth, all of the Broadhalfpenny Brigands Cricket Club; David Barnard and Tony Pay of the Harting Cricket Club; Tony Robinson, Chris Box-Grainger and Geoffrey Coppinger of the Cricket Society; David Frith, then editor of *Wisden Cricket Monthly*; William Powell of the Cricket Memorabilia Society; Michael Gauntlett of Ian Dyer Cricket Books; Richard Madley of Phillips Auctioneers; SR Tomlinson of the Bodleian Library; John Gowen of the Stansted Park Foundation; David Sentance of the Los Angeles Krickets; Bob Murton, the oldest surviving member of the early Wadham Brothers' team; Jeff Hancock at The Oval; and Irving Rosenwater, Colin Ingleby-Mackenzie, Michael Silverman, Keith Evans, Dick Richards, Julian Cartwright, David Smith, Roy Kirby, Geoff Stevens, John Eddowes, David and Lindsay Brown, and Bill Dean from Australia. They all became involved, and helped. My thanks to every one.

It seemed to me at an early stage in my researches that it would be particularly interesting, and useful, to find a benchmark by which to judge in today's terms the true value of the stakes put up by patrons for the great matches during the glory days. Such a benchmark would also provide a modern value of the costs incurred by spectators and players. Eventually I found what I was looking for. I am indebted to the work and advice of Robert Pretcher, an American financial historian and analyst, who has plotted the real change in the buying power of money back to the South Sea Bubble of 1720. The consequences of his findings when applied to the figures we have about the cost of bats, liquor and gate charges are shown in the appropriate places, and tally with satisfying closeness to the cost of many of those items today. It is only when we extrapolate his findings to the stake moneys put up for many of the great matches that the horrific extravagance of the patrons of cricket in the late eighteenth century becomes startlingly clear. Incredible though the value of those stakes may now seem when measured against the financial realities of today, Mr Pretcher's painstaking work suggests that they are broadly valid. If nothing else, they illuminate a dark corner of the motivation behind many of the great matches.

Finally, a number of other individuals must be singled out. Chris Bazalgette has contributed to the narrative with information, suggestions and, perhaps to the astonishment of his colleagues but not to him, with his personal cricketing achievements on Broadhalfpenny Down. Richard Stilgoe has kindly given permission for the reproduction of his poem 'It All Began At Hambledon'. My old friend Chris Turner, with typical generosity, brought an architect's perspective to a cricket-lover's problem, and re-visualized the lodge from little more than a tiny indistinct sketch, historical knowledge and a deep understanding of the game. Christine Pardoe and her husband Mike lavished hospitality and the run of her grandfather's papers in equal measure. Colin Ingleby-Mackenzie kindly allowed himself to get involved again towards the end and wrote a generous foreword. Both he and the talented Philip Hodkin, who so painstakingly recreated some of the more memorable images from pre-camera days, deserve special acknowledgement; as do the entire editorial team at Robson Books, so ably led by Kate Mills. To them all, a heartfelt thank-you.

But perhaps the real heroes of the production of this book are the stalwarts who rashly agreed – offered in some cases – to read the first and subsequent drafts. Without the critical eyes, knowledge, and astounding attention to detail they have all contributed, this book would be a mere shadow of what it is. Clive Barnett, Hubert Doggart, Pauline Taylor, Alan Ground, Douglas Hudson and Jim Lyons have my unqualified thanks, as do Bob Beagley, Bryan Burns and Glenn Duggan, who read specific sections. My wife Nicky, as fierce a critic of the written word as I have ever encountered, has not only made the book more readable, but has also put up with many months of living with a single-issue husband.

What can I say? To you all – thank you. I trust the final volume meets with your approval, gives you some pleasure, and is a worthy testament to our collective efforts. Any mistakes still remaining are mine alone. Any credit can be enjoyed collectively.

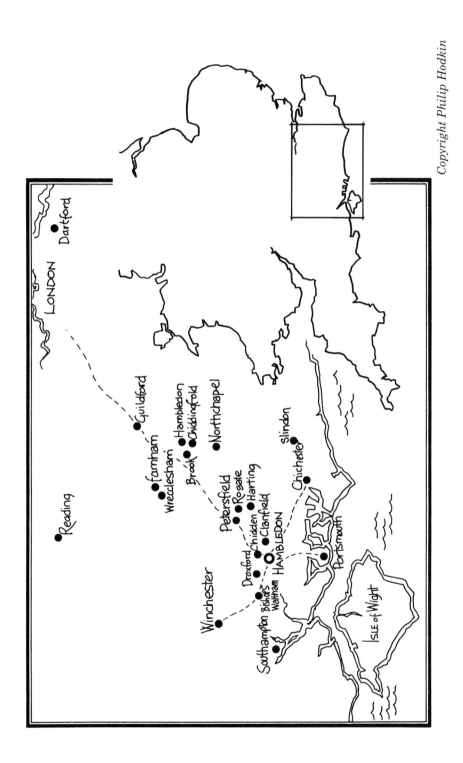

Foreword

By Colin Ingleby-Mackenzie
President, Marylebone Cricket Club 1997
Captain, Hampshire County Cricket Club 1958-65

Richard Nyren, Hambledon's rumbustious captain throughout the glory days, was a born leader. He set an example for us all to follow. He loved his cricket, and played for fun, and after reading this excellent book I feel we had a number of characteristics in common.

I am very lucky to have combined being Hampshire Captain and President of MCC. In both capacities I am happy to sing the praises of Hambledon. But it is ironical that it was Thomas Lord's patron and one of the founders of MCC, Lord Winchelsea, who did much to undermine the supremacy of the great club Hambledon, even while he was its President.

I am thrilled to learn from Ashley Mote's most interesting and readable book that my great friend and mentor, Harry Altham, did so much to restore and maintain the fortunes of Broadhalfpenny Down, the club's original ground.

All cricket lovers are in debt to Ashley Mote for passing on his knowledge and well-researched history of this greatest early centre of the game.

Preparing the Ground

Broadhalfpenny Down is not where cricket started. But it is where the game grew up.

The misconception that it is the place where cricket started is one of the quaintly enduring myths in English sporting history. For myth it is.

Over the years, many thousands of visitors to Broadhalfpenny Down have asked those of us who play there, 'Is this where cricket started?' The words are almost always the same, so entrenched in the cricketing public's mind is this particular, if misguided, notion.

Happily, the answer is more romantic and intriguing than a simple negative. For what happened on this otherwise un-remarkable piece of Hampshire downland fires the imagination sometimes to the point of disbelief at the great events that took place here over 200 years ago.

For if this is not where cricket started, it is most certainly the game's spiritual home, fortified by a popular misconception which is now so entrenched that nothing will shift it. And while the comforting accuracy of facts may not be on its side, there are plenty of other reasons why Broadhalfpenny Down deserves its unique place in English sporting history. It is the place where a simple country pastime finally left its origins behind and showed the first unmistakable signs of becoming a national sport. It is the place where the crude techniques of the first players were discarded for subtler skills. It is the place where enthusiastic amateurs became professional sportsmen.

In the years between the mid 1750s and late 1780s, Broadhalfpenny Down became the olympic stadium of its time. It staged many of the biggest matches, it fielded the most famous team, and that team was the stuff of legends. Originally, they were just a collection of humble country folk, but they, and the players who joined them, could and did beat everybody in sight. Time and again, the whole of Hampshire and beyond would metaphorically hold its collective breath as 'little' Hambledon took on the might of 'all' England. And time and again they won. The crowds loved it, and time and again they came back for more. This was David and Goliath stuff, and it has always appealed to the English psyche. There had been better cricket grounds, grander teams and more exciting matches long before Hambledon's fame spread far beyond Broadhalfpenny Down. But the contests on this unprepossessing stretch of Hampshire turf saw sporting contests of epic proportions and, most importantly, they were the first to become so visible to the rest of the world.

After it was all over, but still within living memory, they were captured for all time when John Nyren, the son of the club captain, wrote his reminiscences so eloquently that he bequeathed permanence to what he called 'the glory days'. The legend of Broadhalfpenny Down was born and, by definition, legends are for ever. This

John Nyren as a young man. (Reproduced by kind permission of the MCC/the Bat and Ball)

humble stretch of downland had inspired John Nyren to write the first book in the now vast and distinguished library of cricket literature. It was a masterpiece. On this specific point, Broadhalfpenny Down stands supreme.

And there is more. Mighty changes in the game were pioneered on Broadhalfpenny Down. They flowed from the genius of the club's captain, Richard Nyren, the first man to think deeply about the game and how it could be played better, and who combined that remarkable talent with an even rarer one – an extraordinary ability to lead and inspire the players around him. It was here on Broadhalfpenny Down that Richard Nyren first had the vision and skill to devise and develop length bowling, a technique later perfected by David Harris. It was here that John Small senior, followed by William (Silver Billy) Beldham, had the vision and skill to counter it with straight bats and fast footwork. These men of Hambledon adopted a thoroughly professional approach

Probable birthplace of Richard Nyren, as it is today. The Newland/Nyren families lived in The Grange, Slindon, Sussex, during the early part of the 18th century. Uncle Richard Newland, the England captain at the time, probably had his recently married sister's family living under the same roof when young Richard was born. The Georgian facade to the building was added later, of course.

towards improving their game. Their striving for perfection never ceased. But while they may have embarked on an endless pursuit of advantage over their opponents, what they discovered was a fundamentally better game.

So much of the credit for this most important of achievements properly belongs to the club captain. Leading by example, Richard Nyren constantly encouraged his players to exercise their minds and analyse the basics of the game as it was then played. By chance, these were men with an independent turn of mind, and they readily responded to his daring. Like the greatest players of any sport at any time, they came to ignore the current norms, and revealed a talent, confidence and flair which eventually rewrote what then passed for the coaching manuals. They found the skill and conviction to persevere with the new ideas they gradually developed until, ultimately, this handful of Hambledon cricketers perfected totally new methods and techniques which were far removed from the original. They went on to produce performances of breathtaking originality, moments of magic which inspired lyrical praise, and left treasured memories in the minds of all those lucky enough to witness them. In the process, they had inadvertently unveiled an altogether more demanding, subtle, elegant and satisfying game.

They also discovered that they could earn their living playing cricket. The 'professionalism' which the Hambledon players displayed in developing the techniques of the game eventually translated into professionalism in the game itself. Professional players had been around in small numbers since the 1720s, but Hambledon produced cricket's first fully professional team and Broadhalfpenny Down was the home of cricket's first fully professional club.

A two-innings game, usually between eleven players on each side, was the well-established norm for virtually all important matches by the mid-eighteenth century. But the arrangements for these 'great' matches, as they were called, developed on Broadhalfpenny Down and have since become the norm in the modern first-class game. The members had their own pavilion – although it was then called the lodge. The teams each had their own (tented) changing-rooms. The president and committee members had their own hospitality tents. The press and the bookmakers were accommodated separately. And there were catering and viewing facilities all around the ground for the general public. The style in which these great matches were conducted on Broadhalfpenny Down over 200 years ago simply evolved to cope with demand and the social niceties of the period. But the Hambledon club started a tradition which is still strictly observed in the first-class game today.

During the course of this huge and unplanned revolution in the game, the Hambledon club became the most powerful in the land and it simultaneously found itself adopting the mantle of responsibility for the laws of cricket. Increasingly, in the years leading up to the founding of the MCC in 1787, this little country village governed the sport, and made all the important decisions about the way the game was played.

All of which are yet more reasons why Broadhalfpenny Down is unique. That is why so many people make the pilgrimage to see it, why cricketers today love to play on it, and why this ground will forever be cricket's spiritual home. It may have taken centuries for the game of cricket to germinate; but its first full flowering took about thirty-five years. And it happened on Broadhalfpenny Down.

Nowadays we do not see twenty thousand people at a match, but they came in those numbers in the 1770s and 80s. It is difficult to imagine how the club would have coped with the sheer logistics of parking thousands of wagons; handling thousands of horses, all needing water; supplying and serving ale and food from one tiny pub across the track to a veritable multitude. Such demands on resources would still stretch the capability of even the largest catering company today.

In those days the burly, shrewd and affable Richard Nyren was also the landlord of the Bat and Ball Inn. This was business on an enormous scale, and he appears to have thrived on it. A cynic today might dare to suggest that cricket was just his way of developing the business of an obscure pub in the middle of nowhere. But twentieth-century marketing techniques had no place in the unsophisticated world of rural Hampshire then. In any case, Richard Nyren was a cricket fanatic. He was the driving force behind this incredible club and its astonishing feats on Broadhalfpenny Down. During those early years, the huge crowds came for good reason.

Before the glory days, Broadhalfpenny Down was just another cricket field. For over 100 years afterwards, it was totally forgotten. When the legendary men who made Hambledon the most famous and powerful cricket club in the country first forsook it for nearby Windmill Down, and then left the area altogether, Broadhalfpenny Down was not even claimed for farming. It was left to grow thistles and docks. It provided rough grazing for sheep and horses, while the riders slaked their thirst at the Bat and Ball just across the road. Later in the nineteenth century, it was ploughed up and used to grow corn. The remains of the old lodge (pavilion), on the far side of the ground, were first vandalized, then allowed to disintegrate, and finally the remnants were removed to make way for the plough. For much of the next hundred years, Broadhalfpenny Down was just a ploughed field. The magic was gone. Only the memories were left. But what memories they were, and still are to this day.

From this distance in time, it is quite impossible to determine exactly how and where cricket started. There have even been tongue-in-cheek suggestions that it started half a million years ago since a number of what looked like prehistoric cricket balls were discovered in West Sussex, beside the bones of an Ancient Briton. He was certainly in the right place. Others, only marginally more serious, have suggested that cricket started in France, of all places. It is certainly true that the French were playing a game with a club and a ball by the fifteenth century. They called it *criquet*. This might be a forerunner of croquet or stool-ball, depending on whether the truth lies in the name or the method of play. The curious idea that the French invented cricket might also have gained some credence at one time from the anglicizing of the French words *non pair*, meaning 'man without equal', or 'arbitrator', which became the word 'umpire'. However, there is little else to justify these odd claims. We can safely ignore them.

Other theories put the origin of the game in Iceland – would you believe – and Flanders. The old Flemish word *krik* meant stick. From the twelfth century the Flemish played a game with a ball and a crooked stick. Did they export both their game and their products when Flemish weavers first settled in Kent? In which case it is but a small step to the long-held view that the game of cricket first evolved among the shepherd boys on the Weald of Kent. This was anything up to 500 years earlier than the pinnacles of achievement by the Hambledon club in the late 1700s.

Their invention was the product of boredom. Perhaps inspired by their new Flemish neighbours, perhaps not, did these young shepherds start throwing stones at the 'wickets', or gates, through which the sheep passed into their pens? On either side was a 'stump', and over the top was a removable 'bail' which otherwise held the gate square and steady. The wicket gate was slightly wider than a sheep. Even today, Australian sheep-farmers still refer to the crosspiece, or slip-rail, over their wicket gates as the 'bail'.

It is not difficult to imagine, again perhaps from boredom, a game developing between two boys. One of them tries to throw a missile through the wicket gate, or at a stump or bail. He could equally have been throwing his missile at a tree stump. His companion uses the nearest thing to hand – his shepherd's crick, or crook – to fend the missile away. It is easy to see how one thing could lead to another, how more boys might join in, how the need for some way of measuring the success of the boy 'batting' led to the idea of running a fixed distance while the 'ball' was retrieved. A simple ball of tree-bark wound with string quickly replaced the stone, for obvious reasons. Later, local cobblers assembled balls from cork cores inside wool combings, all stuffed into outer cases made of leather. From such simple beginnings, a slow process of evolution went on over many decades, centuries even, and still only as a means of amusement and to pass the time. Ultimately, of course, as we all now know, a structured game emerged – a contest between two sides playing under agreed rules. Yet that was a huge leap forward. It must have taken many lifetimes. As Harry Altham pointed out in his masterly book, *A History of Cricket*, the game 'just growed'.

Supposing something like this sequence of events did occur, it is already plain to see where all the technical terms came from. Added to which, Dr Johnson had no doubts, in his first dictionary of the English language, that the Saxon word 'crick', variously spelt 'cryce', 'creag' or 'cricce', meant 'stick'. Modern scholars dispute much of Johnson's original work, but there can be little doubt that this simple, ancient word became the root of the game's name, and reveals cricket's true origins. This link also reminds us that cricket is, and always has been, a peculiarly Anglo-Saxon game. Centuries later it is still true that the successful import of cricket by other countries and cultures is invariably via deep links with the Anglo-Saxon world.

Exactly when this long period of primary germination occurred is anybody's guess. We could even be back in the Dark Ages. Not that it matters that much. All we need to know is that it occurred before the thirteenth century, and that this innocent game slowly spread itself among the farming communities along the South Downs, across Sussex and Surrey, and into Hampshire. It is likely that the hop-growers of the region played an important part in the migration of the game at this time. They were more itinerant than the shepherds, and their hop fairs were a regular feature of rural life, as well as an important opportunity for the growers to meet, trade and discuss their problems.

A thirteenth-century wall painting in Cocking Church, on the edge of the South Downs in Sussex, is claimed to depict two shepherds carrying what appear to be cricket bats. It is possible that these slightly curved and shaped sticks were intended for play rather than work. However, close inspection suggests that they were little more than shepherd's crooks. A Decretal of Pope Gregory IX from about 1230 is more promising. This apparently depicts an older man demonstrating a stroke to a young man holding a bat and ball. Was this the first recorded coaching lesson? Either way, by the beginning of the fourteenth century there is solid evidence to show that this fascinating game was now a recognized part of life in southern England. It may have started as just a simple country pastime invented by shepherd boys to amuse themselves on summer afternoons. But it had by then become more widely known and practised, even by royalty. The royal household budget in 1300 included money allocated for costs incurred by Prince Edward, son of Edward I, when playing cricket.

A manuscript in the Bodleian Library, Oxford, dated 1344 and quoted by the Rev. James Pycroft in his book *The Cricket Field*, shows a woman in the act of throwing what looks like a cricket ball at a man holding a straight bat. Other figures, of both sexes, stand about in attitudes which suggest their being ready to catch or stop the ball after it has been struck.

In the sixteenth century Henry VIII had cricket outlawed. Along with many other 'new' sports, cricket was banned in an attempt to force men back to archery, which skill had become 'sore decayed' and on which the defence of the realm rested. This particular act remained on the statute book until 1845, although it was widely ignored for many generations. However, it means that everything that happened on Broadhalfpenny Down during the glory days and, for that matter, at Lord's in its early years, was technically illegal.

About the year 1550, one John Derrick attended the Free School in Guildford, Surrey. In 1598 he confirmed that he had,

This illumination from a manuscript in the Bodleian Library, Oxford, is dated 1344. The lady must have bowled a mean outswinger to justify a slip cordon of four, although the manner in which the monk is holding his bat suggests that he was not a good player of fast bowling.
(Copyright Bodleian Library, Oxford)

This document refers to a certain John Derrick who had been at the Free School, Guildford, about 1550, when he had been involved in 'creckett and other plaies'.
(Reproduced by kind permission of the MCC)

The Rev. James Pycroft, author of The Cricket Field. *(Reproduced by kind permission of the MCC)*

while there, been involved in 'creckett and other plaies'. A copy of the documentary proof is to be found today on the stairwell behind the Long Room at Lord's. By 1560, the Duke firm of ball-makers was already in existence. Over the next 200 years or so, we find numerous references to cricket in the literature of the time, many of them in poetical works. Pycroft's book documents several of them. One, in particular, is revealing. In 1598, Stow's *Survey of London* lists cricket as an amusement of the lower classes. It reads: 'The modern sports of the citizens, *besides drinking(!)* [Pycroft's emphasis] are cock-fighting, bowling upon greens....The lower classes divert themselves at foot-ball, wrestling, cudgels, ninepins, shovel-board, cricket....' So, at that time, cricket was not in illustrious company, it seems, and no doubt the gentry stayed well clear. But how that was to change over the years ahead.

That same year, 1598, the word cricket was translated in an English/Italian dictionary, and thirteen years later we find it again, this time translated in an English/ French dictionary.

By this time, the Sevenoaks club in Kent already boasted a powerful and famous cricket team. It included the great-great-grandfather of a future key figure in the game, Sir Horace Mann, of whom more later. But by 1622 the sport was already beginning to cause social trouble. At Goodwood in Sussex, a group of parishioners were arraigned before the local magistrate for playing cricket in a nearby churchyard on a Sunday. (Contemporary records fail to explain how they managed to set up a pitch with so many obstructions in the way.) While great issue was made of the fact that this game represented a desecration of the Sabbath, the chief complaint was about the damage to the church windows and the risk that a little child might 'have her braynes beaten out with a cricket batte'. It must have been comforting to the accused to know that the local authorities at least had their priorities right. The good burghers of Maidstone in Kent were having more persistent trouble. Their rector was making regular complaints of cricket being played on the Lord's Day throughout the 1630s and 1640s. He clearly had great difficulty stopping it.

About this time, in 1638 to be precise, the first cricket ground of importance came into being. It was presented to the Honourable Artillery Company (HAC), at Finsbury Square, London. The Artillery Ground, as it was known, also became the home ground for London and Middlesex sides for over 100 years. Desmond Eagar, that stalwart of Hampshire cricket for so many years, described the Artillery Ground as cricket's first Mecca, and it was here, in 1744, that the members took the initiative and called a meeting of the leading clubs of the day to draw up the first laws of the game.

Back in 1647, the boys of Winchester College were playing the game. They were reported to have staged a game on St Catherine's Hill. Seven years later, at Eltham in Kent, the churchwardens and overseers of the parish recorded a curious incident in the parish accounts of that year. During the summer, five gentlemen of the parish were each fined two shillings for the 'misdemeanour' of playing cricket on the Lord's Day. One was only a lad, but his tender age apparently made no difference. Perhaps they should have tried playing at Goodwood or Maidstone instead.

That same year, 1654, a young man who rejoiced in the name Jasper Vinall was reportedly killed while playing cricket. He was about to catch the ball when he was struck a blow with the bat as the batsman tried to prevent his dismissal. Clearly the laws of the game had not yet addressed this hazard and poor Master Vinall paid a terrible price for the omission.

Our next piece of evidence about the game in the days before Hambledon again comes from Winchester. In 1656, Thomas

Ken was a schoolboy at Winchester College, an institution which was to play an important part in the story of Broadhalfpenny Down, and is still doing so today. But in that year, young master Ken was found 'attempting to wield a cricket bat'. Like the long line of distinguished churchmen who were to follow in his footsteps, the Bishop of Bath and Wells, as he became, had been drawn to the game of cricket in his youth, although the use of the phrase 'attempting to' suggests he lacked a natural flair for it. It also suggests he accidentally hit something more precious and more delicate than a cricket ball.

Or it might simply have been the fact that cricket was still strongly associated with dissolute behaviour. When Oliver Cromwell came to power in 1653, his enemies tried to blacken his name by suggesting that he had played cricket as a youth. As they were doing so, his own army officers were banning cricket in Ireland, and ordering the common hangman to burn all sticks and balls. Meanwhile, the defeated Cavaliers had retired to their country estates and took to cricket, initially as a diversion. Being the sort of men they were, they soon saw its potential as a vehicle for gambling and it was not long before the early game's links with the seamier side of the betting world had been welded together. It was a connection that was to plague the game for generations to come.

The gentry were now much more openly and widely involved in the game. By 1666, John Churchill, later to become the first Duke of Marlborough, was playing cricket at Old St Paul's School. To the north of London, sufficient interest in the game justified the formation of a club at St Albans. Meanwhile, the Ram Inn at Smithfield in London was being rated for local tax purposes as having the facility to stage cricket matches. Even now, we are still 100 years from Broadhalfpenny Down.

The Royal Navy, no less, was involved in spreading the game around the globe at a very early stage in its history. We shall hear much more of the Royal Navy before our story is done, and the senior service makes an early appearance now. At the beginning of the summer of 1676, the Royal Navy was playing 'Krickett' at the eastern end of the Mediterranean.

Accompanied by the local English consul, they and forty local English residents from Antioch, in Turkey, rode some forty miles further inland, across the desert. They were making for a wide, lush valley near Aleppo, in what is now Syria, where they erected a tented pavilion and spent the day playing cricket. They were nothing if not well organized, it seems. But what three ships' companies of the Royal Navy were doing there in the first place, nobody now knows. The fact that they were playing cricket was, however, regarded as important enough to be logged by the chaplain with them, Henry Teonge. Perhaps we should not be too surprised; cricket was evidently much more fun than being on naval exercises.

The colonists in America were enjoying cricket by this time, too. Descendants of Puritan fathers they may have been, but cricket was now played regularly and with great gusto. So much so, in fact, that a certain William Byrd of Williamsburg, Virginia, must be forever acknowledged as the first overseas batsman to retire with a strained backside. The incident occurred in 1710.

Back in England, cricket's popularity was continuing to grow. The first reference to a match, as such, appeared in *The Foreign Post* on 17 July 1697. It referred to 'a great match' in Sussex for a stake of £55 (about £27,500 at today's values). Yet such games must already have been commonplace. Three years later, in 1700, matches were certainly popular enough to justify the advertising of forthcoming matches. *The Post Boy*, a London newspaper, carried an announcement in March that year of a series of five games to be staged on Clapham Common, starting on Easter Monday. A game this early in the season was not as odd as it might seem. The calendar had not yet been adjusted to bring the date into line with the seasons. In fact, by 1700, the seasons were permanently some two weeks ahead of the date. This problem was to be corrected half a century later.

Some twelve years after the game on Easter Monday there was more trouble with cricket on the Sabbath, this time at Maidenhead in Berkshire. It resulted in the dramatic death of two of the players and the unconsciousness for four days of another two. Contemporary accounts speak of cricket as 'a hellish pastime'. The victims were found 'with their faces looking black, their hair singed, their skin looking as if it was scorched, and stunk most nauseously of sulphur and brimstone'. A more detached view, with the hindsight of nearly 300 years, might lead us to consider that they had been struck by lightning – a catastrophe which has sadly befallen many other cricketers since. Yet another cricket death was recorded at Chailey in Sussex in 1737, when a certain John Boots was batting. He died after colliding with his partner as they were running a quick single.

It is at about this time that we find the first references to county cricket, or at least to teams taking the field under the umbrella of a county name. (We are still a long way from county cricket proper, let alone the concept of the first-class game.) The first of these contests appears to have occurred when Kent lost to a London XI by 21 runs in 1719. They were quickly followed by sides calling themselves Sussex, Middlesex and Surrey, all of which were active before 1730. Indeed, on 24 June 1728, Kent beat Sussex at an unknown venue. Just over a year later, on 5 September 1729 to be precise, 'a great cricket match' was played at Penshurst Place in Kent, between Kent and a team calling themselves 'Sussex, Surrey and Hampshire'. Both sides fielded eleven men, which was not always the case in those days. A stake of £105 was put up, equivalent to about £50,000 today. A crowd of 'some thousands' watched what was obviously an exciting match. The result is officially given as 'Kent gave in', as vivid a description of the outcome of a match as we could want, and much more revealing than mere numbers. Sadly, it is not a form of words to be found later in *Wisden* or anywhere else.

From about this time onwards, records of these 'great' matches come increasingly thick and fast. They were the precursors of the first-class game, played for serious money between teams calling themselves clubs or counties – often the same thing. In 1727, the Duke of Richmond and a Mr Alan Brodrick of Peper Harow, Surrey, agreed to play a twelve-a-side match on a pitch 23 yards long, under a set of rules which amounted to little more than an incomplete set of instructions. Meanwhile, more physical evidence of the pre-Hambledon days is to found at The Oval. Surrey County Cricket Club has in its possession a cricket bat – of the old style, of course – which once belonged to left-handed John Chitty, of Knaphill, near Woking. It is inscribed JC 1729, and weighs 2¼lb – less than half the weight of the great club made in 1771 and now preserved at Lord's.

As we have already seen, cricket was inextricably linked with gambling from its earliest beginnings. In those days, of course, betting on the outcome of contests of all kinds was a normal part of everyday life. Cricket was no exception, but its fast-growing popularity, and the size of the wagers and stake moneys put up, did cause considerable trouble and dissent at times. By 1748, at least one such dispute was having to be settled in the High Court in London, when the King's Bench happily ignored the statute of Henry VIII and described cricket as 'a very manly game, not bad in itself, but only in the ill use made of it by betting more than ten pounds on it; but that was bad and against the law'.

Views were also being expressed by now about the desirability, or otherwise, of the aristocracy and the gentry mixing freely with their social inferiors on the cricket field. One critical commentator, writing in *The British Champion* in 1743, reminded his readers that the game had reduced 'lords, gentlemen clergy and lawyers' to associate with butchers, cobblers and tinkers. This was unseemly and ridiculous, he wrote. It propagated idleness, he suggested, it was a shameless breach of the law (true) and was an open encouragement to gambling (also true). Fisticuffs and broken heads were nowadays not unusual as a result of disputes on the cricket field. However, gentlemen of distinction fought out their cricket quarrels, as they did when their honour was in doubt, with duelling pistols. So cricket was breaking down social structures, and it was encouraging violence on the streets. Both consequences were frowned on by the rest of society. But worse was to come. In 1746, when Kent beat England by a single run, Lord John Sackville was on the winning side. It was captained by his gardener. This was horrifyingly unacceptable, and met with seriously mixed opinions. This was not the way things should be. The players knew differently, of course, even if the attitudes of the rest of the world were still far behind. With a few hardened and vocal exceptions, they were soon to catch up.

The first first-class game of which we have any detailed knowledge occurred on the Artillery Ground in Finsbury Square, London, on 18 June 1744. Kent beat England by one wicket. England scored 39 and 57, Kent scored 53 and 44 for 9. The result, in hindsight, turned on one sensational moment. Richard Newland, the England captain, who was regarded at the time as the best batsman in the country, was going well in England's second innings, and they were building up a good score. Then, when he had scored 15, Newland attempted a huge hit into the outfield. His fears of being caught as he saw Lord John Sackville struggling to get under it were captured later by James Dance, writing under the pseudonym James Love. He was an eye-witness at the match, and committed the whole of it to verse. Of this deciding moment, he wrote:

> O mighty Jove, and all ye powers above
> Let my regarded prayer your pity move!
> Grant me but this. Whatever youth shall dare
> Snatch at the prize, descending thro' the air
> Lay him extended on the grassy plain
> And make his bold ambitious effort vain.

Jove was having none of it. But he does seem to have enjoyed a little mischief at Newland's expense. Lord John did indeed slip and spread-eagled himself on the ground in his efforts to hold the ball – but hold it he did, in one hand and with his arm outstretched. It was as spectacular a catch as anybody had seen, and it effectively won the match for Kent. It was much talked of for many years. Lord John Sackville eventually became the second Duke of Dorset. Within a year of that remarkable catch, a nephew was born who inherited his love of cricket and, in 1769, his title as well. The third Duke of Dorset became a vigorous patron of the game, as well as a fine player. He was an active supporter of Hambledon during the glory days, and of the MCC later.

Richard Newland is, himself, an important figure in our story, for a far more direct reason than his involvement in the first recorded first-class game: he was Richard Nyren's uncle. They both lived in Slindon, Sussex, and it was Richard Newland who taught his young nephew to play cricket, without which the heroics on Broadhalfpenny Down might never have happened.

These two cricketing nephews of cricketing uncles were to find themselves even more closely locked together through cricket than their uncles had been. They enjoyed a long and successful association throughout the glory days on Broadhalfpenny Down, yet it was that same third Duke of Dorset who was eventually to persuade Nyren and the Hambledon club to leave Broadhalfpenny Down. Uncle had dismissed uncle, and now nephew dismissed nephew. Two profoundly different events, certainly, but both brought great disappointment in their different ways to the Newland/Nyren family. It is curious how such coincidences weave their way through such stories as ours. There will be many others before we are done.

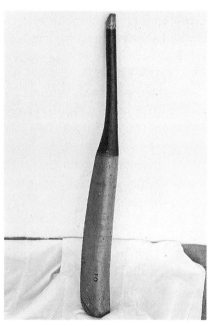

The first specific reference to the Hambledon club comes from a bat at Winchester College, to which is attached a note, written in 1931, stating that the club was probably founded in about 1742. The bat itself was the property of John

John Osmond Miles's bat, questionably dated 1742 but unquestionably from that era, and now owned by Winchester College.

Osmond Miles, who, according to his descendants, used it 'in the first match played on Broadhalfpenny Down by the Hambledon club'. None of which clarifies the relationship, if there was one, with the team which reportedly then played at Broadhalfpenny Down under the name of Squire Land's Club. (Land's name is often misspelled Lamb in early records.) Squire Land was a local landowner, who took his position in local society seriously. That he should raise a village cricket team is entirely in keeping with his place in the community, and his team pre-dated the Hambledon club by some years. The one almost certainly sired the other, particularly bearing in mind the fact that the Hambledon club was still being referred to as Squire Land's club as late as 1764.

That was some years after the first reference to the Hambledon club as such, which appeared in the press in 1756, when a match was reported on Broadhalfpenny Down against Dartford, Kent. A list of players first appeared ten years later. Reports of matches at Broadhalfpenny Down occur with increasing frequency from 1764 onwards, and by 1766 the

Miles's bat, a ball claimed to be contemporary, and the notes which accompanied the gift of these items to Winchester College in 1931.

press were reporting that Hambledon, playing as 'Hampshire', had beaten Sussex after trailing so badly on the first innings that odds of 40–1 were available against a local win. In those days, Hampshire and Hambledon were one and the same side, and they were rapidly establishing themselves as the strongest in the land. Over the next few years they played and beat Surrey, Sussex and Kent many times. The victories over Kent were of particular significance, since that county had as early as 1739 enjoyed the status of 'the unconquerable county'. However, at least one of Kent's early matches against England had been abandoned in uproar when disputes could not be resolved. Such outcomes were not unusual.

But we are getting ahead of ourselves. We must go back to 1750 or thereabouts, shortly before the young Richard Nyren took over the tiny inn which had already stood at Broadhalfpenny Down for some twenty years, and which was then known – with good reason – as 'The Hutt'. He was to change more than its name.

When he arrived, in the middle of the eighteenth century, and we find these first references to the Hambledon club at Broadhalfpenny Down, cricket was already much more than a country pastime. It was also spreading with some vigour to other parts of England. There were signs of the game producing its first heroes, and people regularly went in considerable numbers to watch cricket, as well as to play. These important developments set the stage for an acceleration of the maturing process, so that, by the end of the eighteenth century, the game and its place in English life were set firm. In a little over fifty years it had been transformed from a country amusement to the national game we know today. What happened on Broadhalfpenny Down was a catalyst. Not the only catalyst, but certainly the most talked about, and the most impressive from this distance.

Spanning some thirty-five of those years, two great teams successively represented Hambledon on Broadhalfpenny Down. They were strong enough and consistent enough to notch up a long succession of wins which made them, their club and their ground everlastingly famous. The cusp between these two sides occurred quite dramatically, during the early to mid-1780s. Up to that time, the 'old' team had established itself as the strongest in Hampshire, well able to beat sides from other counties. It had long attracted the interest and attention of both patrons and great players from further afield. This process appears to have accelerated once the ground at Windmill Down was in use, when the proportion of players from outside the village increased noticeably. But we must not forget that, in the normal course of events over a period of many years, players would have come and gone. Individuals would have good years and bad ones. Players suffered injuries and had to stop playing for a few weeks or months. Rarely did exactly the same side play in a succession of matches. In any case, the original side's abilities were eventually and understandably going to fall into decline, the unavoidable result of age eroding fleetness of foot and quickness of eye. So over that entire period, literally dozens of combinations of players formed the single entity which we now blithely refer to as *the* Hambledon team. It was never like that.

Some years earlier, between 1769 and 1771, a poor run of results produced a crisis of confidence. There was even a serious debate about the club folding. But they decided to carry on and within a year or so, a team with a few new faces was producing even more stunning results than before. The people and their performances come later in our tale; for the moment, the important point is the length and scale of their successes. Over the next twenty years or so, from 1771, according to John Nyren, Hambledon played England fifty-one times, and beat them on twenty-nine occasions. From records available to us today we can confirm twenty-eight of those victories, from forty-seven matches. Such a trivial discrepancy hardly matters. This was the pinnacle. It was also the brief yet critical period during which the game changed profoundly, and much for the better.

There are a number of curious coincidences about cricket on Broadhalfpenny Down and the people who have graced it over the centuries. We have seen one already. Of the several others, one is outstanding. It is the shared personal characteristics of some of the great players in the glory days of the Hambledon club. So many of the team were outgoing, fun-loving people. Generosity of spirit seems to have been the norm, with only a few minor exceptions, if John Nyren is to be believed. Mind you, Nyren himself was sufficiently fun-loving and generous of spirit to indulge the people he described. Surely, though, we can believe him when he suggests that not only did they play the game better than anybody else, they also had enormous fun doing it. As for the celebrations, to say nothing of their prodigious consumption of liquor, they were as uninhibited in the pub as were their performances on the field across the road. And here is yet another coincidence: at least seven of the players were innkeepers themselves. Liquor was in the blood, in more ways than one. Casting our memories forward, even to the present day, it has to be said that the vast majority of cricketers can still claim to be outgoing, fun-loving, generous-hearted people; and more than a few are, or have been, publicans. It may not be entirely by chance that a brewer is presently chairman of the Brigands – the club which today plays on Broadhalfpenny Down.

The great Hambledon teams of the late eighteenth century shared other characteristics, too. A disproportionate number of them lived to an immense age, particularly bearing in mind that life expectancy at the time was barely forty years. Of the twenty-six Hambledon players described later, and for whom we have dates, seventeen saw their sixty-fifth birthdays, fourteen saw their seventieth, five saw their eightieth and Silver Billy Beldham lived into his ninety-seventh year. Six of Hambledon's twelve regular England opponents – those about whom we have any personal details – also lived beyond their sixty-fifth birthdays, and a third of them lived beyond eighty. The fact that this tiny group of men should share cricket and longevity is enough to give a statistician nightmares. In those days, long life was a singularly rare event. It was most unusual. Life was expected to be hard and short.

Another common factor between these men, much less surprisingly, was their involvement with the countryside. So many of them were countrymen of one sort or another. They farmed, laboured, or were employed as huntsmen, bailiffs, whippers-in, game-keepers and the like, even though some of them had employment of that kind only as a reward for their success during the summer on the cricket field. Their patrons gave them winter employment from enlightened self-interest. But their potential earnings during the summers were colossal, even by today's standards.

Cricket has always taken time. It is a game which evolves. The contest between bat and ball is also a contest between two heads. It is a test of patience and ingenuity, of courage and skill. It is essentially a team game, but at any one moment it always consists of a contest between two individuals. Furthermore, the battle between them is directly affected by the state of the game at that moment. The same players batting and bowling will have entirely different perceptions of their role, and the importance of it in the context of the game, as the situations they find themselves in differ. The last pair at the wicket and ten runs to win will set up one set of pressures, attitudes, split-second decisions. A huge stand between two batsmen, and the match slipping away, will produce entirely different responses from the batsmen and bowlers. Those utterly different situations might, in large part, involve the same players. But they will behave as if they were playing a totally different game.

Their actions, and their success or failure, will be determined by something else as well – their self-confidence at that precise moment. Not how they felt yesterday or this morning, but how they feel now. Have they the courage and the self-belief in their own skills and talent to dominate the man at the other end of the pitch? Can the bowler now produce that deceptively-flighted ball, and put it on the right spot? Is the batsman now relaxed enough to swing through the line of the ball with certainty and power? Cricket is a game played in the mind as well as on the field. It is played best when instinct prevails. But it is always amenable to shrewd, conscious decisions, made and implemented quickly and based on insight and an understanding of the game. The successful cricketer is the one who can find the right balance between instinct and conscious thought at each moment on the field.

Cricket is also great fun. People first take to cricket because they find they enjoy it. Most go on playing for just the same reason. Even hardened professionals have been known to admit that they still enjoy it. But they know better than any of us that it is not an easy game to master. The joy is in trying, and succeeding from time to time. Of course, success for the professional has very different connotations. But even the average club player has his moments – a brilliant catch, a few scorching drives through the covers, or the ball which does finally turn a country mile and take the off bail with it. Suddenly, all that effort has been worthwhile. It is still fun. Cricket is such a marvellously intricate game – at one and the same time fundamentally simple yet infinitely elusive.

All these subtleties, which make cricket the unique game it is, were fully understood by the players on Broadhalfpenny Down in the latter half of the eighteenth century. Their matches were spread over several days, just as our first-class fixtures are today. They allowed the game to unfold at its natural pace, even if that was, on occasion, tediously slow. We still struggle with the same problem, balancing the interests of the game with the need for action and entertainment. So we share the same experiences and go through the same ups and downs on the cricket field as they did. Despite all the superficial differences, and there are many, in its essentials the game we play today is the same as the one played out so often by Richard Nyren and his heroes all those years ago. The shades that walk today on Broadhalfpenny Down would have liked that, and so should we.

Much has been written about the exploits of the Hambledon club during the latter part of the eighteenth century. But most of it has been drawn from just a few precious and well-studied sources. Richard Nyren's son John recorded his childhood reminiscences some fifty years later with breathtaking vividness, assisted by Charles Cowden Clarke, who appears to have acted as his literary agent and scribe. They performed a feat of physical endurance, patience and memory which puts

The mature John Nyren.
(Reproduced by kind permission of the Bat and Ball)

us all forever in their debt. Some ten years later still, the memories of the last surviving player from the glory days on Broadhalfpenny Down, William (Silver Billy) Beldham, were so carefully written down by the Rev. James Pycroft. These two slim volumes have served as the start and finish for most people mildly interested in the history of cricket. The less well-read but painstakingly-researched early history of the game by Arthur Haygarth, published in the second half of the nineteenth century, completes the trilogy of original sources. There is little else, largely as a result of two catastrophic fires. In 1825, a great fire at Lord's destroyed all the early records of the game, including much material about the Hambledon club. Then in 1908, the country seat of the Earl of Winchilsea also went up in flames. The eighth Earl was a past president of the Hambledon club, and a founder member of the MCC in 1787. The flames at Burley consumed yet more precious records of the Hambledon club and the early days of the game.

The three surviving manuscripts, and numerous later books which owe much to them as sources, are among the very best works in cricket literature. In writing this book, my purpose was not to rewrite such unique material; but there was a case, it seemed to me, to present it in a more accessible and up-to-date form, tailored to a wider audience. Not everyone interested in the history of the game has the time or inclination to struggle with books written and published over a hundred years ago, even if they could obtain copies at a reasonable cost. I hope they will find this an acceptable alternative, at least so far as Broadhalfpenny Down is concerned.

To those, like me, who enjoy the pleasures of hunting through original books and documents, digging out little-known facts and adding to their own sum of knowledge from primary material, I hope my efforts to draw together the tale of Broadhalfpenny Down, and bring it right up to date, will not offend their sensibilities too much. There must be one further word of explanation, too. At an early stage, I took the decision to interpret the scope of this book to embrace material which was germane to Broadhalfpenny Down, and the Hambledon club in its early days, whether or not the events had actually occurred there. Any events relating to, or directly affecting, the side for whom Broadhalfpenny Down was 'home' seemed sufficient justification for inclusion. The outstanding example of my dilemma, and decision, was the great match at Sevenoaks when Hambledon beat England by an innings and 168 runs, and Aylward scored his incredible 167 over three days. How could that be omitted? It isn't!

If, in the course of this book, some of the great characters whose skill and exuberance graced the game at Broadhalfpenny Down more than 200 years ago, live again – however briefly – in our minds, then my efforts will not have been in vain. Immortality takes many forms. The most satisfying must be to live in the minds of generations to come. I have been fortunate enough to come to know as friends some of the men who stride through these pages, and I have greatly enjoyed their company. I have been lucky enough to see the ball in the air – again; cheer the winning run – again; fight my way into a Bat and Ball throbbing with celebration – again! I have basked in yet another famous victory – again; even shared the sore heads next morning – again! Imagination? Of course; where would we be without it? What I am saying is this: it has been entirely a privilege for me to write this book. My only hope now is that I have captured at least some of those experiences and shared them, and the pleasure they bring, with you, my reader.

THE GLORY DAYS
Part 1: The Way It Was

Whichever way you approach it, Broadhalfpenny Down looms above you. Down it may be; but to get to it...is up.

It is two miles from the village of Hambledon with which it will be forever linked. Despite its now apparently isolated location, the village was once something of a crossroads on the cattle drovers' north–south route from Petersfield to Portsmouth, and the pilgrims' west–east route from Winchester to Chichester. In the late eighteenth century it was a thriving village with more than a dozen inns to meet the demand for food, drink and lodging from those passing through.

The cricket ground stands, all four-and-a-half acres of it, high above the village, almost at one end of the great sweep of the South Downs. It is on one of the many outcrops from the southern slopes of the downs which terminate in an elevated and rounded crown. Strictly speaking, the ground itself is not on the pinnacle of what is known to geographers as Broadhalfpenny Down. The ground is, in Hampshire parlance, a hanger, a ridge just below the summit. *Mudie's Hampshire* says of them all: 'They are very bleak on their summits, with little or no soil.' None who have played there, from the Duke of Dorset on, would disagree. Barely six inches of light loam cover a mountain of chalk. It does well to hold the rainfall long enough to feed the slow-growing downland grasses that struggle to survive on it. This combination of fast-draining soil and a hillside fully exposed to the prevailing south-westerlies coming straight off the Solent, makes life almost impossible for most other vegetation. There are few trees standing on Broadhalfpenny Down, except in the more sheltered spots nearby. When the weather is unkind, it takes a hardy sort of cricketer to enjoy playing up here.

But when the weather is good, it is – to this day – the quintessential cricket ground. It is not difficult to stand here and appreciate why Richard Nyren and his men enjoyed playing on this particular spot. It deserves its place in cricket history. Can there be a more typical early English cricket ground in all the land? When the sun is on your back, and a soft breeze fans the face, it is next to perfect.

To the south, the broad sweep of the Meon valley carries the eye over Hambledon to the sea, the Solent and the Isle of Wight. To the west, the great downs roll on and out of sight. Nearby, to the north and east, and in the lea of Butser Hill, the downs briefly give way to farmland, where the animals graze and gigantic modern farm-machinery cultivates fields the size of small continents. It is our loss that they have replaced the half-wild orchards which used to grow on the lower slopes and lavish the sights and smells of spring blossom over the landscape at the start of every season.

That apart, not much has changed in 250 years. On the whole, we see what Nyren saw. We can enjoy it as he did. The myriad shades of green from the fields and woodland below as the sun moves from east to west through the day, the vivid colours of the changing seasons, the glint of sunlight off the sea when the air is crystal clear, the haze in the valleys when it's not. We hear those same hovering skylarks, and the scurrying pheasants in the woods beyond. Only the sheep are farther away. They no longer mow the outfield.

As we have seen, cricket was fairly well-established, if still technically illegal, when King George II came to the throne in

1727. He was the last British sovereign to lead his army in battle, and survived the 1745 Jacobite rebellion only to become embroiled in a disastrous war against France in 1756. As the ageing king increasingly left politics to his able, if disliked, prime minister, Pitt the Elder first extricated the country from trouble in Europe and then embarked on a period of huge overseas expansion. General Wolfe was battling towards the creation of a new British colony in Canada, Captain Cook and Lieutenant Bligh were roaming the Pacific, and Clive was in India. Little would the last three have imagined that the humble game of cricket currently burgeoning on Broadhalfpenny Down was destined to follow them as part of the cement which was to keep the British Empire together for so long. With a chronological tidiness that defies belief, Captain Cook first sighted Australia on 19 April 1770, exactly at the start of the cricket season which heralded the greatest decade of Hambledon's glory days. The connection had been made, and England's first great international cricketing opponents were about to be born.

Twenty years earlier, cricket had unknowingly become involved in politics for the first time. The game inadvertently played an astonishing part in the succession to the throne. It also changed the course of history, and started a sequence of events which culminated in the independence of the United States of America. George II's heir was Frederick Louis, Prince of Wales. Among other things he was, by all accounts, an active and enthusiastic cricketer, if not a particularly good one. From his exalted position, he played a pivotal role in the rapid expansion of the game which occurred in the years up to 1750, including his patronage of, and participation in, the Surrey side. But in 1751 the prince was hit by a ball while playing cricket at Cliveden in Buckinghamshire, and died some time later from his injuries. It was said at the time that cricket had lost a keen player and a great patron of the game with his death. But the country's losses were to be far greater – losses which, then, were of truly unimaginable proportions. Because the prince's death meant that his young, and difficult, son was now the heir to the throne. He did not have long to wait.

THE GAME AT CRICKET

As ſettled by the Several
CRICKET-CLUBS,
Particularly that of the
S T A R and G A R T E R
In P a l l - M a l l.

L O N D O N : 1744   Printed 1755

THE
G A M E
AT
C R I C K E T.

THE Pitching the firſt Wicket is to be determined by the Toſs of a Piece of Money. When the firſt Wicket is pitch'd, and the Popping-Creaſe cut, which muſt be exactly Three Feet Ten Inches from the Wicket, the other Wicket is to be pitch'd directly oppoſite, at Twenty-Two Yards Diſtance, and the other Popping-Creaſe cut Three Feet and Ten Inches before it.

The Bowling-Creaſes muſt be cut in a direct Line from each Stump.

The Stumps muſt be Twenty-Two Inches long, and the Bail Six Inches.

The Ball muſt weigh between Five and Six Ounces.

When the Wickets are both pitch'd, and all the Creaſes cut, the Party that wins the Toſs-up, may order which Side ſhall go inn firſt, at his Option.

L A W S
FOR THE
B O W L E R S.

Four B a l l s and Over.

THE Bowler muſt deliver the Ball, with one Foot behind the Creaſe, even with the Wicket; and when he has bowl'd one Ball, or more, ſhall bowl to the Number of Four before he changes Wickets, and he ſhall change but once in the ſame Innings.

He may order the Player that is inn at his Wicket, to ſtand on which Side of it he pleaſes, at a reaſonable Diſtance.

If he delivers the Ball, with his hinder Foot over the Bowling-Creaſe, the Umpire ſhall call no Ball, tho' it be ſtruck, or the Player be bowl'd out ; which he ſhall do without being aſk'd, and no Perſon ſhall have any Right to queſtion him.

L A W S
FOR THE
S T R I K E R S,
OR
THOSE that are INN.

IF the Wicket is bowl'd down, it's out.

If he ſtrikes, or treads down, or falls himſelf upon his Wicket in ſtriking (but not in over-running) it's out. A Stroke, or Nip, over or under his Bat, or upon his Hands (but not Arms) if the Ball be held before it touches the Ground, though it be hugg'd to the Body, it's out.

If in ſtriking, both his Feet are over the Popping-Creaſe, and his Wicket put down, except his Bat is down within, it's out.

If he runs out of his Ground to hinder a Catch, it's out.

If a Ball is nipp'd up, and he ſtrikes it again wilfully, before it came to the Wicket, it's out.

If the Players have croſs'd each other, he that runs for the Wicket that is put down, is out : If they are not croſs'd, he that returns is out.

If in running a Notch, the Wicket is ſtruck down by a Throw, before his Foot, Hand, or Bat is over the Popping-Creaſe, or a Stump hit by the Ball, though the Ball was down, it's out.

But if the Ball is down before, he that catches the Ball muſt ſtrike a Stump out of the Ground, Ball in Hand, or elſe it's not out.

If the Striker touches, or takes up the Ball before it has lain quite ſtill, unleſs aſk'd by the Bowler, or Wicket-Keeper, it's out.

B A T,
F O O T,
OR
H A N D,
OVER THE
C R E A S E.

WHEN the Ball has been in Hand by one of the Keepers, or Stoppers, and the Player has been at Home, he may go where he pleaſes till the next Ball is bowl'd.

If either of the Strikers is croſs'd, in his running Ground, deſignedly, the ſame muſt be determined by the Umpires.

N. B. The Umpires may order that Notch to be ſcored.

When the Ball is hit up, either of the Strikers may hinder the Catch in his running Ground ; or if it is hit directly acroſs the Wickets, the other Player may place his Body any where within the Swing of the Bat, ſo as to hinder the Bowler from catching it ; but he muſt neither ſtrike at it, nor touch it with his Hands.

If a Striker nips a Ball up juſt before him, he may fall before his Wicket, or pop down his Bat, before it comes to the Wicket, to ſave it.

The Ball hanging on one Stump, though the Ball hit the Wicket, it's not out.

L A W S
FOR THE
W I C K E T - K E E P E R S.

THE Wicket-Keepers ſhall ſtand at a reaſonable Diſtance behind the Wicket, and ſhall not move till the Ball is out of the Bowler's Hand, and ſhall not, by any Noiſe, incommode the Striker ; and if his Hands, Knees, Foot, or Head, be over, or before the Wicket, though the Ball hit it, it ſhall not be out.

L A W S
FOR THE
U M P I R E S.

TO allow Two Minutes for each Man to come inn when one is out, and Ten Minutes between each Hand.

To mark the Ball that it may not be changed.

They are ſole Judges of all Outs and Inns ; of all fair or unfair Play ; of all frivolous Delays ; of all Hurts,

whether real or pretended, and are diſcretionally to allow what Time they think proper before the Game goes on again.

In Caſe of a real Hurt to a Striker, they are to allow another to come inn, and the Perſon hurt to come inn again ; but are not to allow a freſh Man to play, on either Side, on any Account.

They are ſole Judges of all Hindrances ; croſſing the Players in running, and ſtanding unfair to ſtrike, and in Caſe of Hindrance may order a Notch to be ſcor'd.

They are not to order any Man out, unleſs appealed to by one of the Players.

Theſe Laws are to the Umpires jointly.

Each Umpire is the ſole Judge of all Nips and Catches ; Inns and Outs ; good or bad Runs, at his own Wicket, and his Determination ſhall be abſolute ; and he ſhall not be changed for another Umpire, without the Conſent of both Sides.

When the four Balls are bowl'd, he is to call over.

Theſe Laws are ſeparately.

When both Umpires call Play three Times, 'tis at the Peril of giving the Game from them that refuſe to play.

The original laws of cricket, drawn up in 1744 but not printed until 11 years later. Oddly, there is no mention of the purpose of the game – that appears to be taken for granted. These laws deal only with how the game is played.

By 1760, King George II was dead, struck down by a heart attack. His young heir was a very different proposition. The problems he brought to the throne were already well known. He was introverted, petulant and had ambitions to reassert the constitutional rights his grandfather had allowed to lie dormant. To make such a dangerous cocktail much worse, he was later to become vulnerable to terrifying bouts of what appeared to be madness. None of which stopped George III from meddling increasingly in politics as he sought to reign *and* rule with what was later described by the Earl of Chatham as 'all the subtlety of a bull in a china shop'. With a hideous irony, he eventually presided over the greatest loss of royal power ever experienced by a British monarch. After a titanic struggle lasting seven years, and draining ruinous sums of money from the treasuries on both sides of the Atlantic, George Washington finally wrenched the Americas from colonial rule and established the independent United States of America.

Within six years, another revolution – this time on the other side of the English Channel – started a process of violent upheaval in Europe which went on from 1789 to 1815. So violent and socially destructive were the events in France over that long and harrowing period that Professor George Trevelyan later surmised that, if the French noblesse had been capable of playing cricket with their peasants, their chateaux might not have been razed to the ground, and their heads might have remained on their shoulders. So all-embracing were the effects of these events and their consequences on ordinary folk from Russia to the French coast that it was inevitable some of the devastation would touch England too. From our perspective, it must be said that these momentous events even sowed some of the seeds of destruction for the Hambledon club, trivial though that was by comparison with the upheaval in mainland Europe.

Admiral Lord Nelson had finally freed the seas of French and Spanish naval aggression at Trafalgar in 1805, following years of action on the high seas from the eastern Mediterranean and the Baltic to the West Indies. Thousands of young men had been forced into service by the press gangs to achieve those great victories. On land, the wars against Napoleon went on for another ten years, until the Duke of Wellington and General Blucher finally dealt the killer blow at Waterloo in 1815. Again, the cost to the population as a whole was counted in the tens of thousands of previously fit and able-bodied young men. These same years also saw mutiny in the navy over inhumane conditions and rates of pay which had not been increased for a hundred years. It was hardly surprising that Mr Christian had cast Lieutenant Bligh adrift in the South Seas. These were tumultuous times.

There were riots in London, made worse by the fact that they followed a long period of economic depression. Wealth was concentrated in very few hands, just as it had always been. It has been estimated that, during the late eighteenth century, one per cent of the population still owned ninety-nine per cent of the land, and about 400 families had income in excess of £5000 a year (£2.5 million in today's money). Not surprisingly, pickpocketing was rampant. Mass hangings of thieves or the threat of deportation to the Americas, and later to Australia, had little impact on the starving and destitute who prowled the streets and clutched at the clothing of every respectably dressed passer-by.

But life was not all gloom for everybody; far from it. John Wesley was now trying to preach a gospel of personal responsibility. Dr Johnson had finally published his English Dictionary and subsequently found himself a reluctant tourist in the highlands and islands of Scotland. Richard Sheridan, Oliver Goldsmith and David Garrick provided the best entertainment. Ralph Wood made the first Toby jug, John Harrison solved the longitude problem, Thomas Sheraton made furniture for the affluent, while Thomas Gainsborough and Joshua Reynolds painted their portraits. The Royal Academy of Arts was founded, with Reynolds as its first president. By 1791, Thomas Paine had published *The Rights of Man*, and *The Observer* newspaper was about to hit the streets of London, one of more than fifteen newspapers serving a population of less than a million inhabitants.

People had plenty of other diversions as well. In 1752, a couple of weeks of September suddenly disappeared as the calendar in Great Britain was brought into line with the seasons and the rest of Europe. What that did to the fixture-lists that year can readily be imagined. Twenty-four years later the whole of the south of England was hit by another event of cosmic origin, when a violent earthquake rocked the region.

On a more prosaic level, recalcitrant soldiers were flogged in London's Hyde Park, and criminals were regularly hanged at Tyburn. The more debauched of the rich and powerful played lewd games at the Hell Fire Club in Buckinghamshire, including – it was said – the aforementioned Frederick Louis, Prince of Wales. Duelling was still the means by which the gentry settled their more personal quarrels and insults, and a journey to Chelsea or Islington provided plenty of rural shelter for such activities. Even farther out in the wilds, the first Derby was run on Epsom Downs in 1779.

Back in London, the city's footpaths were being paved and lit for the first time; the shops attracted customers from abroad who stood agog at the number of them and the quality of the goods they offered; while the men conducted their business in the taverns and coffee shops which abounded in every quarter. But the noise was intolerable. One visitor to London complained bitterly about his inability to sleep at night when staying there. Every hour was marked by church bells and the calling of the time. The clatter of horses and the chatter of street-traders and passers-by continued until the small hours, and started again before five in the morning. And during the day, the cacophony of inaccurate church bells was joined by street organs on every corner, and the cries of thousands of costermongers plying their wares on every street. He was glad to escape back to the country, where he could sleep at night, hear himself think during the day, live in relative peacefulness, and enjoy the birds and their songs for company.

On the industrial front, chemists had finally split water into its component elements, hydrogen and oxygen, and were beginning experiments to generate, store and control electricity. The basic steam engine had been put to practical use for the first time in 1776. These were important steps forward which, together with the invention of the spinning jenny and the further development of the steam engine, signalled the start of the industrial revolution which was to come to full flower in the next century. But that still lay far ahead.

The nub, from our perspective, is that Broadhalfpenny Down flourished during a period of great economic, political, cultural, industrial and international upheaval. Two of the three most important revolutions the developed world has ever seen occurred during the brief thirty-five or so years covered by the centrepiece of our story. These momentous events had a massive impact on ordinary people. They changed the course of everyday life. After the end of the Seven Years' War in 1763, one critic of the government reported widespread discontent in the country. The roads, he said, were full of penniless wretches who had been paid off by the army and the fleet, but many of them had nowhere to go, and little means of rebuilding their shattered lives. Their country's reward for all their heroism and discomfort appeared to be the right to starve neglected in a ditch. Little wonder, then, that the roads were not safe to travel. Highwaymen were everywhere. And this was just the aftermath of one war. Two more were to follow soon enough. They, too, affected the wealth and well-being of the country as a whole, and of individual families. Parents found themselves increasingly concerned for the physical safety of their young men, battling first on the continent of Europe, then fighting 3000 miles away in North America, and later taking the field of battle again just across the English Channel. Throughout, war on the high seas continued virtually non-stop. So these were far from easy times. They touched everybody – from the greatest to the humblest.

Refugees from the French Revolution were even to be seen in Hambledon village, within a year or so of the start of the crisis just across the English Channel. In 1791, John Nyren's young wife Cleopha, one of the few in the area who spoke French, was helping French priests who had got as far as Portsea and desperately needed assistance. What they must have thought of the English going on with their game of cricket that summer, while barely 100 miles away their own country was tearing itself apart, can only be imagined. They would not have appreciated the subtle but important distinction – to say nothing of safety – between cricket balls flying over Broadhalfpenny Down and buckshot flying on the other side of the Channel.

On the lighter side, one of the chronological quirks of the glory days at Broadhalfpenny Down is that they coincided almost exactly with the equally brief but spectacularly productive life of Wolfgang Amadeus Mozart – a notion which would have been relished by Sir Neville Cardus, who combined a life of musical criticism and cricket writing with such distinction. Mozart was born in Salzburg in 1756 and died in Vienna in 1791, leaving the musical world forever in his debt and much the poorer for his leaving it at such a tragically young age. Were some of his latest 'hits' ever heard in the Bat and Ball, from those uninhibited young tenors George Leer and Tom Sueter? Did they mimic the stammering Don Curzio, or belt out their own rowdy version of Don Giovanni at his worst, not caring for the change of key – and all by way of celebrating a successful day's play? Sadly, we shall never know. What we do know, however, is that they wrote and performed many of their own songs, sometimes assisted by lyricist Richard Nyren (did his talent know no bounds?), over those glorious years. Happily, some of their songs, and lyrics, have been preserved.

Nobody knows when cricket was first played on Broadhalfpenny Down. We can be sure, however, that it was a long time before 1750, when our story properly begins. For over a hundred years, the ground had been an open space where the local people met and traded – something of a cross between a market and a social gathering. That is where the word 'Broadhalfpenny' comes from. It described a place for meeting and trading. 'Brod' is an early version of burgh, or borough. Stall-holders paid the burgh, or the Lord of the Manor, a halfpenny for the right to trade there for the day.

James I granted the Bishop of Winchester the right to hold fairs on this particular piece of open downland, which then became known as Broadhalfpenny Down, early in the seventeenth century. There were many such Broadhalfpennies across the country in those days. Today, only a few have kept their original description and had it converted by the local people into a proper noun. The fact that a small inn, then called the Hutt, stood just across from this particular Broadhalfpenny probably helped to establish its popularity as an occasional meeting-place. Originally, of course, this tiny inn would have been built to cater for those infrequent gatherings. The pub apart, there was little else to commend this lonesome and sometimes bleak spot on the Hampshire downs, high above Hambledon village.

Inevitably, with plenty of space around, and an abundance of small boys to keep occupied while the adults talked and did their business, games of all kinds became a part of the regular social ritual when the villagers met at Broadhalfpenny. The earliest form of cricket would have been one such game, perhaps encouraged by the grown-ups as a means of keeping the young from mischief, and played by the young to pass the time their elders spent gossiping, bargaining and drinking.

But, over the years, the market places at Winchester, Alton, Petersfield and Portsmouth were becoming easier to reach. Better roads, and the wider availability of horse-drawn coaches which offered protection from the weather, made travelling just that little further to market so much easier. These bigger, regular markets offered a better chance of selling your own produce at a good price, and a better chance of finding what you needed for the house, the farm or the family. The need for a local 'Broadhalfpenny' was much diminished by the middle of the eighteenth century.

At the same time, cricket was growing rapidly in popularity throughout the area. It had become an established feature on Broadhalfpenny Down. It seems that a club was started there early in the eighteenth century. Even before 1750 it was sufficiently well-established to have acquired the patronage of the local Squire Land, and been given his name. The young shepherds from the Hampshire downs would have been in the vanguard of this new club's playing strength. Cricket was long since a part of their way of life, and they were good at it. They always had time to practise.

They were strong, too. Men who had handled sheep and worked on farms all their young lives developed big hands, strong forearms and stout thighs. They had great strength and staying power. Throwing or hitting a ball was no trouble to such men. Nor was stamina. The only problem with a cricket match, especially later when they lasted several days, was the neglect of their livelihood.

Over time, more and more local young men, whatever their occupation, were introduced to the sport. They learned to play it with increasing skill, found they enjoyed it, discovered that they could play it well enough as a team to beat other teams in their district, and eventually came to the realization that they might be among the best in the land. Cricket's essential competitiveness, and its unique capacity to generate a challenge both in the head and on the field of play, created a set of circumstances that made inevitable the extraordinary events that occurred at Broadhalfpenny Down during the second half of the eighteenth century. The most that could be said, otherwise, is that if they had not occurred at Hambledon, they would have occurred somewhere else. Logic and hindsight say that these events might have taken place at clubs based in Kent, particularly Sevenoaks, or at either the Artillery Ground or White Conduit Fields, both in London. All these places pre-date Hambledon by anything up to a century. Indeed, logic says that one or other of these three places *ought* to have been the focal point of cricket's full flowering. But they were not.

It just happened to be the Hambledon club playing on Broadhalfpenny Down that first realized that it might be good enough to beat all-comers, and then did something about it. And it had five vital and uniquely combined advantages over those other clubs. First, Hambledon was a small, tight-knit local community, with a sense of focus and pride. Secondly, it was blessed with extraordinary good fortune when the first of cricket's greatest captains joined the club. Thirdly, he found himself leading a team of exceptionally talented, thoughtful and determined men with the potential to become a great side, which it ultimately did under his leadership. Fourthly, the club enjoyed the patronage of several wealthy, influential and shrewd supporters who both funded the stakes Hambledon played for and financed many of its players from their own resources. Last, Hambledon was later to find a scribe who was able to capture for all time the events of those days in vivid and memorable prose.

None of the other leading clubs at that time had all those benefits in such full measure. Hambledon would have set out to test itself in the early 1750s, come what may. But in these particular circumstances, the stage was set for the birth of the legend of Broadhalfpenny Down. They also set in train an expansion of the game at every level. Once the process of challenge and contest was fully under way and had become so highly visible throughout the south of England, an irreversible acceleration in the wider appeal of the game, and participation in it, was inescapable.

In 1750, the strength of cricket still lay in the south-east corner of England. We find the counties of Kent, Sussex, Surrey and Hampshire turning out the strongest sides. Yet these county names are misleading. In reality, Kent was essentially the Sevenoaks club, Sussex was Slindon, Surrey was Chertsey, or Farnham and the nearby villages of Rowledge and Wrecclesham, and Hampshire was Hambledon. The players were justified, in the circumstances of the time, to use the county nomenclature, but only by the absence of any other clubs that might have laid claim to them.

Over the years, and as the fame of the Hambledon club spread far and wide, it was inevitable that good players from other clubs were drawn to Broadhalfpenny Down, to play for what was to become the strongest club in the land. Curiously enough, that cluster of villages around Farnham, on the Surrey–Hampshire border, provided a positive goldmine of talent, including the greatest batsman of them all, William (Silver Billy) Beldham, whom we shall justifiably meet many times in this narrative. Yet Farnham is some twenty-six miles away, and the best a horse might manage over such a distance was about six miles an hour. So a day's cricket, let alone a mere practice, meant at least an eight-hour ride, there and back, on top of whatever sport was to be had once the rider had got himself to Hambledon. Few players today will routinely countenance a journey of that magnitude for a day's cricket. But in the eighteenth century, it was not considered an obstacle to a serious player.

Not that Broadhalfpenny was used only for serious matches. All kinds of social games took place there as well, as they do again these days. Around 1768, for instance, there are indications of a match between ladies from two local villages, Rogate and Harting. This was, apparently, one of a series of three matches, played on different grounds in the area, between these sides. They must have been good, and keen, to embark on such a tournament. The scores are lost, sadly, but the match was umpired by gentlemen from the Hambledon club. We can only hope that the weather was kind. We can also be sure that the Bat and Ball was busy all day, and far into the evening. Matches between mixed teams of ladies and gentlemen, and between uneven numbers of men on one side and women on the other, also took place on Broadhalfpenny Down from time to time. Social contests like these were all part of the regular local entertainment. In July 1772, for instance, the *Reading Mercury* reported that a Hambledon ladies' XI would play a match for £500 (£250,000) against XXII gentlemen 'within the month', and that the betting was already heavily in favour of the ladies.

Such spectacles attracted good-size crowds, too, and had done so for many years. Hard evidence comes in a curious form. The number of spectators attending a match against the renowned Dartford club on Broadhalfpenny Down on Wednesday 18 August 1756 was so great that at least one dog was lost in the multitude, much to the heartbreak of its owner. He had good reason to be fearful, since it was the norm to shoot stray dogs. A forlorn plea for its safe return appeared in the following issue of the *Reading Mercury*.

Reading is some fifty miles from Broadhalfpenny Down – an eight-hour ride. Even allowing for the fact that the newspaper

---

L O S T,

At the Cricket-Match on Broad-Halfpenny, on Wednesday the 18th of August, 1756,

A Yellow and White SPANIEL DOG, of the Setting Kind, about 18 Inches high, with a mottled Nofe, and one very large Spot of Yellow on the Right Side, and anfwers to the Name of ROVER. Whoever will bring the faid Dog to the Rev. Mr. Keats, of Chalton near Petersfield, or give Notice where he may be had again, fhall receive Five Shillings Reward, and all reafonable Charges.

The advertisement for the lost dog, Reading Mercury, 1756.

was one of the few to publish in rural England at that time, this advertisement raises several important issues. Most remarkable is the sheer distance involved, and what that tells us about the appeal of this particular game. Knowledge of it must have been widespread. You don't lose a dog among a handful of spectators. And what is the point in advertising your lost dog so widely if only you and a few other locals were at Hambledon that day? So we can safely conclude that there must have been hundreds of folk present, perhaps thousands, and that many of them had come from far afield.

Yet when all this fuss about a missing dog occurred, the glory days were only just beginning. The club was still a long way from its greatest triumphs. But it was already strong enough to arrange a return fixture against the same powerful Dartford team at the Artillery Ground in London two weeks later, on Saturday 28 August 1756. For both these fixtures, the travelling side was faced with a hazardous two-day journey each way, during which the need to avoid highwaymen was starkly real. But this does not appear to have discouraged them in the least. Perhaps the certainty of huge crowds at both matches helped the teams to cope with the sheer hassle of getting to the opposition's ground. Yet, despite the huge interest at the time, all we know is that Dartford won the return game.

The crowds at some of the bigger matches in those early days were already enormous, even by today's standards. Further impetus came from the ending of the Seven Years' War in 1763. Some semblance of normal life was gradually being restored and cricket once again grew in popularity, both as a sport and as an entertainment. However, that did not stop the cynics carping at these activities. The following year, one newspaper commented on the role of country publicans who promoted sport to line their own pockets. It took the view that their objective was 'to profit themselves by the promotion of idleness and drinking. How often do we see the whole inhabitants of a country village drawn from their harvest work to see a cricket match?' A large part of the population, it reported, 'misspends at least a fourth part of the week'. Fortunately, such criticisms were not voiced to much effect, for the game continued to thrive. Indeed, by 1769, the *Whitehall Evening Post* was driven by the success of the game over the last few years to admit: 'Nothing can exceed the vogue that cricket is in in some parts of Surrey and Hampshire. The people are so fond of it that it is common to ride forty miles to be mere spectators at a cricket match.' Broadhalfpenny Down's time had arrived.

The ground was not laid out as you see it today. The sun sets behind Chidden Down, on the far side of the ground from the Bat and Ball. At the start of each season, Richard Nyren and his team – under the direction of the team's master craftsman, Tom Sueter – constructed a long, low lodge across the south-western side of the ground. Today, of course, it would be called the pavilion, but to our heroes it was always 'the lodge'. It was there for the use of members and remained for the summer. On match days, tents were pitched for each of the two teams, with another exclusively for the use of ladies. The well-being of the ladies watching matches was taken very seriously. They attended regularly and in considerable numbers. William Barber, who followed Richard Nyren as innkeeper at the Bat and Ball, included in one of his advertisements for a match the reassurance to prospective lady spectators that they would be as comfortable as they might be in their own homes. Demand for the ladies' facilities was such that, in 1773, the club decided to purchase sufficient green baize to cover all the chairs in the ladies' tent. Whether this was to re-cover worn-out surfaces, or improve standards, was not recorded in the minutes.

When nobility were present at great matches, they would pitch their own tents. Others were put up to supply the food and drink to all present, and to house the bookmakers, who liked to be sited – for good reason – near the lodge and the players' tents. Over all these structures, permanent or temporary, pennants and flags brought a festive atmosphere to the day's proceedings and at times must have given Broadhalfpenny Down a truly carnival look, somewhat like a medieval tournament.

The lodge provided the ideal vantage point for members, where they could watch with the evening sun at their backs. It

The only known drawing of the original lodge, built by Tom Sueter on Broadhalfpenny Down at the start of each season. It was in the top south-west corner of the ground, protecting the spectators from the prevailing wind and giving them a perfect view of the cricket.

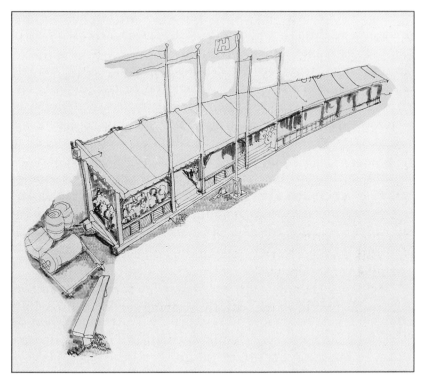

Architect Chris Turner's impression of the original lodge, built each spring by Tom Sueter to house the members of the Hambledon club during the great matches. Was the wooden structure built from ships' timbers hauled up from Portsmouth? (Reproduced by kind permission of Chris Turner)

is still the best place from which to view cricket on Broadhalfpenny Down, and always will be. The rising ground, and the sun behind you, sets up a perfect view. The great matches, of course, called for a huge supplement of facilities. Even more tents were set up all around the ground, to house the bars and catering, to provide additional shelter for the ladies, and protection from the weather and from the inevitable and unceasing wind.

Early records suggest that the centre of the ground was some thirty yards above the present 'square', directly opposite what is now the small porch at the front of the Bat and Ball. In those days, the trees now at the top of the ground were not there (they are less than eighty years old) and the roads were just narrow, muddy tracks. No hedges or fences broke the line of the landscape on this exposed hanger in the downs. The club's use of the pub as a pavilion was entirely logical, since the players, members and spectators could all walk straight out of the bar, across the narrow track and directly on to the ground. The scorers notched their sticks from the comparative shelter of what is now the front porch, but which – then – had an opening at head height to give them direct line-of-sight to the wicket, at least on days when the crowds were not twenty deep all around the ground. At the end of the glory days, their little scorebox window was bricked in; and even as recently as the early 1900s, it was still possible to see where the bricks had been added. Whenever the club was playing one of its great matches, the notchers would sit at a little scoring table at the front of the crowd.

A day's entertainment could be had for gate money of twopence a head, the equivalent of just over £4 today. This would be increased, however, on the big-match days to the equivalent cost we expect nowadays for a Test match. Then, as now, it did not deter spectators, who would fill Broadhalfpenny Down to bursting. For whenever great matches took place at Broadhalfpenny Down, and 'little' Hambledon was pitted against the might of 'all' England, enormous crowds arrived to watch the games. Contemporary reports suggest as many as 20,000 people came from all parts of Hampshire and, as the lost dog advertisement suggested, they came in their droves from much farther afield as well. All roads leading to the ground were packed with horse-drawn traffic – wagons, coaches, carts, individual riders – all trying to get up the hill to the ground in good time; all trying to find a place to tether their animals and give them water; all trying to get a good position for themselves around the ground. Most of the men, of course, would be assessing the odds, listening for the latest news about the teams, and then placing their bets. They would also be disappearing at frequent intervals into the tented bars set up by Richard Nyren to supply the endless demand for ale.

All of which ensured an increasing volume of support from the boundary as the match progressed. Unfortunately, not all of it would have been well-considered encouragement. The ale, and the frustration of those with wagers now at risk, would have seen to that. Every twist and turn of the game, every wicket taken, every catch dropped, every big hit to the boundary and beyond, drew a simultaneous roar of approval and disappointment from the crowds. Any good hit from a Hambledon man was sure to bring forth a great shout in rich Hampshire brogue, 'Go hard, go hard. Tich and turn, tich and turn.' This can be freely translated for those unfamiliar with the language as advice to the running batsmen to ground their bats quickly behind the crease at the other end, and start back for the next run as fast as possible.

Little wonder John Nyren likened these great matches to the meeting of two armies. So intensely was the game followed, ball by ball and over by over, that the very liberty of the spectators might have been hanging on the outcome. But each battle was always fairly fought. Never was a long hit from an England batsman deliberately stopped as it went into the crowd. The spectators would move aside, let their man field it and return it. But he had better hasten, for they were now near enough to let him know if his fielding lacked for speed and a long throw.

By any standards, these matches were a colossal exercise in logistics for Richard Nyren and his family of helpers at the Bat and Ball. In fact, virtually the whole village was involved in the preparations for these great matches. Vast quantities of extra ale and wine had to be ordered well ahead of the game. Gauntlett and Smith, of Winchester, had the contract to supply wines to the club for many years. Carew Gauntlett appears to have extended a particularly generous line of credit to the club, despite the occasional criticism of the quality of his supplies. Understandably, he was held in some regard and the club elected him a member in 1785. When Mr Gauntlett's wine finally arrived, the business of unloading and storing such quantities in this tiny pub must have stretched the cellarman's ingenuity many a time. Manhandling it back to the bar during the match, through a multitude of thirsty spectators all trying to get served at once, was something else. But that would come later. In the kitchens, the same ordering, delivery and storage of several huge sides of beef and venison, great baskets of

Watercolour of the Bat and Ball, by Frederick Gale.
(Reproduced by kind permission of the Bat and Ball)

vegetables and fruit, presented different problems. They all took up more space, but they also demanded careful storage at the right temperature. In summertime, you used the ice-house, if you had one; but there is no evidence of one at the Bat and Ball. There was bread to be made by the hundredweight, and all at the last minute, to serve it fresh. And so the preparations went on, often far into the night before a great match.

On the other side of the track, even before dawn a small army of villagers were busy erecting tents; arranging the seating for spectators; equipping the lodge for the comfort and convenience of members; setting out the tables and chairs in the dining tents; and making sure two special tents were ready for the exclusive use of the players. Nearby, other folk were responsible for the arrangements for the horses, which had to be complete before the first spectators started to arrive. The animals needed rest. Many had made long journeys. Water had to be immediately available in sufficient quantities to cope with the thousands of animals who would arrive tired and then remain there for the day. All the water was drawn from a well outside the back door of the Bat and Ball, in buckets which had to be dropped 325 feet. It was a long, tedious, heavy job, but it had to be done.

They worked from dawn to dusk on the days leading up to a match, and throughout the game. On match days themselves – for many of these games went on for three days and more – the time available to rearrange all the facilities, restock the bars, the tents and the horse-lines was severely reduced. Everything had to be ready again by mid-morning. Yet many of the helpers might have been enjoying the festivities themselves until late the previous night. These matches were big productions by any standards, even when judged next to those of today.

How Richard Nyren ever had time to concentrate on the little matter of leading his beloved Hambledon to victory in such hectic and demanding commercial circumstances defies belief. Of course, in the later years, when he was approaching fifty, he did not always play in these great matches. But up to that time he more often than not played, acted as skipper, and managed the catering for a multitude of spectators and their horses. No wonder his son thought of him as the General.

And when they won...we can only guess at the drinking and celebrating that went on far into the night. The roisterous entertainment and raucous singing was led by the likes of George Leer and Tom Sueter, whose collective vocal talents

Richard Nyren and his helpers prepare for one of the great matches against
England on Broadhalfpenny Down.
(Copyright Philip Hodkin)

'The tiny Bat and Ball Inn stood back at the top of the hill like a brilliant throbbing lantern in the night sky, a single beacon of conviviality in an otherwise desolate landscape.'
(Copyright Philip Hodkin)

were as famous as their exploits on the field opposite. The fun, the singing and the drinking went on until exhaustion, or thoughts of the morrow, finally brought an end to the exuberance, much of which must have been audible two miles away in the village. As the folk who had to depart early rode away, down into the valley, the deafening noise followed them as a reminder of what they were leaving behind. The party was still going on. The tiny Bat and Ball Inn stood back at the top of the hill like a brilliant, throbbing lantern in the night sky, a single beacon of conviviality in an otherwise desolate landscape. It was a sight, and a memory, to fix in the mind.

Meanwhile, for the multitude remaining, the Bat and Ball was still pulsating with bodies all trying to get to the bar, some not even able to get through the door. This humble little place was never built to accommodate such a throng. Conversation was only to be had, even for those who might attempt it, at the top of the voice. Whether your neighbour could hear you mattered not to him, and little to you. What mattered was to enjoy the moment, and the warm glow of satisfaction generated by the day's great events across the track on Broadhalfpenny Down. All reinforced, of course, by the ale.

Despite a minor miracle of forward planning, there was always a danger of what appeared to be half the population of Hampshire drinking the pub dry. Such a calamity must have happened more than once. Seriously good liquor it was, too. Richard Nyren may have been an exceptional and devoted cricketer, but he was an exceptional and devoted innkeeper as well. His punch and ale were as legendary as his exploits on the field across the road. The punch was not 'your modern cat-lap milk punch', John Nyren tells us. No, this was good, unsophisticated John Bull stuff – stark. Punch that could stand on end, make a cat speak! And all at sixpence a bottle. The ale was just as powerful. This was ale that 'would flare like turpentine', turn one man into three. And all for twopence a pint. Even when it was watered down – for there were no weights-and-measures laws in those days – this beer was still potent stuff. And the eating was just as prodigious. Whole sides of beef and venison simply disappeared down scores of gullets in no time at all, copiously washed down with still more beer. There would be a few sore heads next day, without doubt, but nobody minded. Because today, 'little' Hambledon had beaten 'all' England – yet again. What was a sore head, compared to that?

(At the risk of spoiling a good story – and John Nyren's original tells it beautifully – the prices and quantities he quotes are open to question. By today's prices, they equate to £4 for a pint of ale and £12 for a bottle of punch. It must be said, however, that punch was not sold by the bottle then, any more than it ever was. In fact, you bought a *bowl* of punch – which was roughly equal to four normal bottles. It was sufficient to supply a small group of people, at least for a while. Even if his volumes are correct, the prices Nyren quotes – twopence and sixpence – were not commonplace until some 100 years later. Furthermore, on contemporary evidence, the price of admission to Broadhalfpenny Down for a day's play was also quoted at twopence, which is much more likely, and holds up by comparison with today's gate money for county matches. Bearing in mind that the farthing was a useful coin of the realm in the 1750s, and for a long time afterwards, it seems much more likely that the price was actually two- and six-*farthings* a pint and bottle or bowl – about £1 and £3 respectively.)

The club revolved around the Bat and Ball throughout these great days. The Hambledon club, the Bat and Ball and Broadhalfpenny Down were effectively one and the same thing. At most, they were different aspects of a single entity. The clubhouse was an upstairs room in the pub. The landlord was the skipper. The pub supplied all the victuals to the crowds around the cricket field. The cricket kept the pub thriving. It was a triumphant triumvirate. They had their long-term plans, too. Youth cricket was introduced, membership sought from the great and the good from far and wide. This was a club with a track-record, and a mission. Ironically, in the end it was the very uniqueness of the location and circumstances that sowed the seeds for its ultimate demise. As with all dreams, there was finally an awakening. Fortunately for us, that came much later.

For many years, club dinners took place regularly at the Bat and Ball under the watchful eye of mine hosts, Richard and

One of the pair of Richard Nyren's punchbowls in regular use for club functions during the glory days, and used again at lunch on the first day of the 1908 match. This one is now owned by Edward Whalley-Tooker's granddaughter, Christine Pardoe.

The inside of Richard Nyren's punchbowl showed a scene which must capture the spirit of those wondrous Hambledon club functions during the glory days – wine, cricket and song aplenty.
(Reproduced by kind permission of Christine Pardoe)

Frances Nyren. When they moved to the George, in the village itself, in 1771, the club dinners went with them. In the management of their two inns, they were clearly equal partners. Richard ran the bar and oversaw proceedings. Frances managed the catering and was renowned for providing ample good food and drink to a hungry and thirsty club membership. The members of the Hambledon club had an almost inexhaustible capacity for creating conviviality with an abundance of food and drink. It was at least as formidable as anything their team achieved on the field of play, and it appears to have been almost as frequent. Grandson Henry wrote years later that Frances 'was much admired as hostess, whilst her husband and waiters carved the dinner on club days. The dinners were plentiful, and old Richard at the head of it by kindness and good manners made all things go pleasantly.'

One of the oddest features of club dinners was the list of toasts. They were, in order: The Queen's Mother; The King; Hambledon Club; Cricket; To the Immortal Memory of Madge; The President. The first toast is curious, since the Queen was foreign born, and her mother – who would have known nothing of cricket or Hambledon – was dead. On the other hand, it might have been an invitation to the assembly that they might now smoke and take snuff; Queen-Mother was another name for Queen's Herb, a type of tobacco used for snuff. The fifth toast is a real mystery. For generations, no-one knew what it was all about. However, in his recent history of the village, *Hambledon*, the author John Goldsmith, who is a direct descendant from a Hambledon player of the same name, suggests an intriguing, if vulgar, explanation. In polite parlance, this was a toast to the good old days.

Demanding work though it undoubtedly was for them, Richard Nyren and his wife did very well out of the Bat and Ball. They must have been comfortably off by the time they finally gave up the George, after some 30 years' innkeeping in Hambledon. Few publicans can ever have had so many people through the door of one inn, over so many years, as he did at the Bat and Ball. Which was ample reason why, in 1782, Richard was moved to advertise to the local population a word of thanks for their many favours 'during the last 20 years'.

When they moved to the George in 1771, they were no longer swamped by a torrent of thirsty spectators through the door on match days, but they still supplied some of the tents around the ground, now two miles up the road, and throughout the year they were constantly busy with club nights, dinners and meetings. These were heavily attended, for more than one reason. It was much more agreeable to be at a club meeting, and enjoy the hospitality and companionship, than risk a fine. Such gatherings were widely advertised beforehand. There was to be no risk of members pleading ignorance. One such advertisement appeared in the local papers and also in the London paper *The St James Chronicle*, summoning the gentlemen of the club to a special meeting at the George on 7 November 1772. They were advised that dinner would be served at three o'clock. The justification must have been serious business; the outcome would have been quite a party – yet another boisterous night of feasting.

Hugely successful though he was at the Bat and Ball, Richard Nyren never owned it. He was a tenant, and it was not his place to give it another name. In fact, it was still officially known as the Broadhalfpenny Hutt until at least 1797. Locals, and later the whole cricketing world, had by that time long since accepted its new name – the Bat and Ball. Doubtless the title deeds caught up later. At the height of its popularity as a pub, though, its value as a commercial property actually fell – which vividly confirms contemporary reports of economic depression during those times. In 1772, the freehold changed hands for £185 – about £92,000 in today's money. Sixteen years later, in 1788, after probably the most profitable sixteen years any pub has ever had, it changed hands again – this time for a mere two-thirds of its 1772 value. The price paid was only £126 (£63,000).

The Hambledon club in the eighteenth century was not like any village cricket club today. It was marginally akin to today's county clubs. The players were mostly paid professionals. They paid no subscriptions. Only members paid subscriptions, and most of them did not expect to play for the club. Cricket was important, and it became very important. But it was not the be-all and end-all of the club's existence. This was more like a village social club, a glee club even. It provided the local community with opportunities for wining, dining and evening entertainment. All that was an integral part of club life. If singing and song-writing were already part of village life, in the village of Hambledon cricket was to provide the subject-matter. It was no accident that the club motto was 'wine, cricket and song'.

Third Duke of Chandos, president of the Hambledon club 1777, the very pinnacle of the glory days. He was also member of parliament for Winchester, Lord Lieutenant of Hampshire and a Privy Councillor.
(Reproduced by kind permission of Hambledon Cricket Club)

Although the club had clearly been in existence for many years, and certainly from 1742, the first club president we know of was elected to the post in 1773. At a meeting on 4 May, the Rev. Reynell Cotton, a schoolmaster from Winchester who had married a local Hambledon girl some twenty years earlier, was invited to take the post. He was the author of the lyrics used in the now legendary Hambledon song, which can be found at the end of this book.

He was in distinguished company. Hambledon's roll-call of presidents, patrons and supporters over the years comes straight out of Debrett. Together they represent something akin to a quorum of members of the House of Lords, since the list includes the Duke of Dorset, the Duke of Chandos, the Duke of Richmond, the Earl of Winchilsea, the Earl of Tankerville, the Earl of Northington and the Earl of Darnley. In any other company but this, powerful landowners like Sir

Horace Mann, who appears to have spent huge amounts of time and money at Hambledon, would stand out in their own right. But he was mighty welcome for all that. Not that these powerful men were held in awe, far from it. The 1782 president, and local Member of Parliament, Mr JC Jervoise, failed to observe the custom of providing venison for the annual club dinner. He was promptly and unceremoniously fined a whole young buck – in effect, double the quantity of meat he was expected to provide in the first place.

Not everybody in society approved of all these goings-on down in the depths of Hampshire, regardless of the lustre of the company to be found there. Critical comment was rife in some quarters. At the height of the club's fame and fortune, in June 1777 to be exact, an anonymous letter to *The Ladies' and Gentlemen's Magazine* complained bitterly about the conduct of the Duke of Dorset and the Earl of Tankerville on the cricket

(Left) Sir William Benett, steward of the Hambledon club 1778, president 1788, as a young man. The two-stump wicket in the foreground confirms his interest in cricket long before the glory days and his involvement with the club. (Reproduced by kind permission of the Bat and Ball) (Right) Henry Bonham, six times steward of the Hambledon club 1774–1795, sometime secretary, and High Sherriff of Hampshire 1794. (Reproduced by kind permission of Hambledon Cricket Club)

fields of England while the country was in dire trouble – notably in the Americas. This particular letter contained quite a diatribe, and contemporary gossip implicated the Duchess of Devonshire, no less, as the hand holding the pen. She demanded of the two men: 'For God's sake fling away your bats, kick your mob companions out of your houses, and though you can do your bleeding country no service, cease to accumulate insult on misfortune by making it ridiculous.' As if that were not enough, their critic continued in poetry of epic proportions, if not of epic quality:

The Noble Cricketers
Whilst Britain for her slaughter'd legions sighs,
And sunk with wounds her favourite daughter dies;
Whilst pity weeps o'er many a hero's doom,
And death in surly triumph strides the tomb;
O muse, relate the mighty cares that fill
The souls of Dorset and Tankerville...
Far from the cannons' roar, they try at cricket,
'Stead their country, to secure a wicket....
When death (for Lords must die) your doom shall seal,
What sculptur'd honours shall your tomb reveal?
Instead of glory, with a weeping eye,
Instead of virtue pointing to the sky,
Let bats and balls th'affronted stone disgrace,
While farce stands leering by, with Satyr face,
Holding, with forty notches marked, a board
'The Noble Triumph of a Noble Lord'.

There was a great deal more in like vein – twenty-two pages of it to be precise – when the author published the poem in its entirety a year later. The final twist of the dagger already plunged into these two distinguished cricketers was the suggestion that they tell the Good Lord on Judgement Day:

We truants 'midst the Artillery Ground were straying
With shoe-blacks, Barbers' boys, at cricket playing.

THE

NOBLE CRICKETERS:

A POETICAL AND FAMILIAR

E   P   I   S   T   L   E,

ADDRESS'D TO

TWO OF THE IDLEST LORDS

IN HIS MAJESTY's

THREE KINGDOMS.

Ovo prognatus eodem.

LONDON Printed:

SOLD BY J: BEW, NO. 28, PATERNOSTER ROW, 1778.

[PRICE ONE SHILLING.]

The frontispiece to the diatribe against the Duke of Dorset and the Earl of Tankerville, 1778.

The author's own forecast of the Good Lord's Judgement was delivered in equally dire terms:

> Soon as the Judge his frighted ear believes,
> Guess at the sentence, that his justice gives –
> That sentence, hear the Sybil muse foretell,
> 'Damn ye for fools, my Lords – away to Hell'

Apart from their smug satisfaction at having been credited with forty notches by this fiercest of critics – an irony which was doubtless lost on the Duchess herself – we can assume a certain amount of embarrassment in the demeanour of her two victims when they next faced their friends. Amused embarrassment, perhaps, but embarrassment none the less. But nothing a few glasses of wine could not put right, to be sure, the next time they walked into the Bat and Ball. Not that the Duke of Dorset was likely to be doing that in the near future. Lampooned perhaps, but he was off to Paris as His Majesty's Ambassador.

In any case, these two sporting aristocrats were – and had been for some time – in very grand company. Five years earlier, in 1772, appearing merely among the list of newly-elected Hambledon members – nothing fancy like the presidency, of course – was Lord Palmerston, father of the future prime minister, and a certain Bysshe Shelley, grandfather of the poet. All of which makes the appearance of Thomas Paine, author of *The Rights of Man*, at a meeting of members in 1796 less unlikely than it might appear at first sight. It was obviously the practice of the club to offer membership to the great and the good, even to the great and the controversial, as a matter of routine; it must have done the coffers a power of good as well. Quite what Mr Paine was doing in England at all at that time is difficult to surmise. He was officially in France and was threatened with execution for treason in England. So we are left with three possible conclusions – the record of his presence is wrong, his enthusiasm for cricket far exceeded his sense of self-preservation, or the club was now in the hands of wartime conspirators.

In the eighteenth century, the season started and finished later than nowadays. The last game was usually at the end of September. But the club did not reconvene for the beginning of the next season until the first Tuesday in May, when they staged a practice game and a get-together before the first matches. So that nobody was in any doubt, the start of the season was well-advertised locally, telling all the players when to report to the ground. These advertisements were even published as far afield as Salisbury in Wiltshire, presumably to keep non-playing members and prospective supporters at the early games abreast of the club's pre-season activities. Tuesday was nominated for practice matches, since it was market day in Hambledon at that time. It was plainly the best day of the week to meet. Players were expected to turn up on every Tuesday throughout the season, regardless of the fixtures in prospect. Apart from the value of the practice itself, there was money at stake. There were also special rules for practice matches. Any man scoring 30 had to retire, whatever the state of the game or the risk to his earnings. The winners got four shillings (about £100) and the losers three shillings. Discipline was rigid. Late arrivals, let alone absences, were serious matters, too. A fine was imposed even if a man were late; the fate of missing players on their next appearance can only be guessed at. The very least any of these miscreants might get away with was a round of drinks. Those who continued to argue about the laws of the game after a dispute had been settled, or who failed to fall silent when called upon by the president, were in danger of forfeiting a case of claret.

Money appears to have been no object throughout this period in the club's history, although there was a chronic problem with the collection of subscriptions. Both Richard Nyren and William Barber were at various times paid commission on the subscriptions, particularly for those in arrears, that they succeeded in collecting from members with deep pockets but short arms. One member was eventually eight years behind with his subscription. He tendered his resignation with the arrears. Even a former president, the Earl of Darnley, was four years in arrears at one time, living proof of aristocratic penury.

All this aggravation with subscriptions was partially, if not substantially, offset by the club's backers and their winnings on the cricket field. How else could it afford to pay bowlers ten shillings a day (now fifty pence, equal to £250) to bowl at the batsmen, just to give them practice? Even on the county circuit today, such a prospect is unthinkable. The England batsman Ranjitsinhji hired professional bowlers 100 years later, but even he didn't spend that kind of money.

By 1773, the club was wealthy enough to investigate the purchase of a 'machine to convey the cricketers to distant parts'. This was a controversial decision and a ballot had to be arranged to establish the balance of opinions within the club. The motion was carried, and the fine new machine immediately took the strain off the players when they were playing away. It was, however, a precarious contraption and it was to be the cause of much mirth.

Money flowed through the club like the wine consumed by

members. Club dinners, swirling with liquor as they inevitably were, seem to have been based on the assumption that the cost of all this serious enjoyment was immaterial. Members were faced with a fine if they failed to turn up for a dinner, equal to the cost of their place at the table. And on one well-reported occasion, only three members arrived for a meeting of the club, on a dismal wet day. They consumed nine bottles of wine between them. Whether they conducted any business, or were coherent enough afterwards to remember what decisions had been taken, never got as far as the minutes – which tells us all we need to know about the meeting.

The year 1770 saw something of a crisis, when a series of defeats brought the issue of the club's future to a head. We can deduce that some of the more influential members of the club,

'The whole cargo unshipped' from Hambledon's 'machine', which was especially built to carry the team and their equipment to away matches. Peter Stewart refused to get out afterwards. 'One good turn deserves another,' he bellowed from within.
(Copyright Philip Hodkin)

the aristocrats and gentry who had by now become deeply involved in the success of the club, played a big hand in its almost instant recovery. Within a season, it was winning again, but over the next few years the side was sometimes seeded with 'given men'. Lumpy Stevens, who had first played on Broadhalfpenny Down as an England bowler, came to love the place and often played for Hambledon as a given man in later years. These men were the itinerant professionals of the day. They were 'given' in the sense that the club proposing to hire them for a match was granted permission for them to play by the opposition. Because they were so good, these wandering professionals were handsomely paid for their services, match by match and club by club.

In the wintertime, they would live off their summer earnings on the cricket field. If they were lucky, and only the very best players were, they might be offered employment by one of the gentlemen patrons of the clubs who engaged them during the summer. They were in many cases employed – at least during the winters – on the great estates owned by their employers. But the likes of the Duke of Dorset, the Earl of Tankerville, the Earl of Winchilsea and Sir Horace Mann – to name but a few – were also cricket 'nuts'. It was their pleasure and privilege to act as patrons to the great cricket talents of the day if those individuals had no other means of support. At least three of these men were active members of Hambledon, even though Sir Horace spent much of his time trying to raise England sides to beat them. So it is no surprise that they were able to field one of the best sides ever to play the game. John Nyren said of the last and greatest side Hambledon ever fielded that they could beat any XXII in England. They might have beaten any XI that ever took the field anywhere, at any time. A truism it may be, but it is also the truth: the great of one generation would always have held their own in another.

Of course, when we talk about the Hambledon club, we are actually talking about at least two distinctively different sides. The side which took the club to its early successes was led by the 'General', Richard Nyren, until about the mid 1780s. His last games coincided with the start of the careers of the young

John Small and the Walker brothers, among others. John
Nyren also started to play at about the same time. It is entirely
likely that the two pairs of father and son – Nyren and Small
– appeared together for Hambledon in the same matches, at
least occasionally, around that time. From the mid 1780s, of
course, the newcomers included David Harris and Silver Billy
Beldham. So far as cricket itself was concerned, the baton had
been well and truly passed from the original team to the new
one. The tragedy is that this new team played together for a
mere three or four years, before the crumbling of the club's
support, from a variety of causes, started the disintegration of
John Nyren's greatest side.

Most of this new team were not local men. Several of them
were from the hot-bed of cricket talent at that time – Farnham.
For if Hampshire cricket actually meant Hambledon, then
Surrey cricket meant Farnham and the villages nearby. Of
course, the financial incentives to make the twenty-six-mile
journey from Farnham to Hambledon were considerable. For
them, a game of cricket also meant money, as well as a total of
eight or nine hours in the saddle or the cart. Beldham told the
Rev. James Pycroft that he often made the journey there and
back in a single day, to play in a match. The regulars from
Farnham who accepted this inconvenience, and who apparently
made light of it, formed a mighty backbone in the new
Hambledon team. Any side with Beldham, Harris, Wells and
Robinson in it was likely to do well against any opposition. Noah
Mann came almost as far. He lived in Northchapel, Sussex.

The club took a fairly stern view of its regular professionals'
understandable inclination to earn additional income by
playing for other clubs and scratch teams. Opportunities –
temptations might be a better word – were now becoming more
frequent, and the new arrivals appear to have exacerbated the
problem. With the advent of the MCC in 1787, and the offers
then made to Hambledon players from that quarter, the issue
came to a head. It was regarded as so serious that a resolution
was passed the following year which forbade players from such
moonlighting, without the specific permission of the stewards
of the club. The only exception made was for teams being

raised by Hambledon members, specifically the Duke of Dorset and Sir Horace Mann.

Big money pervades this story. Hambledon regularly played for stake money of £500, roughly equivalent to £250,000 today. But it was not always like that. In 1764, just as life was beginning to recover from the war just ended, a stake of £20 was regarded as 'a great sum of money', and Richard Nyren left a six-months pregnant wife behind for several days while he led his team to win it. Towards the end of the glory days, the figures occasionally went to extremes – stakes were sometimes the then-enormous sum of £1050 (£525,000 today). At the time, the law limited wagers to a maximum of £500, but this was contemptuously ignored by the rich and powerful men who gambled on cricket matches. In any case, the stakes were only the start. The whole world, it seemed, was present at these great matches and gambled on the result, and on individual performances.

Over the twenty years or so from 1770, FS Ashley-Cooper, one of cricket's greatest students, calculated that the Hambledon club was known to have played for a total of £32,527.50 and won £22,497.50 of it. That is the modern equivalent of winning £11,250,000 out of a total stake amounting to some £16,250,000. But many match records were lost. Such calculations as this, fascinating though they are, must be tempered by the knowledge that stake monies put up for great matches were sometimes for a whole series, not for a single game. Such tournaments might consist of a pair of games, or three, or five. There was no regular pattern. If, however, we accept John Nyren's total number of wins as correct, and allow at least some latitude for stake monies occasionally covering several games, the club's true winnings would still have been much higher. In the match reports that follow, almost two-thirds of the Hambledon v England records do not state the prize money at stake. Neither do they support Ashley-Cooper's figure, by a margin of nearly fifty per cent. Assuming the two discrepancies to some extent cancel each other out, we are probably left with an underestimate by

Ashley-Cooper of some twenty-five per cent. That would put the stakes played for by the Hambledon club at over £40,000 (£20 million), and their winnings at some £28,000 (£14 million).

Not that the professionals saw much of these huge sums. They went to the stakeholders first, some went to the club, and we know that the players got their hands on a few worthwhile bonuses on top of their match fees. These frequently amounted to considerably more than just a few free drinks, paid for by grateful backers. By the standards of the time, the professionals did pretty well out of cricket, which helps to explain the willingness of our heroes to make those tedious journeys. The real financial killings were made in side betting, and there were no restrictions on individual players betting on themselves, other players' performances, their team's scores, or the result of the match.

Sadly, but not surprisingly, this brings us to the irresistible temptations faced by the players to throw matches and fix results. Few games were played just for the sport, although one, played on 14 July 1783, was for a prize of 'eleven pairs of white corded dimity breeches and eleven handsome striped pink waistcoats'. Normally, however, the value put on such sartorial elegance was as nothing compared with the side wagers on a game. They commonly exceeded the stake money by more than tenfold. So we can estimate that the 20,000 people present on the ground for one of the great Hambledon v England matches would have wagered in excess of £2 million at today's values, the equivalent of over £100 for every man, woman and child present. Beldham freely admitted that corruption was an everyday occurrence, and that he had – to his shame – been directly involved at least once.

Right in front of the lodge sat the bookmakers. They would do business with all-comers – players, stakeholders and spectators alike. So the stakeholders could easily lay off their risk, if they wished. Little wonder that the early laws of the game covered the basic rules for determining the result of a match. And the mischief was of Machiavellian proportions. Players were hidden from view until the last minute; rumours were spread about their health, or lack of it; players' wives were said to be dead or dying; bribes and back-handers were commonplace. Double-bluff was not uncommon either. A strong side might start a rumour that they had been bribed to throw the game, then place their own bets at much better odds and eventually play to win.

For humble country folk, for whom a few shillings a week was a good living-wage, these sums of money and temptations were often too great to resist. Even the gentry found the gambling opportunities the game offered too much to withstand, and were just as foolhardy as their more humble neighbours. They made the same mistakes and took the same risks, but with more noughts on the end of the numbers involved. It is highly likely that Sir Horace Mann, who had effectively fulfilled the role of self-appointed England manager in his efforts to raise a side strong enough to beat Hambledon, brought about his own financial ruin, which ended in bankruptcy, as a direct result of his antics on the cricket field and in the gambling dens around the grounds.

The likes of Lord Frederick Beauclerk, on the other hand, made personal fortunes from the game. He was supposed to be the vicar of Redbourne, near St Albans, but he appears to have spent most of his time on the cricket field and in the saddle – from which he delivered sermons, so as not to waste precious hunting time. He claimed that he made some 600 guineas (£315,000) a year from cricket. Since he was supposedly a gentleman, he would not have been paid to play. Can we really believe that there was no boot-money in those days? Even so, most of his income came from gambling on the results of matches in which he played.

All this villainy should colour our view of the scorecards and results with a large helping of scepticism. And we have to admit that, just possibly, Hambledon were not quite as good as we thought. When we look at their performances on the field of play, we are not just looking at sporting achievements; we are looking at gambling skulduggery as well. Black though this aspect of the game was at that time, and the truth demands that we at least doff our cap to it, equally we cannot now allow it to spoil our pleasure at the great events which took place on Broadhalfpenny Down.

Before we go any further, we need to look at the changes and improvements that took place in the way the game was played, and how the laws responded to these changes. In certain respects, the importance of Broadhalfpenny Down in the history of the game and its development lies in this part of our story.

In the earliest days, even before 1700, there are indications that the batsmen completed a run by touching the umpires at either end. This is why the umpire at the batsman's end appears in contemporary pictures to be standing suicidally close at leg slip! It also explains why both umpires held bats, a tradition which suddenly had a fresh purpose after the law on bat-width was introduced in 1771. Originally, however, it was how the umpires avoided the risk of physical assault in the batsman's rush to 'tich and turn'. They could touch the umpire's bat instead. The introduction of the popping-hole between the stumps changed all that, but the tradition of the umpire holding a bat went on, without practical purpose, even into the twentieth century at club and school level.

So, to reduce further the risk of personal injury to the umpires, eventually a hole was cut in the ground between the stumps to accommodate the ball, or the butt-end of the bat – but not both at once. If the batsman got his bat into the hole before the fielder 'popped' the ball there, he had completed his run. If the ball was popped in first, he was run out. All this might have saved the umpires from injury, but it merely shifted the risk onto the players. It took many a broken hand before the 'popping' crease was moved forward, by the length of an arrow, close to where it is today, and the run-out determined by the bat failing to cross the crease before the bail was removed by the ball, or a hand holding it. That change in the law appears to have been made before 1700.

Of course, the umpires still had a thankless and sometimes risky task to perform. Physical danger had gone, but aggression and verbal abuse remained. Disputes were commonplace, and if the players on one side or the other did not agree with the umpires' decision when argument arose, notwithstanding that one of the two was always their own man, then play might cease indefinitely until the matter was resolved to the disputatious side's satisfaction. Before 1774, the umpires were obliged to call 'play' three times after a set time-limit. If play did not then restart, the game was awarded to whichever side was willing to continue. After 1774, the call for 'play' had to be made only once. Sadly, the sight of teams walking off in the middle of a match was depressingly frequent, and they often took their own umpire with them, forcibly if necessary. They were not prepared to risk his reneging on them with the other umpire.

The bowling was strictly underarm, initially as fast as possible, and all along the ground. The ground itself was uneven at best and downright mountainous at worst. We shall encounter a good deal of talk later about bowling, and the introduction and perfection of length bowling by David Harris. He was tutored originally by Richard Nyren, who had been the first to realize its value and develop a technique that worked. Fast deliveries all along the ground suddenly became balls dropped on a length and allowed to bounce, fly off or skid through, depending on the terrain at that point. These changes had a profound influence on batting techniques, and they ultimately helped to move the game forward to methods of batting and bowling more akin to those of today. But whatever the underarm delivery method during the glory days, some of it was devastatingly effective. Tom Walker attempted to introduce a type of round-arm action in about 1788, but it failed to gain support or approval. It was not until 1828 that round-arm bowling was legitimized by the MCC, and it was 1864 before full overarm actions were finally accepted; by which time, Broadhalfpenny Down was covered in thistles and the Hambledon club was as dormant as Sleeping Beauty.

These changes and improvements happened rapidly during the glory days, especially the 1770s. Length bowling was evolving, and batting techniques had to change to cope with it. The shape of the bat changed, too. Over those few years, the original game, with curved bats flailing at fast deliveries all along the ground and scores over ten runs being something of an achievement, became a game played with skill and thoughtfulness. Better bowling, with the ball being dropped on a length and bouncing up or skidding through, demanded a straight bat and straight play. Gradually, batsmen discovered that they could survive in this new environment, and that they could accumulate runs and make big scores if they were patient and watchful. This improvement spurred the bowlers on to even greater efforts to dismiss them. Each bred technical improvements in the other.

At the forefront of these developments was the Hambledon team as a whole, and four of the team's greatest players in particular – the bowlers Richard Nyren and David Harris, and the batsmen old John Small and Silver Billy Beldham. Their place in the history of cricket is unique; what they did to the game was of supreme importance, and its impact has been everlasting. Of them all, John Small perhaps contributed most, but that does not diminish the crucial roles of the others. John Small was credited by his contemporaries as being the first batsman to work out how to play cricket in his head, and then apply it effectively at the wicket. He discovered the art of playing straight to counter the new bowling; of keeping the ball down by playing with his head over the ball and his left elbow forward and bent. He was among the first to move his feet to the pitch of this new bowling; and it was in his Petersfield workshop that he first fashioned a straight bat which would enable him to play down the line of each delivery. In effect, he conducted a one-man cricket revolution, and no man since has single-handedly made a bigger contribution to the game. Beldham later took these techniques to new heights of achievement and turned himself into one of the greatest run-makers the game has ever seen.

For as long as the game has been played, the wickets have normally been pitched 22 yards apart. Originally, the stumps were made up of three sticks, two set vertically, one foot high and two-feet apart, with the third across the top. A batsman was bowled out only when the bail was dislodged. The difficulty this gave the bowler was to become one of the great issues during the glory days at Broadhalfpenny Down.

Given this wicket format, the batsman had every reason to attack every delivery. The chances of a ball dislodging the bail completely were minimal. Defensive batting was unknown – and pointless. The ball was most likely to pass through the wicket, or possibly bounce over it. Furthermore, the curved and thickened end of the bat – which was not dissimilar to a hockey stick – was not suitable for blocking the ball down the line of delivery. All this was to change quite soon, but in the earliest days of our story the very idea of defence, of playing out a maiden over to await better scoring opportunities later, was completely unknown – inconceivable, even. Jumping out to drive was equally unknown. The batsman in those earliest days simply stood at his wicket intent on hitting as many balls as far as he could before he was dismissed, one way or another. His was expected to be a short life at the wicket, but a merry one. The concept of building an innings came later.

The runs, called notches until at least 1823, were cut into the bark of a small branch, kept for the purpose and discarded immediately after the match. To speed up calculations, every tenth notch was cut somewhat deeper. These scoring sticks were still in use until about 1811 but they were gradually being replaced, originally with a system of brass markers moved along a device like a cribbage board. Pen and paper records came soon enough. But – even then – the details recorded were still sparse. No bowling analysis. The catcher's name was recorded, but not the bowler who forced the batsman's error. There was no distinction between stumping and run out, and the wicket-keeper was credited with neither. Curiously, though, even from these earliest of days, cricket was played as a two-innings game. Both sides had the opportunity to bat twice. Even the idea of following on, if the side batting second was too far behind after the first innings, emerged very early.

When we look at the scorecards for the matches which took place on Broadhalfpenny Down in the late eighteenth century, to the modern eye there is a lack of balance about them. We are used to scorecards being, in effect, top heavy. Not always, of course, but usually we expect the top order to score more than those who follow. And tail-enders... well, they have always been tail-enders. Anything they contribute is a bonus.

But we must not look at the scorecards of the 1750s, or even those up to 1800, in the same way. In those days, the scorecard was usually constructed by social standing. It had nothing to do with batting ability. The gentlemen were listed at the top, with the professionals and rustics at the bottom. Sometimes a line was drawn between the two groups, just in case any reader might be in doubt. Later, the card was occasionally set out in descending order of runs scored, the precursor to the scorecard we see today. Much as we might wish to imagine that James Aylward really had gone in at number ten in June 1777 and scored 167 while supported by his fellow tail-enders, the truth is somewhat less dramatic. He opened the batting, and the correct batting order is to be found in the first volume of Haygarth's *Scores and Biographies*. But Aylward was a humble professional, and a rustic, so he found himself at the bottom of the scorecard which was widely reproduced afterwards and which hangs on many a cricket enthusiast's

wall. There is even a copy at the Bat and Ball. Those same early cards also sometimes describe the not-out batsman at the end of an innings as 'last man in', even if he had opened the innings and carried his bat. All of which can be very confusing to the modern eye. The change in the structure of the scorecard evolved slowly over the years around the turn of the century, and it is not clear, except by such deduction as might be possible, which method was used in scoring each match. By 1822, however, the modern con- struction appears finally to

Arthur Haygarth, who compiled the monumental Scores and Biographies. *(Reproduced by kind permission of the MCC)*

have prevailed, and the Gentlemen v Players match of that year certainly uses the modern method.

From earliest times, and certainly right through the glory days, great matches were always played out to a finish. There was no such proposition as a draw. Most games would be expected to continue for several days, but interruptions for rain often obliged the players to carry on longer than they first expected, regardless of the neglect to their duties at home, on the farm, or elsewhere. Not only had the idea of fixing the maximum time for a match simply not occurred to them, but the money at stake and placed in side bets with the book-makers made unthinkable the notion of stopping before a result was obtained.

The earliest laws of the game of which we have any detailed knowledge were drawn up in 1744, at a meeting initiated by the Royal Artillery Company in London. These gentlemen, together with invited representatives from other leading clubs, took it upon themselves to regularize and commit to paper the then prevailing norm. What they agreed and published was a set of laws which encapsulated the rules of engagement which had been commonplace for some fifty years. Variations were not unusual, especially when gambling was involved. But before the HAC regularized matters, games were normally played under rules agreed and signed by the parties before each match – a cumbersome practice which was also rapidly becoming utterly impractical. On occasion, even the length of the pitch was altered to 23 yards, or some other measurement.

Proper publication seems to have been delayed for some reason, and it is not until 1755 that we find a version of the 1744 laws, modified by changes of language rather than substance, in full circulation. The laws were re-issued in 1767, unchanged.

The essentials of the 1744 laws bear a striking resemblance to the fundamental laws of the game today, and completely capture the substance of the game as we know it. But there is one extraordinary omission. Nowhere in these laws is the underlying purpose of the game spelled out. They assume that the reader already knows that each side will bat twice, and that the winner will be the side scoring the most notches. The first set of cricket laws were concerned only with the mechanics of the game.

The pitch was set at 22 yards, with the popping crease 3ft 10in in front. The two stumps were 22in high and 6in apart. The ball must weigh between 5–6oz. The winner of the toss had the choice of innings, and the right to pitch the stumps. The back-foot no-ball law and the scoring of extras were included, as was the dead-ball concept. Overs consisted of four deliveries. Curiously, the over had originally consisted of six deliveries, but the reduction to four, with the captains free to agree to six if they wished, was common practice even before 1744. It remained the norm for over 150 years.

Batsmen were dismissed if they were bowled (with the bail falling to the ground), caught, stumped or run out. A batsman could also be given out for 'standing unfair to strike', an early version of the lbw law. They were also out if they hit their own wicket, if they handled the ball, hit the ball twice, or obstructed a catch. A little late for master Vinall, perhaps, but the practice of allowing the batsman to obstruct a fielder from making a catch had long since been curbed to prevent further deaths, and the 1744 laws confirm that it had by then been eliminated altogether. The batsman was not out, however, if he obstructed a catch when running a notch. He could also hit the ball twice in defence of his wicket. One of the few laws of 1744 which disappeared between then and now was the ordering of extra notches by the umpires if the fielders hindered the batsmen while they were running between the wickets.

Other laws, which we still observe today, prevented the wicket-keeper from moving or making a noise when the bowler made his delivery, and from getting any part of his person over or in front of the stumps. Batsmen could retire hurt and resume their innings later, but no replacement of players was permitted. Umpires could give batsmen out only if there were an appeal from the fielding side, and they were charged with being solely responsible for all the decisions required at their end. This included judgements on what constituted fair or unfair play, and the settlement of disputes.

Over the next half-century, particularly as Hambledon came to dominate the game and Broadhalfpenny Down became the focus of the cricket world, the increasing skills and ingenuity of the players brought to light some serious gaps in the laws. Cricket was new and fast-growing. As with all such phenomena, during the early stages of development the changes and improvements come thick and fast. Only later, when the refinements have themselves helped the maturing process, does the pace of change slow down. The second half of the eighteenth century was this crucial time for cricket. Almost all the fundamental changes to the laws and methods of play took place over that period, and produced the game we recognize today.

That same time-span covers all of Hambledon's glory days, and during the greatest of those days, the Hambledon club also became the sole source of decision and arbitration on matters pertaining to the laws of the game of cricket. Hambledon found itself, almost by default, responsible for the maintenance of the laws and their amendment to cope with changing circumstances and new developments. The club also had to deal with the sometimes dramatic and expensive consequences of a few mischievous players trying to take advantage of what proved to be several crucial omissions in the laws.

The width of the bat was one such great issue. This was brought dramatically to a head when Hambledon played Surrey on 23 September 1771. This was a crucial match for Hambledon; it took place at the end of their worst season in years and with the very future of the club in the balance. If Hambledon were to lose, the club might not survive, such was the mood. Victory mattered even more than the stake money on this particular occasion. So the arrival at the wicket of the Surrey and England batsman Shock White with a bat the full width of his stumps was...well, a shock! At the time, there was nothing in the laws to outlaw such a mighty club as this. It is not difficult to imagine the mirth in the tent as his team-mates realized what he was about to do, nor the smirk on his face which he tried desperately to suppress as he walked as nonchalantly as possible out to the wicket. His team-mates were mighty amused, but perhaps some of them were also

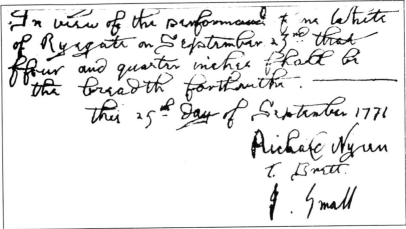

Minutes of the meeting of the Hambledon Club, 25 September 1771, which determined the maximum size of the bat at 4¼ inches. That meeting was held two days after Shock White came to the wicket with a bat the full width of his stumps. Signed by Richard Nyren, Tom Brett and John Small senior.
(Reproduced by kind permission of the MCC/The Bat and Ball)

faintly embarrassed that one of their number could do something so flagrantly against the spirit of the game, if not the letter. Uproar greeted Shock White at the wicket, according to at least one account of this dramatic event, and some of the Hambledon players immediately seized him and his monstrous bat. Others rushed off to find a carpenter's plane, and instantly shaved his bat to more normal proportions before he was allowed to start his innings.

All of which did him no good, at least not in the context of the match. Hambledon won, and by a single run. They survived and went on to record the greatest period in their already illustrious history. And Shock White's little escapade produced a swift and decisive response. A mere two days later, Hambledon passed a law limiting the width of a bat to 4¼in. It was signed by Richard Nyren, as captain; John Small, as bat-maker and the club's leading run-scorer; and Thomas Brett, the club's leading wicket-taker. A copy of the original minutes hangs in the Bat and Ball to this day.

From the beginning of the following season, umpires always carried with them a bat of the approved maximum width, so that they could instantly adjudicate if a batsman arrived at the wicket with a suspect blade. Many drawings of the period show this curiosity, with what appear to be four batsmen on the field, a left-over from the days before the popping crease. But now there was good reason for bats of the correct size to be immediately to hand. There were to be no more pranks by the likes of Shock White. One shock was quite enough. After the new law was passed, Hambledon even went so far as to have a special iron grid made up to gauge every bat in doubt, and that unique iron frame hung for over 100 years in the Bat and Ball.

Perhaps fearing that anyone who could think of using a bat as wide as the stumps might, next week, turn up with a ball the size of a cannon shot or a marble, Hambledon quickly decided that cricket balls should weigh between $5\frac{1}{2}$ and $5\frac{3}{4}$ ounces – nothing more and nothing less. They were not going to be caught out again. At least, not in that way. The 1744 law suggesting a ball between five and six oz was held to be far too vague.

The other great issue of the time was the width and format of the wicket. Despite the fact that the wicket had been modified on more than one occasion by the time the 1744 laws were agreed, it was still made up of only two stumps. At least the overall shape was now higher than it was wide. In fact, it was 22in high and only 6in wide. This still left the bowler with a severe problem, which finally came to a head in one of the great England v Hambledon matches.

This momentous event, which forced a profound change in the laws and consequently in the nature of the game, took place not on Broadhalfpenny Down, but on the Artillery Ground in London on 22 May 1775. Five of Hambledon were playing a single-wicket match against five of Kent. The stake was 50 guineas, about £27,500 in today's money. Lumpy Stevens, playing for All England, bowled a ball straight through old John Small's stumps without dislodging the bail, not once but *three* times.

We should not underestimate just what an achievement this was, nor the frustration for the bowler. John Small senior was regarded as just about the best batsman in England at that time. He rarely lost his wicket by being bowled out. Lumpy had managed it on two occasions some years earlier, and both had been the subject of critical acclaim. So to get the ball past Small's bat and through the wicket once was a source of real satisfaction for the bowler. To do it three times...well, this was bordering on the sensational.

But not once did the bail drop. Unjust is hardly the word. Lumpy must have been a bitterly disappointed man, notwithstanding his habitual good humour. Neither his finances nor his humour were improved by the fact that old John Small went on to make the fourteen runs he needed (in two and three-quarter hours, it must be said) to win the match. By common consent, Lumpy was hard done-by.

Of course, there had been many other occasions when such incidents had occurred, but this was a high-profile match, with huge sums of money at stake and plenty more wagered on the side. So it is hardly surprising that this particular injustice prompted a review of the laws of the game – at the hands of the Hambledon club who had, ironically, been the beneficiaries of Lumpy's misfortune. But such is the spirit of the game – then and now – that the issue was taken up with vigour and in the certain knowledge that 'something must be done'. As a result, the Hambledon club decided to introduce the third stump. It was in use when James Aylward recorded his great innings in June 1777. By 1780, three stumps, now 22in x 6in, had become the norm everywhere.

In 1788, the wicket was again increased in size, from 22in x 6in to 24in x 7in. Over the next few years it was variously set at 26in x 7in and then 26in x 8in. Two bails were first mentioned in the records in 1786, but their requirement was not made part of the laws for another thirty years. The last modification to the size of the wicket, this time to 27in x 8in, occurred in about 1817, when all the fiddling about finally came to an end. The MCC had at last arrived more or less at the format we all recognize today, although there was to be one final, minor change made in 1931. The last adjustment in the early 1800s also included the specification of two bails and a demand that the stumps should be of sufficient size to ensure that the ball could not pass through the wicket. The popping crease was moved two inches farther forward at the same time. It was put at four feet exactly from the base of the wicket, to allow for the additional height of the stumps.

A year before the great issue of the third stump arose, the increasingly obvious need for another comprehensive review of the laws had become so pressing that a meeting was called at the Star and Garter in Pall Mall, London, on 25 February 1774. The leading figures from all the major cricket counties of the day – Hampshire, Sussex, Kent, Surrey, Middlesex and London – were invited. Among others, the Duke of Dorset, the Earl of Winchilsea, the Earl of Tankerville and Sir Horace Mann all attended. So did the Rev. Charles Powlett, a longstanding patron of the Hambledon club, and his friend and fellow member Philip Dehaney. Charles Coles, who was to become a member of the Hambledon club at the start of the following season, was also present. So Hambledon's views and interests were strongly represented, which reflected their standing in the game at the time. As might be expected with that delegation, their opinions on all the matters under discussion carried great weight. Hambledon was a power in the land.

During the course of their deliberations, the committee made seven significant alterations to the 1744 laws, mostly by way of better definitions. The maximum width of the bat and the permitted weight-range of the ball were written into the laws for the first time. The lbw dismissal was defined more explicitly, and the forfeit of a notch for a short run appeared for the first time. Two other changes of substance were also agreed, one of which was to last and the other not. Today, it is still permitted for substitutes to field in place of injured players. That dispensation first appeared in the 1774 laws.

They also determined that visitors should choose the site of the pitch and have the choice of innings. Previously, it had been decided by the toss of a coin or bat. Now, the visiting side had the right to pick the place where the wickets were to be pitched. The only constraint was an imaginary circle thirty yards from the centre of the field; the wickets must be within that. If the game was being played on a neutral ground, then the leading bowlers on each side tossed up to decide which should have the choice. This often had an enormous impact on the outcome of the game, particularly when a skilled eye selected the site of the pitch. Some bowlers became quite cunning at judging just the right spot to suit their particular types of delivery. As David Harris and Lumpy Stevens had already proved, the right to choose the site of the wicket was a crucial part of the tactics of the game. Now that it was the automatic right of the visiting team, it suddenly became even more important. Pitch preparation, if we can call it that, was negligible until it finally began to dawn on home sides that the flatter the centre of the ground, the more likely they were to negate the advantage of choosing where to put the stumps. As for the outfield, that was mown by the sheep, a method which was still in use within living memory.

The 1774 laws covered one other vital aspect of the game which has fortunately fallen into disuse. Arrangements for games with uneven numbers of players on each side, and for so-called single-wicket competitions, were well-established at the time. These were then the equivalent of today's one-day first-class games in terms of spectacle and popular following. The problem was betting. So entrenched was betting as a part of the game, that the laws now included regulations on the way in which wagers on the outcome of a match should be determined. In a two-innings match, for instance, the combined totals only would decide the winner of a wager, regardless of the scores after the first innings. Bets on individual scores must stand on the score made in the first innings only.

Finally, it is said that the 1774 meeting set up a council of the Hambledon club to settle disputes and legislate on the laws of the game henceforth. Which is why the stump issue was resolved so promptly the following year.

The concept of the boundary line, and the introduction of the four and six hits, depending on the point at which the ball first lands, all came in a hundred years later. During the glory days, the boundary was merely the imaginary line about fifty yards from the wickets, behind which the spectators were supposed to stay while the game was in progress. If the ball went beyond that line and disappeared into the crowd, or over a fence, or beyond, the fielder was obliged to give chase and return it as fast as possible, while the batsmen just kept running. In 1787, Silver Billy Beldham ran ten while the ball was being fetched from one of his hits. By 1823, however, a call of 'lost ball' resulted in six runs being added to the batsman's score. If more than six runs had already been completed when the call was made that number was added instead. To score a 'six', as we now understand it, the batsman had to hit the ball completely out of the ground.

As the game grew in popularity and became much more of a national sport, the first mutterings were heard about the laws of the game being in the hands of a few rustics in deepest Hampshire. In particular, these were coming from the more aristocratic voices in London. Here were the first signs of power, if not playing power, beginning to slip from 'little' Hambledon north-eastwards towards the capital. Not that there is any evidence of ill-feeling between Hambledon and the gentlemen from London. Many of them had close links that went back many years. Instead, attitudes and expectations were gradually changing, while darkening economic and social circumstances were gathering strength, too. They were to play their part in due course.

By 1787, the Marylebone Cricket Club – that 'self-appointed Privy Council of cricket', as cricket correspondent Reg Hayter once described it – had been formed and the following year it had taken over the role of law-makers in perpetuity. It wasted no time in establishing its powers. As early as May 1788, less than a year after its formation, the MCC held a meeting to revise the laws of the game, for implementation that same summer.

They tidied up the lbw law, they specifically legitimized the preparation of pitches, and they made two important changes to the laws relating to catches. Now a batsman could be given out for obstructing a catch whether he was running or not, and all runs made while the ball was in the air were to be disallowed if the ball was caught cleanly. Fielders were in future to forfeit five runs to the batsman if they used top hats or any other piece of clothing or equipment to stop the ball while the batsmen were running notches. And soon after this first meeting, the MCC also allowed a new ball at the start of each innings.

As little as three years after that first MCC meeting to review the laws, in 1791 to be precise, Hambledon actually asked the MCC to adjudicate on an umpiring decision involving a bump ball – something that would have been unthinkable ten years earlier.

After the demise of the Hambledon club's influence over the game, the MCC found itself with a never-ending and often thankless task. A comprehensive set of laws covering every aspect of the game in one era is inevitably not adequate for the next. Cricket and cricketers change. Techniques change. That forces other changes, and the law is always trying to catch up. We see these pressures still today. Hambledon probably bowed out of this awesome responsibility none too soon.

Appearance was important when playing a game of cricket in the eighteenth century. It mattered as much, if not more, then as now. The gentlemen – gentry might be the better description – always wore dark breeches which fastened just below the knee, and silk stockings. Trousers were regarded as unsuitable, since they might impede the batsman when playing the ball. Batting pads, and gloves for that matter, were still a long way off. Smart silver-buckle shoes completed the outfit. Wigs were removed. In their place, wide-brimmed hats were sometimes preferred, particularly by the England sides, but Hambledon sported the velvet tricorn, which was provided by the club from 1781 and bedecked with gold lace colours. It was from this form of headgear that the jockey cap must have evolved later. For a short time at the start of the nineteenth century, top hats and later straw hats became much favoured, particularly by the gentlemen players. But they in turn proved cumbersome accoutrements and were discarded eventually in favour of the cap.

Hambledon also sported light-blue coats with black velvet collars, and the letters 'CC' (cricket club) emblazoned on their buttons. Of course, all this finery was removed for the match itself, as were the smocks and coats worn by their opponents. The matches were contested with everybody stripped to white shirts and breeches, which were sometimes coloured. The gentlemen's shirts might have ruffed sleeves and sport a finer cut by their tailors, but basically all the players looked much the same as each other. The umpires wore cocked hats and frock coats.

The players (euphemism for 'not gentlemen'), who were paid for their services, were obliged to wear hats with the colours of their team bound around the brim. Presumably this was to ensure that everybody knew at a glance which side this particular hired-hand might be on today.

Contemporary pictures often show one of the fielders wearing a handkerchief around the calf of one leg, tied loosely just below the knee. He was the long-stop. He was also a rustic, unable to afford the price of a pair of breeches. And even if he could afford them, he certainly would not risk spoiling them on the cricket field. He was obliged to wear trousers, and he used the handkerchief to hitch up and tie his trouser on the leg he normally bent when kneeling down to stop the ball. It was a habit borrowed from everyday country life. Labourers would use string tied below each knee for much the same purpose – to make it easier for them to stoop down. When, gradually, trousers began to be made looser, and crouching became easier, the handkerchief disappeared. For the gentry, in their fine knee breeches and silk stockings, none of this was necessary, of course. Who could imagine an aristocrat being long-stop, anyway?

The equipment of the day was positively primitive. Bats were carved in the shape of the hockey stick from solid pieces of ash or alder, without any forming of the blade to provide a sweet-spot. The handle was a mere extension of the blade, carved to fit a man's hand. There was no sprung handle attached. The shuddering impact of the ball on the toe of such a club can only be imagined with horror. Separate, sprung handles made of cane were not introduced until the 1850s. The ball, meantime, had already become something like the ball we still use – a core of cork inside wadding, all of which was stuffed into an outer skin of leather dyed a vivid red.

Protective pads and gloves – such as they were – were also introduced during the mid-nineteenth century. Pathetic by today's standards, they were far better than nothing. But they came long after Broadhalfpenny Down had become a ploughed field. Prior to these innovations, the most batsmen might do to protect their legs was to stuff wool-padding down the front of their stockings when they went out to bat. Ironically, Robert Robinson had experimented with pads, and spiked shoes, on Broadhalfpenny Down some seventy-five years earlier, and been laughed into abandoning them for fear of further embarrassing himself in front of the rest of the team.

And quite a collection of characters they were, too; everything from country bumpkins to young bucks of the day. A few even made the transformation from one category to the other, and they did it on the cricket field, just as Yorkshire miners were to do it a hundred years later.

But it is time to meet these men of Hambledon properly.

THE GLORY DAYS
Part 2: The Players

John Arlott was probably the first to point out that John Nyren's little masterpiece, captured so skilfully by Charles Cowden Clarke, not only tells the story of a remarkable cricket club at its zenith, but also offers a vivid insight into peasant life in late-eighteenth-century southern England. These men, he observed, might just as easily have walked off the pages of early Thomas Hardy.

When Clarke captured John Nyren's memories of the glory days of the Hambledon club, he was capturing the memories of a child. Nyren was born in 1764, at Hambledon. His father had been landlord of the Bat and Ball from about 1762, as well as being the power behind the club which played on Broadhalfpenny Down. The club played there probably as early as 1742, but certainly from the early 1750s until the 1790s. From 1782 it moved increasingly to Windmill Down, which had the twin virtues of being nearer the village and less windswept and bleak. By the end of that decade, however, the club was in terminal decline.

So Nyren's memories were from a boyhood some sixty years before. They are frustratingly incomplete, they raise more questions and spark more flights of imagination than they should; but they are all we have by way of a first-hand account.

They tell a story of men who, at the time and apart from their cricket, would certainly have regarded themselves as unremarkable country folk, struggling to support their families in difficult and often uncertain circumstances. But for their cricket, no-one would now know or care about them. But their success on the field of play made them famous, if not rich, and John Nyren's recollections, incomplete and undoubtedly rose-coloured though they are, immortalized them. They are, almost to a man, spectacular, larger-than-life figures, who earned the fame they have.

But John Nyren did not start the story at the beginning. For that, we have to turn to the few match reports remaining from the earliest days of the club. We glimpse a handful of men who are sadly condemned to remain little more than shadows. But we at least have some names, starting of course with Squire Land. Perhaps he was the captain of a team which included Edmeads, Bayton, John and Edgar Woolgar, Ridge, Purdy, Glazier, and the owner of the Hambledon bat of 1742, John Osmond Miles, who appears to have been referred to simply as Osmond. Squire Land and Miles were men of the 1740s and 50s. Edmeads and Ridge played into the early 1770s but then dropped out, probably as they reached the end of their natural playing days.

These few players are not even sufficient to form one team, let alone meet the needs of a growing and increasingly successful club which, over some twenty-five years or so, must have called on the cricketing skills of several dozen men. Of them, we know nothing whatsoever, not even their names. All of them pre-date the glory days. Yet they were successful enough to have laid the foundation for the extraordinary events which were to follow. These shadowy figures were also fortunate to benefit from the burgeoning talents of Richard Nyren, John Small senior, William Barber and William Hogsflesh. These four men all played from the mid 1750s onwards, and went on to form the nucleus of the first great Hambledon side – the one ultimately led so gloriously by Richard Nyren during the 1770s.

John Nyren described two teams from his childhood memories: the side which first brought fame to Broadhalfpenny Down and the formidable side which emerged just at the end of the glory days. Both were essentially inspired by one man.

Richard Nyren (1734 or 35 – 1797)

Richard Nyren was the greatest of them all. The inspiration and the driving force behind all that happened at Broadhalfpenny Down between the late 1750s and 1791, when he left the village. The man who is, ultimately, responsible for all that happens there to this day, and in the foreseeable future. As long as cricket is played, and cricketers want to see its early roots, Broadhalfpenny Down will be a living memorial to Richard Nyren. Indeed, this book would not have been written were it not for his achievements there over 200 years ago.

In fact, Richard Nyren was not a local man. He came from Slindon, in what is now West Sussex. He learned his cricket from his uncle, the surgeon Richard Newland, that famous and revered player of his day, captain of Slindon and England, whom we met earlier. This tutoring by his uncle would have taken place during the 1740s, when young Richard was in his teens. He may have visited Hambledon for the first time during the early 1750s, when he was still only in his twenties. There is some evidence to suggest that a Nyren family connection with Hambledon already existed. The words 'J Nyren 1743' were uncovered on the wall of a old building in the village during renovations in the 1970s. Was this another uncle, perhaps, who lived there already and who invited his young nephew to visit? Knowing of the lad's interest in cricket, and with a burgeoning cricket team on Broadhalfpenny Down, this would have been an entirely understandable invitation from a caring relative. Richard's decision in 1764 to name his own son John would tend to reinforce the notion. It would have been a fitting tribute to the uncle who first gave him the opportunity to play for a club with a growing reputation.

Certainly cricket was already being played on

Broadhalfpenny Down, opposite the pub, before he got there. After he married Frances Pennicud, a Quaker girl, at Slindon in November 1758, the young couple moved permanently to Hambledon, where Richard eventually farmed and kept the Bat and Ball Inn. Richard might have taken over the pub when the chance first arose around the year 1760, the year the previous tenant moved out. It is more likely, however, that he took over in 1762. Whichever date it was, his taking the tenancy sealed a commitment to the Hambledon club that he had already made in his mind years earlier. Whatever the reasoning, or the timing, the consequences were to be dramatic. He was now permanently near this splendid ground and club. In due course, he took over responsibility for the upkeep of Broadhalfpenny Down and he continued to help look after it, as he later looked after Windmill Down, as long as he lived in the area – until 1791. He was to become 'the club's head and right arm', in his son's words.

Back at the beginning of the glory days, however, these were exciting times. Richard Nyren had arrived at a moment when the club was increasingly able to field a strong side. Suddenly, and apparently out of the blue, the club found itself with an exceptional cricketing talent; four skills in one man. He was a good left-handed bowler, a safe attacking batsman, a born tactician on the field of play, and a natural leader of men.

We know little more of Richard Nyren as a player than his son tells us. He was a useful all-rounder, by all accounts, and usually batted in the middle of the order. He bowled left-handed, had a high delivery, kept a good length, and was 'provokingly deceitful' through the air. It was Richard Nyren who first experimented with length bowling, as opposed to the previous norm of deliveries all along the ground. He worked on this idea until he was able to use his new method to great effect on the field of play. Later, he was to nurture David Harris in these same black arts of bowling, and see him take them to new heights of skill and achievement.

But it was as a captain that Richard Nyren excelled. Here was the ideal man: a player fully worth his place in the side; one who could out-think the opposition; a man who could earn and keep the devotion of his team; and a man with the ability to marshal their collective resources to deliver victory time and again. Many's the side since, even at the very pinnacle of the modern first-class game, that has wished for such a player.

He also had an exceptional knowledge of the game and was one of the most influential contributors to any discussion of the laws. And amendments to the laws were quite a regular occurrence in these formative days. 'He was consulted on all questions of law and precedent; and I never knew an exception taken against his opinion, or a decision reversed,' his son tells us. He had a rare skill in his dealings with other people on these potentially tricky occasions, and his talent for negotiation on the merits of an issue would have been invaluable. These were the days when peasants and gentry knew their places; they all lived together, yes, but in a decidedly structured society. It could have been no light matter to have to express, and defend, his opinion to an aristocrat like the Duke of Dorset, or to Sir Horace Mann, when an issue of cricket law arose. But Richard Nyren would do it with tact, directness and a conviction self-evidently based on a deep understanding of the game. Aristocrat or rustic, they all respected his judgement and listened to his opinions. Afterwards, they all equally offered him their hands in appreciation and friendship.

So Richard Nyren was a rare man indeed. He was also a very stout man, but uncommonly active, according to his son. He may not have been the best player in the team, but he was as good as any, better than some, and unique as a captain. The nickname 'General' obviously suited him well, and it was a title he wore lightly. It must have amused him, too.

But he was a tough man on the cricket field. His son tells of an incident during a Hambledon v Surrey match on Broadhalfpenny Down in 1775, when Surrey had set a big score and Hambledon appeared to be in trouble at 'five out for very few runs'. A number of heavy wagers had been placed on Surrey's winning, and money previously placed on Hambledon was frantically being laid off, at the best odds the gamblers could get. At the fall of the fifth wicket, Richard Nyren joined old John Small at the wicket. Small had opened the innings and was well set, but needed someone to stay with him. Who better than the General? And so it was. The two of them rebuilt the innings, and then created the platform for a win. Eventually, Nyren was out for 98, his highest recorded score for the club.

As he left the field of play, he was accosted by a couple of gamblers. They vigorously complained that he had turned the game at their considerable expense. Nyren was horrified. The two men were none other than Charles Powlett and Powlett's close friend from their days at Westminster School, Philip Dehaney. Both were supposedly distinguished members of the Hambledon club. Powlett was not only a reverend gentleman, he had been a steward of the club the previous year and was a longstanding patron. Dehaney was later to become a Member of Parliament. Both had been at the Star and Garter the previous year as part of the Hambledon delegation to the committee which revised the laws of the game. But the loyalty these two opportunists showed to the club that day was pretty threadbare. They had wagered heavily against a Hambledon win when the game looked lost. Nyren was glad of the outcome and their losses, he told them, adding: 'Another time, don't bet your money against such men as we are.' John Small finished with 136 not out, and the match was won.

Richard Nyren's talents as an innkeeper were almost as legendary as his exploits on the cricket field. He was clearly the life and soul of the Bat and Ball, and turned it into a vibrant centre of local entertainment. His ales were the heartiest a man could drink, with a never-ending supply to slake the driest thirst. Dinners of an evening were so indulgent that memories of over-eating and gluttony flooded back vividly to his son over fifty years later.

When Richard Nyren and his local friends weren't thrashing the hide off an England XI, they were out to all hours hunting, shooting and fishing. These were men who lived life to the full. Winter was not going to be dull, just different. And after the sport, what else but back to the warmth of the pub, where they set about entertaining themselves with music and their own songs? Richard was a good violinist, and also wrote lyrics.

He was a man of enterprise, too. He would advertise the great matches at Broadhalfpenny Down in the *Hampshire Chronicle*, inviting the crowds to come and watch Hambledon take on the greatest cricket teams from all over England. On match days, the ground would be furnished with refreshment booths, freely re-supplied from the pub across the track for as long as the match continued. And although Richard Nyren must have become a wealthy man on the back of all that trade over so many years, he might also have found the pace too much as he got older. Perhaps this was why he and his family eventually moved out of the Bat and Ball, leaving it in the capable hands of his long-standing friend and fellow cricketer William Barber. He also unloaded at least some of the responsibility for maintaining Broadhalfpenny Down on to Barber. In 1771, Richard Nyren took over the George Inn, two miles down the road in the village of Hambledon itself. The club moved its meetings there, too, so it would not have been any quieter in the winter than it had been at the Bat and Ball. And during the summers, his wife and he would continue to supply tents pitched up on Broadhalfpenny Down during the great matches with yet more food and drink – but now that involved a two-mile journey each way. It was hardly an easier life.

In 1791, when this thirty-five-year-long party was finally all over, Richard Nyren moved to London, where he continued to play cricket from time to time. After he died only six years later, his widow moved back to Hambledon to live in a cottage owned by their son. She lived to be over ninety years old.

The team which Richard Nyren originally joined, and later captained, took Hambledon to glory and made Broadhalfpenny Down famous.

Not in batting order, John Nyren lists it as:

> Richard Nyren, captain
> Thomas Brett

William Barber
William Hogsflesh
John Small senior
Tom Sueter
George Leer
Edward Aburrow
Peter Stewart
William Lamborn
Tom Taylor

Tom Taylor was the sole survivor of this original side to get into John Nyren's later team, which he regarded as Hambledon's finest. We should not forget, though, that the 'original' team should also have included Noah Mann, who was playing regularly throughout the glory days of the 1770s, as well as later. He, with Taylor and John Small senior, carried on playing, and became part of Hambledon's second great team.

Thomas Brett (1747 – 1809)

Thomas Brett was Hambledon's first strike bowler. He was the fastest and the straightest bowler in the club. The ball came out of his hand like a bullet at point-blank range, delivered with a high action. He got even more velocity than those bowlers of the day who used a jerking action, which was permitted under the laws at that time and was also regarded as the quickest method of delivery. But Thomas Brett was faster. He took a huge number of wickets over the years. Despite his speed, many a batsman lost his wicket to Thomas Brett by being stumped, although the credit for such spectacular wicket-keeping properly belongs to Tom Sueter, of whom more later.

Thomas Brett was a dark, strong man, with a short arm, which made his speed of delivery all the more remarkable. When he was called upon to bat, his team-mates held no great hope of his contribution to the score. Like so many tail-enders since, Thomas Brett slashed mightily at the bowling and scored a few if he was lucky, but more often than not lost his wicket quite quickly. He was also something of an embarrassment in the field, according to John Nyren.

Thomas Brett was a local man, born into a farming family who owned Tine Heads Farm at Catherington, some five miles from Hambledon. His family was related by marriage to the family of William Barber. Thomas Brett played at Broadhalfpenny Down until 1778. He was only thirty-one when he left the area for Portsmouth, where he spent the rest of his life. His departure at such an early stage in a fine cricketing career must have been a severe blow to the club but for the fact that David Harris arrived in that same year. Perhaps the benefits of exchanging one great bowler for another, in what appear to be somewhat fortuitous circumstances, were not immediately apparent – but they soon enough became so.

William Barber (1734 – 1805)

Together with William Hogsflesh, William Barber was one of the two regular first-change bowlers at Broadhalfpenny Down. These two, with Thomas Brett and Richard Nyren, formed the front-line quartet of bowlers at the club for many of the early years of success.

Barber was a committed member of the club, and involved himself in many aspects of its management over a considerable period of time. He helped with maintenance of the ground, collected subscription arrears, collected vast numbers of empties for return to the wine merchant and, after he took over the Bat and Ball from Richard Nyren in 1771, always took great trouble to keep up the standard of catering and service both in the pub and on the ground across the road. It was one of his advertisements in support of a great match on Broadhalfpenny Down that told lady readers that his tents would put them 'as much at their ease as if they were in their own dressing-room'.

Although William Barber was not strong, he was good enough to bowl a steady length, and he did so from a high delivery action. While he may not have been as fast as many bowlers at a time when fast bowling was the norm – indeed, the faster the better – that apparent shortcoming did nothing to diminish his success with the ball.

William Barber's immediate family came from the Chichester area of Sussex, but he knew Hambledon through the Brett family. They had inter-married over the generations. He was originally a shoemaker. Barber's last recorded game at Broadhalfpenny Down was in 1777, when he was forty-three. He moved to Horndean, not far from Hambledon, and continued to play cricket for Horndean for some years. Arthur Haygarth suggests that Barber was enticed away from Broadhalfpenny Down by supporters of the Horndean club, who needed a bowler of his calibre. After he left for Horndean, his family kept the Bat and Ball for another six years. They gave it up in 1783, just as the club was starting to move its centre of activities up to Windmill Down. They must have been alarmed at the commercial implications of that trend and decided to move on as well.

William Hogsflesh (1744 – 1818)

According to John Nyren, almost all that he said to describe William Barber was also true of this last member of the bowling quartet. William Hogsflesh was slower than the others, but could bowl a steady length from a high delivery action. In his day, which probably covered the 1760s and certainly extended up to 1776, he was famous for his success with the ball, but little more is known about him. He was a local man.

John Small senior (1737 – 1826)

A batsman of the first magnitude, John Small senior thrived in an era before batting became a defensive science as well as one of controlled aggression. He was the first batsman to work the game out in his head and formulate a method of scoring runs heavily, despite the difficulties of playing – in his early days –

against fast bowling all along uneven ground. Old John Small, as he became known to distinguish him from his son, made runs under all conditions, such was his eye and skill with a bat. According to Pycroft, once when he was playing for Hambledon against All England, John Small senior batted for three days without losing his wicket. Regrettably, the score is lost. It is most likely Pycroft meant that he was not out in both innings of the game. Either way, it was a prodigious achievement on the uneven pitches of those days.

This great player has often been credited with the unique distinction of scoring the first recorded century in great matches – the forerunners of the first-class game. It happened in 1768, when he scored over 140 on Broadhalfpenny Down against Kent. This score is sometimes claimed to have been his total in a single innings, but since Hambledon only scored 131 in their first innings and 194 in their second, it is much more likely to have been his total over both innings. Even that was remarkable enough, given the likely condition of the pitch. Seven years later, playing against Surrey on the same ground, he made 136 not out, and followed it with 85 in the corresponding match the next summer. With performances like these, it is hardly surprising that old John Small played the anchor role when Hambledon were batting, certainly until the arrival much later of Tom Walker. But John Small was more than an anchor. He was the rock the anchor lodged under as well. Richard Nyren knew that his trusted friend, this brilliantly talented batsman, could be relied on at the start of every innings to get it away securely. And more often than not, he would still be batting hours later.

John Small senior was already thirty-eight years old, and his career ought to have been past its peak, when the third stump was added in 1775. This, together with the new length bowling of David Harris and his like over the next few years, demanded a profound change in batting technique and equipment. Small senior probably had a great deal to do with the rapid alteration of the bat's shape from the original curve to the straight 'pod'. This was needed to deal with length bowling effectively. None of these huge changes in method or equipment seemed to faze old

Small, notwithstanding an inclination to edge the ball to the wicket-keeper which developed later in his career. Otherwise, his success at the popping crease continued as if nothing had happened. But something fundamental had happened.

He now played very straight, with the bat down the line of flight. Balls dropping short of a length, outside the off-stump, were met with his front foot taking his body well across and keeping it balanced. His shots were evidently made with great control over the ball. The fact that he played the rising short ball off the front foot – which only the best players attempt today, and then only when they are batting on a fast, true wicket – suggests that Small's co-ordination and timing must have been of the very highest order. His foot movements were so quick and took him across to the line of delivery so early that he appeared to have ample time for his shot – another indication of his class. He got so well over the length ball, too. And when he did play an attacking shot, he hit the ball with great power and momentum from the strength in his wrists.

To achieve all this, he must have seen the ball very early in its flight, like all great batsmen since. In fact, we know he had a keen eye because he is credited by John Nyren with being the first man to develop a talent for the quick single, which he exploited as a matter of routine ever afterwards. Not only could he judge the chances of making his ground with precision, but he did so simultaneously with his shot, rather as Jack Hobbs was to do so famously over 100 years later. Old Small's speed across those twenty-two yards was equally impressive.

This speed and judgement were just as valuable in the field, where he normally stood at cover or mid-wicket. John Nyren says he was 'as active as a hare'. He was also a thinking man, and developed a deep insight into the game. When Richard Nyren became captain, he would regularly consult John Small on the finer points of the game, or on the laws themselves, if he wanted a second opinion.

The high regard in which John Small was held by his captain and the rest of the team did not, however, prevent his wife from contributing her highly visible and vocal support from the

Mrs Small – complete with immense umbrella – roars encouragement to her menfolk.
(Copyright Philip Hodkin)

boundary, assistance she was to inflict on their son later. Mrs Small was no cricket widow. In fact, there is some evidence to suggest that she was both a knowledgeable and enthusiastic follower of the game at its highest level. She was certainly a regular, if spectacular, supporter at Broadhalfpenny Down in those days, waving a gigantic green umbrella from the boundary and shouting encouragement to her menfolk. This was no shrinking violet. Support was what they needed, and support they got. Mrs Small was not to be trifled with, and any player achieving less than she considered right, especially if he were either her husband or son, had better beware of her wrath afterwards.

The imagination boggles at the prospect of such antics at Lord's or the Artillery Ground, for Mrs Small went to many of the great games elsewhere, especially if her husband or son were playing. Perhaps they made allowance for this strange and vocal lady up from the country, who seems to have adopted this self-appointed role quite early in her husband's career.

She was apparently convinced that Hambledon had a better chance of winning when she was present. Given the style of her interventions, we can believe it.

Despite the enduring presence of his family's support – for his wife doubtless brought young John along to matches as soon as he could walk – John Small senior was a man at peace with himself. He was also a man of great integrity and quick wits. Two stories about him reveal much of his character. In 1775, the Duke of Dorset had watched Small battle for over two hours to score the fourteen runs needed to win a match between five of Kent and five of Hambledon, played at the Artillery Ground in London. This was the game in which Lumpy Stevens 'bowled' Small three times without dislodging the bail, as a direct result of which the third stump was introduced shortly afterwards. The Duke much admired old Small's determination and batting skills on this tense occasion, and decided to show his appreciation. He knew that this fine batsman was also something of a musician. (He played the fiddle, and later took up the double bass as well.) After this nail-biting finish, the Duke sent him a fine new violin, carriage paid, as a token of his esteem. Small was touched by the gesture, but he perhaps felt beholden to his Lordship as a consequence. Whatever the reason, or his thinking, old Small clearly felt the need to reciprocate. He was, by this time, a well-known maker of bats and balls at his small Petersfield workshop. So he sent the Duke two bats and some balls – also carriage paid.

The aforesaid violin features in the other story told by John Nyren. Small was crossing some fields on his way one evening to a musical party when he suddenly found himself faced with a raging bull. With true English *sang-froid*, and astonishingly quick thinking, he put his violin to his chin and started playing to the beast as he slowly edged his way towards the nearest stile. It did the trick. The bull stopped, listened, approved, lost interest, and finally wandered off. The violin-player got to the stile, and to the party.

Mention has been made of old John Small's bat-making skills. He has to be regarded as one of the pioneers of modern bat-making. Indeed, he would have an important place in the annals of the game on that account alone, had he not been such a fine batsman as well. But as a bat-maker, with a workshop some six miles from Broadhalfpenny Down, he started making bats when they were still fashioned after the shape of a hockey stick and from a single piece of ash or alder. As the new-length bowling demanded a straighter bat, so John Small developed the new shape in his workshop, introduced the shoulder at the top of the blade, and made a bat which would meet the length ball better, but one which also drove and pulled the ball better. As with so many successful innovations in any walk of life, once the benefits became widely apparent and fully appreciated, Small was swamped with orders and had great difficulty in meeting demand. Even through the winters, he would work long into the evenings every day of the week, just to keep up with demand. In those days, a top-quality bat cost four shillings, or 20 pence as we now call it. Taking inflation into account, one of John Small's best bats cost roughly £100 at today's prices, a sum satisfyingly close to the actual cost of a good bat today. Whether he made the giant 5lb bat, manufactured in 1771 and now kept at Lord's, is not known. But it does prove that heavyweight bats are nothing new to the game, as some commentators would have us believe.

In those days, if you wanted to buy a bat or some balls from old John Small, it was not difficult to find his house and workshop in Dragon Street, Petersfield. Outside it hung a painted sign. It read:

> Here lives John Small,
> Makes bats and balls,
> Pitches a wicket, plays at cricket
> With any man in England.

John Small senior first played for Hambledon in about 1755 when he was eighteen years old, according to Arthur Haygarth. He probably saw cricket played on Broadhalfpenny Down when he was a boy, and it was still known as Squire Land's club. He went on playing, at county level no less, until he was past sixty. His last recorded match was for Hampshire against MCC in

1798. He started life as a shoemaker, but gave that up to pursue a life on the cricket field. Cobbler to ball-maker was a tiny step in those days. Perhaps that was why his cricket balls were particularly sought-after. He took up bat-making somewhat later, and he and his son continued to make these items at their shop in Petersfield for many years. When old John Small turned eighty, he sold the last six balls he ever made to Edward Budd, who was subsequently offered a guinea each for them by William Ward. Both gentlemen were well-known and successful cricketers during the early part of the nineteenth century.

John Small senior was also a gamekeeper, and an excellent shot. He finally gave up gamekeeping when he was past seventy, when he at last admitted to himself that seven-mile walks around the grounds were getting too much. Even so, he continued to follow the hounds on foot until he was past eighty-five. In addition to all his other talents and achievements, he was a good skater and regularly skated on Petersfield lake in winter. He had taught himself to play the double bass, and often played his tenor violin in Petersfield church. He was able to do this without the aid of spectacles until the very last year of his life. He was born in Empshott, not far from Petersfield, to where his family moved when he was six years old. He lived there all his life.

Pierce Egan's much quoted eulogy says it all:

> Here lies, bowled out by Death's unerring ball,
> A Cricketer renowned, by name John Small.
> But though his name was Small, yet great his fame,
> For nobly did he play the noble game;
> His life was like his innings, long and good,
> Full ninety summers he did death withstood.
> At length, the ninetieth winter came, when (fate
> Not leaving him one solitary mate)
> This last of Hambledonians, old John Small,
> Gave up his bat and ball, his leather, wax and all.

A fitting tribute, words of admiration and affection, which leave us just a small insight into the remarkable man he must have been. There is another clue in this poem about the overlapping of the two great Hambledon teams. William Beldham died many years after old John Small, but he was not regarded – by Egan, at least – as being part of the original club. Beldham was just another of those johnny-come-latelies.

Tom Sueter (1749 – 1827)

Wicket-keeper *par excellence*. Nothing – well, very little – passed him. 'For coolness and nerve in this trying and responsible post, I never saw his equal,' John Nyren tells us. Tom Sueter was not a small man, as so many wicket-keepers are today. But he had big, safe hands, an eagle's eye, and the reactions of a cheetah. Proof of his skill, speed and courage is provided by the astonishing and regular stumpings he made off Thomas Brett's ferocious bowling. It must have been tough enough to face Brett at his fastest, but to have to worry about being stumped off it as well...this was too much for many batsmen. There can be little doubt that Tom Sueter set the standards for wicket-keeping in those early days, and developed many of the techniques that wicket-keepers now take for granted.

Tom Sueter had such a good eye and such fast reactions that he was inevitably a good bat, too. He was a left-hander, a hard-hitting, gloriously straight driver of the ball, at least in part because his nimbleness behind the wicket also served him so well in front of it. He would get like lightning to the pitch of many a delivery that others might not have attempted to drive. In fact, he was the first player regularly to jump forward from his crease to attack the ball, a sight which stunned other players when they first saw it. But his success attracted imitators soon enough, although not all of them had his fleetness of foot. He had all the other strokes, and played the cut particularly well. But whatever stroke he played, it was sure to be played with style as well as strength. He could run, too, and was famous for his quick singles; although as he was such a fast-scoring hitter of the ball, we are left wondering why quick singles mattered that much to him, especially as they took him away from the strike. Either way, he could be relied on to score fast, faster in fact than any other man in the side, which was often as valuable an asset to Hambledon as the runs themselves.

So he was a formidable batsman. A newspaper report many years after his death mentioned that, when only seventeen years old, Tom Sueter had batted for three days when playing in a match for the Earl of Tankerville. Sadly, the scores are lost.

Tom Sueter was a local Hambledon man, an architect and surveyor by profession. It was he, each year, who was asked to build the lodge at Broadhalfpenny Down at the start of the season. He must have been a craftsman of some quality, for he was also given the responsibility for major restoration work on Hambledon village church in 1788, when he was assisted by Richard Flood. He regularly sang tenor in the church choir, and he was not averse to singing even more lustily in the Bat and Ball, opposite Broadhalfpenny Down. Many was the time, after a match, when Tom sang to entertain the players, their visitors and guests in the Bat and Ball. FS Ashley-Cooper, in his enchanting book *Cricket Highways and Byways*, muses about Tom Sueter smashing England's best bowling all over Broadhalfpenny Down on a Saturday, entertaining the teams in the pub after the match, and then singing solo like an angel next morning in Hambledon village church. Little wonder, then, that Tom Sueter was one of the most popular men in the club, especially as he was also blessed with an amiable disposition and a kind-hearted honesty never doubted by a soul, even when he was appealing to the umpire for a stumping. If Tom Sueter appealed, it was because he genuinely thought the batsman was out.

When Tom Sueter died, he left a sovereign to pay for the singing of an anthem over his corpse in the church he loved so much, and which he had so painstakingly helped to rebuild.

George Leer (1749 – 1812)

There is some dispute about the spelling of Leer's surname. John Nyren and all the old scores show it as Lear, but Arthur

Haygarth insisted that it should be spelt Leer, and that is certainly the spelling on his tombstone in Hambledon churchyard. Either way, he was universally known at the time as Little George.

What was not in doubt was his ability as long-stop, behind Tom Sueter and in the face of the gale-force bowling from the other end in the form of Thomas Brett. George Leer covered vast areas of the outfield behind the wicket-keeper and the slips with a speed which defied belief at times. 'The ground that man would cover was quite extraordinary,' according to John Nyren, who thought him as safe 'as a sand-bank'. On many occasions, no more than two runs would be taken to him during the entire innings of the other side, a truly astonishing feat when you bear in mind that long-stop had no gloves, and the game was played on an uneven pitch and a bumpy outfield. He worked a ruse with Noah Mann for years, and they took scores of wickets with it. Noah would stand behind long-stop, George Leer's specialist position, and slip. Noah would be there to cover both men, effectively at short third-man in today's parlance. From time to time, George would tip Noah the wink and Noah would creep up close behind him. Then, when the ball came through from the wicket, George would deliberately fumble it and let it pass. The batsmen, seeing it go past George, would set off for a bye. But Noah's swoop had the ball back with the wicket-keeper in a flash, running out the on-coming batsman, often by yards. Little George was a cunning cricketer, as well as a quick one.

His batting average was not high – Nyren estimates it at between ten and twenty – but he recorded several big fifties over the years in great matches. So he was well worth his place in the side, especially as any occasional shortcomings with the bat were more than made up in the field, where he had no peer as long-stop.

George Leer was a counter-tenor, peculiarly apposite since the wicket-keeper in front of him was a tenor. Did they ever sing duet to lull the batsman in front of them into a false sense of security at the wicket as Brett ran in to bowl? The laws forbade it, of course, certainly after 1777. But such mischief was bound to have crossed their minds, especially when they were enjoying a glass of ale in the pub after a game. And it was there, and then, that they regularly and legitimately let their singing talents shine. After a day's play, Tom and George entertained the assembled crowds of players and spectators throughout the evening, with their own and other popular songs of the day.

Little George was a local man, like so many of the original team at Hambledon. But he moved the six miles to Petersfield later in his life, where he was a brewer.

Edward Aburrow (1747 – 1835)

Known to one and all as 'Curry', though no-one now knows why, Edward Aburrow was a local Hambledon man, a shoemaker by trade, and yet another of the original team who lived to a great age.

He was an exceptionally fine out-fielder, fast across the ground, and he had a long, quick throw to the wicket-keeper which discouraged batsmen from taking liberties when the ball went in his direction. He was a 'safe and steady batter', according to John Nyren, and a useful change bowler.

His last recorded game at Broadhalfpenny Down was in 1782, when he was still only thirty-five. While so many of his contemporaries went on playing for much longer, Edward Aburrow dropped out. Perhaps he found it increasingly difficult to hold his place in the side, especially as so many of the new team were by then establishing themselves at Broadhalfpenny Down. Whatever the explanation, he was still relatively young when his name disappeared from the club's records.

Peter Stewart (17?? – 1796)

Like George Leer earlier, there is some dispute about the way in which Peter Stewart spelt his name. Arthur Haygarth suggested that John Nyren's version 'Steward' was wrong, and there seems some validity in that argument. This time, it is not his tombstone but his entry in Hambledon's burial register that Haygarth quotes as proof. There is no disputing Peter Stewart's nickname, however. Everybody called him 'Buck'.

He, too, was a good out-fielder, and a steady bat. His particular strength was the cut, though John Nyren thought Tom Sueter played the shot better (Beldham and Robinson played it better still). But Buck was a good team player, and clearly worth his place in the early days. By 1779, however, he had stopped playing for the club, perhaps for the same reason as Edward Aburrow; did he, too, find it difficult to hold a place in an increasingly powerful side? Or was he simply too old?

Peter Stewart was a member of a local family, and other Stewarts also played for the club. He was a carpenter and shoemaker by trade, and also kept the Green Man pub in Hambledon village for a time. Later, his son John took over the New Inn in the village.

Buck was something of a wag. At least, that was how he liked the rest of the team to think of him. He certainly proved to be a source of unsophisticated amusement on many an occasion, and Nyren thought highly enough of one incident to preserve it forever. Hambledon were playing away, and planned to travel to the match in the 'machine' specially built for them. It was large enough to accommodate the whole team, all its gear, the umpire and the scorer. It is not difficult to imagine such an unwieldy, cumbersome structure, supported on hard-rimmed wheels, loaded almost to the roof with bodies and kit, being hauled precariously by a team of exhausted horses over the rough, rutted tracks that passed for main roads in those days. Getting anywhere from Broadhalfpenny Down by such transport must have been a minor achievement in its own right. Not surprisingly, mishaps were commonplace. On this particular occasion, the entire, laden contraption had fallen over in a ditch, with everybody and everything inside it. As Nyren puts it, so succinctly, 'the whole cargo unshipped'. Everybody struggled out into the road – except Buck. He refused to come out, insisting instead that the rest of them should right the vehicle with him still in it. 'One good turn deserves another,' he shrieked at them from inside, amid howls of laughter from the whole party. Nyren wrote: 'This repartee was admired for a week.' But he does not tell us what state the team was in when it finally got to its destination, nor what happened during the match. We are left to imagine that too.

William Lamborn (dates unknown)

Little is known about the man they called the Little Farmer, perhaps because John Nyren spelt his name Lambert – Arthur Haygarth could only find references to Lamborn in the old Hambledon records and concluded that they were one and the same man. Lamborn first bowled on Broadhalfpenny Down in 1777 as a visitor playing for England. But like that other great bowler, Lumpy Stevens, he was soon invited to change sides and play for Hambledon. He continued to appear for the club until 1781 and then disappeared. Yet in that brief time, this gentle country bumpkin earned a lasting place in the annals of the game. He was an exceptional, if not unique, bowler – though he was certainly unique in his time, for he is undoubtedly the father of 'the wrong 'un'. His right-handed delivery was 'the most extraordinary I ever saw', John Nyren tells us.

In the days when underarm bowling was fast and still all along the ground, the natural right-handed movement of the fingers as the ball was released helped to turn it from leg to off. (That same action, when overarm bowling was introduced later, became the leg-break – which is much less natural to a right-hander as the arm is brought over the head.) Lamborn bowled the off-break *underarm* – which is equally unnatural to a right-handed bowler, hence Nyren's remark. Lamborn was the first man to master this extraordinary delivery technique and he took buckets full of wickets with it. On more than one occasion, he bowled his way through England sides and set up victory for Hambledon. The batsmen 'tumbled out as if they had been picked off by a rifle corps'.

The Little Farmer was actually a shepherd, and he would set up a couple of sheep-hurdles as wickets and bowl away at them for hours while he was supposed to be looking after his father's flock. Lamborn's finely-honed ability to turn the ball the wrong way reaped huge rewards, both for the bowler and for the team. Once, when he was bowling to the Duke of Dorset, no less, he completely bamboozled his Lordship with a ball which started straight and then turned across him, missing the leg stump by a hair's breadth. Forgetting himself for a moment – and Nyren provides evidence to suggest that Lamborn was not blessed with the sharpest brain the game has ever known – he bawled out in his rich Hampshire brogue, 'Ah! That was *tedious* near you, Sir!' Fortunately, his aristocratic foe laughed as much as the rest of the assembled multitude at this blissfully direct, but utterly unintended, familiarity.

So, Lamborn was a match-winner with the ball, but he sadly contributed little with a bat and even less with his intellect. Here, truly, was John Arlott's quintessential cricketer from the pages of Thomas Hardy.

Thomas Taylor (1753 – 1806)

Tom Taylor shares with old John Small and Noah Mann the distinction of playing for the original team which first brought Hambledon to greatness and going on to play with their successors. He held his place right through the 1770s and 1780s, against all-comers. Yet he was a risk-taking batsman who got himself out more than he should by attempting to cut balls bowled straight at his wicket. He was a fine batsman, nonetheless, and made a great many runs for the club over the years.

He has an enduring, if questionable, claim to fame, however. Tom Taylor is held responsible for the introduction of the lbw law. As Silver Billy Beldham put it many years later, he was 'shabby enough' to put his leg in the way of balls which might hit the wicket. Given his rash inclination to cut at straight bowling, this is hardly surprising to the objective cricketer. But whatever Tom Taylor's motive, and it is difficult to think it was other than a deliberate act, the Hambledon club became increasingly concerned at this practice. Not surprisingly, it was quickly copied by others and eventually became widespread, despite the risk of injury such behaviour involved. But this was 'not cricket'.

Here we have a problem of dates. The first record of Tom Taylor's playing for Hambledon is 1774, according to Arthur Haygarth. Prior to that year there was an lbw law of sorts, which appears not to have been uniformly applied. Sometimes it was not applied at all. But immediately before the 1774 season, the special meeting in London reviewed and amended the laws of the game. The use of the leg to defend the wicket was one of the issues it decided to clarify. The meeting took the view that the law should be considerably tightened to allow the umpire to give the batsman out if – in his opinion – the ball would have hit the wicket had it not hit the batsman first. If Haygarth is correct, then Tom Taylor's actions were not directly responsible for this change and Beldham was wrong. It is most likely, however, that Taylor was already a regular Hambledon player and that the events are correctly reported. Haygarth was the first to admit that a great many records had been lost prior to the 1770s.

There are happier, undisputed reasons – as a fielder – that this short, stocky man is best remembered. John Nyren thought him one of the finest he ever saw. He moved like a cat, and was as watchful as one. He would lurk in the covers, ostensibly to save a second run. But his speed to the ball and quickness with the return of the ball to the wicket-keeper, were such that he ran out many a batsman. Often, the batsmen were still going for the first run when they realized the crisis facing them. Getting two to Tom Taylor was a dangerous occupation, more likely to end in the loss of a wicket than an addition to the score.

Tom Taylor was born in Ropley, near Winchester, but lived at various times at Alresford and Alton. Like the great General himself, Richard Nyren – and William Beldham, Peter Stewart and Noah Mann – Tom Taylor was a publican, and kept the Globe Inn at Alresford for many years.

So that was the original team, although it has some serious omissions in it, which we shall rectify shortly. But assuming it was the team which first took Hambledon to greatness, what would Richard Nyren's batting order have been, leaving aside rank and social status? Perhaps like this:

1. John Small senior
2. Peter Stewart
3. Tom Sueter, wicket-keeper
4. Tom Taylor
5. George Leer
6. Richard Nyren, captain
7. Edward Aburrow
8. William Hogsflesh
9. William Barber
10. William Lamborn
11. Thomas Brett

In his *The Cricketers of my Time*, John Nyren described two sides, which overlapped during the early 1780s, when the 'old' team was getting past its best, and the 'new' team was still coming together. There is little doubt that the 'new' team was the stronger of the two. The strong players who joined at that time, many of whom came from that hot-bed of talent at Farnham, twenty-six miles away, made Hambledon almost invincible as well as a living legend. But they could be regarded as johnny-come-latelies, at least to the extent that they joined a strong club *because* it was strong. In the short term, they made it even stronger; but they also failed to hold the club together when times got tough. Because this was the side which ironically saw the Hambledon club to its demise. It was the 'old' team which had taken the club to its pinnacle of success, over a period which started some twenty years earlier. The 'new' side eventually dropped the ball.

John Nyren listed this new and stronger side now playing on

Broadhalfpenny Down (inevitably not in batting order) as:

> David Harris
> John Wells
> Richard Purchase
> William (Silver Billy) Beldham
> John Small junior
> Harry Walker
> Tom Walker
> Robert Robinson
> Noah Mann
> Thomas Scott
> Thomas Taylor

No XI in England, he went on, could have had any chance with these men. 'I think they might have beaten any XXII.' Yet this side is curious for a number of reasons. It omits all but one of the original Hambledon side which brought the club to fame in the first place. Remarkably, it omits no less a key player than the General himself, Richard Nyren. Noah Mann is included here but was not listed in the original team, for which he played regularly. And John Small senior is omitted here, yet he – like Mann – played regularly for both sides. Admittedly, old Small was past his best by the mid 1780s, and his son was now playing in his place. But it is an odd omission for all that. Taylor, old Small and Mann are the three players who span the two sides, and who played regularly in both. John Nyren's memories of his great side appear to focus on the years around 1786, when he would have been twenty-two. Is there an element of hero-worship here? Perhaps he did not include old Small or his own father in his great side because at that time they were both in their fifties and well past their prime.

As with all clubs, always, Hambledon's players came and went, reached their peaks at different times, declined or moved away in no predictable pattern. It is just possible that this dream team did take the field together around 1786, but it most certainly did not do so with everyone at their respective best, particularly bearing in mind the difference in their ages of thirteen years. Which is not to say that these famous men were anything less than the greatest cricketers in England in their day.

So what did these men do on the cricket field, and off it?

The records we have from John Nyren, from the Rev. James Pycroft, who interviewed an ageing Silver Billy Beldham in 1837, from the Rev. John Mitford, who had also visited Beldham a few years earlier, and from Arthur Haygarth's first volume of *Scores and Biographies*, published in 1862 and covering the game as best as he was able back to 1744, enable us to build up a picture of this extraordinary team, and the other players in what today would be called the first-team squad.

David Harris (1755 – 1803)

David Harris is at the top of John Nyren's later team for very good reason. Not because he could bat; quite the reverse. He was the most feared bowler of his day, the most difficult to score off, the most accurate and the most testing for any batsman to face. He literally changed the course of cricket history single-handed. This muscular, angular man was a bowler without peer.

He was also a kind, scrupulously honest man, whose goodness showed in his face, according to Nyren. He generated affection from all about him and was a staunch friend to those in need. 'I never heard even a suspicion breathed against his integrity, and I knew him long and intimately,' John Nyren said.

But Harris was a formidable foe on the cricket field. He generated a colossal speed from a highly-ritualized delivery technique. He started as upright as a soldier. Then, with a graceful curve of his right arm he raised the ball to his forehead, drew back his right foot and started his run with his left. This routine never changed. At the point of delivery his arm would twist almost up to his armpit, and the ball would appear as if pushed from his hand. It had the height of delivery and speed of lift that overarm bowling generates today, but it was so straight and precisely on a length that, sometimes, he would wear the pitch bald of grass at that point. This combination of pace, pitch and lift was altogether new as a method of bowling, and it forced a new and better method of batting from his opponents.

When he first joined Hambledon, Harris was too often inclined to bowl full tosses, but endless practice ensured that he became, and remained, a consistently steady bowler to a full length, who rarely over-pitched. Richard Nyren had already developed a length ball before Harris's arrival at Broadhalfpenny Down. He quickly recognized David Harris's natural aptitude as a bowler and actively encouraged him to try this new technique. In the end, David Harris did far more than that. He took length bowling to new heights. He would practise all winter long, and at night after dinner, whatever the season of the year. 'Many a Hampshire barn was heard to resound with bats and balls as well as threshing' when David Harris was around.

Such was his method of delivery that the ball flew off the ground with the lightest of bounces. Yet his style, and choice of wickets, endangered the batsman who failed to block the cannon-ball he faced – he was at risk of having his fingers ground to dust, his bones pulverised and blood spread over the ground. 'Many a time I have seen blood drawn in this way,' Nyren says.

It is to the skill and precision of Harris's bowling, which brought this new-found technique of length bowling to perfection, that Nyren attributes the improvement in defensive batting which occurred at the same time. Shown the way by Hambledon's own Tom Walker, defensive play developed rapidly against such accurate and aggressive bowling. Once, when they were on opposing sides, David Harris bowled 170 balls to Tom Walker and conceded only a single in all that time. There were matches in which the batting side might score 70 or 80, but less than ten would come from David Harris's bowling. Sneakers and half-volleys were no longer on the menu. David Harris was a veritable miser where runs were concerned. He allowed them out of his grasp as he might yield gold bars to total strangers.

Harris's bowling was the severest test of any batsman, and Silver Billy Beldham facing David Harris was a memory John

*David Harris, 'after George Shepheard', 1790
(Reproduced by kind permission of the MCC)*

Nyren still relished half a lifetime later: 'Unless a batter were of the very first class, and accustomed to the best style of stopping, he could do little or nothing with Harris.' For John Nyren, David Harris was simply the best bowler he ever saw, and his arrival at Broadhalfpenny Down in 1778 or thereabouts further strengthened this already immensely strong side.

The remarkable claims made for the achievements of David Harris in changing the course of cricket history come from contemporary accounts. They describe a veritable revolution in the game. From a backward, slashing game, it changed to a forward and defensive game. Eventually, in 1788, the stumps were made higher by two inches, to take account of the new bowling method he perfected. But long before that, the bat had already changed shape. This new-fangled style of bowling required a straight bat in the hand, as well as a straight method of wielding it. Indeed, these improvements to the game and the way it was beginning to be played led to the claim that David Harris was the true father of modern cricket. What went before was still a relic of the country pastime. What he left was recognizably today's game.

When he first started playing in great matches, innings totals dropped and the speed of run-getting dropped too. But as the better batsmen learned to cope with this new bowling and adopted new bats and methods, they also gradually acquired the skill and patience to accumulate big scores. Lord Frederick Beauclerk, no mean performer himself, only encountered Harris's bowling when the great man was towards the end of his playing days. He had already suffered several fits of gout and was by now 'slow and feeble', but his lordship described Harris's bowling even then as the grandest of its kind he had ever seen.

Such, too, was the skill David Harris retained towards the end of his illustrious career, and the esteem he commanded, that he was encouraged to play even when his terrible gout prevented him from so much as standing. He would make his way to the ground on crutches and, once warmed up, would bowl as well as ever. A great armchair was provided at the bowler's end so that he could rest between deliveries, and he did so with the aplomb of a king at court, as if this was the manner in which he always conducted himself upon the field of play.

From his earliest involvement in the game, David Harris obviously thought deeply about tactics as well as performance. These were the days when the side winning the toss – or, later, playing away – had the right to choose where the wickets were to be pitched. In his prime, Harris would go to the ground at Broadhalfpenny Down at six in the morning before a match and consider where the pitching of the wickets would best suit his bowling. But, being the man he was, he also thought about the needs of the other bowlers in the side that day, and where their interests might best be served. His objective was to win the game, not just to take the most wickets.

By contrast, that other outstanding bowler of the period, Lumpy Stevens, had no such thoughts. When Lumpy chose a wicket, it was to ensure that his potential success was maximised. Any other bowlers in the side had to make what they could of it. But David Harris's attention to such details bordered on genius. He looked for slightly rising ground to pitch the ball against. With the rising ball coming at the batsmen at such speed, most of Harris' wickets fell to catches; another illustration of his shrewdness. In the early days, with a lower, wider wicket of two stumps, topped by a single bail, bowling a man out was difficult at the best of times. Harris's choice of a pitch which encouraged catches made great sense tactically.

David Harris's gout obliged him to sit down between deliveries towards the end of his career. 'Slow and feeble' he might have been, but Lord Frederick Beauclerk still thought Harris's bowling the grandest of its kind he had ever seen. (Copyright Philip Hodkin)

Like so many fine bowlers who came after him, David Harris had no great talent as a left-handed batsman, and might perhaps be described as the very first president of the Number Eleven Club. He was no great fielder either, although he always got his body behind the ball in the field. And he often fielded at slip.

David Harris lived in Crookham, not far from Farnham, and was a potter by trade.

John Wells (1759 – 1835)

Here was another master tactician, whose opinions were sought both during matches and off the field. He had a keen appreciation of the game and its finer points. But here, too, was a work-horse of a man, an all-rounder who could be relied on as a quickish stock bowler and asked to hit out or defend when batting, as the circumstances demanded.

From John Nyren's description of John Wells, we can sense the strength and dependability of the man, the tough professional who would give his all, and more, throughout the match. But he was never expected to win the man-of-the-match award. The glory generally went to others.

Except when it came to fielding. He could throw down a single stump to run a batsman out, and did so many times. In single-wicket contests, his ability in the field off his own bowling was much feared. But it cost him a fingernail once, when he tore it off against the buckle of his shoe while fielding. Despite the lack of protective clothing and equipment in those days, it was one of the few nasty injuries Silver Billy Beldham ever saw on a cricket field.

John Wells's first recorded match for Hambledon was in 1783. But he would have been twenty-four by then; so he might have been playing well before that. He was known as 'Honest John Wells', and shared with David Harris those qualities of personal integrity which 'render man useful to society as well as happy in himself', in the words of John Nyren, who perhaps captured a whole way of eighteenth century rural life in such a perspicacious phrase. John Wells also came from that early cradle of cricket, Farnham, and was a baker by trade. He would travel the twenty-six miles to and from the ground on the day of each match, starting early and getting home late. He often travelled with Silver Billy Beldham, whose sister he married. At one time the two brothers-in-law thought about building a cart for the journey, since they both came from Farnham, but the new tax on carts, introduced in 1785, soon put an end to that idea.

Richard Purchase (1756 – 1837)

A 'slowish' bowler, who could bowl to a length and get the ball to lift at the batsman. This slim, dark man had no guile about him, John Nyren recalled, 'nor was he up to the tricks of the game.' But he could bat, and was a 'tolerably good field'.

As an innocent young man, he was selected to play for Hambledon against England when Thomas Brett, the club's most feared bowler at the time, was unavailable. The date was 4 August 1773. He was just sixteen. Despite his youth, inexperience and naivety, he still managed to bowl four England batsmen out in the match, which England won by nine wickets. He might even have had a hand in some of the other dismissals as well. But, as usual for the time, the scorecard does not reveal the bowler when a catch was made. Curiously, having played so remarkably well in illustrious company for one so young, Richard Purchase then disappeared. There is no record of his having played for the club between 1775 and 1781, years when he would have been in his prime.

Despite Nyren's verdict that he was only 'a fair hitter', Purchase did once open the second innings of a match, with William Harding of Frensham, and they put on 200 for the first wicket. After they had been parted, the rest of the side was skittled out for less than thirty more, and their total of 228 proved insufficient to win the match. All of which suggests that he was, in fact, no mug with a bat. An opening stand of over 200 on a wicket which defeats all but one of the rest of the team indicates an ability to concentrate, play straight and build an innings.

Richard Purchase lived all his life at Liss, near Petersfield, was a blacksmith by trade, but died a poor man at the age of eighty. Towards the end of his life, he used to bleed the villagers when they were ill and became known locally as Old Doctor Purchase.

William (Silver Billy) Beldham (1766 – 1862)

The finest batsman of his age, 'perhaps of any age', according to John Nyren. A close-set, active man, with a crop of flaxen hair – which turned silver in his later years – over a handsome and intelligent face. He was the complete right-handed batsman, both in defence and attack.

He had learnt to play cricket from Harry Hall, a baker at Farnham, where the Beldham family lived. Whether his brother George, who played briefly for Hambledon, also took lessons is not known; what is certain is the unique natural ability Hall found in young William. Hall was no great player himself, but he had a great talent for teaching the game; and in William Beldham he found a star pupil, with a rare aptitude which fed avidly off Hall's tutoring.

It was Hall who first devised the instruction to right-handed batsman 'to keep the left elbow up'. That, and a straight bat, keeps the length ball out of your wicket and the ball on the ground when you play it, he taught. Beldham learned fast.

He was still a young man when he first joined the Hambledon club and started playing at Broadhalfpenny Down. Long before he was out of his teens he was regarded as a club professional, entitled to draw expenses even for practice matches. In those days, the early 1780s, the bowling was still generally fast but no longer always along the ground. During his long career, both the bowling, and the batting skills needed to master it, were to evolve out of all recognition, and Beldham's contribution to the development of batting techniques during that crucial period of profound change cannot be underestimated.

It is hardly surprising that, at certain times in his career, the purists of the day would criticize him, particularly his inclination to play the cut shot to deliveries which other batsmen would have played with a straighter bat. But this was now the master at work, and he made his own decisions about which shot to play at which ball. His astonishing batting achievements over so many years were the complete answer to his critics.

When he arrived at Hambledon, a mere lad of fourteen, he already had a firm grasp of the art of batting and was seen immediately as a truly exceptional talent. The older and more worldly men in the team seized on this young man and carefully nurtured his skill into full bloom over the next few years, by sharing with him their own knowledge and experience. It was not lost on such a bright lad.

In no time, his name and batting achievements were being widely talked about. He was soon to be acknowledged as the best batsman anyone had ever seen or heard of. The best bowlers wanted to measure themselves against him. His wicket was the most prized; dismiss him and you might have changed the course of a game. At times, the fielding side's best prospect of getting his wicket was by running him out – something that happened to him more times in the later part of his career than he cared to admit.

'No-one could stop a ball better, or make more brilliant hits all over the ground. Wherever the ball was bowled, it was hit away in the most severe, venomous style.' His technique was so secure that Nyren considered it 'safer than a bank'. All bowling came as one to William Beldham: fast or slow, short, good or full length, high or low, turning or swinging, the ball would fly from his bat 'like an eagle on the wing'. The severity of his hitting, particularly his playing of the cut shot, became a legend even in his own lifetime. Says Nyren: 'When he could cut at the point of his bat, he was in his glory. The speed (of the ball) was the speed of thought.' It was like the cut of a racket, his wrists 'seemed to turn on springs of the finest steel', the Rev. John Mitford reported. He took the ball not a moment too soon or too late.

But he was not only a powerful hitter; he was an elegant batsman, a true artist at the crease, as well. Before the ball was delivered, Beldham stood calmly, composed and with a piercing focus of the eyes. He was in command. And at the moment of attack, his movements were a lethal mixture of gracefulness, animation and concentrated energy. The speed of his bat was electric. And his courage and fleetness of foot got him to the pitch of any ball capable of being turned into a half-volley. He was also an exceptionally good judge of a quick single, particularly in his younger days.

Had there been national first-class batting averages kept in those distant days, all the contemporary reports of William Beldham suggest that he would have been in the top few, if not at the very top, for something approaching thirty-five years in succession. He never missed a season. And he told the Rev.

James Pycroft that he had calculated his own average over one thirteen-year period at 43 runs per innings. He did not mention whether he had made any distinction between innings when he was out and those when he carried his bat. We can suppose not. Had he done so, his average would almost certainly have exceeded 50. He also made the point to Pycroft that he was at his best as a batsman only when there was pressure on him to make runs. Concentration was hard for him when the outcome of the match was not at stake. But when it was, then the fielding side had a problem on their hands. Such a consistent

William (Silver Billy) Beldham, 'after George Shepheard', 1790 (Reproduced by kind permission of the MCC)

performance against the very best opposition, over so many years, gives some credence to the proposition that this man must be counted among the greatest batsmen of them all. Beldham stands in the front rank, along with Grace, Trumper, Hobbs, Bradman, and perhaps a mere handful of others.

In terms of sheer ability, only Lord Frederick Beauclerk of his contemporaries could stand comparison with William Beldham. Nyren remembers one occasion when the two of them were batting together: 'The display of talent that was exhibited between them that day was the most interesting sight of its kind I ever witnessed.'

Another great batsman, of a slightly later era, Felix (Nicholas Wanostrocht), described Silver Billy Beldham's bat as 'the sceptre of delight', and when the Rev. John Mitford visited Beldham at his home at Oak Cottage, Tilford, near

Farnham, when he was over sixty-five, Mitford was thrilled to be allowed to touch the bat which still hung in Beldham's smoke-laden kitchen at that time. 'I trembled when I touched it. It seemed an act of profaneness, of violation. I pressed it to my lips and returned it to its sanctuary.' And that was the act, and reaction, of a vicar...

William Beldham was almost as outstanding a fielder as he was a batsman. As a man with unusually fast reactions and co-ordination, he had a safe pair of hands and it was perhaps inevitable that he should find his natural place in the field at slip, particularly in his later years. But in his prime he could field anywhere, and often did. He would even keep wicket from time to time.

He was a useful medium-pace change bowler, prone to bowling full-tosses too frequently for comfort on occasions. But Beldham could read a batsman's skills – or lack of them – quickly enough, and would then try to bowl to the man's weaknesses. So as a change bowler, he had a useful role to play, especially when his captain was trying to break a big partnership. He would come on for a short spell, and if he took a wicket, so much the better. But he rarely bowled for long spells.

He was not above using all the tricks he could devise to take a wicket. Did he ever at Broadhalfpenny Down perpetrate the trick that he used at Lord's in 1806, when he was bowling to Lord Frederick Beauclerk in a single-wicket contest? Sawdust had recently been introduced to assist players in keeping their feet when the ground was wet. Unseen by the batsman, who had been batting for some time and showed every sign of winning the game, Beldham picked up a lump of wet dirt and sawdust, stuck it onto the ball, and bowled a delivery which landed on the dirt, turned violently and took Lord Frederick's wicket. He freely admitted the ruse later, and the result of the match stood unchallenged.

Of course, these were the days when the tens of thousands of spectators who came to watch their heroes on the cricket field were all safely behind the boundary some eighty yards away, or more. There was no close-up of his hand working the dirt onto the ball to fill the television screens in millions of homes, a fate which was to befall an England captain nearly 200 years later, with all the attendant fuss that followed. We can only wonder what the television age would have made of such goings-on at Lord's in 1806.

William Beldham went on playing first-class cricket for some forty years after he first played at Broadhalfpenny Down. At the age of fifty-three he scored 73 in a single-wicket match and reduced poor Browne of Brighton, a hitherto much-feared fast bowler, to a point where he hardly dared to bowl within Beldham's reach.

*An elderly Silver Billy Beldham muses on the glory days.
(Reproduced by kind permission of the MCC/The Bat and Ball)*

His last recorded first-class match was at Lords in 1821 when, at the age of fifty-five, he was selected for the Players versus Gentlemen game and finished with 23 not out; an appropriate outcome for the great man's last innings. There is some suggestion, however, that this last great match was not much to his liking. EV Lucas discovered that, even when he was between sixty and seventy years of age, Beldham was formally barred from playing in county matches. Whether this was for his own safety, or to protect bowlers from further indignities at the hands of an old man, is not clear. But we can guess.

William Beldham was born at Wrecclesham, near Farnham, where his family had a farm. After he retired from cricket he kept a public-house at Tilford where, from 1821, he lived for the rest of his long life. In 1852, when he was already eighty-six years old, Beldham walked the seven miles to Godalming to watch the local club play an England XI. And he walked home again in the evening.

When Beldham was ninety-two, Arthur Haygarth found him working in his garden at eight in the morning, still upright, in good health, and fit enough to walk without the aid of a stick. He finally died at the great age of ninety-six, the last of the immortals of Broadhalfpenny Down to pass away, having lived long enough to see cricket become the international sport we know today. He had been born just before the greatest of the glory days on Broadhalfpenny Down. By the time of his death in 1862, the first-class county system was well-established, John Wisden was just about to start his cricket almanack, and the first English touring team had already been to North America.

John Small junior (1765 – 1836)

John Small junior was a chip off the old block. His father was a close friend and contemporary of Richard Nyren. He had played for Hambledon from the early days, and had a fine reputation as a batsman. The son stood comparison with his father as batsman, fielder and friend. The family friendship on and off the cricket field simply passed down to the next generation.

Young Nyren and Small were boys together, watched their fathers play for Hambledon when they were children and grew up to take their places. As Richard Nyren and John Small senior were retiring from the Hambledon side, their offspring were ready to step into their shoes. But there the similarities ended, for John Small junior earned a place in his friend's greatest team, and John Nyren was realistic enough, and modest enough, not to award himself a place. His immortality came from his unique record of these events and people.

That childhood friendship between young John Small and John Nyren lasted a lifetime. Nyren's affectionate memories of his old friend positively spring from his pages, written so long after the events but with a warmth undimmed by the passage of time. He reminisces – in his late sixties – 'I think we could give some of the young whipsters a little trouble even now...it is my opinion we could bother them yet. They would find some trouble to bowl down our stumps.' Two old men, still dreaming dreams.

John Small junior first played at Broadhalfpenny Down in 1785, when he was nineteen years old. He was an outstanding opening batsman who played straight and correctly. He was an opening bat for good reason: he could build an innings, and see off the most demanding bowling. He was also reputed to be the best judge of a quick single in the entire club, Silver Billy Beldham thought. On one occasion, recalled by John Nyren, Small opened an innings with John Hammond at Lord's, when they needed 40 to win the match. They decided to take a run whenever the ball passed the wicket-keeper, such was their confidence and their judgement of the quick single. They got the 40 runs and won by ten wickets. In the event, all but one came from the bat. The exception was indeed a bye.

John Small junior was a strong, stocky man, just like his father. His inherited ability with a bat was recognized very early on in his life, by his mother as well as his father. As we have seen, she was one of his most ardent supporters, and would regularly attend the matches in which he was playing, just as she had done for her husband years before, still roaring her menfolk on. What father and son Small made of it all is not recorded. We can be certain, however, that all three of them – mother, father and son – would have been mighty proud and pleased whenever the two men played together for the same team, and this they did many times during the ten years or so from 1785, when young Small turned twenty and father was forty-eight.

The younger John Small was a first-class field, a specialist at cover, like his father before him. But he did not go on playing at the highest level for as long as his father had done. His name last appears in a match report when he was forty-six years old, compared with his father's last county game at the age of sixty-one.

John Small junior lived in Petersfield and helped to run the family business making cricket bats and balls. At times, the game must have seemed to fill just about every waking hour in the Small household, all year round.

Harry Walker (1760 – 1805)

Harry Walker and his younger brother Tom joined the Hambledon club together. Of the two, Tom became the better known, but this did not diminish the devotion of the older brother for the younger. Harry held his young hero Tom in awe, and modelled his batting on Tom's style. But there the similarity ended. As Silver Billy Beldham put it, 'Harry's half-hour was as good as Tom's afternoon.' He was a terrific hitter of the ball and could be relied on to score his runs fast. He batted left-handed and would fight his corner with real determination if runs were hard to come by. He was also as difficult to get out as his more illustrious brother.

Harry Walker is credited by Beldham as being the first man to bring the cut stroke to perfection. Robert Robinson ran him a close second, but Harry Walker pioneered the stroke as a means of dealing positively with the short, lifting ball on the off-side. He would wait until the ball was almost past his wicket and then cut down on it 'with great force'. Harry was also an excellent fielder.

Harry Walker's name first appears in existing records in 1784, when he was already twenty-four, but he was probably a player of some note before then. He was born at Churt, near Frensham, Surrey, where the family owned a farm. They also farmed at Hindhead, near the Devil's Punch Bowl. In his later years, Harry Walker moved to Brook, Surrey, where he traded as a maltster. He sadly hastened his end by consuming too much of the finished product.

Tom Walker (1762 – 1831)

The truth is that Tom Walker and his brother Harry were a couple of country bumpkins. As John Nyren put it: 'Never came two such unadulterated rustics into a civilized community.' Tom, in particular, was the constant source of amusement to the rest of the team, such was his un-sophisticated and ungainly manner. He was a bundle of bones held together by a skin which was textured like the bark of an old oak tree. His legs held him up like bean sticks, and Nyren's opinion was that the good Lord had omitted muscle when Tom Walker was under construction. He relied only on his tendons to hold himself together and to keep his limbs moving – which they consequently did in a somewhat rigid and awkward manner. When he ran – which was not very often – his arms and legs whirled in uncoordinated confusion. Nyren questioned what he had in his veins, as well. Even when his knuckles were rapped by the bowling of David Harris and others, the bones crunched, the skin split...but there was scarcely any blood to be seen. He dealt with the little there was by rubbing the back of his hand in the dirt. Tom Walker was a hard man, by all accounts. He obviously looked it, too. When he was twenty he looked forty, a predicament that never left him. Little wonder, then, that he became the butt of so much mirth. Perhaps it was the only way his team, and opponents, could cope with his awesome single-mindedness.

Whatever his physical shortcomings, this bean-stick of a man was as immovable as granite on the cricket field. Not only did he have little in the way of blood; he had little in the way of nerves, either. He must have wiped many a tear of laughter from many an opponent's eye during the course of matches in which he played. Yet here is a right-handed opening bat to compare with any since. He would start an innings on the assumption that he would still be there at the end. He very often was. He went by the nickname of 'Old Everlasting', and for good reason. He may not have scored quickly, but he would hold the innings together, and drive the bowlers half-crazy with frustration. Nothing ruffled him, nothing dented his concentration, nothing was going to stop his game-plan. As Nyren put it, he was 'devilish troublesome' to get out. As we saw earlier, David Harris once bowled 170 balls to Tom Walker, who scored only a single off them all. But he was still there at the end.

His concentration was absolute. When he was batting he became incoherent with concentration, committed to the struggle, body and soul. The most anyone got out of him was a grunt, a noise of personal disapproval if something had gone wrong or was not to his liking – a ball played not where he wanted, or one which beat him, perhaps. A fearsome sound it was, too. It was described to the Rev. John Mitford as being 'like a broken-winded horse, only of a deeper bass'.

Whatever the state of the game, whatever the score, or time remaining, Tom Walker continued to play his own game, regardless of all that was going on around him. First over or last over, they all came the same to him. Neither did he let his own humble background influence his response when he faced the bowling of an aristocrat. This was batsman versus bowler; not yokel versus peer of the realm. Which was how he once brought Lord Frederick Beauclerk to a frenzy of anger when he blocked a succession of deliveries. Eventually his lordship threw down his white hat and called Tom Walker 'a confounded old beast'. Said Walker: 'I doan't care what ee zays,' and carried on in his own phlegmatic way as if nothing had happened.

Tom Walker, 'after George Shepheard', 1790
(Reproduced by kind permission of the MCC)

Like all successful openers, Tom Walker played straight. He had a sound technique, which he worked on constantly. Like David Harris, he would practise in a barn on his farm, in all weathers, and all through the year. Like most straight players, he drove the ball well, both to off and leg, and always along the ground. There were few easy catches to be had off Tom Walker.

In 1786, playing in a six-a-side game for Hambledon against Kent, he took nearly five hours to score 26 in the first innings. In the second innings he received 321 deliveries, off which he struck a mere 12 runs. The whole match produced only 169 runs, and it took four days to complete. Whether there were any spectators left to take the slightest interest in the outcome is doubtful.

Yet Tom Walker's scoring was substantial. Having driven the Kent bowling to despair earlier in the season, he found himself playing Kent again, later in 1786. This time he was playing for the White Conduit Club. The match was at Canterbury. Now he set records of a very different kind. In the first innings he scored 95 not out (out of a total of 183) and in the second 102, a total of 197 for once out, in the days when wickets were not prepared for batting as they are now. The bat he used in the first innings is preserved to this day at Lord's, and inscribed 'Walker 95,'86'. There is no record of anyone else getting so close to a century in both innings of a match before that time. Indeed, another thirty-four years were to pass before, in July 1817, the Sussex all-rounder William Lambert became the first man to score two separate centuries in a single game. He made 107 not out and 157 against Surrey, playing at Lord's.

Not surprisingly, Tom Walker regularly finished a season with one of Hambledon's highest aggregates, despite his legendary reputation for stone-walling. His average would have been the envy of many others, too, had they been kept then as they are today. In these respects, perhaps only Beldham was his peer. In yet another appearance against Kent in 1786, Tom Walker made 56 out of 116; and for Surrey in 1788, he made 93 out of 197. So he could clearly score runs at a reasonable pace once he was 'set', especially if wickets were going down at the other end.

There is little doubt that Tom Walker was a cricketer to be taken seriously. Indeed, he was a wily old fox, who could see and take an advantage on the cricket field whenever one was offered by his opponents. He had a thorough knowledge of the game and a nimble mind behind those gaunt features. But his nimbleness did not extend to his running between the wickets. Once, when he was batting with the fleet-footed Noah Mann, they were running what proved to be a 'four' and Noah lapped Tom Walker. Both of them were now making for the same end.

Noah patted Tom on the shoulder and commented: 'Good name for you – Walker. You never were a runner.'

Tom Walker has a unique place in the annals of cricket, not as a batsman but as a bowler. He was not a regular bowler, nor even a change bowler except on rare occasions. Yet he revolutionized bowling. He was the first man to bowl round-arm. This was in 1792, before which all bowling had been underarm. When he first 'threw' the ball, as Nyren puts it, the Hambledon club was so thunderstruck that a meeting was called to review the situation. It was decided that this method of delivery was 'foul play', due to the tremendous pace that such bowling generated. Yet, twenty years later, John Willes of Kent reinvented it and soon it was the norm, eventually evolving into overarm. The game had changed forever.

Tom Walker also experimented with bowling slow, high lobs which would scarcely reach the wicket at the other end, often to the embarrassment of the facing batsman. Even good batsmen of the day were not used to such childish lobs, and they complained bitterly that such bowling made them look foolish and was difficult to score off. Two hundred years later, batsmen are still complaining about the problems of playing slow bowling. Perhaps it's true – nothing ever changes.

Like his brother Harry, Tom was born and brought up on the family farms near Hindhead. He played regularly until he was fifty years old, occasionally appearing for the MCC against Surrey towards the end of his career. He gave up farming and became a gamekeeper for a few years, before he and his wife moved to Chiddingfold, Surrey, just south of Haslemere, where they kept a grocer's shop. He was sixty-eight when he died.

(Harry and Tom Walker had a younger brother, John (1768-1835), who played a few games for Hambledon around 1789.)

Robert Robinson (1765 – 1822)

Although Robert Robinson's name appears in Nyren's great XI, he makes no other reference to this player in his recollections.

Robert Robinson's primitive shin-guards anticipated modern pads by many decades, but his team-mates' mirth embarrassed him into abandoning them.
(Copyright Philip Hodkin)

Nor does the name appear in any match accounts from the glory days. But Arthur Haygarth describes him as a terrific hitter, with a vicious cut. Beldham considered Robert Robinson to be one of the fathers of the cut. He would wait until the ball was almost past him, and then cut with great force.

Robert Robinson was born in 1765, so he would have been one of the late-comers to Broadhalfpenny Down. He was a big man, a farmer's son, and he batted left-handed. For several years, Arthur Haygarth tells us, he was 'one of the best in England'. Yet, as a child, his right hand – the more important of the two for a left-hander – had been severely damaged in a fire, which had stunted the growth of his fingers and caused the loss of one of them. As a result, his bat handle had to be specially modified for him, with grooving to fit the deformity, strengthened by iron let into the remaining wood. One of Robert Robinson's unique bats is still to be seen at Lord's.

He was known as 'Long Bob', and 'Three-Fingered Jack', both nicknames being brutally to the point. But he had yet another claim to fame. Robert Robinson had an inventive turn of mind, and he sought practical solutions to problems he encountered on the cricket field. He did not simply complain about the pain suffered when the ball hit his legs; he did something about it. He invented the leg-guard, or pads as they are now universally called. His invention consisted of two thin boards, held wrapped around the leg. The ball would ricochet off these primitive contraptions with such a clatter that his contemporaries could not contain their laughter. Such was his embarrassment that, sadly, he felt obliged to stop using them.

But his ingenuity did not stop there. Robinson is also credited with the introduction of spikes, although his original idea was to have them on one shoe only. They were of such enormous length that they must have slowed him up, although they gave the extra grip he sought. Despite such early difficulties, his originality of thought and ingenuity predated by many decades the equipment we all take for granted today.

Robert Robinson played professionally for Surrey later in his career, had a benefit match in 1816 and went on playing until he was fifty-four, only three years before his death. Even by the standards of the day, to continue to such an age was unusual.

He lived most of his life at Ash, near Farnham, where he was born and died. So here was yet another first-class player from this nursery of talent during the latter half of the eighteenth century.

Noah Mann (1756 – 1789)

The fastest man in the side. No-one ever beat him in a running race, and he was often challenged. So quick was he around the field, and in his thinking, that he ran out many a batsman who failed to judge his speed and reactions. He was all muscle, broad-chested, large at the hips, but had legs like a spider. Yet they carried him as fast as any man. He was truly hyperactive, with boundless energy to boot.

Noah Mann arrives at the Bat and Ball, still collecting handkerchiefs at full gallop.
(Copyright Philip Hodkin)

He needed it, too. Every Tuesday, to practise, and on match days, he would set off on horseback from Northchapel, a village near Petworth and over twenty-five miles from Broadhalfpenny Down. He made the fifty-plus miles round trip without giving it a thought. He obviously loved riding, and was something of a skilled horseman anyway. On some occasions – as he approached the Bat and Ball up the long sloping road from the east – his team-mates, already gathered at the top of the hill, would place handkerchiefs on the ground for him to collect by leaning from his horse at full gallop. He rarely missed one.

On the cricket field he was something of an all-rounder, and the ideal man for a crisis. In addition to his contributions in the field, he could bat anywhere and was a useful change bowler. And he did everything left-handed. The General (Richard Nyren) often asked Noah Mann to come on for a few overs when Hambledon were having trouble breaking up a partnership. Noah rarely let him down. He had that happy knack of taking wickets just when they were most needed. He could put a curve on the ball that was sufficiently deceptive to the batsman that it would lure him into a false stroke, often enough a fatal one. His delivery of the ball involved a vigorous twist of the wrist and hand. Watching him bowl was like watching a juggler, by all accounts. Two or three overs of his mesmeric bowling usually did the trick.

He was equally effective with a bat in his hand. Given his hyperactivity and his brute strength, it is not surprising that he was a fearsome hitter of the ball. Once, when he was batting with John Nyren, he hit a full toss over his shoulder so far that they ran ten.

Like many great hitters since, Noah Mann liked to bat well up the order and did not take kindly to the skipper putting him further down. But Richard Nyren knew his man, and his value in a crisis. On one famous occasion, Hambledon were chasing a huge total set them by England. Nyren kept Mann back to bat at number eleven, despite constant pleas from Noah to be allowed in sooner. When he finally got to the wicket, ten runs were still needed to win, with now only the last wicket left. Thousands around the boundary could hardly bear the tension. Old men chewed the ends off their staves; an agitated Sir Horace Mann, the gentleman farmer from Kent, was to be seen outside the ground scything daisies with the end of his walking stick; he could hardly bear to look. Not only was he the *de facto* England manager on this particular day, but he was heavily indebted to the bookies. The whole multitude held its breath.

Lumpy Stevens was bowling for England and had just taken the previous wicket. His first two balls to Noah Mann (who was no relation to the anxious England manager) were straight, of good length, and the batsman just pushed them back. Still ten wanted. The next was a full toss; Noah got underneath it and, with a mighty swing of the bat hit the ball clean out of the ground. Six! Broadhalfpenny Down erupted. John Nyren never heard a roar like it. They eventually got the remaining four in singles and won the game, after a titanic tussle, by a single wicket. Afterwards, Noah Mann again complained to Richard Nyren that he should have gone in earlier, but the General had his answer ready. He told Noah that he was the one man in the side with the nerve and confidence to make those runs, whatever the pressure. Nyren could be sure of him, as of no other. Noah accepted the compliment, and the decision, since it had demonstrably won the game. Sadly, the records of the game are lost.

But it was as a fielder that Noah Mann earned his greatest renown. He darted around the field like lightning and covered an area normally allocated to two men. And he was the other half of the long-stop run-out trap which he worked so successfully with George Leer for so many years. The initiative always came from George, who would tip Noah the wink when he was going to let a ball go by, or appear to go by. Noah then came in close behind, and as the batsmen set off for what they thought was a safe bye, Noah would swoop on the ball and have it into Tom Sueter's hands in a flash. They ensnared many an unwitting batsman with that ploy.

Noah Mann never wore a hat, or any other head-covering, on the cricket field. In its day, this was odd behaviour. Gentlemen wore wide-brimmed hats, players wore tricorns. But not Noah Mann. Whatever the weather, he was never seen with anything on his head. Nobody tells us why. Maybe he simply liked to feel the sun.

Noah Mann was born in Northchapel and lived there all his life. He was a shoemaker, and kept the Half Moon pub there to his end – and a sad and untimely end it was. It came in December 1789. Noah and friends had had a wild night at the bar, following a day's shooting, and he was so far past caring that no-one could persuade him to go up to bed. Instead, he fell asleep in a chair in front of the open fire. As usual, all the ashes were heaped together on the hearth, to keep the fire in for the morning. During the night, he fell off his chair onto the embers, and was so paralytically asleep that he got severely burned all down one side. He was dead from his injuries within the day. He was only thirty-three.

Thomas Scott (1766 – 1799)

Although Thomas Scott is listed in John Nyren's all-time best XI, he tells us nothing about him. Arthur Haygarth discovered that he was a 'very successful batsman' who played for the club for several seasons. He was a glover by trade, and his family lived in Alton.

Like Noah Mann, he died an untimely death at the early age of thirty-three; no-one knows why. But their short lives are in sharp contrast with so many other cricketers of these glory days, who lived to an extraordinary age for those times.

So if that was John Nyren's best team, it was definitely not listed in what we would today regard as the right batting order (nor would it have been at the time). However, given the knowledge we have of these superb cricketers, and ignoring – for a moment – the chronological inexactitude, who do we suppose would be the captain, and what would his true batting order have been? Some of the match records give us clues. Perhaps this XI would have batted thus:

1. John Small junior
2. Tom Walker
3. Silver Billy Beldham
4. Robert Robinson
5. Harry Walker
6. Thomas Scott
7. John Wells
8. Tom Taylor
9. Richard Purchase
10. Noah Mann
11. David Harris

But if this was John Nyren's best side from the players he saw at Broadhalfpenny Down, it is alarmingly unbalanced. For a start, it has no regular wicket-keeper. Beldham, who occasionally kept, would have had to fill the role. It is also somewhat short on bowling, but we have to remember that bowling was not regarded then as important as batting when picking a side. Even so, this team lacks at least one strong opening-bowler. It is well-enough supplied with change bowlers, and Richard Purchase and Noah Mann can supply the spin, if required.

Its supreme strength is in its batting, of course. No wonder Nyren claimed that this side could beat any XXII in England at the time. Maybe the shortage of one more bowler at the expense of a middle-order batsman would have been more than made up in the colossal scoring power this team had. If crowds of 20,000 came to watch Hambledon play England at Broadhalfpenny Down when only a fraction of that team was on view on any one day, we can only wonder at the crowds the full side would have attracted. Perhaps the Elysian Fields have already seen such a spectacular event, in which case the scorecard would be a collectors' item, even in that exalted realm.

More seriously, though, there is another question over this team: who would have been the captain? Richard Nyren is not there to act as General. Perhaps David Harris would have been elected skipper. These days, bowlers are not often asked to captain a side, mainly because they find making decisions in the field, especially about their own bowling, so difficult and distracting from their own performance. But David Harris appears, from what we know of all these men, to have had the tactical shrewdness, man-management skills, and sheer ability to read a game. He would have been the man to lead it.

But while this was, according to John Nyren, the finest team Hambledon might ever have fielded, there is sadly no evidence from match records that it ever played as a unit on any single occasion. It was certainly possible. Bearing in mind the thirteen-year age difference between the oldest and youngest members of this side, at best they might have played together at opposite ends of their playing days, with skills and fitness to match.

Of course, many other players appeared for Hambledon during the glory days on Broadhalfpenny Down. Some might reasonably have expected to appear in one, if not both, of the teams we have looked at so far. Yet more players – perhaps we should call them occasionals – played for the club from time to time. As we have seen, it was also the practice of the day to form sides which included 'given men', meaning that they were strengthened by players who did not normally represent them. These players were itinerant professionals, with loyalty strictly limited to whichever club was paying them for that day's sport. Such funds were forthcoming either from the club itself or, more likely, from a benefactor of the club. Many of the men we have already met fall into the category of professional, by that measure at least. And the men who originally became famous for their exploits on Broadhalfpenny Down, as did Silver Billy Beldham, Tom Walker, David Harris, Robert Robinson and John Small junior, all went on to earn their livings as cricketers for much of their active lives.

Among the other cricketers who played for Hambledon at that time, whether regularly, as guests, or as given men, were several more great names from the period. They make an odd assortment, but cricket then was a great social leveller, as we have seen repeatedly.

So these men were also members of what might be described as the Hambledon squad.

Richard Veck (1756 – 1823)

It is a complete mystery why John Nyren made no mention of Richard Veck in his memoirs, since Veck was one of the regular players at Broadhalfpenny Down during the glory days. He was a useful batsman and played for some nine seasons, although little is known of him. He was born at Alresford, near Alton. He took a draper's shop in 1783 at Bishop's Waltham, not far from Hambledon, but gave up playing cricket the following year, under pressure from his young wife and from the demands of his business.

James Aylward (1741 – 1827)

A safe left-handed batsman, with a sound defence, who will always be remembered for the greatest innings the club ever saw, the one which set up its biggest-ever win over England. The three-day game started on 18 June 1777 and James Aylward batted with great determination and correctness over three days. He scored 167 runs out of a total of 403, against the finest bowling-attack of the day, led by Lumpy Stevens. England were overwhelmed, losing by an innings and 168 runs – one more than Aylward's score. (The match is described in more detail in the next chapter.)

A couple of years or so after his great feat, Aylward was 'poached' from Hambledon by Sir Horace Mann, who offered him a post as bailiff on his estate in Kent. He accepted, and played for Sir Horace's sides, including his 'All-England' teams, thereafter. He repaid Sir Horace's generosity many times, even if the daisies did continue to suffer. At Bishopsbourne, Kent, in 1786, VI of Kent were playing VI of Hambledon. Sir Horace was playing for Kent that day, and he skippered the side as well. Aylward went to the wicket when Kent's penultimate wicket fell. They now needed two runs to win, with the last pair batting. He was dropped by Taylor before he had scored, but did not allow that to break his concentration. In the end, it took Aylward ninety-four deliveries to get those two runs, but get them he did.

John Nyren tells us little of James Aylward, apart from his clumsiness in the field. He was, however, known for his fussy, somewhat grand manner. When he felt so inclined, he might call for a lemon to quench his thirst after he had been batting for a while, and would not be best pleased to receive little more than a round of derogatory laughter instead. It has been suggested by the cricket writer GD Martineau, among others, that Aylward's penchant for the public consumption of lemon is the origin of the phrase 'looking a lemon', as a description of public embarrassment.

Some three or four years after his great innings against England, James Aylward returned to play again on Broadhalfpenny Down – this time as England's skipper. He played first-class cricket until he was in his sixties, his last known game being at the end of the 1802 season. Even in death, he made a poignant connection between the beginnings of the modern game and its maturity. Having made the greatest score for Hambledon, when the club had its biggest win over England, he was to be buried in St John's Wood churchyard, right next door to Lord's cricket ground.

The Earl of Winchilsea (1752 – 1826)

An enthusiastic supporter of the club, who played occasionally in the 1780s and made a few good scores in his time. After the demise of the Hambledon club, he was credited – if that is the right word – with attempting the introduction of a fourth stump, and a wicket two inches taller. This 'improvement', he claimed, would shorten the game. Fortunately for the rest of us, the idea was not taken up. The Earl was a founder member of the MCC.

Richard Francis (dates unknown)

Richard Francis was something of a carpet-bagging cricketer. He was originally a Surrey man, who first moved to Hambledon for the opportunity to play on Broadhalfpenny Down. Then, later in his life, he moved to Essex, where he continued to play for some years, according to Beldham's recollections. Richard Francis first encountered the Hambledon club when he played against it for Surrey. He was already a well-known bowler, who delivered the ball with a pronounced jerk – a legitimate action then.

He moved himself to Hambledon, expressly with the intention of joining the club. He had scarcely finished moving in when he encountered John Nyren, then still a boy, in the village street. Young John recognized him at once and rushed back to the George to tell his father whom he had just met in the village. Richard Francis was enlisted at once.

Francis played at Broadhalfpenny Down, and later at Windmill Down, for some years. He and David Harris, who started playing there a short time later, were a powerful addition to an already formidably-strong team. Richard Francis was also a useful bat, and could be expected to make a contribution to the score fairly regularly.

John Freemantle (1758 – 1831)

A useful, quickish bowler, with a high delivery action. Compared to the abundance of talent in the club at the time, John Freemantle does not rate highly, according to John Nyren, but he was a handy man to have in the side, nonetheless. He could be relied on for a few runs, too, and more than made up for his limited natural talent as a player with a great determination and commitment on the field; in short, he was a John Bull of a man.

Andrew Freemantle (1768/9(?) – 1837)

A sound, effective, left-handed batsman who played cricket for some twenty-three years. How many of them were spent at Broadhalfpenny Down is not clear from the remaining records, which confirm his presence in only two seasons at the very end of the glory days. He had an exceptionally good defence and was a good hitter, too. Once he had played himself in, 'it was a deuced hard matter to get him out,' according to John Nyren. He was equally dependable in the field, where he was normally positioned in the deep.

When he moved to the Winchester area about the turn of the century, he took a pub at Easton. It, too, was called the Bat and Ball Inn.

So these were the men who gave a little Hampshire village the strongest cricket team in all England. It was a distinction they held for some thirty-five years. The original side had one of the greatest captains of all time, and it took the club from obscurity to fame. Surely that feat is just as remarkable as that achieved by its successor, which built the club's reputation to even greater heights. Little wonder, then, that John Nyren described the men of Hambledon as only 'a little lower than angels'.

At the risk of committing an act of sacrilege, there is an irresistible temptation to review these two sides again, discard the totally understandable childhood distortions of perspective that John Nyren revealed when he named his best side, and try to assemble the greatest team from the glory days, regardless of dates. There would seem to be a persuasive case for the inclusion of Richard Nyren as captain, Brett as the fastest bowler of them all, Tom Sueter to keep wicket, and old John Small, in any XI picked from the club's total playing strength over the years. But who goes from John Nyren's later side? This is not an easy decision. Perhaps inevitably, old John Small replaces his son. He was clearly the better player of the two. Thomas Scott has to make way for Brett, and the inclusion of the wicket-keeper supreme, Tom Sueter, who is also well able to hold his place as a fast-scoring middle-order batsman, has to displace Tom Taylor. Richard Nyren must edge out Harry Walker, despite the latter's potential for quick scoring. This side has more than enough batsmen already. His going makes way for the brains and the all-round skills of the General.

In batting order, then, this would seem to be the ultimate Hambledon team:

1. John Small senior
2. Tom Walker
3. William Beldham
4. Robert Robinson
5. Tom Sueter, wicket-keeper
6. Richard Nyren, captain
7. John Wells
8. Noah Mann
9. Richard Purchase
10. David Harris
11. Thomas Brett

There would be no price too high to see that team take the field. The only problem might be to find a team worthy of opposing them. Happily, in these entirely speculative circumstances we can ignore such realities. We can simply enjoy the thought. Only the bookmakers would not relish this spectacle. The odds would be out of sight.

Not before time, we must now pay tribute to the man who first brought these remarkable men and their astonishing achievements to our notice.

John Nyren (15 December 1764 – 30 June 1837)

Son of the finest cricket captain of his day. He was born when his parents were living at the Bat and Ball. For John, cricket was a part of his life from the time he could stand up and take notice. In due course, he too played for Hambledon, and later for England. His first few formative years were lived directly opposite Broadhalfpenny Down, and they had a profound effect on him. Much later, he found his place in history as the recorder of the great men he watched as a child, and of their exploits across the road. Yet he was modest enough not to include his own efforts in his memoirs. Nor did he attempt to rank his own achievements as he ranked all the others, a self-imposed task he performed with affection as well as considerable objectivity.

Here was a supreme observer, a man without envy, who had been steeped in the game from childhood and understood it to the very depths of his being. He was a true lover of the game of cricket and all it stood for. He knew its infinite capacity to thrill and surprise, to bring out aspects of character from the players, and the spectators, which might otherwise have lain hidden. Above all, he was able to capture it on paper, with the sensitive help of Charles Cowden Clarke. Between them, they produced the very first, and possibly still the very best, piece of cricket literature in what is now a vast library. In his own way, John Nyren made himself as much one of the immortals of cricket as any of the men he wrote about. Seventy years after Nyren's death, EV Lucas – author of *The Hambledon Men*, the next great book about the glory days – described *The Cricketers of my Time* as a masterpiece:

Nyren's book stands alone in English literature. It had no predecessor; it has no successor. The only piece of writing that I can find worthy to place beside it is Hazlitt's description of Cavanagh, the Fives player, which is full of gusto – the gusto that comes from admiration and love.

Self-evidently, John Nyren was a thinker as well as a writer, a predictable chip off the old block – and what a block Richard Nyren was. His son clearly inherited his father's shrewdness, observation, tact, and infinite capacity to influence events. John was a thinking cricketer, too, and no slouch on the field of play. He was a useful left-handed batsman, and a fielder who could always be relied upon, particularly at point, where he took many a catch off defensive strokes that the batsmen might have thought safe. He was also an exceptional judge of the high catch. He ran with his back to a high hit, unlike most fielders who struggle to run backwards while they keep their eye on the ball. But not John Nyren. He would turn at just the right moment, steady himself in the right spot and take the catch cleanly; a rare skill, even today.

John Nyren formally joined the Hambledon club in 1778, when he was still only thirteen. He must have thought of membership as his birthright, since he had had cricket and the players as part of his home life from the beginning. He went on playing for the club until 1791, when his father moved to London and the glory days were effectively brought to an end. Even so, son John continued to play cricket beyond his sixtieth birthday. He was over fifty-two when he played his last recorded first-class match. It took place at Lord's, where he was known as 'young Hambledon', on 18 June 1817 – forty years to the day after James Aylward's immortal innings.

His first direct experience of what was then the first-class game came in 1787 when, at the age of twenty-two, he suddenly found himself playing for England, and against Hambledon no less. James Aylward skippered the England side and John Nyren's inclusion was simply to make up the numbers. Suddenly, and unexpectedly, here he was on his home ground playing against his own club. It must have been an overwhelming experience, playing with and against so many of his boyhood heroes. Whether he endeared himself to his home club is doubtful, since England won and the young Nyren succeeded in running out two of the Hambledon batsmen. But father would have been proud, even though he might not have cared much for the result.

We know little about John Nyren beyond the researches of Haygarth and the biographical sketches by EV Lucas, published in 1907. For students of the game, Lucas's *The Hambledon Men* has long been strongly recommended. It was the primary source for this chapter, but contains infinitely more detail for those readers seeking additional information. It takes a more expansive view and offers the leisurely reader the sheer pleasure of fine writing by a master essayist of a bygone age. What Lucas does tell us, mainly through the memories of John Nyren's grand-daughter, is that he was a truly cultivated man with wide artistic interests. She confirms what we already knew – that he was a perspicacious and thoughtful man. He was also much given to helping others, often at his own expense. Personal kindness was part of his nature.

Now, briefly, let's look at some of the men Hambledon played against and who, sometimes, also played for the club. To some extent using social rank as our yardstick, in the manner of the times, we must start thus:

Sir Horace Mann (1744 – 1814)

One of the earliest of the great patrons of the game, Sir Horace Mann seems to have spent most, if not all, of his life enjoying cricket, especially in and around his estates in Kent. He was known as 'The King of Cricket', but like many a monarch before him he ultimately found his crown an expensive burden. He sometimes played, but more often than not he was the match manager, in today's parlance, and the team manager as well, especially when Hambledon was the opposition. It is

Sir Horace Mann scythes the daisies once again, as the events on Broadhalfpenny Down put his wager increasingly at risk.
(Copyright Philip Hodkin)

almost fair to say that Sir Horace appears to have spent a large part of his adult life trying to raise an England side good enough to beat Hambledon on Broadhalfpenny Down, or anywhere else for that matter. He didn't have much success. Given his habit of scything daisies with his stick when things weren't going well, he must have cleared quite an acreage in the course of his cricketing days.

Despite more than his share of disappointments, nothing should detract from his huge and continuing generosity towards the game and those who could play it to the highest standards. At a critical point in its growth from a country pastime to the towering game it became, Sir Horace Mann's financial and social influence on cricket was of fundamental importance. Ironically, and sadly, that same crucial support – indeed extravagance – must have played its own part in his ultimate bankruptcy. Certainly he was better known for his indulgence in sport in general, and cricket in particular, than he ever was for any interest in business. His financial ruin must, too, have been accelerated by his penchant for gambling.

Sir Horace regularly wagered wildly excessive sums of money on the outcome of matches, which must have helped reduce the daisy population still further.

The Mann family later changed its name to Cornwallis, and eventually rebuilt its fortunes. Even today, the family is still closely associated with cricket in general, and with Kent County Cricket Club in particular. Sir Horace Mann was a Carthusian, and must be one of the earliest-known cricketers to emerge from Charterhouse School, that distinguished source of so many fine players since, including – much later – the England captain Peter May.

John Frederick, third Duke of Dorset (1745 – 1799)

The third Duke of Dorset was not in the same league as that other cricketing aristocrat, Lord Frederick Beauclerk, but he was a useful player all the same. He was an exceptional fielder in his younger days, a talent which appears to have run in the family, as we saw earlier with his uncle's catch in the deep to dismiss Richard Nyren's uncle. The Duke's patronage of the game was of infinitely greater value to cricket as a whole, to say nothing of the particular clubs he supported, than all the runs he scored when he was an active participant. Sevenoaks Vine is particularly indebted to the Dorset family, since they gave the club its ground in perpetuity.

When the Earl of Tankerville was not playing in the same side, the Duke of Dorset preferred to field at slip, where he had an odd habit of standing with his head resting to one side as he relaxed between deliveries. Nobody appears to have argued much with his right to decide where he wanted to field, captain included. His uncle might have indulged his gardener, but not this Duke.

His playing days were captured in *The Gentleman's Magazine*, which published this panegyric in 1773, four years before the famous lampoon penned by the Duchess of Devonshire. This earlier comment on the Duke's cricketing abilities and interests was definitely not from her pen:

> His Grace for bowling cannot yield
> To none but Lumpy in the field.
> He firmly stands with bat upright
> And strikes with his athletic might;
> Sends forth the ball across the mead
> And scores six notches for the deed.

The Duke of Dorset was a great advocate of the game and was deeply involved in it throughout his life. He raised, and supported with his money, his presence, and his active participation, many of the great teams of the day, particularly the team that first gloried under the name 'All-England'.

He must also be credited with the first attempt to raise an international touring side. At the time, 1789, he had been His Majesty's Ambassador to France for a short time, watching local unrest boiling up to the climactic outbreak of the French Revolution later that year. At the beginning of the year, however, his lordship was struck with a brilliant idea. He wrote to the then England captain, William Yalden, and suggested that he should put a side together to visit France in the summer and show the game to the French with a match in the Bois de Boulogne. Yalden did as he was asked. The team included the Earl of Tankerville and Lumpy Stevens. A place was also left for the Duke himself. Yalden and his team set off for Paris with a mixture of excitement and trepidation. Many of the players, certainly those whose idea of a long journey was a two-day ride to the other side of London for a cricket match, had certainly never been abroad before. Anticipation was running high. Yalden finally got his team as far as Dover, where they awaited the next sailing to Calais. When the boat docked, who should disembark but an ashen-faced Duke of Dorset, coming hot-foot in the opposite direction. He had just escaped with his life from the beginnings of the French Revolution. Needless to say, the tour went no further, but it pre-dated the next international touring side – and the first to get beyond the coastline of England – by some seventy years, when a touring team set sail for Montreal and Philadelphia in 1859.

The Duke was a member of the Hambledon club, although he sometimes played against the club or raised teams to do so. He was a member of the club's committee and led the Hambledon delegation to the meeting in London which drew up the first comprehensive revision of the laws governing the game, in 1774.

Sadly, John Frederick, third Duke of Dorset, will also forever be remembered for having had a direct hand in Hambledon's decision gradually to abandon Broadhalfpenny Down from 1782 onwards. His views on the place as being increasingly unsuitable for cricket played a decisive part in the club's ultimate demise.

The Earl of Tankerville (1743 – 1822)

The Earl of Tankerville was another aristocratic batsman and alternative slip-field to the Duke of Dorset. What a wonderful image of social levelling is conjured up by the vision of the Duke and the Earl standing at first and second slip to the bowling of the humble but demonic Lumpy Stevens. There must have been times when the yokels watching from the boundary wondered whether they were seeing things. Lumpy would not have been averse to moving their lordships into just the right position for possible catches and, no doubt, expressing himself with glee – or chagrin, depending on the outcome – in the event of a sharp edge to his aristocratic slip-cordon.

There is little doubt that the Earl indulged Lumpy. He was his patron and kept him well-stocked with goodies from the baronial kitchens and cellars. So dropping a catch – were such an unlikely calamity to occur – might be recompensed with a good bottle or two afterwards. In fact, the Earl did far more than that, both for Lumpy Stevens and for several other great but humble players of the day. He supported them financially and gave them jobs which were, in reality, sinecures during the cricket season. After Lumpy retired from the game, the Earl gave him a full-time job as gardener at his seat at Walton-on-

Thames, Surrey. The Earl was, with Sir Horace Mann and the third Duke of Dorset, one of the game's first great patrons and, in the case of the Earl's esteemed friend and much-favoured bowler, he extended his patronage even to the erection of a tombstone over Lumpy's grave.

Edward 'Lumpy' Stevens (1735 – 1819)

Lumpy is so inextricably bound up with his patron, the Earl of Tankerville, that they belong together even here. Lumpy was a short, stout, genial and straightforward man. He came from Surrey and, so far as the records now tell us, first played at Broadhalfpenny Down as a member of the England side on 23 June 1772. He was already thirty-seven years old, so it would not be unreasonable to suppose that he had played there before then. On this occasion, Hambledon won by 53 runs. Lumpy's disappointment at the result does not appear to have spoilt his view of the ground, however. He came to love the place, and played there regularly over many years. Some of his greatest bowling feats were achieved on this ground. In fact, he became so popular with the Hambledon club – for he was a man of great good humour as well as a fiend with a ball in his hand – that he was invited to become a member. He played for the club from time to time, and attended many Hambledon functions over the years. It is fair to say that Broadhalfpenny Down became Lumpy Stevens's spiritual home, such was his affection for it.

He was a much-feared bowler who liked nothing more than to bowl a batsman out with a delivery that shot all along the ground after pitching and took off the bail in a flash. John Nyren thought Lumpy almost as good as David Harris in his ability to pitch the ball consistently in the right place. But he lacked Harris's pace and his shrewdness. Lumpy pitched his wickets – when the choice was his – so that his deliveries might shoot forward along the ground. This obliged him to get his wickets by hitting the wicket, which was not easy when there were only two stumps to aim at – a situation that did not change until 1775, when Lumpy had already passed his fortieth birthday. This change in the laws was, of course, Lumpy's greatest claim to fame. He bowled a ball through old John Small's stumps three times in a single innings, an achievement which triggered the introduction of the third stump. Some seasons earlier he had twice bowled out John Small senior, once in a match played at Bishopsbourne, Kent, while the other occasion was on Broadhalfpenny Down. Prior to that, the batsman had rarely lost his bail in many years, and Lumpy's two successes were held in awe for some time afterwards.

Lumpy Stevens, who first played cricket on Broadhalfpenny Down for England and came to love the place. This portrait is believed to be by Almond, an itinerant painter, in 1783 when Lumpy was 48 years old. (Reproduced by kind permission of the MCC/The Bat and Ball)

Lumpy's approach to bowling was significantly different from that of his young rival, David Harris. Harris, as we have already seen, pitched his wickets so that he could get lift from the pitch and thus increase the chances of getting batsmen out caught. It also made scoring runs safely more difficult. Lumpy normally sought to dislodge the bail. Despite this apparent disadvantage, Lumpy was a regular England bowler for many years and took wickets season after season. He might even have taken more than Harris over the years, but at a greater cost. Lumpy Stevens's bowling average, good though it must have been, was not even close to that of David Harris. That did not stop the Earl of Tankerville wagering an incredible £100 (£50,000 today) on Lumpy's bowling an over of four balls and hitting a small feather on the ground at least once. He did it, and the Earl won his bet.

Lumpy was good enough to play for England until well into his fifties. He was fifty-four when he played his last recorded match. After his playing days were over, he was invited by the

Earl of Tankerville to take up a job as gardener on the Earl's estate at Walton-on-Thames.

Despite the distance involved – now over fifty miles – Lumpy would, from time to time, return to Broadhalfpenny Down and the scene of some of his greatest exploits, just to drink in the atmosphere – and in the Bat and Ball, no doubt. He was a great trencherman. Yet there is some question about how he came by his famous nickname. He was short and reputedly round. However, there must be some doubt about his being overweight. Drawings of him made during his lifetime suggest that he had a lumpiness about his face, which was not particularly chubby. His appearance is the first of at least three possible reasons offered by various commentators of the time to explain how he acquired the name Lumpy. The second was his alleged single-handed consumption of an enormous apple pie at a Hambledon club dinner at the Bat and Ball. Finally, there was his particular habit of choosing a lumpy piece of ground to bowl at, so that the ball might shoot. Perhaps all three explanations contributed to this, the most renowned of all cricketing nicknames and one which is still instantly recognized two centuries later. He would have liked that.

Reverend Lord Frederick Beauclerk (1773 – 1850)

Lord Frederick Beauclerk was the best of the nobility playing regularly at the turn of the century, and certainly one of the best batsmen of his day. John Nyren thought Beauclerk the second-best batsman in the game after Silver Billy Beldham, which is some accolade. He was also a useful slow bowler, at least until the more fleet-footed batsmen got after him. In the field he was, oddly enough, something of a problem. He fielded in the slips generally, but not with any notable success.

But there is some doubt about Lord Frederick's ever having played at Broadhalfpenny Down. He came to prominence while quite young, but he would still have been in his teens when the ground fell into disuse. He properly belongs to the next generation of greats and sadly cannot detain us here, especially

as we have already encountered his legendary gambling on
the outcome of cricket matches
in which he played. Man of the
cloth he may have been, but his
true vocation was as a
professional gambler.

John Frame
(1733 – 1796)

Another short, stout, fast
bowler, John Frame looked
just like Lumpy Stevens, with
whom he often used to open
the bowling for England.
Frame was particularly quick,
despite his girth. What a sight
the two of them must have
made, the very antithesis of
what we now think opening
fast-bowlers should look like. Frame came from the Dartford
area of Kent, but was born in Warlingham, Surrey.

*Lord Frederick Beauclerk, 'after
George Shepheard', 1790.
(Reproduced by kind permission of the
MCC)*

Thomas 'Shock' White (1740 – 1831)

A formidable all-rounder, a forcing batsman and the third of
the short, stout triumvirate of England fast bowlers. He used
to come on as first change. Unlike the other two, however,
Shock White was expected to score runs. The manner in which
he attempted to do so in September 1771 made him one of the
immortals of the game and changed the laws of cricket for ever.

Every batsman who has ever walked out to bat since Shock
White's never-to-be-forgotten day of mischief has carried a
blade exactly 4¼in wide; narrower if the blade-maker has erred

Shock White arrives at the wicket with a bat the width of the stumps,
23 September 1771.
(Copyright Philip Hodkin)

with the knife, but never wider. Because that day, Shock White attempted to take guard in front of his wicket with a bat as wide as the stumps. This was not acceptable and the law was changed within days. What had previously been an unspoken understanding about the size of the bat was instantly enshrined in the laws.

Whether Shock White (who was also known as Daddy White) got his nickname as a result of this caper, or for some other reason, is not known. The use of 'Daddy' might, of course, have evolved much later, since he lived to see his ninety-first birthday. Thomas White came from Reigate, Surrey.

John Wood (dates unknown)

The fourth, regular England bowler, described by John Nyren as 'tall, stout and bony'. (Quite what picture he was trying to conjure up is difficult to imagine, since there seems some mutual contradiction in such a description.) John Wood was a useful all-rounder, but was never regarded as being among the best. He came from Sevenoaks, Kent.

William Fennex (1763/4 – 1839)

A man of immense strength and stamina, William Fennex appears to have played cricket at the highest level for some forty years, certainly well into his sixties. He was an all-rounder and made something of a reputation for himself as a single-wicket player. He played against Hambledon for the first time in 1786, but most of his life was spent to the north of London, in Middlesex, Buckinghamshire and Suffolk.

As a batsman, he was a free-flowing, elegant player, particularly fond of getting onto the front foot to drive. As a fast underhand bowler, his action was exceptionally high, almost shoulder-level when he delivered the ball at great speed. He was still bowling regularly when he turned seventy, but not in top-class matches.

His fielding ability made him a complete cricketer. According to *The Sporting Magazine*, about the time he first played against Hambledon he beat the three greatest cricketers of the day in a single-wicket competition, 'alone and unassisted'. He would have been about twenty-two at the time. Over fifty years later, his phenomenal strength was still in evidence. He was over sixty-eight when he accepted a job as a cricket coach in Suffolk, a post which he held until the end of his days. At the age of seventy-five, and only shortly before his death, he walked ninety miles in three days carrying an umbrella, his clothing and three cricket bats. Where he was going, and for what purpose, is not recorded. But he got there.

Minshull (dates unknown)

One of England's best batsmen of the time, with a good, sound defence and an ability to score runs, Minshull regularly opened the batting for England. His style, however, was a touch awkward – 'uncouth' was Nyren's word. Of course, he was playing at a time when moving forward to drive off the front foot was still somewhat novel. As an archetypal opener, Minshull would have eschewed risk, and probably preferred to play most deliveries from the crease. He evidently had a somewhat inflated opinion of his own abilities, which he did little to hide. It was not shared by his Hambledon opponents.

Minshull, whose name was variously spelt Minshall and Minchin in the scores and records of the time, was believed to come from Middlesex. He was employed by the Duke of Dorset.

Joseph Miller (17?? – 1799)

Minshull's opening partner, but a more elegant bat. Miller had a good technique and was a fine cutter of the ball. 'As steady as the pyramids,' Nyren said of him. He was as stockily built as his partner, but was by far the more active of the two men. Miller was also the more popular of the two among their Hambledon foe. He was freely acknowledged as being particularly amiable and good-hearted, and they enjoyed his company in the bar afterwards. Joseph Miller came from Kent.

William Yalden (1740 – 1824)

England's regular wicket-keeper, albeit not in quite the same league as Tom Sueter. His appealing for run-outs and stumpings left something to be desired, according to John Nyren, particularly by comparison with Tom Sueter's scrupulous standards.

Yalden gave up cricket at one time from failing eye-sight. After a season out of the game, he was urged to try again by the Earl of Tankerville. He did, and much to their collective astonishment, he was even more successful than before. Once, when he was fielding in the deep, he jumped a fence, fell on his back and still managed to catch the ball before it hit the ground.

William Yalden was also expected to score some runs and he was useful enough with a bat to make a contribution more often than not. He was a licensed victualler and came from the Chertsey area of Surrey.

In 1778, a Mr Yalden was proposed for membership of the Hambledon club and was duly elected. It is likely that this was a gesture of goodwill to a powerful, influential and long-standing opponent, who was also a former England captain. Unfortunately there is no conclusive proof that they are one and the same person, but the unusual surname encourages the thought.

John Ring (1758 – 1800)

One of the best batsmen in the country, John Ring came from Kent and first appeared against Hambledon in 1782. He was technically sound, watchful and scored a high proportion of his runs through powerful hitting on the leg-side. In the field, he was a fine cover-point.

His brother George was also a good cricketer and is alleged to have been indirectly responsible for his brother's early death. Both were employed by Sir Horace Mann and during a light-hearted practice one day, George was bowling to John when a delivery suddenly reared up and broke his brother's nose. Some weeks later, John died of complications following his injuries.

Robert Clifford (dates unknown)

A regular in the England side over many years, Robert Clifford was a useful all-rounder. He batted left-handed but his particular success came mainly with the ball, which he delivered right-handed. As a child, he suffered a terrible accident to his right hand which resulted in the two smallest fingers remaining twisted inside the palm of his hand. This must have created great problems for him when batting and fielding, but might also have been the source of some of the considerable spin he was able to impart on the ball when he bowled his slow lobs.

There were many other players who feature in records of the time, but about whom little is now known. Quiddington was the England long-stop for several matches, but he was not in the same league as George Leer. Certainly he never had to cope with Thomas Brett's express deliveries. But he was good, for all that, according to John Nyren. He was a batsman and held his place in the side to score runs.

The England team boasted several other good batsmen who appeared in great matches against Hambledon. Booker and Boorman were both athletic left-handers who also bowled. Brazier was another useful all-rounder who hit the ball particularly hard, as was Bullen who bowled extremely fast. William Bowra, James Bayley, Pattenden, Simmons, Colchin and a number of others appeared in quite a few of the matches for which the records have survived, although little is now known about them. Another name leaves us with an unanswerable problem: May. We find Richard and Thomas. Which of the two played in which match? The usual omission of initials from the already spartan scoresheets of the day makes it impossible to say.

Is that really an England squad, allowing that the term can loosely be applied to the cricketers we know played – at least from time to time – on Broadhalfpenny Down and elsewhere against Hambledon? Certainly, many of them took part in several of the great matches. They offer us the prospect of good games, depending on the team selected from those 'available'. Even allowing for John Nyren's slightly less generous observations about these fine players, they must have been a formidable side and certainly more than a match for most other teams, including Hambledon on many occasions. The fact that they sometimes struggled against Hambledon might account for at least some of Nyren's apparently less generous objectivity when describing his beloved club's opponents. But we must not forget that England won a good proportion of these matches. They were never a pushover. No Goliath ever is.

So, as we have done before, let's suppose we can pick the England side for a match against Hambledon from the squad we have; perhaps it might bat like this:

1. Miller
2. Minchull
3. Ring
4. Earl of Tankerville, captain
5. Fennex
6. Booker
7. Yalden, wicket-keeper
8. White
9. Clifford
10. Frame
11. Lumpy Stevens

So, if that was Hambledon's playing strength – and principal opposition – over the years between the mid 1750s and the late 1780s, what exactly did they achieve on the field of play, and particularly on Broadhalfpenny Down? After all, their performances have never been equalled in the whole history of the game. There is not a national, county, provincial or state side that can hold so much as a candle to the record of the Hambledon club over those thirty-five years or so. Neither first-class nor any other level of cricket has ever seen the like since. Nor is it likely to do so in the future.

According to John Nyren, Hambledon beat England a record twenty-nine times in fifty-one matches played over the seasons from 1771. It was a total that stood unbeaten for over 100 years. Even then, it took the might of the Australian Test sides over thirty-four years and ninety-eight matches to capture that record from Hambledon. They finally recorded their thirtieth win over England at Adelaide in 1908, the same year that the monument to Hambledon's exploits was unveiled on Broadhalfpenny Down. The record had passed on, but it had left behind for all time the extraordinary achievement of the men of Hambledon, the men who played on Broadhalfpenny Down.

We have met the men. Now it is time to see exactly what they did on the cricket field.

THE GLORY DAYS
Part 3: The Matches

It is widely believed that the glory days, as John Nyren called them, extended from about 1750 to 1787. Those are the dates carved into the monument on Broadhalfpenny Down. But they are not strictly correct – at least, they do not tell the whole story. The note bequeathed with the old bat at Winchester College claims that the Hambledon club was formed in 1742. The evidence of the 'lost dog' advertisement and the matches against Dartford in 1756 tell us that the club was already quite a force in the land by the middle of that decade. By 1771, it was so well-established and powerful that it held responsibility for the laws of the game, apparently by common consent. Over those thirty years, though we know little else, we can safely assume that the club made gradual progress which finally accelerated into formidable strength and success. How that translated into results is obscure; the first known match was played in 1756, but from that season to 1767 we have no more than a few indistinct snapshots.

Only when we get to the dramas of 1769-71 does the mist begin to clear. We have no less a guide through this critical period than John Nyren himself. However, he was only a boy of five in 1769, so considerable allowance must be made for his memory of events nearly sixty years later. He suggests, however, that results and playing strength were so bad that the Hambledon club was nearly wound up. A succession of heavy defeats during 1771 was the climax to a period of near-terminal decline. John Nyren does little to clarify the reasons, perhaps because he was not clear about them himself. We can make some deductions, however, from the few solid facts available to guide us. For a start, we know that only John Small senior, Richard Nyren and William Barber were over thirty. All the rest of the first great team we know about were in their early twenties. Most played in 1769, and they were all playing from 1771 onwards. Who played during the intervening two seasons is unknown, but it is difficult to imagine that they all suddenly disappeared and then came back. There would have been continuity.

The evidence suggests that there were regular sides from the mid 1740s, the last one of which was now getting past its best. This team, like its predecessors, was made up of people about whom we now know literally nothing, apart from a few names. They had regularly represented the club for many years and, by 1769 or so, the inevitable was beginning to happen. They were now losing more matches than the club could tolerate. A successful club required a successful cricket team.

Of course, we do not know, either, when Richard Nyren was first elected captain of the Hambledon cricket team. Was it around this period of change and upheaval? Was it his inspiration that first got the show back on the road, and then took the club to its greatest heights? Was there a meeting at the Bat and Ball when Richard Nyren pleaded with the committee to appoint him captain? Or did one of their number make an inspired proposal, based on his judgement of Nyren's shrewdness and motivational skills? There is a good deal of circumstantial evidence to suggest a sequence of events along these lines, though it remains pure conjecture. The ages of the personalities who were about to have such an impact on the cricket world certainly support this possibility. Of the great side which Richard Nyren led, Leer and Sueter were both just twenty in 1769, Brett and Aburrow only twenty-three, and Taylor a mere seventeen. Hogsflesh was twenty-five. We can probably assume that Stewart was also about twenty-five, but Lamborn was almost certainly younger. We know for certain that Hogsflesh, Stewart, Sueter and Brett were all playing in 1769, despite their youth and inexperience. Old John Small, Nyren and Barber had older heads, experience hardened on the field of play, and they provided continuity with the club's past.

The turning point for this new and relatively inexperienced side came at the very end of the 1771 season. Hambledon were playing Surrey away from home and won the game by a single run. It was a memorable and important match for quite another reason as well: it was the match in which Shock White of Reigate came in to bat carrying a blade as wide as his stumps. For both reasons, this was not a date Hambledon was ever to forget; it was 23 September 1771. A week later, on 30 September 1771, playing Surrey again but this time at Broad-halfpenny Down, they won again – now by ten wickets.

These successes were to prove crucial. Honour, and that most precious of cricketing commodities, confidence, were restored. From the start of the 1772 season, and over the next few summers, John Nyren claimed that Hambledon played fifty-one matches against England and won twenty-nine of them. We have solid proof of twenty-eight wins from forty-seven matches played from 1771 to the end of the glory days. According to the match records that follow, Hambledon played England thirty-four times between 1772 and 1781, and won nineteen. They also won another game, against XXII of England. They won three out of the four single-wicket matches played against England during those same ten seasons. Over the longer period, 1772 to 1796, forty matches were played against England, with twenty-two victories. Two other matches, when England fielded more than eleven players, were also won. In five of the six single-wicket games against England, the Hambledon club were again successful.

Curiously, their record against county sides was less impressive. After 1771, Hambledon are known to have played sixty-eight county matches, and won thirty-two. There were twenty-eight played against Kent, with Hambledon winning thirteen and tying one; fifteen against Surrey, winning eight and one result unknown. Of an assortment of other matches played over the same period, according to Ashley-Cooper, Hambledon won forty-eight out of 105 games, with sixteen results unknown.

Another ironic and extraordinary fact emerges from the match records which follow. Hambledon played better, and won more great victories, when playing away. Broadhalfpenny Down might have been the club's home, but its greatest triumphs generally happened elsewhere. In the following records, the club won only three of the seven matches played against England on Broadhalfpenny Down.

Reports of matches from contemporary sources vary from non-existent through sparse to partial and incomplete. But that is not all. Far too often for comfort, reports of apparently the same match offer conflicting details – dates being the most frequent area of doubt. Just occasionally we have full undisputed details. This lack of clear information sometimes extends even to the venue. Such records leave the compiler to best guess the truth, and much of what follows is unavoidably based on that approach. Further digging among primary sources is always open to readers with an inclination to search for even greater exactitude.

This paucity of detail is further undermined by questionable accuracy. Despite the best endeavours of some of cricket's finest and most thorough historians over the last 200 years, this particular writer is left with two other specific problems. First and most importantly, bearing in mind that this book is essentially a biography of a cricket ground, what to do about matches which highlight the glory days but which are known not to have taken place on Broadhalfpenny Down. Secondly, what to do about matches where the venue is unknown or doubtful. It would have been counter-productive to take a pedantic view and omit them simply because Broadhalfpennny Down was not, or might not have been, the venue. So, both categories are included where they form an integral part of the glory days of the Hambledon club – a period which embraces the years when the club was based on Broadhalfpenny Down. As a result, during the years between 1782 and 1792, when both Broadhalfpenny Down and Windmill Down were in use, all known 'home' games have been included.

Despite the frustrating shortage of detail, particularly about some of the most important matches, there is an abundance of games about which at least something is known. So here was another choice. Do they all get a mention, or only some? And if selection is to be made, on what basis should it be exercised? This was never intended to be a reference book *per se*, nor even a compendium. But at least one decision was easy. The whole thrust of the story of the glory days is about the achievements of 'little' Hambledon when it faced the might of 'all' England. All those matches should be included, regardless of venue. As much as is available about those matches is shown in full. Using Nyren's calculations, only four are missing altogether.

Beyond the Hambledon v England matches, it seemed right to be more selective. So all the other great matches – which we would today regard as first-class county matches – known to have been played by the club, whether home or away, are included. Summaries of the scores are given where they are known, and highlights of individual performance added whenever interest or memorability justifies them. Sometimes these great matches were between Hambledon (effectively Hampshire) and other counties playing collectively (XXII of Hertfordshire and Essex, for instance). Often, both sides had 'given men' in their teams – itinerant professionals, paid for their services match by match. In some cases the balance of the sides was uneven, and teams did not always field an 'eleven'. Again, where these details are known they are included.

Some of the scoresheets were not recorded as we would write them today, and in that respect two important differences are apparent. First, the credit for a wicket went to one individual on the fielding side, even if two were involved in the dismissal. In particular this was hard on the bowler when a batsman was caught or stumped. In these cases, only the catcher or stumper was credited with the dismissal. So an original match analysis might record, say, a bowler taking four wickets, three bowled and one caught (by him). In those days, he had taken four wickets. In this book he still does.

The second difference relates to the batting order. As we have seen, social status usually determined a batsman's place in the list, a method which is particularly confusing and unhelpful to the modern eye. So, in the following accounts, the actual batting order is given where it is known or can be deduced with certainty.

Finally, a word about the time taken over matches during the glory days. With stakes as high as they were, and because it had not occurred to anyone that matches could, or should, be played over a fixed period of time, games were played to a finish, however long that took. So where the number of days taken to complete a match is stated, the game was not necessarily arranged to last that length of time, it simply happened to last that many days before a result was achieved. According to surviving records, over the entire period of the glory days only two matches involving Hambledon were left unfinished. They occurred in 1783 and 1789, and both were eventually abandoned because of persistent bad weather.

18 August 1756
HAMBLEDON v DARTFORD (KENT)
Played at Broadhalfpenny Down. No details.

This is the first recorded match played by Hambledon. It was the match at which the dog Rover was lost. People came to this match in droves, possibly from over forty miles away. Their presence in such numbers provides confirmation, if it were needed, of the standing of the Hambledon club, even by this time. There can be no doubt that Hambledon was already a force in the cricket world. Such reputations are not gained overnight, which in turn suggests that the club had been playing and winning for some years before this date.

28 August 1756
DARTFORD (KENT) v HAMBLEDON

The Artillery Ground, Finsbury Square, London. Dartford won. Stake £50.

There are no further details of this match. However, the fact that the team travelled some sixty miles over two days to play this return game would indicate that the first match was a successful and perhaps close encounter.

FS Ashley-Cooper's researches in the early 1900s revealed a five-a-side match on the same ground, and on the same day, between England and Hambledon, for a stake of £20. No details were found, but it suggests that a single-wicket competition followed the Dartford game.

10 September 1764 (two days)
SURREY v HAMBLEDON

Laleham Burway, Chertsey, Surrey. Hambledon won by four wickets. 'Great sums of money depending' on the outcome, reported to be £20.

Surrey 48 and 127. Hambledon 76 and 100 for 6.

The visitors set off for this match two days earlier, and it was obviously an important game, financially if for no other reason, for the captain left a six-months pregnant wife behind (John Nyren was born that December). The Hambledon team was believed to be: Nyren, Small, Stewart, Hogsflesh, Barber, Bayton, Osmond, John and Edward Woolgar, Ridge and Squire Land. In 1764, the club was still occasionally being referred to as Squire Land's club. Surrey, which was largely the Chertsey club, included Shock White and players from Dartford.

The game was fraught with incidents and injuries. Surrey had three men hurt and Hambledon lost two, although Stewart played on with a knee-strain and a broken finger. There was a crisis at the start of Hambledon's second innings. Wanting 100 to win, they quickly slumped to 3 runs for four wickets, but recovered to get the other 97 runs for the loss of only two more wickets.

17 September 1764 (two days)
HAMBLEDON v SURREY

Broadhalfpenny Down. Surrey won by two wickets. No details.

This is believed to have been a return match against a Surrey side chiefly made up of Chertsey players, following the game a week earlier. After this second match, with the score one-all, the clubs agreed to play a decider, but no record exists of the match ever taking place.

17 June 1766 SUSSEX v HAMBLEDON

Venue uncertain, possibly Goodwood, Sussex. Hambledon won. No details.

This was the match at which odds of 40–1 against Hambledon were to be had after they trailed badly on the first innings.

4 August 1767 (two days)
HAMBLEDON v SUSSEX

Broadhalfpenny Down. Hambledon won. No details.

8 August 1767 HAMBLEDON v SUSSEX

Broadhalfpenny Down. Hambledon won. No details.

This was the second of a series of five matches, but nothing is known of the others.

September 1767 SURREY v HAMBLEDON

Duppas Hill, near Croydon, Surrey. Hambledon won by 262 runs. Stake £210.

There are no other details, beyond the fact that Hambledon's openers – believed to be Aburrow and Sueter – put on 192 for the first wicket in three-and-a-half hours. Their partnership was 'the greatest thing ever known'. At the time, Sueter was only eighteen years old. Lumpy played for Surrey.

28 September 1767 (two days)
HAMBLEDON v SURREY

Broadhalfpenny Down. Hambledon won by 224 runs. No details.

This was believed to a be a return match, following the game near Croydon a week or so earlier. Hambledon again proved much too strong for their opponents.

14 October 1767
CATERHAM (SURREY) v HAMBLEDON

Caterham, Surrey. Caterham won. Stake £100. No details.

30 August 1768 (four days) HAMBLEDON v KENT

Broadhalfpenny Down. Hambledon won by 144 runs. 'Considerable stake'.

Hambledon 131 and 194. Kent 141 and 40.

Reports talked of an 'easy' victory, mainly due to the remarkable batting of old John Small, whose personal score exceeded 140. This has often been claimed as the first century recorded in great matches and is held to be the first first-class hundred in the history of the game. However, it is more likely to have been the total of his score in both innings. Had it been scored out of a total of 194 in Hambledon's second innings, it would have been a truly astonishing performance.

Some accounts of this match date it 23 August, and others 6 September. But this is unlikely, since the following game would still have been in progress.

5 September 1768 (two days)
HAMBLEDON v SUSSEX

Broadhalfpenny Down. Hambledon won by seven wickets. 'Large' stake. No details.

John Small scored 80 not out, as his good form with the bat continued.

12 September 1768 SUSSEX v HAMBLEDON

Venue unknown, possibly Goodwood, Sussex. Sussex won. Stake £1000. No details.

29 June 1769 HAMBLEDON v SURREY

Broadhalfpenny Down. No details.

31 July 1769 (two days) SURREY v HAMBLEDON

Guildford, Surrey. Hambledon won by four wickets.

Surrey 104 and 137. Hambledon 99 and 143 for 6.

This was widely regarded as a decisive match between these two sides, following several in the recent past. Whether there was a substantial stake at risk, which was to be determined by the result of this one match, is not known. But the attendance of over 20,000 spectators at the game suggests the result was of some importance.

Surrey was largely represented by the Caterham club, and in some reports this is the name given to Hambledon's opponents. Old John Small batted well in both innings. The Hambledon team was: Nyren, Small, Brett, Hogsflesh, Stewart, Sueter, Barber, Purdy, Ridge, Bayton and Glazier. The last four belong to the largely-unknown previous generation of Hambledon players. When this match was played, the club's new wicket-keeper Sueter was still only twenty, while Brett, Hogsflesh and Stewart were all in their early twenties.

14 September 1769 (three days) SURREY v HAMBLEDON

Guildford, Surrey. Result unknown. Played for 'a considerable sum'.

28 September 1769 (two days) SURREY v HAMBLEDON

Broadhalfpenny Down. Hambledon won by an innings and 41 runs. No details.

Sueter and Leer reportedly put on 128 for Hambledon's first wicket.

4 October 1770
HAMBLEDON v CATERHAM (SURREY)
Broadhalfpenny Down. Hambledon won by 57 runs.
Hambledon 104 and 105. Caterham 74 and 78.

May 1771
HAMBLEDON v (Not known – Men of Wiltshire?)
Venue unknown. Hambledon lost by ten wickets. *The Salisbury Journal* reported that, as a result of this match, 'several thousand pounds' changed hands.

12 August 1771 (two days)
ENGLAND v HAMBLEDON
Guildford, Surrey. England won by ten wickets. Stake 'several thousand pounds'.
Hambledon 65 and 90. England 146 and 10 for 0.
This is the first match between England and Hambledon for which any record still remains. It would be surprising if it were the first such game, since it took place towards the end of one of the club's worst seasons for many years.

20 August 1771 HAMBLEDON v SUSSEX
Broadhalfpenny Down. Sussex won by eight wickets.
Hambledon 65 and 128. Sussex 93 and 101 for 2.
'None but gentlemen will play in this match,' said an advertisement beforehand.

23 August 1771 SUSSEX v HAMBLEDON
Valdo Corner, Goodwood, Sussex. Sussex won by an innings and 74 runs.
Hambledon 21 and 48. Sussex 143.

23 September 1771 SURREY v HAMBLEDON

Laleham Burway, Chertsey, Surrey. Hambledon won by one run. Stake £50.

Hambledon 218. Surrey 217.

This was the notorious match in which Shock White arrived at the crease with a bat the width of his stumps. It was also the match which turned Hambledon's fortunes after a run of poor results, as the figures immediately above suggest. Had they lost this match at Chertsey, Hambledon were in danger of folding. This win, by the smallest possible margin, set them on the road to their most successful decade of all.

30 September 1771 HAMBLEDON v SURREY

Broadhalfpenny Down. Hambledon won by ten wickets.

Surrey 117 and 126. Hambledon 230 and 14 for 0.

1 June 1772 V of HAMBLEDON v V of KENT

The Artillery Ground, Finsbury Square, London. Kent won by one wicket.

Hambledon 11 and 46 (Nyren 29). Kent 35 (Minshull 26) and 23 for 4.

A reported crowd of some 20,000 crammed into the ground to watch this match.

15 June 1772 (three days)
XI of HAMBLEDON v XXII of OTHER COUNTIES

Moulsey Hurst, Surrey. Hambledon won 'all hollow'.

A triumph for the smaller side. The terminology used to describe the result suggests it was a huge win. It was not unusual in those days for teams of unequal numbers to compete against one another, but this is the first recorded instance of XI of Hambledon beating XXII of England.

23 June 1772 (three days)
HAMBLEDON v ENGLAND
Broadhalfpenny Down. Hambledon won by 53 runs. Stake £525.

No extras were allowed in this match. The difference between the sides was John Small, who dominated both Hambledon innings and scored half the team's total in the match. This is the first recorded occasion when Lumpy Stevens played at Broadhalfpenny Down.

Hambledon				England		
	1st inns	2nd inns			1st inns	2nd inns
Brett	11	2	White		35	6
Yalden	5	9	Fuggles		5	12
Small	78	34	Minshull		16	1
Sueter	2	9	Miller		11	0
Nyren	9	4	Gill		5	2
Leer	1	0	Palmer		13	8
Edmeads	0	6	May		15	18
Stewart	12	11	Childs		2	0
Aburrow	27	0	Frame		2	4
Hogsflesh	0	4	Lumpy		5	7
Barber	1	0	May		0	5
Total	**146**	**79**	**Total**		**109**	**63**

23 July 1772 (three days)
ENGLAND v HAMBLEDON
Guildford, Surrey. Hambledon won by 72 runs. Stake £525.

There are two versions of the scores in this match. This scorecard excludes extras. The other version shows amended totals and the inclusion of 11 byes to Hambledon and 21 to England. The scores are given as: Hambledon 152 and 122; England 126 and 60. That version records a win for Hambledon by 88 runs. Other records place this match in August 1772, rather than July.

Both Yalden and Sueter were playing for Hambledon, but it is not known which one of them kept wicket. It was likely to have been Tom Sueter, who was generally regarded as the better of the two behind the stumps. Yalden's scores also suggest that he played as a batsman.

Hambledon			England		
Brett	3	2	Lumpy	0	1
Yalden	68	49	Fuggles	21	3
Small	1	30	Simmons	27	3
Sueter	21	5	Minshull	0	13
Nyren	16	0	Miller	30	26
Leer	2	0	Boorman	18	0
Edmeads	5	17	Pattenden	15	4
Stewart	11	7	T May	5	3
Aburrow	10	0	Frame	1	10
Barber	5	0	Page	0	3
Hogsflesh	2	8	R May	0	7
Total	**144**	**118**	**Total**	**117**	**73**

10 August 1772 HAMBLEDON + SUSSEX v KENT
Broadhalfpenny Down. Hambledon + Sussex won by 50 runs. Stake £210. No details.

19 August 1772 (two days) ENGLAND v HAMBLEDON
Bishopsbourne, Kent. England won by two wickets.

Richard Nyren was not able to play in this match. It was estimated that some 20,000 people were there on the first day. Lumpy achieved the rare feat of bowling old John Small out, something that had not happened for some years. Brett bowled very fast, but not well enough to salvage a victory. According to *The Kent Messenger* there were some seven hours play on each day.

Hambledon			England		
Brett	11	11	Lumpy	14	12
Sueter	26	0	R May	3	did not bat
Leer	29	7	Wood	0	20
Small	22	48	Pattenden	20	4
Stewart	13	12	Minshull	24	9
Ridge	4	8	Simmons	3	1
Barber	0	2	Fuggles	0	1
Hogsflesh	0	1	Miller	14	not out 17
Yalden	4	1	White	8	5
Edmeads	7	4	Palmer	29	14
Aburrow	0	6	Boorman	0	not out 2
byes	7	13		21	16
Total	**123**	**113**	**Total**	**136**	**101**
					for 8 wickets

28 August 1772 SURREY v HAMBLEDON

Guildford, Surrey. Hambledon won by 45 runs. No details.

2 June 1773 (two days)
V of ENGLAND v V of HAMBLEDON

The Artillery Ground, Finsbury Square, London. England won by one wicket.

Hambledon 24 and 33. England 31 and 27 for 4.

The Duke of Dorset raised the England side, and Horace (later Sir Horace) Mann sponsored the Hambledon team. Over 20,000 spectators watched the game, which produced a cliff-hanging finish. With three wickets down, England still needed 19 to win. Lumpy was next in, a man not noted for his batting. But he got 8 before losing his wicket. That left Miller, a strong batsman who played commendably straight and who usually opened the innings in normal matches, to get the last 11. He was helped by the fact that, crucially, Brett was unable to bowl in England's second innings, having sustained a nasty blow on the foot earlier in the game. Miller finally got the runs.

21 June 1773 (two days)
ENGLAND v HAMBLEDON

Sevenoaks, Kent. England won by an innings and 51 runs

Another huge crowd attended this match, and saw the England side play exceptionally well. They played, according the *The Kentish Gazette*, in 'as masterly a manner as ever was known, not making one mistake, nor losing one bye-run'. Brett was still unfit but decided to play. Miller's opening partner Minshull was out for 15, hit wicket – the first recorded dismissal of this kind in great matches. The next did not occur for thirteen years. When Hambledon were batting they were intimidated by some very aggressive field-placings, particularly with Simmons standing very close.

Hambledon

Brett	b Lumpy	26	c Minshull	1
Leer	run out	14	not out	15
Sueter	b Lumpy	11	c Lumpy	9
Stewart	run out	5	b Wood	0
Yalden	b Wood	5	b Lumpy	0
Aylward	c Minshull	4	b Lumpy	13
Hogsflesh	c Simmons	4	c Wood	0
Small	c Lumpy	3	run out	4
Nyren	c White	2	c Minshull	5
Aburrow	not out	2	b Lumpy	2
Barber	b R May	1	b Wood	0
byes		0		0
Total		**77**		**49**

England

Miller	c Barber	73
Simmons	b Brett	20
T May	b Barber	16
Minshull	hit wicket	15
J Wood	b Hogsflesh	14
T Wood	b Hogsflesh	12
R May	not out	10
T White	b Nyren	7
Pattenden	c Hogsflesh	1
Lumpy	b Brett	6
Childs	b Hogsflesh	1
byes		2
Total		**177**

2 July 1773 (two days) ENGLAND v HAMBLEDON

The Artillery Ground, Finsbury Square, London. England won by six wickets.

Brett did not play for Hambledon. He was continuing to suffer the after-effects of the severe blow from a ball during the five-a-side game played in June at the Artillery Ground and decided to give his injury more time to heal. England's first innings total includes 17 byes, an extraordinary number with Tom Sueter behind the stumps and George Leer at long-stop. This was a day they both preferred to forget, no doubt. One of the England batsmen shown as 'did not bat' must have been '0 not out', but which one is not recorded.

Hambledon			England		
Brett	1	14	Lumpy	5	did not bat
Nyren	0	14	Frame	11	did not bat
Sueter	29	32	T Wood	15	did not bat
Small	58	25	Childs	38	did not bat
Aylward	8	1	White	24	1
Hogsflesh	2	14	Colchin	1	9
Stewart	10	5	Boorman	5	55
Yalden	4	2	J Wood	5	did not bat
Aburrow	0	3	Bullen	1	1
Barber	15	25	Read	13	did not bat
Leer	0	3	Palmer	not out 52	not out 30
byes	5	16	byes	17	4
Total	**132**	**154**	**Total**	**187**	**100**
					for 4 wickets

9 July 1773 (two days) ENGLAND v HAMBLEDON

The Artillery Ground, Finsbury Square, London. England won by two wickets. 'Great sums depending'. No details.

Brett was still troubled by his injury and unable to play.

12 July 1773 (two days) ENGLAND v HAMBLEDON

Laleham Burway, Chertsey, Surrey. England won by 114 runs. Stake £105. No details.

4 August 1773 (two days)
HAMBLEDON v ENGLAND

Broadhalfpenny Down. England won by nine wickets. Stake
£510.

Brett was still unfit, and the sixteen-year-old Richard
Purchase was invited to play instead. He took four wickets.
Simmons, batting for England, made one hit for seven runs.
The Duke of Dorset distinguished himself by bowling six
batsmen in the two Hambledon innings. Lumpy hit the stumps
seven times, including bowling old Small again.

Hambledon

Ridge	b Dorset	0	c Yalden	24
Hogsflesh	b Lumpy	6	b Dorset	0
Purchase	b Lumpy	1	c Miller	17
Small	b Lumpy	16	run out	22
Sueter	b Dorset	2	b Dorset	39
Nyren	b Dorset	5	not out	6
Leer	b Dorset	2	c Simmons	13
Francis	b Wood	2	c Palmer	6
Davis	run out	30	b Lumpy	7
Barber	not out	2	b Lumpy	1
Aylward	b Lumpy	18	b Lumpy	4
byes		5		1
Total		**89**		**140**

England

Stone	b Hogsflesh	0	did not bat	
Palmer	c Ridge	68	did not bat	
Minshull	c Ridge	11	did not bat	
White	b Purchase	69	did not bat	
Miller	b Hogsflesh	18	did not bat	
Dorset	c Barber	3	did not bat	
Yalden	b Purchase	0	not out	10
Simmons	c Nyren	3	c Hogsflesh	13
Pattenden	b Purchase	1	not out	4
Lumpy	b Purchase	1	did not bat	
Wood	not out	17	did not bat	
byes		11		1
Total		**202**	**28 for 1 wicket**	

23 August 1773 (four days)
HAMBLEDON v SURREY

Broadhalfpenny Down. Surrey won by six wickets. Stake £105.
   Hambledon 103 and 51. Surrey 131 and 24 for 4.

Brett and old John Small were both unavailable for this match. There was some heavy side-betting on individual scores in this match, much of it against the scores of the Rev. Reynell Cotton, the club's president, playing for Hambledon. The bookies had a bad day. The presidency did nothing for his batting technique; he got 0 and 2. In Hambledon's second innings, George Leer scored 29 of the side's total of 51.

16 September 1773 (five days)
SURREY v HAMBLEDON

Laleham Burway, Chertsey, Surrey. Surrey won by eight wickets. 'Greater sums depending than ever before'.
   Hambledon 38 and 145. Surrey 120 and 64 for 2.

This match was badly affected by the rain and this is the first recorded occasion when a great match took five days to complete.

27 September 1773 (two days)
HAMBLEDON v SURREY

Broadhalfpenny Down. Surrey won by an innings and 60 runs.
   Hambledon 83 (Bayley 24, Sueter 22) and 82 (Aylward 33). Surrey 225 (Yalden 88, Miller 39).

Hambledon fielded a strong side for this match, including Nyren, old Small, Purchase, Brett, Leer, Stewart and Frame as a given man. But the Surrey side included six regular England players – Lumpy, Shock White, Yalden, Miller, Minshull and Francis.

6 June 1774 (two days)
V of HAMBLEDON v V of KENT

Moulsey Hurst, Surrey. Hambledon won by 188 runs.

Hambledon 118 (Small 49) and 127 (Sueter 74). Kent 21 and 36 (Minshull 29).

This was an enormous win in a single-wicket match, where the scores were more usually less than 50 for each side's innings.

21 June 1774 (three days)
HAMBLEDON v ENGLAND

Broadhalfpenny Down. Hambledon won by an innings and 52 runs.

Hambledon had Lumpy Stevens playing for them as a given man. Batting first, and assuming Minshull and Miller opened the innings – England were in trouble from early on, and they fell away further once the openers were out. Hambledon's batting was solid from top to bottom, with only two players failing to reach double figures and seven batsmen each scoring more than 20. John Small showed the way, as ever, and Hambledon must have passed England's first-innings score with only three or four wickets down. Later on, Tom Sueter hit out powerfully for 67, scored in double-quick time. It was an innings which knocked the heart out of the England side, who collapsed for the second time in the match once the leading batsmen were dismissed. This match is believed to be the first in which a single innings exceeded 300 runs.

Some accounts of this match suggest that it took place at Laleham Burway, and not on Broadhalfpenny Down.

England			Hambledon	
Dorset	19	6	Aburrow	9
Tankerville	18	35	J Small snr	47
Stone	14	4	Lumpy	22
Minshull	37	38	Leer	12
May	7	6	Sueter	67
Miller	3	26	Nyren	21
Wood	10	0	Aylward	37
White	5	0	Francis	29
Palmer	0	6	Stewart	11
Childs	2	6	Purchase	37
Yalden	1	0	Brett	9
byes	6	6		6
Total	**122**	**133**	**Total**	**307**

8 July 1774 (two days) ENGLAND v HAMBLEDON

Sevenoaks, Kent. Hambledon won by 169 runs.

This victory was the result of a fine team effort by the Hambledon side. They batted, fielded and bowled well, with virtually everybody in the side contributing during the match. Richard Nyren master-minded the strategy as usual, and brought home another famous victory.

Hambledon

Aylward	run out	29	c Minshull	61
Francis	b Bullen	4	b Wood	1
Small	b Bullen	10	run out	20
Sueter	c Bullen	12	b Bullen	30
Leer	b Frame	28	b Wood	14
Nyren	b Bullen	10	c Minshull	18
Stewart	not out	14	b Colchin	7
Lumpy	c Wood	21	b Colchin	11
Aburrow	b Bullen	8	b Wood	7
Brett	b Bullen	2	not out	4
Purchase	c White	0	b Colchin	0
byes		1		9
Total		**139**		**182**

England

Tankerville	c Small	1	b Lumpy	5
Stone	c Small	0	b Brett	3
Bullen	b Lumpy	7	b Lumpy	1
Minshull	b Purchase	6	b Lumpy	8
Miller	b Nyren	16	c Sueter	12
Colchin	not out	10	c Leer	19
White	b Brett	17	c Nyren	4
Palmer	c Small	3	b Lumpy	5
J Wood	b Nyren	27	c Brett	3
Frame	b Brett	1	b Purchase	3
T Wood	b Lumpy	0	not out	0
byes		0		1
Total		**88**		**64**

13 July 1774 HAMBLEDON v KENT

Broadhalfpenny Down. Hambledon won by ten wickets. Stake £525. No details.

The Kent side included Lumpy, Shock White and Colchin as given men. Immediately after this resounding defeat, Kent challenged Hambledon to play two matches for £1050, on condition that Kent's teams for both matches would include three given men, of whom Lumpy would be one. The challenge was promptly accepted, and the matches were started on 8 and 15 August 1774 (see below). Other accounts suggest that this challenge was made to the Surrey side, at Guildford, after the following match. However, apart from one other game at the very end of the season for a purse one-tenth the size, Hambledon did not play Surrey again that year.

20 July 1774 (two days) SURREY v HAMBLEDON

Guildford, Surrey. Hambledon won by seven wickets. Stake £50.

Surrey 61 and 77. Hambledon 91 and 48 for 3.

Brett's ferocious bowling broke the Surrey batsmen and left them bemused. He took nine wickets in the match, all bowled.

8 August 1774 (three days) KENT v HAMBLEDON

Sevenoaks, Kent. Kent won by an innings and 35 runs.

Hambledon 46 and 159 (Small 55 not out). Kent 240 (Miller 95, Dorset 77).

This was the first of the two matches agreed between the clubs after the terrible drubbing Hambledon gave Kent three weeks previously. First blood to Kent, not least through the efforts of the Duke of Dorset, who clearly had a great deal of money at stake. The second match was scheduled to start a week later.

15 August 1774 (three days)
HAMBLEDON v KENT

Broadhalfpenny Down. Kent won by four wickets.

Hambledon 174 (Small 45) and 129. Kent 168 and 136 for 6 (White 50).

The Duke of Dorset was said to have won 'a considerable sum of money' on the result of this match – presumably the £1050 (£525,000 at today's values) put up a month earlier. Barber was unable to bowl in Kent's second innings as he had strained a leg, and the Duke allowed Hogsflesh to take his place. It was an extraordinarily generous and gentlemanly gesture in the circumstances, but it did not affect the outcome.

27 September 1774 SURREY v HAMBLEDON

Laleham Burway, Chertsey, Surrey. Stake £100. No details.

22 May 1775 (two days)
V of KENT v V of HAMBLEDON

The Artillery Ground, Finsbury Square, London. Hambledon won by one wicket. Stake £52.50.

Kent 37 and 102 (Bullen 56). Hambledon 92 (Small 75) and 48 for 4.

The Hambledon side consisted of Small, Brett, Sueter and Leer, with Shock White a given man. Kent included Lumpy as a given man. This was the famous match in which old Small stayed in for 165 minutes to get the last 14 runs needed to win, after which the Duke of Dorset sent him a violin as a token of his esteem. While Small was batting, Lumpy put the ball through the stumps three times without removing the bail. This brought the issue of adding a third stump to a head, since Lumpy clearly deserved the wicket, but ended up on the losing side. The third stump was added shortly after this match, which was watched by a huge crowd.

14 June 1775 (two days) KENT v HAMBLEDON
Sevenoaks, Kent. Kent won by 110 runs.

Kent 104 and 194 (Pattenden 72). Hambledon 157 and 31 (Lumpy bowled 5)

The financial and cricketing events of the previous summer played a part in this fixture. Hambledon would have been looking for revenge, but failed to achieve it. Once again, Lumpy was their undoing. Contemporary reports tell us that this match attracted more side-betting than ever: 'More money was won and lost than ever before.'

27 June 1775 HAMBLEDON v KENT
Broadhalfpenny Down. Hambledon won by nine wickets.

Kent 84 and 147 (Miller 71). Hambledon 219 (Leer 79) and 18 for 1.

6 July 1775 (three days) SURREY v HAMBLEDON
Laleham Burway, Chertsey, Surrey. Surrey won by 69 runs.

Surrey 76 and 163. Hambledon 51 and 119.

Although he was on the losing side, the man of the match was Thomas Brett, who took 12 wickets in the game, bowling eleven and catching one.

13 July 1775 (four days) HAMBLEDON v SURREY
Broadhalfpenny Down. Hambledon won by 296 runs.

Hambledon 168 (Small 38) and 357 (Small 136 not out, Nyren 98, Brett 68). Surrey 151 and 78 for 3.

By common consent, this was one of the greatest matches ever seen. Play continued on the third day, a Saturday, until eight o'clock in the evening. On the Monday, when play resumed, Surrey found themselves struggling. They finally 'gave in' when their third wicket fell and they were still nearly 300 runs behind. *The Kentish Gazette* described Small after this match as 'the best cricketer the world ever produced'.

This was also the match which produced that famous crisis among the gamblers, when Hambledon had lost five second-innings wickets having scarcely built on their small first-innings lead. Richard Nyren then joined John Small and they put together one of the greatest partnerships the game had ever seen, which set up a famous victory. As he came off, having made his highest score for the club, Nyren was confronted by two distinguished and supposedly loyal club members who bitterly complained at their losses, having backed Surrey to win. Nyren's reply is now part of the history of the game. The story is told in full in his biography in the previous chapter.

3 August 1775 KENT v HAMBLEDON

Guildford, Surrey. Kent won. No details.

5 June 1776 (three days)
ENGLAND v HAMBLEDON

Moulsey Hurst, Surrey. Hambledon won by 152 runs. Stake £525.

This was yet another fine all-round performance, with Richard Nyren directing operations to great effect. The Duke of Dorset played for the England side in this match, and again took wickets. For Hambledon, William Barber hit the stumps five times. R May took seven wickets in the match, including five catches.

Hambledon

Veck	c Bowra	6	c May	12
Aylward	b Dorset	13	c Miller	30
Sueter	b May	36	b May	4
Small	c Bowra	38	c Bullen	44
Taylor	run out	0	b White	41
Nyren	c May	18	c Bullen	13
Francis	b May	10	b Dorset	16
Brett	c Colchin	43	c White	0
Davis	c Bullen	40	b Dorset	13
Stewart	not out	15	not out	7
Barber	b May	0	b May	3
byes		6		3
Total		**225**		**186**

England

Palmer	b Barber	2	b Barber	0
Pattenden	b Barber	0	b Brett	38
Miller	c Sueter	15	b Brett	39
Bowra	c Veck	2	b Nyren	19
White	b Barber	3	b Brett	0
Dorset	run out	3	c Sueter	3
Brazier	b Nyren	3	b Brett	49
Colchin	c Barber	0	b Taylor	14
Booker	c Stewart	4	run out	15
R May	run out	12	not out	16
Bullen	not out	10	c Small	3
byes		1		8
Total		**55**		**204**

26 June 1776 ENGLAND v HAMBLEDON

Sevenoaks, Kent. Hambledon won by 75 runs.

Strong batting in Hambledon's first innings, led by a fine 70 from the General himself, set up a good win for the visitors. England looked to be getting on terms towards the end of their first innings, but then fell away during the rest of the match.

Hambledon

Aylward	b Dorset	6	b White	3
Small	b Dorset	45	c Bullen	7
Leer	b Lumpy	0	c Bowra	1
Sueter	c Booker	5	run out	13
Brett	c Bullen	3	not out	1
Aburrow	c Bowra	8	c Brazier	5
Francis	c Booker	47	b White	9
Taylor	c Booker	42	c Booker	14
Barber	not out	4	c Boorman	0
Nyren	c Dorset	70	c Bullen	19
Veck	c Bullen	0	b Lumpy	10
byes		11		2
Total		**241**		**84**

England

Dorset	b Brett	6	c Nyren	2
Lumpy	b Nyren	6	b Barber	2
Miller	c Small	4	c Sueter	6
Bowra	b Brett	1	c Small	20
Bullen	c Francis	29	b Brett	0
Brazier	c Veck	34	not out	19
Pattenden	c Small	0	c Aburrow	6
Boorman	not out	13	c Francis	9
Booker	run out	41	c Taylor	6
White	hit wicket	23	c Sueter	0
Wood	b Nyren	9	b Nyren	2
byes		7		5
Total		**173**		**77**

2 July 1776 HAMBLEDON v ENGLAND

Broadhalfpenny Down. England won by four wickets.

Having notched up two good away wins against England in the previous month, Hambledon failed to make it three in a row on their home ground. They found Lumpy's bowling difficult on Broadhalfpenny Down and, despite a fine second-innings score, failed to stop England getting home with four wickets to spare.

There is more than one version of the scorecard for this match, but the following appears to be the most credible.

Hambledon

Aylward	c Wood	5	b Lumpy	19
Small	c Bowra	12	b White	57
Leer	b Lumpy	21	b White	23
Sueter	c Wood	6	c White	16
Brett	not out	0	not out	0
Aburrow	b Lumpy	0	b Wood	7
Francis	b Lumpy	3	b Wood	13
Taylor	c Bullen	20	b White	22
Nyren	b Lumpy	6	b Lumpy	36
Veck	c Brazier	14	b Lumpy	14
Barber	c Bullen	0	b White	8
byes		0		6
Total		**87**		**221**

England

Dorset	c Barber	34	b Francis	1
Lumpy	not out	0	did not bat	
Miller	c Leer	16	c Sueter	12
Bowra	b Francis	31	b Francis	0
Bullen	b Brett	3	did not bat	
Brazier	b Brett	36	b Francis	17
Pattenden	b Brett	20	b Francis	14
Boorman	c Sueter	0	not out	38
Booker	b Taylor	6	not out	17
White	b Taylor	4	b Brett	38
Wood	b Barber	4	did not bat	
byes		9		9
Total		**163**		**146**
				for 6 wickets

15 July 1776 ENGLAND v HAMBLEDON

Sevenoaks, Kent. Hambledon won by six wickets.

Playing away again, once more Hambledon won against England. John Small produced another of his classic anchor innings, which effectively set up the win. Some determined batting in Hambledon's second innings between Leer and Nyren, who shared an unfinished fifth-wicket partnership of about 50 runs, saw Hambledon home by a flatteringly large margin. Some reports of this match show the England side as Kent.

England

Dorset	c Aylward	9	b Francis	0
Lumpy	b Nyren	8	not out	0
Miller	c Nyren	27	c Veck	21
Bowra	c Veck	37	b Francis	8
Bullen	b Brett	4	run out	0
Brazier	c Taylor	33	c Francis	17
Pattenden	c Small	8	b Brett	3
Boorman	not out	5	b Brett	6
Booker	c Small	1	c Taylor	2
White	c Leer	9	run out	11
Wood	b Nyren	7	c Leer	0
byes		6		1
Total		**154**		**69**

Hambledon

Aylward	c Bullen	13	c Boorman	0
Small	not out	59	c Wood	2
Leer	c Lumpy	5	not out	47
Sueter	c Lumpy	8	c Wood	13
Brett	b Wood	5	did not bat	
Aburrow	b Lumpy	5	did not bat	
Francis	c Boorman	9	c Bowra	5
Taylor	b Wood	8	did not bat	
Davis	b Wood	1	did not bat	
Nyren	b Lumpy	5	not out	22
Veck	c Lumpy	10	did not bat	
byes		2		5
Total		**130**		**94**
				for 4 wickets

22 July 1776 (three days)
HAMBLEDON v ENGLAND

Holt Common, between Broadhalfpenny Down and the village of Chidden. England won by five wickets.

This use of an alternative ground for a home match appears to have been Hambledon's first attempt to find a replacement for the somewhat exposed Broadhalfpenny Down. The *Salisbury Journal* reported that the ground was more sheltered from all the winds. The tiny hamlet of Chidden is cosily tucked in the folds of the downs, and is certainly lower-lying than Broadhalfpenny Down. The surrounding terrain has a better soil cover and lusher vegetation. Despite these advantages, Holt Common was never used on a regular basis. England succeeded in reversing the result of a fortnight before, playing with a largely unchanged side.

Hambledon

Aylward	b Lumpy	13	c Boorman	9
Small	b Wood	20	b Lumpy	10
Leer	c Wood	0	b Lumpy	18
Sueter	run out	2	c White	11
Brett	c Booker	0	c Booker	0
Aburrow	c Wood	6	not out	25
Francis	b Lumpy	12	c Booker	9
Taylor	b Lumpy	0	c Booker	5
Veck	not out	13	c Yalden	8
Nyren	b White	15	b White	12
Barber	c Pattenden	4	c Yalden	3
byes		3		3
Total		**88**		**113**

England

Dorset	b Brett	5	not out	13
Lumpy	not out	16	did not bat	
Yalden	b Brett	31	b Brett	15
Bowra	c Francis	36	did not bat	
Bayton	b Brett	5	did not bat	
Brazier	b Francis	6	not out	19
Pattenden	c Sueter	1	c Small	4
Boorman	b Brett	0	c Brett	12
Booker	c Taylor	2	c Barber	0
White	c Nyren	15	c Francis	3
Wood	c Small	3	did not bat	
byes		15		1
Total		**135**		**67**
			for 5 wickets	

5 August 1776 (four days)
SURREY v HAMBLEDON

Laleham Burway, Chertsey, Surrey. Surrey won by one wicket.

Hambledon 94 and 176 (Aylward 82 not out). Surrey 141 (White 58) and 130 for 9.

Most of the details of this nail-bitingly exciting match are lost. Surrey, with the Earl of Tankerville in their side, led Hambledon by 47 runs on the first innings. Then, needing 130 to win, Surrey lost their ninth wicket with only 87 scored. Hambledon were confident of victory. The last Surrey pair, Wood and Lumpy, not only had to face Brett's fastest bowling just to save the match, they still needed 43 runs for an unlikely victory.

The odds against a Surrey victory when the ninth wicket fell were astronomic. Hambledon were as near a certainty as the gamblers had ever been offered. Spectators were placing bets for a Hambledon win all round the ground. Some people risked over £6 (£3000) to win the equivalent of 12¹/₂ pence (£62.50) – odds of 50–1 on. Other wagers were placed at even worse odds.

The outcome had a hideous inevitability about it. Lumpy and Wood not only survived against all the odds and expectations, they oh-so-slowly crept the score up and up towards that precious 130 target. Then, at last, when the tension was bordering on the unbearable, with the aid of no less than 12 byes past Tom Sueter and George Leer, they snatched victory by the narrowest of margins. Both batsmen finished with 19 not out.

The Kentish Gazette said of this match that it was 'the most extraordinary game of cricket that ever was played' – an opinion the editor might have conceded to the events almost exactly 205 years later, at Headingley, when odds of 500–1 were offered against an equally unlikely England victory.

26 August 1776 HAMBLEDON v SURREY

Broadhalfpenny Down. Hambledon won by 198 runs. Stake £1050.

Hambledon 273 (Small 85, Veck 46) and 155 (Aylward 59). Surrey 82 (Nyren 5 wickets) and 148.

During this game two Surrey players, Bowra and Minshull, became ill. In Surrey's second innings, Quiddenden and Yalden were allowed to bat in their places. After the match, Hambledon challenged England to a match within a fortnight, for 'any sum over £50' (£25,000). There were no takers.

1777

This was a truly amazing year for the Hambledon club. During the course of it, they beat England five times in seven matches.

Altogether, they played ten great matches during the season, won seven, gained one by default of the opposition, and lost two. Several of the scorecards are lost.

29 May 1777 (two days)
V of ENGLAND v V of HAMBLEDON

The Artillery Ground, Finsbury Square, London. Hambledon won by 15 runs. Stake £525.

Hambledon 32 and 44. England 41 and 20.

Thomas Brett was the man of the match. In both of England's innings, he bowled out three of their five batsmen. *The Hampshire Chronicle* wrote afterwards that this was the best match ever played by the Hambledon club in London. At one time the betting against them stood at 4–1.

18 June 1777 (three days)
HAMBLEDON v ENGLAND

Sevenoaks, Kent. Hambledon won by an innings and 168 runs. Stake £1050.

This remarkable match gave Hambledon their greatest ever win over England. James Aylward's 167 was the highest individual score ever made in what then passed for the first-class game. It was not exceeded for forty-three years. This was also one of the first major games to be played under the new third-stump law, which makes Aylward's triumph all the more impressive. Its introduction meant that defence suddenly became as important a part of the game as attack. To survive for any length of time, let alone bat continuously for nearly two days, a batsman now had to be technically sound, and play straight to avoid being bowled.

This game is sometimes erroneously credited with being the first won by Hambledon when they were playing on level terms with England. At one time it was thought that in all previous games won by Hambledon they were dependent on 'given men'. Recent research has shown this not to be the case. One other curiosity stands out in this scorecard: Lumpy played for

England, while his great friend and patron, the Earl of Tankerville, played for Hambledon

Batting first, England's first four batsmen scored heavily, but something of a collapse saw the home side finally dismissed for 166 by late afternoon on the first day. The Hambledon reply, led by Aylward, was beyond anything previously seen in great matches. Aylward went on batting as his partners came and went, not one of them failing to stay with him and put on a good number of runs before losing his wicket. It was a solid batting performance all the way down the order. It is said that Aylward started batting at about 5pm on the Wednesday, stayed in throughout Thursday, and was finally dismissed at 3pm on Friday. The best partnership was between Aylward and Sueter, and must have been worth 100 or so. England's first-innings total was probably passed with only three wickets down. Even Brett, batting last as usual, managed to add 9 runs of his own. England faced a huge deficit, but they must have been totally demoralized by Aylward's *tour de force*. Hambledon overwhelmed them for 69, thus winning the match by the biggest margin – an innings and 168 runs – ever recorded.

Sadly, and despite its fame as the greatest of all the great matches, at least three versions of the scorecard for this game are known to exist. Not even the totals are undisputed. Batting orders and dismissals vary widely. For instance, in England's first innings, Bullen is variously reported as being bowled by Tankerville, caught by Brett and caught by Taylor. Only his score of 13 is unchanged. Epps reported the match as starting on 28 May, which is unlikely. He also recorded the victory by an innings and 170 runs, having deprived Lumpy of his meagre 2 in England's second innings.

The batting order and scorecard details shown here come from Haygarth's painstakingly-considered record in his *Scores and Biographies*. It is more likely to be correct than the different versions often seen on reprints of what purport to be the original scorecard, which usually set out the batsmen by social status. For the first time in Hambledon matches, Haygarth records both the catcher and the bowler when a batsmen is dismissed 'caught'. The whole of the Hambledon innings is shown in this way, but unfortunately he was unable to find the information for either of the England innings.

England

Bullen	b Tankerville	13	b Nyren	2
Pattenden	b Brett	38	c Sueter	0
Miller	c Small	27	b Brett	23
Minshull	not out	60	b Taylor	12
White	c Veck	8	run out	10
Dorset	b Brett	0	c Tankerville	5
Yalden	c Small	6	c Nyren	8
Bowra	b Brett	2	b Taylor	4
Booker	c Brett	8	b Brett	2
Lumpy	b Brett	1	not out	2
Wood	b Brett	1	b Nyren	1
byes		2		0
Total		**166**		**69**

Hambledon

Veck	b Lumpy	16
Aylward	b Bullen	167
Small	c White b Lumpy	33
Tankerville	b Wood	3
Sueter	b Wood	46
Leer	b Wood	7
Taylor	c Bullen b Wood	32
Nyren	b Lumpy	37
Francis	c & b Wood	26
Aburrow	c Minshull b Bullen	22
Brett	not out	9
byes		5
Total		**403**

7 July 1777 (four days)
HAMBLEDON v ENGLAND

Broadhalfpenny Down. England won by 28 runs.

This was a classic example of the team dominating the first innings subsequently letting their opponents first get back into the game and then go on to win it. Hambledon were 134 runs ahead on the first innings but still managed to lose the match. Veck, who had made 54 in the first innings, was injured during

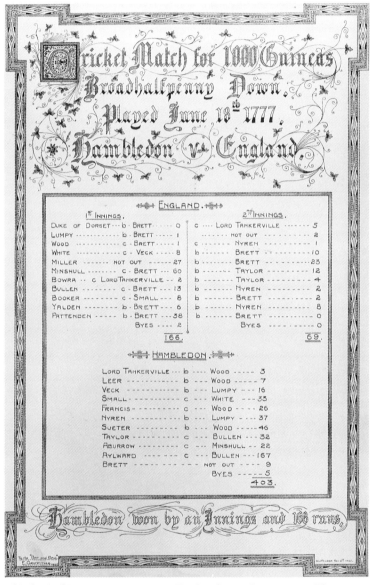

Cricket Match for 1000 Guineas
Broadhalfpenny Down.
Played June 18th 1777.
Hambledon v. England.

❖ ENGLAND. ❖

1st INNINGS.		2nd INNINGS.	
DUKE OF DORSET ··· b · BRETT ······ 0		c ····· LORD TANKERVILLE ······· 5	
LUMPY ··············· b · BRETT ····· 1		········ NOT OUT ··········· 2	
WOOD ············· c · BRETT ····· 1		c ········ NYREN ··········· 1	
WHITE ············· c · VECK ···· 8		b ········ BRETT ········· 10	
MILLER ······· NOT OUT ······ 27		b ········ BRETT ········· 23	
MINSHULL ········ c · BRETT ··· 60		b ······· TAYLOR ········· 12	
BOWRA ·· c LORD TANKERVILLE ·· 2		b ········ TAYLOR ········· 4	
BULLEN ·········· c · BRETT ··· 13		b ········ NYREN ········· 2	
BOOKER ········· c · SMALL ··· 8		b ········ BRETT ········· 2	
YALDEN ········ b · BRETT ··· 6		b ······· NYREN ········· 8	
PATTENDEN ····· b · BRETT ··· 38		b ········ BRETT ········· 0	
BYES ···· 2		BYES ·········· 0	
166.		69.	

❖ HAMBLEDON. ❖

LORD TANKERVILLE ··· b ···· WOOD ····· 3		
LEER ············· b ···· WOOD ····· 7		
VECK ············· b ···· LUMPY ··· 16		
SMALL ············ c ··· WHITE ··· 33		
FRANCIS ·········· c ··· WOOD ··· 26		
NYREN ············ b ··· LUMPY ··· 37		
SUETER ·········· b ··· WOOD ····· 46		
TAYLOR ·········· c ··· BULLEN ··· 32		
ABURROW ·········· c ··· MINSHULL ·· 22		
AYLWARD ········ c ··· BULLEN ··· 167		
BRETT ············ NOT OUT ···· 9		
BYES ····· 5		
403.		

Hambledon won by an Innings and 168 runs.

Hambledon's biggest win against England, 18 June 1777. There are two errors on this illuminated scorecard. It claims that the game was played at Broadhalfpenny Down. In fact it was played at Sevenoaks Vine. And it lists the players by social rank, as was the custom of the day. Yet this version of the scorecard was probably produced many years after the game and at a time when the batting order was known and was by then the norm.

the England second innings, and was obliged to go in as last man. Hambledon needed only 74 to win, but were dismissed for 45, despite a determined rearguard action by the captain. Considering the massive defeat England had suffered in the previous game, and the dreadful start they made in this one, the outcome must have been sweet indeed for the England team.

Epps places this match a month later, and reports the victory by 25 runs. He also indicates odds of 1-8 on a Hambledon win at the end of the England second innings. What odds were offered on an England victory, and whether anyone took them, he omitted to mention.

England

Yalden	b Brett	1	c Taylor	44
Wood	b Francis	9	b Small	0
Miller	b Francis	4	b Brett	65
Minshull	b Brett	21	b Brett	16
Bowra	run out	2	b Francis	6
Bullen	b Brett	1	c Sueter	27
Dorset	c Tankerville	2	b Small	0
Clifford	b Brett	7	run out	4
White	b Nyren	3	b Small	3
Booker	b Nyren	5	c Nyren	29
Lumpy	not out	1	not out	5
byes		4		8
Total		**60**		**207**

Hambledon

Aylward	c Miller	16	b Wood	0
Veck	b White	54	not out	0
Small	b Wood	3	run out	8
Sueter	c Wood	21	c Yalden	1
Leer	c Yalden	15	c Wood	0
Tankerville	run out	0	c Miller	7
Taylor	b Lumpy	0	b Lumpy	2
Nyren	b White	18	c Yalden	17
Aburrow	b Lumpy	25	run out	2
Francis	b Dorset	35	b Lumpy	6
Brett	not out	6	c Bullen	1
byes		1		1
Total		**194**		**45**

22 July 1777 (five days)
ENGLAND v HAMBLEDON

Laleham Burway, Chertsey, Surrey. Hambledon won by 30 runs.

Minshull had to retire having hurt his knee in England's first innings. He was unable to continue in the match, and the Hambledon side allowed Atfield to take his place. This included allowing him to bat in the first innings, as a continuation of Minshull's knock. Brett took eight wickets in the match, which took five days to complete, partly due to the weather.

Hambledon

Dorset	b Lamborn	37	c Tankerville	16
Small	c Edmeads	28	b Lumpy	14
Aylward	c Edmeads	17	c Tankerville	0
Veck	b Lamborn	2	c Edmeads	9
Sueter	c Yalden	7	b Wood	20
Taylor	not out	0	c Yalden	20
Leer	b Wood	0	b Wood	69
Nyren	b Lamborn	10	c Bullen	9
Francis	c Wood	0	run out	4
Aburrow	c White	0	b Lumpy	22
Brett	b Lumpy	6	not out	0
byes		8		4
Total		**115**		**187**

England

Tankerville	b Dorset	34	b Nyren	21
Edmeads	c Sueter	16	b Brett	4
Yalden	c Veck	1	not out	32
Lumpy	not out	6	b Brett	3
Minshull	retired hurt	7	did not bat	
Atfield[1]	run out	16	b Brett	0
Wood	b Brett	5	run out	4
Miller	c Francis	0	c Francis	2
Bowra	b Brett	29	b Nyren	8
Bullen	b Brett	3	c Aburrow	36
Lamborn	b Brett	0	b Brett	8
White	b Dorset	22	c Small	10
byes		4		1
Total		**143**		**129**

[1] batting for Minshull

18 August 1777 (three days)
ENGLAND v HAMBLEDON

Guildford, Surrey. Hambledon won by one wicket. Stake £1050 + £52.50 from Guildford.

This keenly-fought match had an extra financial edge to it. To encourage the organizers to stage the match in the town, the local council added 50 guineas to the stake money, the first time this is known to have occurred. Once again, Richard Nyren was responsible for seeing his side safely home. He and Sueter scored the last few runs, old heads in a desperately tight situation, well able to cope with the pressure of being the last-wicket pair.

This match was Noah Mann's first, and William Barber's last, for the club. Wood's dismissal, 'thrown out' Brett, in England's first innings is taken to mean that he was run out by a direct hit on the wicket from a fielder in the deep – in other words, run out.

England

Bullen	b Nyren	0	b Mann	20
Minshull	not out	33	b Mann	0
Tankerville	b Brett	1	b Nyren	45
Miller	run out	2	b Mann	64
Yalden	c Taylor	6	b Francis	42
Bowra	b Nyren	3	run out	12
Edmeads	b Brett	1	c Francis	7
Phillips	b Nyren	0	c Veck	19
Lumpy	run out	1	not out	5
Wood	b Brett	0	'thrown out' Brett	17
Lamborn	b Nyren	0	c Aylward	9
byes		3		9
Total		**50**		**249**

Hambledon

Veck	c Yalden	1	c Bullen		16
Francis	c Tankerville	15	b Lamborn		9
Aylward	c Bowra	30	b Lumpy		0
Small	c Minshull	14	c Wood		35
Sueter	b Wood	14	not out		9
Mann	c Bullen	23	c Edmeads		11
Taylor	c Edmeads	20	c Wood		62
Aburrow	b Lumpy	6	b Lumpy		8
Nyren	b Lumpy	4	not out		4
Brett	not out	3	b Bullen		4
Barber	b Lumpy	0	b Lumpy		0
byes		3			9
Total		**133**			**167**
					for 9 wickets

8 September 1777 (three days)
HAMBLEDON v ENGLAND

Broadhalfpenny Down. England won by 54 runs. Stake £52.50.

Hambledon were always struggling in this match, and needed a fourth-innings total higher than any of the previous three to win the game. Despite the bonus of 22 byes in their second innings, they failed by 54 runs. This was the first Hambledon match to list a substitute fielder, a dispensation which had been introduced into the game by the revision of the laws three years earlier.

England

Bowra	b Nyren	4	b Nyren		19
Bullen	c Leer	46	b Francis		31
Tankerville	b Brett	13	b Mann		21
Miller	b Mann	51	b Veck		39
Yalden	b Mann	8	c Brett		10
Bayton	b Brett	1	c Francis		13
Edmeads	b Brett	10	not out		33
Colchin	c Francis	2	c Mann		4
Bedster	not out	5	run out		0
Lumpy	b Brett	2	c Francis		5
Lamborn	b Brett	2	c Francis		2
byes		2			10
Total		**146**			**187**

Hambledon

Veck	c Edmeads	15	b Colchin	16
Taylor	c Bayton	1	b Lamborn	13
Aylward	b Lumpy	29	c sub (Goodwin)	47
Small	b Lamborn	16	b Lumpy	30
Sueter	c Bullen	5	b Colchin	0
Leer	b Lamborn	9	c Tankerville	3
Francis	c Bullen	24	b Lamborn	1
Mann	b Lumpy	5	b Lumpy	9
Nyren	b Lamborn	5	not out	15
Aburrow	b Lamborn	0	b Colchin	5
Brett	not out	1	c Bullen	1
byes		7		22
Total		**117**		**162**

15 September 1777 (three days)
ENGLAND v HAMBLEDON

The Artillery Ground, Finsbury Square, London. Hambledon won by 131 runs. Stake £52.50.

Catches dominated this match. Nineteen of the forty batsmen dismissed went to catches. Lumpy hit the stumps seven times. This was the last game the Hambledon club played on the ground of the Honourable Artillery Company in London.

Hambledon

Veck	c Bullen	18	c Lumpy	79
Aburrow	b Lumpy	5	not out	1
Aylward	c Yalden	56	c Edmeads	28
Small	c Yalden	4	c Yalden	1
Sueter	b Lumpy	21	b Colchin	11
Nyren	b Lumpy	16	b Colchin	9
Taylor	b Lumpy	24	c Bullen	9
Leer	b Lumpy	15	b Lumpy	33
Francis	run out	11	c Pemmel	4
Mann	b Lumpy	2	c Edmeads	9
Baker	not out	0	c Edmeads	1
byes		15		27
Total		**187**		**212**

England

Bullen	c Aburrow	5	c Aburrow	2
Bowra	b Mann	8	b Nyren	9
Tankerville	c Francis	13	c Small	22
Miller	c Taylor	22	c Aylward	11
Yalden	b Nyren	0	b Taylor	10
Edmeads	b Taylor	18	b Francis	14
Bedster	b Taylor	22	c Aylward	28
Pemmel	not out	18	b Mann	4
Colchin	run out	27	b Nyren	8
Lumpy	run out	3	c Nyren	6
Lamborn	c Aburrow	7	not out	2
byes		8		1
Total		**151**		**117**

29 June 1778 ENGLAND v HAMBLEDON

Sevenoaks, Kent. Hambledon won by three wickets.

Yet another away win, yet another fine all-round performance, and yet another occasion when Richard Nyren led the way with a determined second-innings knock to set up victory. Veck saw the visitors safely home with the highest score of the match.

England

Clifford	b Francis	10	b Nyren	15
Lumpy	b Mann	11	b Brett	4
Miller	run out	0	b Brett	32
Minshull	c Taylor	0	c Sueter	12
Bowra	run out	14	b Nyren	2
White	b Brett	13	b Mann	11
Wood	b Francis	7	not out	7
Yalden	c Taylor	19	run out	22
Lamborn	not out	2	c Veck	4
Bullen	b Brett	5	c Aburrow	6
Booker	b Mann	0	b Mann	4
byes		7		3
Total		**88**		**122**

Hambledon

Small	c Yalden	1	b Lamborn	6
Sueter	b Lumpy	3	not out	2
Leer	c Yalden	4	did not bat	
Nyren	b Lumpy	3	c Yalden	38
Francis	b Lamborn	24	c Lumpy	0
Veck	c Wood	2	not out	53
Taylor	c Minshull	0	c Wood	5
Aburrow	not out	1	b Lamborn	0
Brett	c Wood	0	did not bat	
Bedster	c Minshull	12	c Yalden	7
Mann	b Lumpy	16	c Yalden	19
byes		5		10
Total		**71**		**140**
				for 7 wickets

6 July 1778 (two days) HAMBLEDON v ENGLAND

Itchen Stoke Down, near Alresford, Hampshire. England won by 45 runs.

Lumpy and Lamborn took twelve of the twenty Hambledon wickets between them, hitting the stumps eleven times. This was the second time the Hambledon club had tried a new home venue, this one some fifteen miles from the village itself. Stoke Down was to become the first-choice home ground for the true Hampshire side which was to emerge towards the end of the century.

England

Bullen	b Nyren	0	not out	12
Bedster	b Francis	3	b Brett	34
Miller	c Sueter	1	b Nyren	9
Minshull	b Taylor	31	run out	0
White	b Taylor	33	b Nyren	16
Bowra	run out	2	run out	29
Yalden	not out	24	c Taylor	10
Booker	b Taylor	2	c Francis	3
Lumpy	c Taylor	19	b Nyren	11
Wood	b Mann	26	c Aburrow	0
Lamborn	b Mann	0	b Nyren	1
byes		2		5
Total		**143**		**130**

Hambledon

Aburrow	b Lamborn	14	b Lamborn	0
Francis	b Lamborn	0	b Lumpy	23
Sueter	b Lamborn	22	not out	17
Veck	c Wood	7	c Lumpy	7
Small	not out	49	b Lumpy	4
Taylor	b Lamborn	1	b Lamborn	5
Mann	c Yalden	7	b Lamborn	0
Leer	b Lumpy	17	c Yalden	2
Nyren	c Miller	5	b Lumpy	3
Stone	run out	0	run out	0
Brett	c Bullen	19	b Wood	12
byes		11		3
Total		**152**		**76**

24 September 1778 (two days)
HAMBLEDON v SURREY

Broadhalfpenny Down. Hambledon won by four wickets. Stake £1100.

Surrey 115 and 165. Hambledon 135 and 149 for 6.

6 October 1778 (three days)
SURREY v HAMBLEDON

Laleham Burway, Chertsey, Surrey. Surrey won by 138 runs.

Surrey 238 (Minshull 75) and 105. Hambledon 116 and 89.

This was Thomas Brett's last game for Hambledon and also saw the first recorded instance of a batsman being 'stumped' out – in Hambledon's second innings, the scorecard reads: Bonham stumped Yalden 9.

14 June 1779 HAMBLEDON v ENGLAND

Itchen Stoke Down, near Alresford, Hampshire. Hambledon won by six wickets.

This was a comparatively rare home win, although Hambledon were not playing at Broadhalfpenny Down. Nyren had a good match with the ball, taking seven wickets in all.

England

Bullen	run out	5	c Sueter		4
Bedster	c Small	23	b Mann		26
Miller	b Nyren	23	c Sueter		25
Minshull	c Small	7	c Small		17
Rimmington	b Nyren	2	b Nyren		18
Bowra	c Aylward	9	c Tankerville		9
Mills	b Nyren	5	b Nyren		34
Clifford	b Nyren	3	c Tankerville		34
Booker	not out	1	c Aburrow		7
Lumpy	run out	0	not out		4
Lamborn	b Francis	0	c Nyren		0
byes		2			1
Total		**80**			**179**

Hambledon

Tankerville	c Booker	6	b Lamborn		12
Small	b Lumpy	16	b Lumpy		11
Aylward	b Lamborn	12	b Lumpy		27
Veck	b Lumpy	30	not out		39
Sueter	b Lumpy	44	did not bat		
Taylor	b Lumpy	10	did not bat		
Leer	c Bedster	2	did not bat		
Aburrow	b Lamborn	11	not out		25
Francis	c Bowra	0	did not bat		
Mann	b Lamborn	4	did not bat		
Nyren	not out	0	b Bullen		6
byes		2			5
Total		**137**			**125**
				for 4 wickets	

23 June 1779 (four days)
ENGLAND v HAMBLEDON

Sevenoaks, Kent. Hambledon won by an innings and 89 runs.

Noah Mann was unquestionably the man of the match on this occasion. In addition to his 56 runs, he took nine wickets in the match, five bowled and four caught. This was Shock White's last great match.

England

Bedster	c Small	22	b Francis		37
Mills	b Mann	3	c Sueter		7
Miller	hit wicket	0	b Mann		0
Bullen	b Mann	1	not out		5
Minshull	b Nyren	3	run out		4
Bowra	b Nyren	0	c Mann		11
Yalden	b Nyren	0	c Mann		2
Clifford	b Mann	2	c Veck		12
White	c Taylor	3	b Nyren		6
Lamborn	c Mann	1	b Mann		0
Lumpy	not out	21	b Mann		3
byes		0			0
Total		**56**			**87**

Hambledon

Aburrow	b Bullen	16
Aylward	b Bullen	13
Small	b Lamborn	3
Tankerville	b Lumpy	6
Veck	b Lamborn	79
Mann	b Lamborn	56
Francis	b Lamborn	1
Taylor	b Lamborn	13
Sueter	c Bowra	11
Leer	c Yalden	9
Nyren	not out	14
byes		11
Total		**232**

23 August 1779 HAMBLEDON v ENGLAND

Broadhalfpenny Down. Hambledon won by 149 runs.

For some unexplained reason, only half the dismissals in this game were recorded. However, it is clear that the first-innings partnership between Mann and Small set Hambledon on their way to another win over England. Noah Mann had a particularly good game, since he also took wickets.

Hambledon

Aburrow	2	b Lamborn	9
Mann	45	b Lamborn	23
Small	66	b Lumpy	6
Veck	8	b Bullen	14
Sueter	10	c Bullen	24
Leer	2	c Yalden	58
Taylor	6	b Lamborn	2
Berwick	0	not out	10
Stewart	4	b Lumpy	2
Nyren	1	c Aylward	14
Bowra	16	b Lamborn	12
byes	7		8
Total	**167**		**182**

England

Bedster	8	b Nyren	2
Tankerville	0	c Nyren	12
Yalden	10	b Berwick	0
Atfield	17	c Veck	16
Miller	0	b Mann	37
Minshull	0	b Nyren	4
Lamborn	0	b Mann	0
Bullen	3	b Mann	6
Lumpy	4	not out	1
Clifford	17	c Aburrow	3
Aylward	51	b Nyren	3
byes	2		4
Total	**112**		**88**

13 September 1779 (four days)
ENGLAND v HAMBLEDON

Moulsey Hurst, Surrey. Hambledon won by two wickets.

Again we only have half the dismissals in what was obviously a keenly-fought match. England came back strongly in their second innings and very nearly snatched victory after having trailed badly on the first innings. Once again, some dogged batting by the Hambledon captain and his trusty wicket-keeper kept England at bay towards the end of the match, and finally saw the visitors safely home.

England

Bedster	b Nyren	1	7
Atfield	b Nyren	9	46
Aylward	c Bowra	4	6
Miller	b Mann	7	34
Minshull	b Berwick	0	34
Bullen	c Taylor	35	12
Clifford	c Taylor	33	21
Yalden	c Berwick	0	25
Edmeads	c Veck	0	0
Lumpy	b Nyren	2	52
Lamborn	not out	0	not out 3
byes		0	2
Total		**91**	**242**

Hambledon

Leer	c Bullen	21	10
Taylor	c Bedster	80	3
Mann	b Bedster	38	1
Small	c Yalden	5	9
Veck	c Bedster	3	43
Sueter	b Bullen	5	not out 11
Bowra	b Lumpy	5	6
Aburrow	run out	0	35
Nyren	b Lumpy	2	not out 23
Berwick	b Lumpy	1	19
Stewart	run out	6	did not bat
byes		6	2
Total		**172**	**162**
			for 8 wickets

1780s

During this decade, Hambledon played England seventeen times and won ten, according to the records that survive. Of these, all four of the five- and six-a-side matches were won, as was one game in which XI of Hambledon played XIII of England. All the other matches were between sides of eleven men apiece.

30 August 1780 (three days)
ENGLAND v HAMBLEDON

Bishopsbourne, Kent. England won by 165 runs.

Hambledon never seemed to get into this match. They were having a hard time almost from beginning to end. During one of his two successful innings for England, Yalden scored a total of twelve runs off two successive deliveries. The long-suffering bowler is not known. In some reports, this match is shown as Hambledon v Kent and Surrey.

England

T Rimmington	b Nyren	25		run out	7
Bedster	b Mann	12		b Lamborn	8
Bullen	c Tankerville	7		c Small	12
Aylward	b Nyren	9		b Nyren	24
B Rimmington	b Lamborn	4		c Small	4
Miller	c Small	7		b Aburrow	37
Bowra	b Veck	31		c Mann	1
Yalden	c Freemantle	52		b Lamborn	34
Clifford	b Nyren	25		c Taylor	7
Lumpy	c Sueter	6		not out	4
Berwick	not out	6		b Freemantle	5
byes		13			1
Total		**197**			**144**

Hambledon

Aburrow	c Bullen	0		b Lumpy	36
Atfield	b Clifford	13		run out	0
Mann	b Lumpy	6		b Clifford	33
Taylor	b Clifford	2		c T Rimmington	0
Small	c Lumpy	22		b Lumpy	19
Nyren	c Bullen	4		c Bowra	0
Veck	c Aylward	7		b Clifford	2
Lamborn	b Clifford	2		not out	3
Sueter	c Berwick	14		b Clifford	0
Tankerville	b Clifford	4		c Aylward	1
J Freemantle	not out	1		c Aylward	0
byes		5			2
Total		**80**			**96**

2 September 1780 V of
ENGLAND v V of HAMBLEDON

Bishopsbourne, Kent. Hambledon won by one run.

Hambledon 23. England 22.

This match followed immediately after the three-day game at Bishopsbourne. It was a one-day game, five-a-side to bat and bowl. It was the first such arrangement and juxtaposition of fixtures for twenty-four years, although it is possible that the records are lost of similar back-to-back fixtures in the intervening years.

20 September 1780 (three days)
HAMBLEDON v ENGLAND

Itchen Stoke Down, near Alresford, Hampshire. England won by 51 runs. Stake £1050.

Surrey players were added to both teams, and in some reports the teams were described as Hambledon with Surrey divided v Kent with Surrey divided. Neverthless, the Hambledon side included nine regular players, who, on this occasion, did not fare too well.

England

B Rimmington	b Lamborn	7	b Nyren	38
Bullen	b Lamborn	0	b Freemantle	15
Miller	c Mann	50	c Small	3
Aylward	c Nyren	26	b Nyren	3
T Rimmington	c Mann	0	b Lamborn	3
Bedster	c Mann	24	c Nyren	10
Yalden	b Lamborn	0	b Nyren	4
Berwick	c Wood	2	not out	4
Bowra	c Freemantle	3	run out	1
Clifford	not out	33	b Nyren	12
Lumpy	b Lamborn	31	b Nyren	4
byes		3		4
Total		**179**		**101**

Hambledon

Small	c Yalden	0	b Lumpy	6
Tankerville	b Clifford	3	c Aylward	2
Veck	b Lumpy	16	c Bullen	23
Mann	c Clifford	30	b Lumpy	10
Aburrow	run out	42	run out	1
Nyren	b Lumpy	11	not out	4
Taylor	c Lumpy	17	b Lumpy	2
Sueter	b Lumpy	36	b Clifford	6
J Freemantle	b Clifford	4	b Lumpy	0
Wood	b Lumpy	5	b Lumpy	1
Lamborn	not out	0	b Lumpy	4
byes		5		1
Total		**169**		**60**

28 May 1781 (two days)
V of ENGLAND v V of HAMBLEDON

Moulsey Hurst, Surrey. Hambledon won by 78 runs.

Hambledon 36 and 112 (Mann 67). England 30 and 40.

Once again, Noah Mann was man of the match. His second-innings 67 was higher than England's total in either innings, and almost more than their combined totals. In addition to his success with the bat, Mann also dismissed five England batsmen with catches.

6 June 1781 (four days) HAMBLEDON v ENGLAND

Itchen Stoke Down, near Alresford, Hampshire. Hambledon won by eight wickets.

This match is sometimes referred to as being between Hambledon and Kent. Certainly Kent were strongly represented. Haygarth has little doubt, however, that this was an England side. The game itself produced some high scoring and was keenly fought, despite the size of Hambledon's margin at the end. The scores themselves, and the fact that this was the fourth Hambledon home game to be played on this ground in as many years, suggest that Stoke Down was already proving itself to be a better pitch than Broadhalfpenny Down.

In England's first innings, all the batsmen were bowled out, Lamborn taking seven and Mann the other three.

England

Miller	b Mann	16	c Taylor	14
T Rimmington	b Lamborn	0	b Mann	4
Aylward	b Lamborn	25	c Bedster	73
M Rimmington	b Lamborn	2	not out	16
Bullen	b Mann	16	b Mann	1
Clifford	b Lamborn	22	b Lamborn	48
B Rimmington	b Lamborn	1	b Nyren	31
Bowra	not out	13	b Mann	8
Yalden	b Mann	0	b Nyren	7
Boorman	b Lamborn	1	b Freemantle	17
Lumpy	b Lamborn	1	b Mann	12
byes		4		1
Total		**101**		**232**

Hambledon

Bedster	c Yalden	5	b Bowra	49
Mann	b Clifford	10	b Lumpy	73
Taylor	c Yalden	12	not out	1
J Freemantle	not out	19	not out	5
Aburrow	c Clifford	11	did not bat	
Small	b Lumpy	47	did not bat	
Veck	c B Rimmington	12	did not bat	
Sueter	c M Rimmington	66	did not bat	
Leer	c Bullen	15	did not bat	
Nyren	b Lumpy	8	did not bat	
Lamborn	c Clifford	0	did not bat	
byes		1		0
Total		**206**		**128**
				for 2 wickets

18 July 1781 (three days)
ENGLAND v HAMBLEDON

Bishopsbourne, Kent. England won by 150 runs.

This match, too, is sometimes referred to as a match between Kent and Hambledon. Lumpy and Clifford kept the Hambledon batsmen struggling all through this game and effectively won it for the England side, whose own batsmen collectively put up two solid scores. Clifford had an outstanding game, scoring 26 and 57, and taking seven wickets (two bowled). Lumpy also took seven, hitting the stumps six times.

England

Bullen	c Sueter	4	b Nyren	13
Clifford	b Nyren	26	b Freemantle	57
Aylward	c Veck	29	c Sueter	25
Webb	b Lamborn	8	c Taylor	2
Bowra	b Lamborn	15	b Freemantle	10
B Rimmington	b Lamborn	11	c Sueter	20
Pattenden	c Taylor	15	c Taylor	16
Hogben	b Nyren	13	c Aburrow	15
Yalden	not out	18	b Mann	0
Lumpy	b Freemantle	7	not out	10
Miller	c Nyren	29	run out	14
byes		6		4
Total		**181**		**186**

Hambledon

Bedster	b Lumpy	0	c Clifford	3
Aburrow	b Lumpy	5	c Yalden	5
Taylor	b Clifford	6	b Lumpy	3
Veck	c Yalden	2	c Lumpy	26
Small	c Clifford	7	c Yalden	17
Sueter	c Clifford	3	run out	14
Mann	c Bullen	2	c Yalden	7
Nyren	b Clifford	5	b Lumpy	22
J Freemantle	c Clifford	1	b Lumpy	6
Lamborn	c Clifford	8	not out	0
Leer	not out	14	b Lumpy	53
byes		6		2
Total		**59**		**158**

30 July 1781 (three days) HAMBLEDON v KENT

Broadhalfpenny Down. Kent won by 38 runs.

Kent 218 (Clifford 66) and 188. Hambledon 185 (Mann 49) and 183 (Veck 44, Mann 41 not out).

This game was Richard Nyren's and Hambledon's last recorded great match on Broadhalfpenny Down. The General scored eight runs in total and took six wickets, five of them bowled.

15 August 1781
HAMBLEDON v PETERSFIELD AND BURITON

Broadhalfpenny Down. Result unknown. Stake £525.

What two local village sides were doing at Broadhalfpenny Down playing against the mighty Hambledon team for a prize worth the modern equivalent of over a quarter of a miilion pounds is anybody's guess. So is the result, which is long since lost.

27 August 1781 (two days) KENT v HAMBLEDON

Bishopsbourne, Kent. Hambledon won by eight runs.

Hambledon 60 and 106. Kent 88 and 70.

In Hambledon's second innings, Sueter was dismissed 'c Sim v (*sic*) Boreman 13'. This is taken to mean that Sim was substituting for Boreman in the field, and took a catch which should be credited to the original player.

1782

It was around this time that the Windmill Down wicket first came into use. The club did not make a clean break with Broadhalfpenny Down, especially since there were initially no facilities at Windmill Down, and no pub just across the track. New pitches take time to come good, but John Nyren eventually came to think highly of it. He considered it a better place for cricket. Gradually, the club switched more and more of its games and social activities to Windmill Down, and later built a new clubhouse on the ground. For the sake of completeness, the games at both grounds during the rest of the glory days are included here.

3 July 1782 KENT v HAMBLEDON

Sevenoaks, Kent. Kent won by four wickets. Stake £1050.
Hambledon 87 (Harris 27) and 140 (Sueter 48). Kent 102 and 127 for 6 (Bowra 48).

11 July 1782 (four days) HAMBLEDON v KENT

Itchen Stoke Down, near Alresford, Hampshire. Kent won by 142 runs.

Kent 257 (Aylward 75, Bedster 63, Bowra 50) and 72. Hambledon 121 and 66.

This match was marred by bad weather, which spread the game over four days and almost certainly influenced the outcome. Kent's first innings, which was played in good conditions, eventually proved decisive.

25 July 1782 (two days)
ENGLAND v HAMBLEDON

Bishopsbourne, Kent. Hambledon won by nine runs.

This is another of those matches which is sometimes referred to as being between Kent and Hambledon. Again, Haygarth clearly shows it as an England game. The England player Clifford was unlucky to be on the losing side, since he was plainly the man of the match. In addition to his impressive 46 out of 99 in England's second innings, he also took ten wickets in the match, bowling six in the first innings and another, plus three catches, in Hambledon's second attempt.

In what was obviously a tense, low-scoring game, Richard Nyren had a great deal to do with Hambledon's narrow victory. He was already forty-eight years old when this match was played, but age did not prevent him from taking seven England wickets in the match, five bowled and two caught.

Hambledon

Nyren	b Clifford	0	b Bullen	13
Mann	b Bullen	5	b Clifford	21
Sueter	b Clifford	2	c Clifford	6
Small	b Francis	15	c Bullen	3
Purchase	b Clifford	33	c Clifford	2
Veck	b Clifford	12	c Aylward	4
Aburrow	b Clifford	0	b Bullen	32
Taylor	b Clifford	0	c Aylward	2
Harris	b Clifford	1	run out	4
Lumpy	b Bullen	3	not out	6
Leer	not out	15	b Bedster	23
byes		2		12
Total		**88**		**128**

England

Francis	b Lumpy	17	b Lumpy	1
Bedster	c Sueter	0	c Nyren	0
Bullen	c Nyren	11	b Nyren	2
Brazier	b Lumpy	26	run out	23
Aylward	b Lumpy	0	c Veck	4
Bowra	c Veck	6	b Nyren	0
Hogben	c Taylor	1	b Nyren	0
Ring	b Nyren	3	c Taylor	7
Pattenden	b Lumpy	1	not out	7
Clifford	c Taylor	28	c Veck	46
Booker	not out	11	b Nyren	6
byes		4		3
Total		**108**		**99**

8 August 1782 HAMBLEDON v ENGLAND

Windmill Down. England won by 147 runs.

This is the first recorded match at Windmill Down, although one account places it at Broadhalfpenny Down. Assuming it was played on their new ground, Hambledon made a somewhat inauspicious start. This was a heavy defeat, even with Lumpy Stevens playing for them and taking six wickets. Hambledon were never in the game. In neither innings did they manage much more than half the England total.

England

Miller	b Nyren	1	c Harris	25
Bowra	run out	0	c Lumpy	15
Clifford	c Purchase	1	b Lumpy	31
Ring	c Small	10	b Lumpy	9
Yalden	not out	24	b Nyren	16
Aylward	c Sueter	19	stumped Sueter	18
Bedster	c Sueter	11	b Nyren	0
Francis	b Lumpy	21	c Small	4
Brazier	b Lumpy	2	b Lumpy	39
Bullen	c Sueter	16	c Purchase	28
Booker	b Nyren	10	not out	3
byes		0		1
Total		**115**		**189**

Hambledon

Mann	b Bullen	2	run out	44
Purchase	b Clifford	3	c Bedster	23
Leer	c Bullen	2	b Clifford	6
Sueter	c Yalden	14	b Bullen	0
Small	c Bowra	0	c Yalden	8
Veck	b Bullen	4	b Clifford	3
Aburrow	not out	21	run out	0
Nyren	b Clifford	3	b Bullen	1
Taylor	c Aylward	9	b Clifford	0
Lumpy	b Bullen	4	c Francis	2
Harris	b Clifford	0	not out	2
byes		2		4
Total		**64**		**93**

28 August 1782 (three days)
VI of KENT v VI of HAMBLEDON

Moulsey Hurst, Surrey. Hambledon won by 47 runs.

Hambledon 35 (Small 25) and 66 (Veck 26). Kent 35 (Aylward 20) and 19.

A match total of 155 runs scored over three days does not appear to have offered much entertainment to the spectators. But with both sides playing away from home, it is quite likely that few were present. The absentees did not miss much, although the margin of the result was exceptionally high for a six-a-side match, especially after the teams had been level on the first innings.

5 September 1782 HAMBLEDON v SUSSEX
Windmill Down. No details.

8 July 1783 (two days) HAMBLEDON v KENT
Windmill Down. Matched tied.

Kent 111 and 91. Hambledon 140 (Taylor 51, Sueter 42) and 62.

Nobody could recall a great match ending in a tie before this game. However, there was a dispute about the final score, and it seems likely that Kent won by one run. Pratt, the Kent scorer, made a habit of cutting every tenth notch deeper, so that he could tally up more quickly. But he had made one of his tenth (deep) notches on the eleventh mark. So Kent had actually scored one run more. By the time this error was discovered, the Hambledon scorer had conveniently 'lost' his stick. The result was declared a tie – a unique occurrence in great matches up to that time.

14 July 1783 HAMBLEDON INTER-CLUB MATCH
Broadhalfpenny Down.

This was probably a practice match of sorts. The prize offered to the winning team was 'eleven pairs of white corded dimity breeches and eleven handsome striped pink waistcoats'.

6 August 1783 (four days) KENT v HAMBLEDON
Bishopsbourne, Kent. Hambledon won by 85 runs.

Hambledon 160 (Small 52) and 192 (Taylor 66). Kent 204 (Ring 82, Bedster 61) and 63.

In Kent's second innings, the wickets were shared by Taylor, Harris and Lumpy. Bullen got 23 of Kent's 63 and none of the other batsmen reached double figures.

26 August 1783 (four days)
HAMBLEDON v ENGLAND
Windmill Down. Match drawn.

With Hambledon having moved to Windmill Down because of the better playing conditions it was ironic that this match, the second against England to be staged there, should be abandoned as a draw due to inclement weather. This was the first time a great match involving Hambledon had not been finished, according to surviving records, and it therefore appears as the club's first draw.

Hambledon might have been glad of it. They were beginning to struggle and, with half their side dismissed, they still needed another 70 to win. The 46-year-old John Small was run out in both innings, but he was still good enough to make one of the highest scores of the match. Some records show this as a match against Kent, and once again that county certainly provided most of the England team.

England

Aylward	hit wicket	18	c Taylor	18
Brazier	c Small	79	b Harris	9
Ring	b Harris	7	c Taylor	27
Bedster	b Lumpy	15	c Taylor	6
Clifford	b Nyren	19	c Harris	0
Dorset	b Lumpy	3	c Francis	3
Booker	b Lumpy	25	b Lumpy	21
Townsend	b Francis	14	c Taylor	22
Wood	not out	7	c Small	5
Yalden	c Lumpy	22	not out	11
Bullen	b Harris	6	b Harris	9
byes		3		2
Total		**218**		**133**

Hambledon

Small snr	run out	78	run out	13
Mann	c Yalden	18	b Brazier	32
Taylor	b Brazier	16	did not bat	
Veck	b Bullen	13	b Bullen	14
Sueter	c Ring	53	did not bat	
Francis	b Bullen	0	b Brazier	0
Nyren	b Brazier	22	did not bat	
Purchase	c Dorset	0	c Bullen	0
Wells	b Brazier	4	not out	2
Harris	c Bullen	7	did not bat	
Lumpy	not out	0	did not bat	
byes		6		2
Total		**217**		**63**
			for 5 wickets	

16 September 1783 (four days)
VI of ENGLAND v VI of HAMBLEDON

Bishopsbourne, Kent. Hambledon won by 31 runs.

Hambledon 46 and 55 (Veck 32). England 22 and 48.

In England's second innings, David Harris bowled five of the six batsmen, having bowled the other one (Bullen) in the first innings.

1 June 1784 (two days)
ENGLAND v HAMBLEDON

Sevenoaks, Kent. England won by seven wickets.

This match was a very special occasion for father and son Small, and a source of great pride for their most vocal and enthusiastic family supporter, Mrs Small. For the first time, father John and son John were in the same Hambledon side for a great match. However, apart from James Aylward, this was not a match for the batsmen. In Hambledon's two innings, Clifford and Bullen took fourteen wickets between them, while Francis took six for Hambledon in England's first innings. Unfortunately, he could not repeat the performance in the second. Again, some records show this as a match against Kent.

Hambledon

Mann	c Bowra	1	b Clifford	3
Purchase	b Clifford	0	c Bedster	16
Small snr	b Bullen	3	c Bowra	38
Sueter	not out	35	b Bullen	1
Veck	b Bullen	5	b Clifford	19
Taylor	b Bullen	12	c Bowra	15
Francis	b Bullen	1	c Aylward	8
Nyren	b Clifford	0	c Bullen	8
Cole	c Clifford	4	b Bullen	4
Small jnr	b Bullen	6	c Bedster	0
Lumpy	b Bullen	3	not out	1
byes		0		3
Total		**70**		**116**

England

Bullen	b Francis	14	did not bat	
Clifford	c Francis	31	b Lumpy	0
Hosmer	run out	2	b Francis	11
Ring	b Francis	0	c Taylor	5
Aylward	b Francis	37	not out	28
Bedster	c Taylor	0	not out	18
Brazier	b Lumpy	8	did not bat	
Davison	b Francis	0	did not bat	
Bowra	c Francis	3	did not bat	
Booker	not out	20	did not bat	
Townsend	c Nyren	7	did not bat	
byes		2		1
Total		**124**		**63**
				for 3 wickets

26 July 1784 (three days)
VI of HAMBLEDON v VI of KENT

Itchen Stoke Down, near Alresford, Hampshire. Kent won by 20 runs.

Kent 37 and 39. Hambledon 29 and 27.

Contemporary newspaper reports of this game claimed that it was the first great single-wicket match ever lost by the Hambledon side. They were wrong, of course. Bullen took nine wickets in the match, hitting the stumps eight times.

1785

No match reports for this year.

26 June 1786 (three days) KENT v HAMBLEDON

Sevenoaks, Kent. Kent won by four wickets.

Hambledon 143 (T Walker 43) and 89. Kent 123 and 110 for 6 (Ring 61 not out).

The fleet-footed Noah Mann was run out for 0 in both Hambledon's innings in this match, a questionable achievement which did nothing to endear him to the rest of the team. Some thought his rashness had cost them the game. He would have been somewhat depressed by the experience, too. Sevenoaks was a mighty long way to go for two ducks, to say nothing of the embarrassing dent in his reputation as a runner.

13 July 1786 (three days) HAMBLEDON v KENT
Windmill Down. Hambledon won by one wicket.

Kent 83 and 189 (Booker 55 not out, Aylward 53). Hambledon 163 (H Walker 66, T Walker 55) and 110 for 9.

This match is sometimes referred to as England versus Kent. However, the England side included nine regular Hambledon players, and the match was played on the club's new home ground. The Walker brothers dominated Hambledon's first innings, with 121 out of a total of 163.

3 August 1786 (three days) KENT v HAMBLEDON
Moulsey Hurst, Surrey. Hambledon won by 35 runs.

Hambledon 116 (T Walker 56) and 144. Kent 143 and 82 (Booker 39).

While there is no doubt about the scores or the result, there are three different descriptions given to the two sides. Apart from Kent v Hambledon, the fixture was also described as Earl of Winchilsea's XI v Sir Horace Mann's XI (Kent); and, even more quixotically, as the ABC's XI (Kent) v the Rest of the Alphabet's XI. At least these curious descriptions explain why both sides were apparently playing away from home.

6 September 1786 (four days)
VI of KENT v VI of HAMBLEDON
Bishopsbourne, Kent. Kent won by one wicket.

Hambledon 45 and 39. Kent 19 and 66 for 5.

This must have been one of the most tedious matches ever played. It lasted four days and produced an aggregate of 169 runs in the four innings, two-thirds of them coming from just two batsmen. Ring scored 11 and 57 off 404 deliveries for Kent, while Tom Walker scored 26 off 382 deliveries in five hours in Hambledon's first innings and 12 off 321 deliveries in the second. Altogether, the two men faced 1107 balls and were at the crease for over half the match.

Aylward, last man in for Kent, went in with two runs needed for victory. Before he had scored, he gave Taylor a sharp chance at point, which was dropped! He took sixty-four deliveries to score his first run, and another thirty to get the winning run.

(Later in the season, when playing in a six-a-side match for the White Conduit Club, again against Kent, Tom Walker improved dramatically on his efforts against them recorded in this match. He scored 95 not out and 102, the greatest two-innings scores ever recorded and a mere five runs short of two centuries in a match, a feat which had never been achieved up to that date.)

2 August 1787 (three days)
VI of HAMBLEDON v VI of KENT
Lord's. Kent won by 23 runs.

Kent 53 and 13. Hambledon 27 and 16.

David Harris took eleven of the twelve Kent wickets, all bowled. Noah Mann got the other, also bowled. Eleven Hambledon wickets were bowled down. The only exception in the entire match was Taylor's dismissal in Hambledon's second innings, when he was caught.

7 August 1787 (two days) KENT v HAMBLEDON
Coxheath, near Maidstone, Kent. Hambledon won by two wickets.

Kent 140 (Clifford 50) and 194. Hambledon 256 (T Walker 57, Beldham 42) and 79 for 8.

14 August 1787 (four days)
ENGLAND v HAMBLEDON
Bishopsbourne, Kent. Hambledon won by 266 runs. Stake £1050.

It was the opinion of *The Kentish Gazette* after this overwhelming victory by Hambledon that the Hampshire team had 'arrived at an unequalled degree of perfection'. Few who saw the game would have disagreed with that view. England had been crushed.

Hambledon

Purchase	b Clifford	6	run out	0
Small snr	b Fennex	40	b Boorman	24
Taylor	b Clifford	8	run out	20
T Walker	c Bullen	65	b Fennex	17
H Walker	b Clifford	2	c Brazier	10
Mann	b Fennex	4	b Bullen	12
John Wells	b Clifford	10	b Fennex	13
Small jnr	b Clifford	0	not out	10
Winchilsea	b Fennex	12	c Amherst	20
Beldham	run out	28	b Fennex	42
Harris	not out	8	b Clifford	3
byes		10		3
Total		**193**		**174**

England

Clifford	c Small jnr	5	b Harris	3
Bullen	c Beldham	0	c Winchilsea	1
Fennex	b Harris	0	b Harris	9
Ring	b Harris	24	run out	13
Brazier	c Beldham	21	c H Walker	0
Crozoer	b Harris	0	b Harris	2
Amherst	c Mann	0	c Wells	3
Aylward	b Taylor	2	c T Walker	0
Boorman	b Harris	0	not out	0
Louch	c Taylor	4	c Purchase	0
Booker	not out	0	run out	7
byes		4		3
Total		**60**		**41**

3 September 1787 (three days)
HAMBLEDON v ENGLAND

Windmill Down. England won by 65 runs.

Hambledon lost seven men run out in this match and Silver Billy Beldham had the embarrassing and – for him – very rare

distinction of not troubling the notchers in either innings. This
was the first recorded appearance of John Nyren in a great
match, at the age of twenty-two. England arrived one man
short, and the England skipper, James Aylward, asked him to
make up the numbers. He had the disconcerting experience of
running out two of the Hambledon players, and being on the
winning side against his beloved home club.

England

Aylward	c Purchase	31	c John Wells	65
Clifford	b Taylor	3	b Beldham	2
Ring	c Taylor	14	c H Walker	2
Pilcher	c Taylor	0	run out	13
Brazier	b Harris	3	c John Wells	14
Fennex	b Harris	2	c Taylor	0
Booker	c Beldham	1	run out	15
Louch	not out	21	c Mann	8
Bullen	c Small	2	not out	2
Boorman	c Beldham	23	b Mann	0
John Nyren	c John Wells	3	c Taylor	1
byes		6		1
Total		**109**		**123**

Hambledon

T Walker	b Boorman	7	b Boorman	1
Small snr	c Aylward	3	b Bullen	7
Taylor	run out	1	b Bullen	5
H Walker	b Bullen	1	b Bullen	2
Beldham	c Boorman	0	run out	0
John Wells	run out	6	run out	23
Mann	b Bullen	5	c Bullen	41
Small jnr	run out	4	b Boorman	4
Purchase	run out	0	not out	30
Harris	not out	4	b Bullen	4
James Wells	b Bullen	1	run out	5
byes		5		8
Total		**37**		**130**

31 May 1788

Mr Thomas Lord's new cricket ground in Dorset Square staged its first match.

Around this time, 1788, great matches were increasingly staged with Hambledon men on both sides. Three took place this year alone – on 9 June at Moulsey Hurst, on 2 July in Wiltshire, and on 13 August on Windmill Down, no less. These matches are not included here since the club itself was not involved (apart from providing the ground in one case). These games are, however, the first clear evidence of the disintegration of the Hambledon club as the top players sought income wherever it was to be found.

17 June 1788 (two days)
HAMBLEDON v ENGLAND

Itchen Stoke Down, near Alresford, Hampshire. Hambledon won by an innings and 76 runs.

This match was something of a triumph for the two Hambledon bowlers, Richard Purchase and David Harris. Silver Billy Beldham's 52 was far and away the best innings of the game and set up a big victory for the home side.

Hambledon		
T Walker	run out	6
H Walker	b Clifford	23
Small snr	run out	3
Small jnr	b Lumpy	5
Taylor	c Ingram	22
Beldham	not out	52
John Wells	b Bullen	39
Purchase	b Clifford	3
Harris	b Fennex	21
Mann	c Clifford	0
James Wells	b Lumpy	37
byes		9
Total		**220**

England

Aylward	b Purchase	30	b Purchase	5
Louch	c Harris	2	c Mann	0
Bullen	run out	0	b Purchase	7
Clifford	c James Wells	0	not out	15
Ring	b Harris	6	b Purchase	6
Cole	c Mann	1	b Harris	1
Fennex	b Harris	0	run out	18
Booker	run out	5	b Harris	2
Boorman	c Taylor	17	c Taylor	19
Lumpy	not out	1	b Harris	2
Ingram	b Purchase	1	run out	5
byes		0		1
Total		**63**		**81**

24 July 1788 (two days) ENGLAND v HAMBLEDON

Sevenoaks, Kent. Hambledon won by 53 runs.

This was a bowlers' match. Clifford took nine wickets (four bowled) and Lumpy five (four bowled) in Hambledon's two innings. A score of over 20 was a rarity in the game.

Hambledon

T Walker	b Lumpy	5	c Clifford	9
H Walker	c Louch	8	c Clifford	31
Small snr	c Clifford	10	c Clifford	3
Winchilsea	not out	2	c Lumpy	4
John Wells	c Aylward	0	b Lumpy	29
James Wells	c Louch	12	b Lumpy	0
Taylor	c Bowra	7	b Fennex	3
Beldham	c Clifford	7	b Lumpy	6
Purchase	b Clifford	7	not out	8
Harris	b Clifford	2	b Clifford	0
Mann	c Bowra	15	b Clifford	5
byes		0		4
Total		**75**		**102**

England

Louch	b Taylor	35	c John Wells	0
Aylward	c Beldham	4	b Mann	4
Clifford	b Purchase	6	run out	10
Bullen	c Taylor	1	not out	2
Booker	run out	0	c H Walker	7
Brazier	b Harris	2	c Purchase	1
Fennex	b Taylor	13	c Taylor	2
Bowra	run out	5	b Mann	1
Boorman	c H Walker	9	b Mann	6
Lumpy	not out	3	c Beldham	0
Crawte	run out	12	b Mann	0
byes		1		0
Total		**91**		**33**

21 August 1788 (three days)
VI of ENGLAND v VI of HAMBLEDON

Lord's. Hambledon won by five wickets.

England 8 and 19. Hambledon 24 and 4 for 1.

Once again, David Harris's bowling won the game for Hambledon. He took nine wickets in the match, four in the first innings and five in the second, one of which was a catch.

29 August 1788 (five days)
VI of KENT v VI of HAMBLEDON

Bishopsbourne, Kent. Hambledon won by six runs.

Hambledon 25 and 17. Kent 4 and 32.

How a match yielding 78 runs in total could possibly last five days (and that excludes the Sunday, when there was no play) is beyond modern comprehension. Even if the weather interrupted play, it is difficult to imagine a more boring spectacle when the players were on the field. The stake is unknown, but it must have been immense to have created such a tedious match. Father and son Small both played for Hambledon. Yet again, David Harris was the man of the match, taking seven wickets in the two innings, all bowled, including the last man in, Joseph Ring, whose dismissal won the match.

26 June 1789 (seven days)
XIII of ENGLAND v XI of HAMBLEDON

Lord's. Hambledon won by six wickets.

This is the first recorded match played by a full Hambledon team at Thomas Lord's new cricket ground.

The club's success against the odds owed everything to the truly astonishing performance of the twenty-three-year-old Billy Beldham, who scored a third of all Hambledon's runs. If this batting order is correct – and the evidence supports it – his achievement in Hambledon's first innings must be ranked among the very best. He would have arrived at the wicket with the score at about 20 for 6, chasing an England first innings total of 118. To set up a win from that position was an extraordinary feat of determination and skill.

England

Ring	b Purchase	0	b Purchase	11
White	b Taylor	17	c John Wells	7
Pilcher	c Beldham	4	b Purchase	7
Palmer	b Taylor	2	run out	0
Aylward	b Harris	37	c John Wells	9
Brazier	run out	9	c Beldham	1
Clifford	c Beldham	4	b Purchase	0
Bullen	b Harris	12	c Beldham	2
Fennex	c H Walker	21	run out	0
Ingram	b Harris	9	c Small jnr	33
Boorman	c Beldham	0	not out	0
Lumpy	not out	0	b Harris	0
Louch	b Purchase	0	b Harris	2
byes		3		1
Total		**118**		**73**

Hambledon

T Walker	b Clifford	0	b Fennex	0
H Walker	b Boorman	0	did not bat	
Purchase	b Boorman	39	did not bat	
Taylor	b Boorman	6	b Boorman	4
Small snr	b Boorman	2	not out	6
John Wells	b Clifford	4	b Fennex	0
Mann	b Clifford	1	b Fennex	14
Beldham	b Brazier	94	not out	16
James Wells	b Clifford	1	did not bat	
Small jnr	c Louch	1	did not bat	
Harris	not out	0	did not bat	
byes		2		2
Total		**150**		**42**
				for 4 wickets

9 July 1789 (two days)
VI of HAMBLEDON v VI of KENT

Itchen Stoke Down, near Alresford, Hampshire. Match abandoned.

Kent 66 (Ring 25) and 64. Hambledon 31 and 10 for 2.

David Harris was to have played for Hambledon, but his gout prevented him from taking part. The weather was so bad that the game was not resumed after rain stopped play on the second day.

31 July 1789 (three days)
SURREY v HAMBLEDON

Moulsey Hurst, Surrey. Surrey won by 221 runs. No details.

18 August 1789 KENT v HAMBLEDON

Bishopsbourne, Kent. Hambledon won by 29 runs.

Hambledon 135 (Purchase 59) and 106. Kent 137 and 75.

The bowlers dominated this game for Hambledon. David Harris took eight wickets in the match and hit the stumps six times. Richard Purchase took five of the remaining wickets, including four bowled out.

This was the last great match played at Bishopsbourne.

1790 saw no matches played by the Hambledon club, although many of the club's leading players took part in other games, often split between both sides in the same match.

6 June 1791
XXII of MIDDLESEX v XI HAMBLEDON

Lord's. Middlesex won by three wickets. Stake £1050.

This was the last match played by the original Hambledon side, against the odds and when most players were past their best. To lose by a mere three wickets in such circumstances was a handsome tribute to their ability, courage and determination. They never played together as a team again. Once again, contemporary records suggest more betting on this game than anything known before.

Thomas Lord played for the Middlesex team. In their two innings, the highest individual score was 17. Only six batsmen got to double figures during either Middlesex innings. Tom Taylor kept wicket for Hambledon. He caught six and stumped one. David Harris took ten wickets in the match – seven bowled and three caught.

Hambledon

Small jnr	b Bedster	12	b Fennex	0
Beldham	run out	19	b Fennex	15
T Walker	c Fennex	0	b Fennex	0
Wells	b Fennex	2	b Turner	25
Purchase	b Grange	0	b Fennex	1
H Walker	c Knowles	8	c J White	0
Small snr	b Lord	14	c Cantrell	5
A Freemantle	c J White	10	b Turner	12
Taylor	b Fennex	1	not out	2
Harris	run out	0	b Fennex	0
Scott	not out	49	run out	23
byes		12		7
Total		**127**		**90**

XXII of Middlesex
122 and 96 for 18 wickets.

(As the fates would have it, Hambledon returned to Lord's 198 years later for the final of the 1989 annual village knock-out competition. Unfortunately, the game was ruined by rain, abandoned, and played elsewhere the following day. Hambledon lost.)

June 1792
HAMBLEDON v XXII of HERTFORDSHIRE AND ESSEX
Broadhalfpenny Down. The result is lost.

This is the last recorded match on Broadhalfpenny Down for 116 years.

19 August 1794 (two days)
HAMPSHIRE v KENT AND SURREY
Itchen Stoke Down, near Alresford, Hampshire. Kent and Surrey won by six wickets.

Hampshire 65 and 71. Kent and Surrey 70 and 67 for 4.

The Hampshire side included ten former Hambledon regular players, against a team which included all the three Walker brothers. By this time, the use of the 'Hampshire' nomenclature was becoming the norm, and Hambledon's role in the development of cricket was passing into history.

21 August 1794 (three days)
HAMPSHIRE v KENT AND SURREY
Itchen Stoke Down, near Alresford, Hampshire. Hampshire won by six wickets.

Surrey and Kent 118 and 95. Hampshire 184 (J Wells 75, Beldham 46) and 30 for 4.

This was a return match, back-to-back with the previous match. The teams were virtually unchanged for the second game. The result was exactly reversed.

It was all over. The glory days had come and gone. A set of cricket records had been created over the last fifty years or so, the memories of which would endure in the game forever. The last match had been played on Broadhalfpenny Down for several generations to come, and during that time of neglect a heavy proportion of those records was to be lost through carelessness, lack of interest and fire.

But we have a date for the monument. It was in 1792 that the original Hambledon club played its last game on Broadhalfpenny Down.

Into the Dust

While 'little' Hambledon was enjoying to the full its most glorious of the glory days during the 1770s and 80s, and building a reputation that will last as long as the game of cricket itself, circumstances elsewhere were changing rapidly. In terms of sheer power and influence, the centre of cricket gravity moved gradually and inevitably towards London during those same decades. As the 1780s wore on, the aristocrats involved in the game, as players and as patrons, became increasingly reluctant to ride all the way to Broadhalfpenny Down, or Windmill Down for that matter. Why drag all the way down to Hambledon yet again? It was a tedious and difficult day's journey just to get there. The novelty of playing at Broadhalfpenny Down was wearing thin from all that travelling.

Within ten years it had worn off altogether, encouraged by the increasingly difficult economic conditions of the day. The recession in the 1780s was becoming a depression. This economic downturn further encouraged the aristocrats to reduce their time and expense in travelling back and forth to Hambledon, purely in the pursuit of entertainment. These were tough times and they called for some hard decisions. Attention had to be paid to financial matters, as an increasing priority.

In any case, perfectly good cricket grounds were to be found much closer to home. A fine ground at White Conduit House, in Islington, had been in use for years, and the Artillery Ground in Finsbury Square had been established for almost 150 years. Then, in 1787, with the active encouragement of the Duke of Dorset and others, Thomas Lord opened the third first-class ground in London, this one at Dorset Square. It was to be the last straw for the Hambledon club.

It had been that same Duke of Dorset's suggestion, made just a few years earlier, that Hambledon should move their ground permanently from Broadhalfpenny Down to Windmill Down, just above the village. His lordship considered Broadhalfpenny Down a bleak place to play cricket, despite the fact that the England side he so often patronized generally fared better against Hambledon on that ground than anywhere else. Not surprisingly, given the Duke's place in society, others soon echoed his opinion. Such comments, genuinely held or not, gradually built up a momentum which was to seal the fate of Broadhalfpenny Down. It was a fate that was to last for over 100 years.

The Duke's view that it was a bleak place for cricket had a profound influence in other respects, too. Somehow it downgraded and undermined the independence and stature of the Hambledon club. The Duke had spoken and that was that. Furthermore, purely local considerations reinforced the idea. To move the ground permanently to Windmill Down, just above the village, would be better for everybody. Richard Nyren and his successor William Barber had both left the Bat and Ball Inn. Admittedly, Richard Nyren was still innkeeping at the George, down in the village. It was much easier for him, as it was for everyone else, to get to the ground at Windmill Down than to travel the two miles back to Broadhalfpenny Down. It was less than half the distance, and the ground was much less exposed to the elements. By 1782, Windmill Down was in use. Matches still took place back at Broadhalfpenny Down, but from this season onwards Hambledon's great home matches were played at Windmill Down, or elsewhere in the county.

From the club's point of view, it was singularly unfortunate that the Duke's comments should come within a few years of two other critical events – Richard Nyren's move to London and the formation of the MCC at the new ground created by Thomas Lord. Back in London, the Duke of Dorset, Colonel Charles Lennox, who was later to become the fourth Duke of Richmond, the Earl of Winchilsea, who was the president of the Hambledon club at the time, and several other powerful men with a passion for cricket were all members of the White Conduit Club in Islington. A young man by the name of Thomas Lord was on the club's staff. He was a general factotum, by all accounts, who was known to be a useful cricketer. Indeed, that probably helped him to get the job shortly after he arrived in London from Norfolk, determined to make his way in the world. He was an ambitious young man of considerable initiative, who later became a successful wine merchant. He was also good enough to play cricket for Middlesex. But even while he was still working at the White Conduit Club, he appears to have fulfilled the role of private cricket coach to the Earl of Winchilsea as well. Encouraged by these aristocrats, their protégé was invited to find and make a new cricket ground in London. They offered to guarantee him against any loss on the project. Implicit in their support seems to have been a promise of help for him to stage great matches on his new ground. It was too good an opportunity for this enterprising young man to miss.

He eventually found Dorset Fields, now Dorset Square, and in due course his patrons were as good as their word. The White Conduit Club immediately used Mr Lord's new ground, and very agreeable they found it. Indeed, so good was it that they decided to go further. They would form a new club to use it as a home ground. The meeting at which it was founded took place at the Star and Garter in Pall Mall, that same pleasant institution which had housed the meeting to discuss the laws of cricket some thirteen years earlier. The club was to be called the Marylebone Cricket Club. It had effectively been sired by the White Conduit Club. The year was 1787, and the first ball was bowled at its headquarters, Mr Lord's cricket ground, on

31 May the following year. (The MCC was eventually to move its headquarters to the present ground in St John's Wood in 1814 – but that is another story.)

Within a year, the MCC's powerful and aristocratic membership had quickly swept the administration of the game, and its law-making powers, away from the little country club in deepest Hampshire. The Earl of Winchilsea's blatant conflict of interests in such a situation, which arose through his encouragement of Thomas Lord while he was president of the Hambledon club, would not have crossed his mind. Nor would it have been questioned – the structure of society in those days would not have permitted it. Even if a few humble Hampshire folk might have had doubts, they would not have dared mention them, let alone raise them as an issue. In any case, it was many of these same aristocrats who had been the strength behind the Hambledon club in the first place. They may not have been as visible as the players, but they held the power. Wherever they went, the power went with them. At the time, to be fair, the long-term consequences of the establishment of the MCC and Thomas Lord's new cricket ground were probably unforeseen by all concerned. Even with some foresight, it is probable that most players and members of the MCC and Hambledon clubs would almost certainly have viewed this expansion of the game in London as a good thing anyway.

With all these changing attitudes and priorities, however, pressures were inexorably building up on the Hambledon club. For the first time in living memory, more members were resigning than were being elected. Money had always been tight, but now it was suddenly getting tighter. Across the Channel a revolution was under way, and there were signs of war coming in Europe. Nothing was quite the same any more.

Then in 1791, the well-being of the now struggling Hambledon club suddenly took a dramatic turn for the worse. Richard Nyren decided to move permanently to London. We can only speculate on his motive for the move. It might have been a consequence of the decline in the Hambledon club, and his own decline as a player, which had inevitably occurred a few years before. It might have been his health, and a need to be nearer to the medical attention he required. It might have been the fact that England was now in the grip of a nasty recession. Or it might have been some combination of all three possibilities.

Whatever Richard Nyren's reasons were for moving, it was a moment of drama and sadness for the club. Undoubtedly many of his friends tried to discourage him. But he was adamant. There is one explanation for Nyren's move to London which we can rule out, however. It was not for domestic considerations. All his family were still in or near the village. John had just got married and was, for the time being, living not far away, at Portsea. So Richard's reasons for leaving must have been powerful. But he did not cut his local ties altogether. His links with the village were to remain intact through family and friends. Sadly, Richard Nyren died a mere six years later, in 1797. So perhaps his health did have something to do with it, after all, although he had been well enough to play some cricket during those years. After his death, Richard's widow Frances promptly returned to Hambledon, to live in a house provided by her son.

Meanwhile, the local Squire Powlett, as he now was, took on the thankless task of grappling with the survival of the club. He was nearly seventy years old and no longer full of energy. He had put behind him the regrettable incident in 1775, when he had gambled heavily against a Hambledon win. That was now just a dim and embarrassing memory. As a staunch member of Hambledon, he had always tried to act in the club's best interests, he had been an active supporter throughout the glory days, and now he attempted to come to its rescue in this dark hour. But it was to prove too much even for his committed efforts. Club meetings were relaxed from weekly to fortnightly, but that only seemed to make matters worse. The change merely reflected the diminishing level of interest. It certainly did nothing to bring the people back. From little Hambledon's point of view, events elsewhere had together created an impetus that no-one now had the strength or influence to stop, let alone reverse.

Instead, the unfortunate coincidence of all these circumstances brought the glory days to a precipitous end, made much worse a few years later when the Napoleonic Wars drew many of the local young men away to death or hideous injury. By 1793, war had broken out with France, and within no time the club's support and playing strength was literally scattered to the four winds as members went to war at sea and on the continent of Europe.

By 1796, the club was struggling even to get a quorum of members at its meetings. A meeting called for 29 August that year attracted only four members. Curiously, a larger group of non-members also turned up. They included Thomas Paine, author of *The Rights of Man*, who arrived despite the risks to his personal safety. What he was doing there, if the report is true, is difficult to fathom. Since several of the other non-members present were military folk, an intriguing question arises: was the Hambledon club falling into the hands of revolutionaries; had it become a cover for wartime activities? We shall probably never know, and maybe that's just as well.

A month later, on 21 September 1796 to be exact, the minute book reads forlornly: 'No gentlemen.' It was finally over. These bleak words record the last vestiges of the Hambledon club as it had been.

There is a sad, even wistful footnote to this period of events at Hambledon. A great swansong of a match took place on 6 June 1791, when a team of eleven true old Hambledon players – obviously a long way past their best – took on XXII of Middlesex in a three-day match at Lord's. It was to prove a terrific contest which they lost by a mere three wickets. Father and son Small both played, as did Silver Billy Beldham, the Walker brothers, David Harris, John Wells, Tom Taylor, Tom Scott, Richard Purchase and Andrew Freemantle. It must have been just like old times. It is not clear who skippered the side, but we know that Tom Taylor kept wicket. The Middlesex side included Thomas Lord himself, but only six of their batsmen got to double figures in either innings, and their highest individual score was 17. David Harris bowled seven out and, for good measure, also took three catches. Obviously his gout was not troubling him too much, and the match report makes no reference to an armchair on the field of play. Details of the scores of this memorable, if not epic, encounter were set out in the previous chapter.

Hambledon's heroic failure in this match was a fitting and poignant grand finale. It had brought together again so many of the great players from the glory days, to play as a team for the very last time under the Hambledon banner. We can safely assume that Richard Nyren was there in the pavilion throughout the game, watching and encouraging his old friends as they struggled against these considerable odds. But well as they acquitted themselves, this was their dying gasp as a team, and in truth it was the dying gasp for the club, certainly as a power in the land. For the Hambledon club of old, this was the defining moment at the very end of life. This team never played together again as Hambledon.

A few weeks later, a large party of Richard Nyren's friends gathered back at the Bat and Ball, scene of so many stupendous evenings ten and twenty years before. During the course of the evening of 4 September 1791, Richard Nyren was presented with the most beautifully carved miniature cricket bat, as a memento from all his friends in Hambledon. It was almost certainly made by old John Small, one of Richard's oldest and closest friends since right back in the 1750s, and bat-maker supreme. Very likely it was old John Small who presented it to him. It is difficult to imagine who else would have had precedence, other than a peer of the realm. But we have no evidence that nobility were present that evening. It was essentially a local affair, and it marked, as definitively as anything can, the end of the glory days.

The bat was a mere five inches in length overall, with a blade three-and-a-quarter inches by five-eighths of an inch. A tiny message was etched on the blade. It read: 'Richard Nyren, from old friends, Bat and Ball, Hambledon, September 4th, 1791.' A picture of it, with a caption dated 1951, sits on the walls there to this day. The bat itself is now sadly lost. Nobody at Lord's, the Hampshire County Cricket Club, Hambledon or the Bat and Ball can say what happened to it. Nor has it ever been catalogued or sold through the major auction-houses. Yet it was around long enough to have been photographed, which puts its survival at least to the mid-nineteenth century, and possibly into the twentieth. Whatever its ultimate fate, this beautiful miniature bat, with its heartfelt dedication, marked the departure of Richard Nyren from Hambledon, and the end of an era.

Years later, son John wrote those immortal words: 'When Richard Nyren left Hambledon, the club broke up, and never resumed from that day. The head and right arm were gone.' The baton was passed. As Lord Tennyson was to put it so eloquently some fifty years later: 'The old order changeth, yielding place to new.' Now it was up to the MCC.

Things were never the same again. John Nyren was right when he said that the head and right arm had gone. So had most of the great players, either through age or the attractions of richer pickings elsewhere. The aristocrats had taken more than their own interests to London when they drifted away from Hambledon. They took the best players with them as well. The likes of Silver Billy Beldham, David Harris, the Walkers, Robert Robinson and young John Small still had long careers ahead of them, and they were best pursued on the big

The miniature bat presented to Richard Nyren at the Bat and Ball, 4 September 1791. It was almost certainly made by his old friend John Small senior.
(Reproduced by kind permission of the Bat and Ball)

grounds in London. Being noticed by potential patrons was always crucial for the hired professional. He had no such thing as a long-term contract in his pocket. He could not afford an emotional commitment to Hambledon like the earlier players. If he was to be paid by the match, or offered a sinecure in the winter, he had better be seen scoring runs and taking wickets in all the right places. And that was not on Broadhalfpenny Down any more.

Even as early as July 1793, a Surrey side which included William Beldham, all three Walker brothers, John Wells, James Aylward and the Earl of Winchilsea played against an England side which included father and son Small, David Harris, Andrew Freemantle and Tom Scott. Hambledon's role was merely to provide the ground. The match was played on Windmill Down, of all places. Two years later, a fully-fledged Hampshire county side started playing its home games regularly at Itchen Stoke Down, near Alresford.

Here we have to make an important distinction. The original Hambledon club, the demise of which we have just seen, was a true village club, whose members were generally successful and wealthy men. They employed professional players to represent the club at cricket. The local players who emerged from the wreckage, and who continued to play for a few years after these catastrophic events, were entirely different. They represented a local cricket club, one which would be recognisably the same as the typical village cricket club to be found in most places in England ever since. There are indications that this club continued until 1825, which was also the year of the great fire at Lord's in which so many irreplaceable records of the glory days were lost. But we are no longer comparing like with like. The team was now made up of local men and boys. They played spasmodically against other local sides. We know little of the games they played, but it seems they achieved little of cricketing note. Surviving records are sketchy in the extreme. Even those that do remain confirm that the use of the description 'Hambledon' after about 1792 refers essentially to a local village team which, in reality, bore no cricketing comparison to the great teams of the past which bore that name. This local side was perfectly entitled to call itself Hambledon, but in truth could not claim the pedigree that used to be attached to it. They beat Winchester on Windmill Down by six runs in 1807, but lost heavily three times against sides from the Portsmouth area between 1814 and 1818. What happened afterwards remains something of a mystery. The last game of any kind appears to have taken place about 1825. The cricket club was then dormant until at least the middle of the century. Records start again in 1864.

However, on 26 September 1804, an anniversary match was staged on Windmill Down for 50 guineas (£26,250). It was prominently advertised in *The Hampshire Chronicle*, which mentioned that several of the great players of the past would take part. They included John Small junior, both Freemantle brothers, George Leer, and Shock White. Unfortunately, the advertisement did not state which anniversary was being celebrated. Was it a fiftieth anniversary of the formation of the club in 1754? Possibly, but there is no other evidence to support it. In any case, what evidence we have suggests that the club was founded in 1742, and was already flourishing by 1754. Perhaps the 1804 match was merely a thirtieth anniversary match to mark the club's great win by an innings and 52 runs over England in 1774? That was also the match in which the first ever recorded score of over 300 was achieved by the Hambledon side. Of course, there is another possibility relating to 1774. It was also the year of the important meeting in London to review the laws. Was it that, perhaps, that the 1804 match was commemorating? We shall never know, because *The Hampshire Chronicle* failed to report the 1804 match.

After a splendid dinner in 1819, an unknown gentleman, obviously the worse for a good evening, took hold of an ancient bat. It was one of the originals, the shape of Hercules' club, and had long hung on the walls as a relic of Hambledon's glory days. It had been carefully preserved for over half a century, and had found a last resting-place on the walls of either the Bat and Ball (Ashley-Cooper's account) or the Hambledon

HAMPSHIRE CHRONICLE;

And Winchester, Southampton, Portsmouth and Chichester Journal.

CIRCULATED WITH THE UTMOST EXPEDITION THROUGH THE EXTENSIVE COUNTIES OF

ANTS, WILTS, DORSET, BERKS, SUSSEX, SURREY, *AND THE ISLE OF WIGHT.*

PRINTED BY AND FOR B. LONG, UNDER THE PENT-HOUSE, WINCHESTER.

VOL. XXX. No. 1593. MONDAY, SEPTEMBER 10, 1804. [PRICE SIXPENCE.

CRICKET

A MATCH will be played on Windmill Down, made by Thomas Bonham, Esq. and Charles Clavering, Esq. for 50 Guineas each side, on WEDNESDAY the 26th instant, by the following players, with three Gentlemen each side, viz.

Bennett,	John Bennett,
Barnett,	White,
Windebank,	Morrant,
Small,	Freemantle,
Button,	Pointer,
Knight,	Pink,
Boys,	Littlefield,
Clay.	Lear.

The wickets to be pitched at nine o'Clock, and begin playing at Ten precisely.—On the following day the anniversary of the Hambledon Club will be held at John Stewart's, the New Inn.—Dinner on table at six o'clock.

Announcement for the 1804 match, featuring John Small junior, Shock White, George Leer, and one of the Freemantle brothers. But what was the anniversary?
(Reproduced by kind permission of The Hampshire Chronicle)

clubhouse on Windmill Down (according to a Mr Thomas Smith of nearby Bishop's Waltham, writing to the Rev. James Pycroft). What is not in dispute is what happened next. Our inebriated villain, showing no reverence for this ancient piece of timber, seized it from the display and, before anyone could prevent him, attempted a mighty hit. At which point it flew into a thousand splinters and spread all over the assembled company.

Vandalism of this kind was not unknown in the nineteenth century. The unique iron gauge which had been made in the winter of 1771/2 to measure the legitimacy of a cricket bat had also hung on the walls of the Bat and Ball for more than half a century. It was 'lost' one evening in the 1880s when a customer walked off with it. He 'took a fancy to it', according to FS Ashley-Cooper. It was never seen again.

The Bat and Ball was a pale shadow of its former self early in the 1800s. Almost derelict, it had been neglected for years and saw few customers. Who needed it? The pubs in the village were nearer and more welcoming. There was no cricket across the track in the summer. Its very *raison d'être* was gone. The most the landlord might expect was an occasional visit from the local hunt, whose riders needed liquid refreshment from time to time. There were more birds in the roof than customers in the bar. On the ground across the road, Broadhalfpenny Down grew thistles and docks.

The best that can be said for those early years of the nineteenth century is that John Nyren wrote his book with Charles Cowden Clarke, and the two men of the cloth – the Rev. James Pycroft and to a lesser extent the Rev. John Mitford – researched and recorded what they could of the glory days before it was too late. Even so, and through no fault of their own, they must have missed much that would have been available from first-hand memory only a few years earlier. Later, of course, other historians and cricket aficionados were to take up the baton – some, like Arthur Haygarth, devoting a lifetime to researches which took him all over the country. He must have spent more time in newspaper libraries than almost any other living soul, at least until the likes of FS Ashley-Cooper and a few others followed in his painstaking footsteps.

Ironically, while Broadhalfpenny Down remained uncultivated for so many years, attempts were made to revive and expand the Bat and Ball. In 1837, the first extension to the original building was started, and it opened for business the following year. But by 1857, when the Rev. James Pycroft visited the ground and the pub, he found that Broadhalfpenny Down had been ploughed up and was now being farmed. Arthur Haygarth reported that same year that both Broadhalfpenny Down and Windmilll Down were now under the plough. There was nothing left to indicate where either ground had once been, although EV Lucas wrote later that the rights of the Hambledon club over Broadhalfpenny Down had never lapsed. More recent evidence suggests he was mistaken. About 1857, he says, when Broadhalfpenny Down was about to be ploughed up, a portion of it was allotted as a recreation ground. By the same award, Lucas suggested, this land was exchanged with Winchester College for a piece nearer the village, which now forms the modern ground at Brook Lane.

Lucas claimed that the original award under the Enclosure Act was made to John Foster on 14 January 1857, when Broadhalfpenny Down was 'to be held by him and his heirs...subject to an obligation to preserve the surface in good condition and permitting such land to be at all times used as a place for exercise and recreation for the inhabitants of the said parish (Hambledon) and neighbourhood'. This award was subsequently amended on 20 August 1861, without affecting the substance of the original restriction on use. Lucas drew attention to what he called 'this curious phrase in the wording of the award', in that the grant was made to the village of Hambledon and the neighbourhood. This award, so his reasoning ran, and the exchange of land for the plot at Brook Lane, was to lead eventually to the revival of the Hambledon club. It also gave Broadhalfpenny Down protection from other uses, he argued, in a form which secured its future. At the time, of course, these transactions appeared to have little effect. Nothing changed over the next half-century, except that Windmill Down was planted with fir trees.

Lucas's undoubtedly innocent mistake has been the cause of much confusion since. It is the source of a widespread belief in Hambledon that Broadhalfpenny Down is protected from other uses and is exclusively to be used for recreation. In fact, the enclosure awards made in 1857 and amended in 1861 relate to two other plots, parcels 16 and 36, both in Hambledon district, one of which (16) certainly does form part of the present Hambledon ground at Brook Lane. That much is confirmed by recent access to the original documents. So it is Brook Lane which has that protection, not Broadhalfpenny Down. Much of what Lucas reported came from the then secretary of the Hambledon Cricket Club at the turn of this

Broadhalfpenny Down (parcel 11) from the air, September 1996. Are the indentations in the top right corner of the ground, beyond the present-day boundary, the last vestiges of the original lodge?

century, JA Best. It is possible that there was a small but crucial failure of communication between them. When Mr Best talked of the club's ground, he might have been referring to Brook Lane, while Lucas took him to mean Broadhalfpenny Down. Such a simple mistake would account for all the rumours and confusion which followed publication of Lucas's book *The Hambledon Men*.

In fact, Broadhalfpenny Down was parcel 11 on the original maps and that was granted to James Higgens of Whitedale, Hambledon, also in 1857, but with freehold tenure. There were no restrictions on its use made in the original award, and none known to have been added to the title afterwards. The simple fact is that Broadhalfpenny Down has been in private hands, without restrictions on its use, for as long as the records can tell us. For the best part of the next 100 years, only its limited appeal for farming and non-existent appeal for development saved it from being lost to cricket for ever.

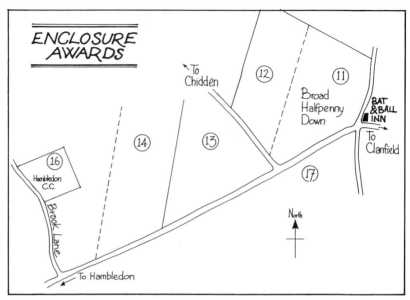

The plots at Broadhalfpenny Down (parcel 11) and Brook Lane (parcel 16).

Whatever the exact sequence of events and ownership of Broadhalfpenny Down during this period of legal turbulence in the middle of the nineteenth century, the revival of the Hambledon club, now properly called the Hambledon Cricket Club, on their new ground at Brook Lane inspired a small group of members to ensure that the connection with Broadhalfpenny Down was not broken. If they could not go to Broadhalfpenny Down, then Broadhalfpenny Down should come to them. It is unlikely that they got the owner's permission for a dawn raid on his land, but what happened next is not in dispute. They carefully cut a huge swathe of rough turf from Broadhalfpenny Down, transported it two miles down the road and relaid it at Brook Lane, where to this day it must still form at least a part of the base of the existing square. The modern Hambledon Cricket Club does indeed still play on Broadhalfpenny Down, at least in one sense.

In 1878, a visitor to Hambledon and Broadhalfpenny Down, the author Frederick Gale, reported that vandals had long since done their worst there. The original pub sign had been burnt as firewood, the clubroom on the first floor of the Bat and Ball was now divided into bedrooms and scarcely any relics of the old days remained. Only the bacon loft was untouched by the ravages of time. Across the road, the ground was growing wheat. That same year, perhaps at the insistence of Frederick Gale, the then owners of the Bat and Ball, the brewers Henty and Constable, responded to some gentle chiding about the state of the pub by promising to make some improvements. They proved to be empty words. Things only got worse.

In August 1893, a certain Mr ETW Fowler, who later wrote of his visit to Hambledon in *Cricket: A Weekly Record*, found the same ploughed field, this time covered with wheat stooks. 'There was not a soul in sight,' he reported. His disappointment took a severe additional nosedive, however, when he walked over to the Bat and Ball and attempted to get a pint of beer and some bread and cheese for lunch. He encountered a fearsome landlady with a manner as crusty as her loaf. This 'far from pleasant-looking' woman told him – in reply to his inevitable question – that 'everything appertaining to cricket has long since gone – to save being bored with questions from gents who collected'. His advice to potential fellow-pilgrims was to think twice before setting off. It might not be worth the candle to see the cradle, he suggested.

Harry Altham, writing in 1926, reported that Broadhalfpenny Down had still been under the plough at the turn of the century. Around the same time, when EV Lucas was working on his book *The Hambledon Men*, he had even more depressing news. As if further deterioration were possible, he found the Bat and Ball 'now very squalid'.

During these long, dormant days at Broadhalfpenny Down, much was going on elsewhere. The world of cricket was fast growing up. The first-class county game was now well-established and growing; Mr Wisden played his first games and was later to become the renowned chronicler of the sport; WG Grace and other great players started on the road to fame and fortune; and the game was being exported all over the globe. It was played in Australia, India, and North America. Many other countries were taking it up as well, and this expansion of the game abroad was helped significantly by the Royal Navy. It is held responsible by no less an authority than FS Ashley-Cooper for the introduction of cricket to Bermuda, the Canary Islands, Gibraltar, the Philippines and scores of other islands around the world from Malta to Samoa and Fiji – which is about as far as you can go from England without leaving the planet. The ships' company of the Royal Yacht *Osborne* even had the temerity to stage a match in St Petersburg, of all places, in 1875. The locals were not impressed, however, and some even demanded an explanation from the local chief of police. They apparently objected to foreign 'warriors' cavorting in their city. Considering what happened there thirty-two years later, Professor Trevelyan could have told them a thing or two about the social advantages of playing cricket.

In England, the MCC was still trying to keep up with developments in the game by amending the laws from time to time. Wides were mentioned as extras for the first time in the early 1800s, umpires gained the long-overdue right to pitch the wickets, the bat was limited to a maximum length of thirty-eight inches, and the follow-on rule was tidied up. By the 1830s, the bowler's name was listed on the scoresheet when a batsman was caught or stumped. Towards the end of the century, boundaries were mentioned for the first time, and in 1900 the over was increased to six balls, from the five introduced eleven years earlier. Thirty years later, yet more (minor) adjustments were made to the size of the wicket and to the circumference of the ball. But we digress.

The plain fact is that Broadhalfpenny Down was ignored throughout the nineteenth century. Queen Victoria, the country's longest-reigning monarch, came...and went. The novelists Jane Austen, Charles Dickens, William Thackeray and the Brontës, the poets John Keats, Percy Bysshe Shelley and the Lords Byron and Tennyson – to say nothing of many other writers – had all picked up their pens for the first time and laid them down for the last. In between those two simple acts, these prolific people had created a veritable mountain of fine literature. Karl Marx had written *Das Kapital* and with it lit a fuse which was to explode the world's third great revolution not long after.

And still Broadhalfpenny Down was ignored. Gladstone and Disraeli changed the face of British politics. The Industrial Revolution changed a way of life. Generations grew up, married, had children, became old and died. Then the next generation did the same. And the next.

And still Broadhalfpenny Down was ignored. Then, finally, as we approach the end of the century, we find a British Empire which had grown to such an extent that the sun literally never set on it. What local skirmishes there were could be dealt with readily enough by military might when moral authority failed. All was well in the world. It was good to be alive. It was good to be English. In London, Oscar Wilde scandalized polite society, and Gilbert and Sullivan entertained just about everybody.

On the cricket grounds around the globe, from Manchester and Headingley to Sydney and Melbourne, the likes of Grace, Fry, Trumper, Ranjitsinhji, Spofforth, MacLaren, FS Jackson, Tom Richardson, Jessop and so many others bestrode the cricket grounds like titans. This was their heyday, and they were watched by tens of thousands of breathless spectators. This was the dawning of cricket's golden age.

Back at Broadhalfpenny Down, something stirred...

A Monumental False Dawn

If Broadhalfpenny Down had been slumbering for over 100 years, it was not as some kind of latter-day Sleeping Beauty. This was the sleep of the neglected. Nobody had cared enough to do anything about its condition, nor that of the Bat and Ball, for generations, and this state of affairs continued into the twentieth century. Then, in the early 1900s, things slowly started to change. Perhaps the huge success cricket was now enjoying, and the astonishing number of exceptionally talented players entertaining vast crowds, encouraged people to start thinking more deeply about the game and its origins.

EV Lucas, for one, was sufficiently intrigued by the Hambledon saga that he embarked on a long and painstaking investigation and assembly of original material and whatever other information and records he could find. Lucas' exhaustive efforts brought together all the most reliable records of the glory days that he could trace, and they were supplemented by his own thorough research among the descendants of some of the original players. It is hardly surprising that his masterpiece has since become a standard reference book on the period. When he finally published *The Hambledon Men* he was clearly meeting a need. It was the first such book on the subject for half a century, and it proved to be a great publishing

The Bat and Ball, circa 1900.
(Reproduced by kind permission of the Bat and Ball)

success when it was eventually released in July 1907. At the time of its publication, the book's purpose was to enable readers to discover the glory days for themselves. But, whether it was intended or not, the book also re-ignited the painful issue of Broadhalfpenny Down's subsequent and chronic neglect.

Within the month, such was the immediate impact of Lucas' work, the London *Evening Standard* published an editorial suggesting that there should be a memorial on Broadhalfpenny Down, and an annual match between Hambledon and a team consisting of 'The Veterans of England'. It went on to propose the building of a residential home, possibly on the ground itself, for elderly ex-professional cricketers, where they 'might husband out life's taper to a close without a fear of being caught or stumped by a cruel adversity'. Warming to his theme, the author continued in equally lyrical terms to argue that the establishment of 'a national asylum for the decayed professional need certainly not interfere with the Cricketers' Benevolent Fund'. Despite the entire article being reproduced in *Cricket: A Weekly Record* at the end of August 1907, the response to the idea of a home for decaying professionals was met with deafening silence. Perhaps nobody could think of themselves, professional or otherwise, as 'decaying', either now or in the future. The article was unsigned, but it is highly likely to have been the work of CB Fry. He had a well-known and highly-developed social conscience, was not averse to lyrical prose and was already a widely-published author.

Hardly allowing time for his socially responsible suggestion to be ignored, this hyperactive future England cricket captain now turned his razor-sharp mind to the celebrations which took place on Broadhalfpenny Down a year later. He had been confronted through Lucas's book with an issue which was instinctively close to his heart, and he was not going to rest until 'something had been done'. Though he might not have realized it at the time, the 'doing' of it was to occupy the next year of his life. Yet he was already tackling another formidable lame-duck of a problem not far from Hambledon. This one was on the Hamble river.

CB Fry became the officer in charge of the training ship *Mercury*, on the Hamble river, within walking distance of Broadhalfpenny Down, in 1908. The previous winter, he had successfully mounted through the courts a rescue of *Mercury* from financial collapse. *Mercury* was an educational facility which gave boys an introduction to classical values and the sea. Having won the right to run the ship, Fry promptly left Sussex and moved to Hampshire, appointed himself 'Commander', and immediately assumed its day-to-day management. It was a self-inflicted task which was to last for the next forty-two years. But here he was now, living just a few miles away from Broadhalfpenny Down. He was in the right place at the right time.

If Lucas's book was an implicit call for action, it was irresistible to Fry, who was already renowned as a jack of all trades, and master of them all as well. He leapt to Broadhalfpenny Down's rescue like a latter-day Prince Charming. Yet Broadhalfpenny Down's Prince Charming was possibly even more unbelievable than most. He was an extraordinary, multi-talented character, unrealistically larger than life, who succeeded at just about everything he chose to

EV Lucas, author of The Hambledon Men, *which inspired the restoration of Broadhalfpenny Down after 116 years of neglect.*
(Copyright Hulton Getty Picture Library)

tackle. He was an accomplished scholar *and* the finest all-round sportsman of his generation. He got a first-class degree at Oxford and went on to became a writer and publisher, as well as an inexhaustible conversationalist whose company was sought by the finest minds of his day. He once stood for Parliament, managed to poll some 20,000 votes, but just failed to get elected.

As a sportsman, he was an amateur who played games simply because he loved them. He was also astonishingly good at them. He won three blues at Oxford, for cricket, football and athletics, and would have won a fourth for rugby. Only an injury deprived him of it. He commanded a place in the Sussex county cricket team as long as he lived there, but switched to the Hampshire side when he moved to the training ship *Mercury*. While he was with Sussex, and still playing for England, he shared with Ranjitsinhji one of the greatest regular batting-partnerships the game has ever known. He played cricket for England twenty-six times between 1895 and 1912. On six occasions he captained the side and never lost a match.

He also played football for Southampton, where he won an FA Cup runners-up medal, and for England. In 1892, he broke the world long-jump record. It stood for twenty-one years. As if all that were not enough, he was a boxer, golfer, sculler and swimmer. He played a good game of tennis, club rugby for Blackheath and, to cap it all, he threw the javelin competitively.

Perhaps the most amazing of all the stories about this astonishing man is his inadvertent flirtation with the crown of Albania in 1919. He was asked by his close friend Ranji to be a deputy in the Indian delegation to the League of Nations. While they were there, Fry wrote a speech for Ranji which was delivered with such effect that it changed the course of European events and 'turned Mussolini out of Corfu'. Its repercussions were even more startling on a personal level. Fry was approached by the Albanian delegation, who were known to be seeking to establish a new dynasty in their country. They offered him their throne, but only if he had sufficient income to finance the appropriate lifestyle. He admitted later that Ranji would almost certainly have funded him, but he did not press his friend for financial help. Fortunately for the training ship *Mercury*, he declined the Albanian offer.

In short, the truth of Fry's life story is more than most novelists would dare to grant to their creations. It was typical of him that he should also prove to be a Prince Charming, for what happened next on Broadhalfpenny Down was almost entirely due to his inspiration and perspiration. CB Fry set about establishing a lasting and proper recognition of the role Broadhalfpenny Down had played in the history of cricket. That other good friend, indefatigable amateur and prodigious hitter of fast centuries, Gilbert Jessop, was roped in to help as well. They were actively supported by WR Wright, who had started *Cricket: A Weekly Record* in 1882 and remained its publisher until 1894. He had long campaigned to rescue Broadhalfpenny Down and now, after thirty years of trying, something was about to happen. The collective hopes of these three men, and others who later joined in the endeavour, were encouragingly high.

Meanwhile, similar considerations had been stirring a few thoughtful minds back at Hambledon itself. Suddenly, as a result of Lucas' book, the village was the centre of attention again. There were two men of power and influence at Hambledon Cricket Club at that time. Together, they dominated its activities, and conducted its affairs with more than a hint of the style of the gentlemen's club which had pervaded its predecessor 120 years before. Captain Thomas (later Sir Thomas) Butler was the president, and Edward Whalley-Tooker, a direct descendant of one of the players of the glory days, was the long-standing club captain. Gentlemen they may have been, but they, too, were now quick off the mark. They reacted with the speed of benevolent dictators to an inspired proposal which came from the very depths of the club.

The idea for the monument seems to have germinated from idle conversation on Saturday 31 August 1907, little more than a month after Lucas' book had been published and the word 'monument' had first appeared in the *Evening Standard* article. Two members of the Hambledon Cricket Club were scoring a match between the Portsmouth Parish Churchboys' Choir XI and Hambledon Choirboys XI. Hambledon scored 84 and then dismissed Portsmouth for 41. It was a quiet game, not an afternoon of high excitement on the pitch. The conversation between the two Hambledon members understandably turned to the Lucas book, and the need to 'do something' about Broadhalfpenny Down. They evidently did not like the idea of a rest home for decaying cricketers, but they did like the idea of a monument. By the end of that afternoon, they had concluded that the word should be taken literally and that what was needed on Hambledon's famous old ground was an obelisk. With nothing else to write on, they scribbled a few notes on the back of the hand-drawn scoresheet they were using for the match. They drafted two different versions of the words to be found on the monument today. One suggested: 'This stone marks the site of the ground of the Hambledon Cricket Club circ. 1750-1787.' The other wrote 'This stone is erected on the ground of the Hambledon Cricket Club dating from about 1750 to 1787.' The first version survived to the stone-cutting stage, with one trivial amendment. There is little doubt that those two members – and nobody now knows who they were – conceived the idea of the monument that day.

Fry's original idea was for a week-long pageant on

Broadhalfpenny Down, the climax of which was to be a three-day match between Hambledon and an England side led by WG Grace. The proposal was discussed by the Hampshire County Cricket Club, and shortly afterwards the county invited Edward Whalley-Tooker and Captain Butler to join them for a further discussion. At that first joint meeting, the idea for the monument was tabled by the Hambledon delegation, and the notion of putting the two proposals together in a single event quickly emerged. After that, things moved fast.

At a Hambledon committee meeting on 15 October 1907, Edward Whalley-Tooker formally proposed the formation of a sub-committee of the club to organise the commissioning, financing and erection of a memorial on Broadhalfpenny Down. Within a month, he had permission from the owner of the ground to erect a monument, and he was already sufficiently confident of the funds to have approached Bernard Cancellor, a well-known local architect and surveyor, for some professional help immediately after the committee meeting. Cancellor was a Wykehamist, he was already the senior partner in his firm Cancellor and Hill, based in Winchester, and he had contributed much to local public life. In 1902, he had been Mayor of Winchester. After the usual preliminary discussions, Whalley-Tooker formally commissioned a design for the monument from Cancellor and Hill. Doubtless he also gave Mr Cancellor the wording developed from the Choirboys scoresheet. They agreed a fee of five guineas.

The owner of Broadhalfpenny Down at this time was a member of the Pease family. They were Quakers, and owned a great deal of farmland in the area at that time. Their land agents were based in Kingston-upon-Hull, of all places, some 300 miles from Broadhalfpenny Down. But Mr Pease and his agents were reasonable men and they agreed to Hambledon's request for permission to erect the stone obelisk, near the fence and just across the road from the Bat and Ball. They had no objection, they said, 'provided that you defray all the costs, including fencing'. They also insisted that the club specifically agree to remove the stones at any time in the future if the owner requested them to do so. These terms were found to be acceptable. It was now November 1907.

By this time, the club and CB Fry were talking publicly of the match at the end of the following season, when the monument was to be unveiled. The Hambledon club undertook to lay and prepare a wicket, and plans were well-advanced for the launch of an appeal to cover the cost of the monument. The money was to be raised by public subscription, organized through the Hambledon Cricket Club. The collection was managed by the then secretary of the club, the Rev. HA Floud, vicar of Hambledon and Denmead. Early in 1908, letters of appeal went out to the cricketing world, including all the national cricket bodies in what were then the colonies. The press were informed. Even the American touring side, the Philadelphians, were approached.

Much to the club's surprise and disappointment, the response was not overwhelming. But they were committed by now. There was no turning back. There followed many months of financial anxiety. During the spring and summer of 1908, Hambledon struggled hard to collect the estimated £105 needed (the equivalent of £6000 today). The MCC contributed five guineas (£5.25), Middlesex County Cricket Club sent two guineas, and several other counties sent a guinea each, as did the Hampshire Hogs. Scores of people also contributed a guinea each – the original maximum permitted from individuals. But it was not enough, and the guinea limit was removed in April. Even the architect sent a guinea, and that was before he had been paid. The financial situation was so

Edward Whalley-Tooker
(Reproduced by kind permission of Christine Pardoe)

serious that four members of the club were eventually obliged to put up personal guarantees for ten pounds each, so that construction work on the monument could start. Otherwise there was a real risk of the unveiling having to be postponed until the following year, with the planned match in September cancelled. Even with the guarantees in place, the fund-raising through that summer remained a constant struggle.

In the end, the total cost of the monument, including all the incidental expenses, amounted to £112, plus a few drinks and a new silver coin. But the club arrived at the match £21 short. And worse was to come. The costs of the match itself were not covered by the receipts. They spent

The draft of the wording for the monument, pencilled on the back of the Choirboys match scoresheet, 31 August 1907. Only one minor change was made during the year that passed between this sketch and the unveiling – 'circ.' became 'circa'.

(Reproduced by kind permission of Hambledon Cricket Club)

£44 on transport for the players, another £40 on catering for the guests, and a total of £176 8s 11d (£176.45 in decimal terms). The sale of enclosure tickets and parking spaces had produced £111 which, together with other receipts, had left the club short by £22 10s (£22.50). It was not until October 1908 that the arrears were finally cleared, and then only after a few generous members had dug a little deeper.

It is possible that one of the fund-raising ideas initiated through increasing desperation involved the production of the now widely-distributed aquatint entitled 'A Match at Hambledon, 1777. The Cradle of Cricket'. The scene was claimed to be 1777, but it was first published on 17 August

1908, just three weeks before the monument was unveiled. This picture is one of several different reproductions of an English School oil-painting, measuring 23 x 37 inches, entitled 'A Game of Cricket, 1777'. The original oil was finally published in Sir Jeremiah Colman's magnificent limited edition, *The Noble Game of Cricket*, in 1941. He rightly makes it clear that none of the various engravings and other reproductions based on it – and there are at least three noticeably different versions – bear any resemblance to Broadhalfpenny Down. In any case, the original title of the work makes no such claim. Sir Jeremiah suggests that the actual location was Sevenoaks Vine, but even that seems unlikely.

What is certain is that this picture has nothing whatever to do with Broadhalfpenny Down and very likely has nothing to do with the Hambledon club either. As a picture of events on Broadhalfpenny Down in 1777, it is a travesty. The geography is wrong, the landscape is wrong and the paucity of spectators is absurd. There were many thousands of people present at all the great matches on Broadhalfpenny Down at that time, and any contemporary painting could not possibly have omitted them. The clothing, particularly the hats worn by the players, tends to confirm the title on the original postcard-size copies made some years earlier, which then described the picture as 'A Game of Cricket, circa 1790'. But that is a side issue. The crux is that it was not painted at Broadhalfpenny Down, and the sole cause of the problem is the caption on the 1908 print editions. Not only is it blatantly wrong, but the use of the phrase 'The Cradle of Cricket' has subsequently helped to perpetuate the notion that this was where cricket started.

The villains here are either the engravers and publishers who rushed out the aquatint with its spurious title in 1908, caring more about revenue than accuracy, or the people who encouraged them. The only mitigation they might claim in retrospect is the help it provided for the monument fund. But these miscreants have caused confusion, added another layer of myth to the Hambledon legend, and disappointed many later generations when they have discovered the truth about this picture. Neither cricket enthusiasts nor buyers of fine art take kindly to the notion that the image now hanging on their walls is not what they thought. And the farther they live from Hampshire, the deeper the disappointment.

Sad to say, artistic sensitivities appear to have been almost as absent in the design of the monument itself. Bernard Cancellor, who had a fine reputation as an architect and surveyor, was regrettably not permitted to build the design he first proposed. His original design of an elegant, tapering column of beautifully-proportioned and polished Portland stone, with an inlaid bronze plaque, was rejected by the Hambledon committee as being too fussy. It was also too expensive. So he sketched a simple drawing on the side of a note which he sent back to the committee, showing an outline much like the structure which stands on Broadhalfpenny Down today. They liked it, and it was affordable – just. In fact, the final cost of the second design was to prove much the same as the original estimate for the first. By the time the Hambledon committee found that out, however, the second

'Hambledon 1777 – The Cradle of Cricket' reads the caption. But it isn't. Place and date are both wrong. This aquatint was produced in August 1908 to help raise funds for the match and the monument. The original oil has been dated c1790, and was possibly painted at Sevenoaks.
(Reproduced by kind permission of Hambledon Cricket Club/the Bat and Ball)

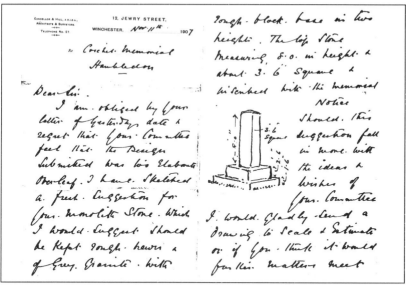

Bernard Cancellor's original design for the monument, rejected on the grounds of cost by Hambledon CC's committee in 1907.
(Restored by Philip Hodkin and reproduced by kind permission of Hambledon Cricket Club)

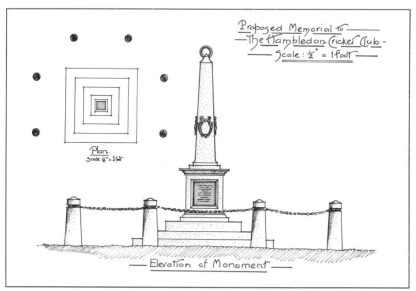

Bernard Cancellor's note, with the only sketch he did of the monument which was finally built, written with ill-suppressed irritation after Hambledon Cricket Club rejected his beautiful original design.
(Reproduced by kind permission of Hambledon Cricket Club)

design was in place.

As it was, Hambledon instructed Cancellor and Hill to go ahead with construction, using this new design. Cancellor knew whom to use. His practice in Winchester had worked before with a local firm of stonemasons, Vokes and Beck. He knew them and trusted them, and he gave them the contract to manufacture and erect the monument.

Cancellor's reluctant, even dismissive, second design is the first sight which greets the visitor to Broadhalfpenny Down today. It is a huge, ugly-looking column of several rough-hewn Cornish granite blocks which perches just inside the fence beside the entrance gate, and immediately across the road from the Bat and Ball. Neither Cornwall nor granite have any direct connections with Broadhalfpenny Down. Apart from cost considerations, this particular material was probably chosen as being the most enduring for a bleak and weather-beaten spot. If so, it was a decision made with good reason. Less than ninety years later, despite the inscription having its back to the prevailing weather, it is already becoming difficult to read. It commemorates the glories of the Hambledon club during its halcyon days, and says: *'This stone marks the site of the ground of the Hambledon Cricket Club, circa 1750 to 1787.'* Of course it was not the Hambledon Cricket Club in those days, and the dates should more accurately have read 1742 to 1792. But it is of no great importance, since the culmination of the glory days is fully covered by the form of words drafted by that unknown scorer at Portsmouth the previous summer.

The structure itself is ten feet square at the base, and just over twelve feet high. The upper column measures eight feet. The whole edifice was cut and prepared at a quarry run by Messrs Sweet of Liskeard. They worked on the instructions of Thomas Beck, head of the stonemasons Vokes and Beck. The company is still trading today, and Thomas Beck's grandson Peter Wheble, himself now in his seventies, remembers his grandfather talking about the struggle he had to get the monument erected in time for the match on 10 September 1908. Once they were ready, the stones were hauled from the Cornish quarry by train as far as Droxford railway station.

Thomas Beck, front left, and his team of stalwarts, with the monument finally in position. The ground around the base is a quagmire.
(Reproduced by kind permission of Peter Wheble)

From there, they were taken up to the ground on steam wagons.

August can often be a wet month in England. Unfortunately, 1908 was one of the wettest. It rained. And how it rained. Day after day it just poured down. The ground quickly became sodden. The team of men entrusted with the assembly on site were sodden as well. When the stones were unloaded from the steam wagons, they were bulky, awkward and very heavy. They, and the rollers used to manoeuvre them, quickly sank into the soft ground. Moving anything big, let alone stones weighing several tons each, was a major problem in such conditions. But the team was working to a deadline which could not be delayed. They had no choice but to carry on. Thomas Beck, at his own considerable and unbudgeted expense, kept the beer flowing from across the road. He was anxious that his team should remain as cheerful as was possible in such atrocious conditions. In fact, he and his men remained positive enough to think of placing a newly-minted silver half-crown between the base and the vertical column, as the last block was hauled into place. Whatever their motives for such extravagant symbolism, the coin is still there today.

When the construction work was finally done, there was mud everywhere. The site was a quagmire. Even cleaning the monument once it was erected only added to the mud already around the base. The ground was so churned up that duck-boards had to be brought in to help tidy up the appearance of the site, if nothing else.

The monument was finally unveiled on time, but still in poor conditions, at lunchtime on Thursday 10 September 1908, the first day of a three-day match between XII of Hambledon and an All-England XII. The previous game recorded there had taken place in 1792. All of 116 years had passed between the two matches.

The unveiling ceremony was to have been performed by the Champion himself, Dr WG Grace. But even he was Hambledon's second choice. They originally wanted the Prince of Wales to perform the ceremony, but he politely declined. Dr Grace might have done better to take the same line. Instead, he first accepted the invitation and then did not turn up either for the game or the ceremony. He had injured a foot in a match at Lord's only a few days before, and was unable to make the journey. At least, that was the official reason. The truth appears to have lain elsewhere, for not all of the English cricket establishment of the time approved of this escapade on Broadhalfpenny Down. The editor of *Cricket: A Weekly Record*, no less a figure than FS Ashley-Cooper, told his readers shortly beforehand: 'I am by no means enamoured of the match. Only one or two players on either side possess any real claim to take part. The North are playing The South at the Oval. MCC are playing an England XI at Uttoxeter at the same time. This match will do nothing to add to the glorious history of Hambledon. Those of us who love the old village for the prominent part it played in the development of the game...regard this twentieth-century venture...almost as a desecration of the soil. Nothing which is enacted there now or in the future can add any fresh lustre to that glorious chapter in its history. Motor cars at Broadhalfpenny Down will be as much out of place as dolphins in a sentry box.' WG Grace's foot was much worse after that diatribe. Such haughty comments surely meant that he should not be seen 'desecrating the soil' at Broadhalfpenny Down. Yes, his foot definitely felt much worse.

In Grace's absence, the stone was unveiled by the Hampshire county captain, EM Sprot, who played in the match for Hambledon. The ceremony was preceded by a hearty lunch for the teams and distinguished guests, presided over by Captain Butler. On the table at lunch were two punch bowls and a dozen dinner-plates used regularly at the Bat and Ball during the glory days, and then in the safe keeping of the Whalley-Tooker family. They had been generously loaned for the occasion, in spite of their delicacy and uniqueness. After lunch came the inevitable speeches. Captain Butler paid handsome tribute to the energy and drive with which CB Fry had ensured the success of the day and the match, and his untiring support and efforts over the previous year. EM Sprot spoke of the 'very proud moment' he had experienced when he first stepped onto the field used by the great Hambledon team over 100 years before, and the knowledge that he was the first player to do so since. Finally, Gilbert Jessop, captain of the England team, thanked the committee of the Hambledon club for their reception on the ground. To great laughter and applause, he observed that all his players would gladly accept a similar invitation in another hundred years' time. And then, well-protected against the windy conditions outside by wine and a meal which would not have disgraced Richard Nyren's kitchen, the party moved over to the monument itself.

As if on cue, the sun came out. But it was not hot. Nobody took their coats off. The wind continued strong and blustery, and there was still a distinct chill in the air. Captain Butler was heard to make a final appeal to the general public crowded around the covered obelisk for funds to help meet its costs. Hard as he might try, Mr Sprot simply could not be heard by most people. Much of what he said was blown away on the wind. Whom he thanked for their efforts to make this day possible few spectators ever knew, but it certainly included the special memorial committee set up by the Hambledon club the previous year to manage the project. What tribute Sprot paid to the men of Hambledon's glory days, 140 years or so before, is also gone forever, apart from his reported admission that his team might not be able to play as well as the giants of old, but they still played with the same keenness. And when he came to it, even his unveiling of the monument itself was something of a technical triumph in such a gale. The sheeting was the size of a large Indian tepee. But in the end all was well, the ceremony was complete, and the Archdeacon of Winchester, Dr Fearon, brought the proceeding to a close with a long speech and a short prayer. Nobody but the good Lord heard that either.

The three days of the match were not without drama of other kinds, too. A report in *The Cricketer*, published in July 1925 but clearly written by someone who was at the 1908 game, referred to the 'many rather amazing blunders' made. He listed some, but implied that there were more. The biggest problem for most of the spectators, and quite a few of the

This poster was produced in 1908 to advertise the first match on Broadhalfpenny Down for 116 years.
(Reproduced by kind permission of Christine Pardoe)

players for that matter, appears to have been the location. Where, exactly, was Hambledon? Next, how do you get there? At least three different answers were pursued by the many drivers trying to find their way to the ground, with the result...chaos. A happy and no doubt smug minority went to the right place and found Broadhalfpenny Down without too much difficulty. Too many others found themselves trailing around various parts of Hampshire like disoriented ants. Into one village, ask the way, back up and turn round, then off again somewhere else, until the latest version of directions inadequately ran out or demonstrably proved themselves wrong. So, start again. Into a village, ask the way, and try once more. An embarrassingly large contingent of other prospective spectators, and players, went to the village of Hambledon near Godalming, Surrey, some twenty-five miles away. Worse, that is a part of the countryside noted for its narrow and winding lanes. Even when the frustrated drivers arriving there had established that they were in the wrong place, they still had the problem of reversing out while others followed in behind them. It was not a good start to the day.

Hundreds of local people walked to and from the match, many of them making journeys of ten miles or more there and back. Many more walked the six miles to and from Droxford railway station each day. When they did eventually all arrive at the ground, *The Hampshire Chronicle* estimated that there were over 5000 people on the ground on the first day. Some estimates put the figure much higher. Over the three days, nearly 18,000 people attended the game. But whatever their numbers, the spectators came determined to enjoy themselves. It mattered little that the weather was unkind, although it did improve during the course of the match. This unique spot might once have been bleak to the Duke of Dorset, but today was a day of celebration on Broadhalfpenny Down. They were here to witness a small piece of history and they were not going to be discouraged by the elements, however historically appropriate they were. Admission to the ground was free, but a contemporary footnote curiously records that the owners of exactly 641 bicycles each paid three pence for parking. Car drivers, who were regarded even in those days as affluent and an easy touch, had to pay eight shillings to park, twice as much as a coach and pair. The owners of single horses paid two shillings to tether their animals for the day with a supply of water. Much of this income went towards meeting the costs of staging the match. The Hambledon club needed every penny it could raise by whatever legitimate means.

The spectators formed a vast protective circle of 200 motorcars and 400 carriages around the perimeter, got out their rugs and picnics, and kept as warm as they could in the conditions. Immediately prior to the match, a team of contractors and local volunteers had spent days preparing for the match, often in very difficult conditions. Their aim was to recreate the atmosphere of the glory days, together with the facilities nowadays expected at a county cricket festival. By all accounts they succeeded triumphantly, and against considerable odds after a Herculean struggle against the elements. At least two of the largest tents had to be erected twice. Each had been blown down in a gale which was so violent that tent-poles snapped like twigs and tarpaulins took off over the downs like demented sails.

As a result of these sterling efforts beforehand, spectators who were willing to pay extra could now enjoy the protection of an enclosure with covered seating along one side of the ground. Not surprisingly, it was fully occupied, as were the stands erected for club members and guests. Two long luncheon-marquees catered for the public, and additional tenting provided facilities for the press, who were present in force, for the teams, the entertainers, and the printers who issued updated scorecards at the fall of every wicket. All this conviviality was noisily reinforced by strolling minstrels and the band from the training ship *Mercury*, which was hired – much to CB Fry's satisfaction – to entertain the crowd at lunchtime and in the other intervals. Together with the huge assembly of vehicles outside and inside the ground, the entire spectacle reminded at least one commentator of Epsom Downs on Derby Day. This carnival atmosphere continued after the close of play each day, when the players moved over the road to

EM Sprot, the Hampshire captain, unveils the monument at lunchtime 10 September 1908. The strength of the wind is apparent from the flags just visible behind the crowd and his struggle with the sheeting.
(Reproduced by kind permission of Hambledon Cricket Club)

(Reproduced by kind permission of Christine Pardoe)

The unveiling ceremony: Captain Butler makes one last appeal for funds from the crowd, but nobody gets too excited about the idea. Many of them can't hear him anyway.
(Reproduced by kind permission of Bob Murton)

The Archdeacon of Winchester, Dr Fearon, brings the ceremony to a close with a long speech and a short prayer. The sun had come out at last.
(Reproduced by kind permission of Bob Murton)

the Bat and Ball, went behind the bar and pulled pints all evening, much to the entertainment of the customers.

The match itself was played on 'reconditioned' turf, a term which *Wisden* did not explain. The *Hampshire Chronicle* reported that the pitch had been laid the previous November by members of the Hambledon club, using turf from a neighbouring down, under the watchful eye of Hampshire's county groundsman at Southampton, referred to in the manner of the day simply as Hopkins. The cricketing press some twenty years later suggested that they also brought in a delivery of Nottingham marl. During the summer of 1908, Hopkins cast a regular supervising eye over progress and spent much of the week before the match on final preparations. Between them, he and the Hambledon club produced an acceptable playing surface. This was no mean feat, since the ground had been neglected or ploughed for over 100 years, 1908 was a wet summer, and the August even wetter. Harry Altham, writing later in Hampshire CCC's official history, described it as 'an excellent wicket' and the scores in the match serve as a lasting testimonial to Hopkins' abilities.

Given Hambledon's habit of beating England, the result was

The Bat and Ball, September 1908, during the match Hambledon v England.
(Reproduced by kind permission of Bob Murton)

Ford and Jessop batting for England against Hambledon on the first day of the 1908 match. England were in some trouble at this stage, and the two of them salvaged what might have been a disastrous first innings. As it was, they were all out for 124, and struggled throughout the rest of the match.
(Reproduced by kind permission of Christine Pardoe)

no surprise. Once again, they won. It must have felt just like old times. The margin was five wickets. In addition to the Hampshire captain, Hambledon's side also included CB Fry, Captain EG Wynyard, Philip Mead and the Rev. WV Jephson, who scored the only hundred of the match. The Hambledon side was captained by the same Edward Whalley-Tooker who had put so much work into making the day possible.

England's side boasted Gilbert Jessop, Albert Trott and Jack Hearne, but trailed Hambledon by 153 runs on the first innings. However, they pulled the game around in their second innings. George Leach was a fast right-arm bowler and free-hitting batsman, but in the first-class game he was still struggling to hold a place in the Sussex side of those days, playing as a lower-order batsman and occasional change bowler. Yet, in such illustrious company, he was now invited by Jessop to open England's second innings and he made a match of it. His 80 was scored in eighty-five minutes out of the 141 added while he was at the wicket. Without this courageous knock, Hambledon all but had the match won. Leach at least ensured that they were set a reasonable target and gave the England bowlers something to defend. Hambledon now needed 157 to win.

Thanks to a fine 84 not out from Fry, they cruised home comfortable winners, despite some alarms on the way. The wicket became difficult after a heavy shower and for a while both the result and the prospect of achieving one looked in doubt. After the restart, Fry had a lucky escape. He had scored 21 when he was caught by Trott off a no-ball. In the end, his innings was, according to one report, 'played with extreme care. He was evidently bent on doing his best to win the match. Fry's innings was a great performance of extraordinary care and resourcefulness, full of vigorous and beautifully-timed hitting.' But perhaps the man of the match was John Newman, a young medium-pace bowler who had only recently earned a regular place in the Hampshire county side. Sadly, later in his career, he earned lasting notoriety when he became one of only three players ever to be sent off the field in a first-class match. But on this much happier occasion, he destroyed the England first innings with a fine spell of sustained seam bowling and finished with 8 for 54, an analysis which still stands nearly ninety years later as the best ever achieved on Broadhalfpenny Down. Newman's final match-analysis was 13 for 120, and he hit the stumps nine times. His victims included Jessop, Trott and Hearne (twice).

The full scorecard for the match reads:

England XII

AE Knight	b Llewellyn	9	c Deer b Newman	13
Mr AW Roberts	b Newman	11	b Newman	69
EH Killick	b Newman	7	run out	2
JT Hearne	b Newman	4	b Newman	2
Mr FGJ Ford	c&b Newman	33	c Newman b Llewellyn	7
Mr G Wilder	b Newman	0	b Newman	43
Mr GL Jessop	b Newman	19	st Stone b Llewellyn	48
AE Trott	c Mead b Newman	4	c Mead b Llewellyn	5
G Leach	lbw b Llewellyn	2	c Wynyard b Langridge	80
G Dennett	not out	26	b Llewellyn	4
HR Butt	b Newman	3	c Fry b Newman	9
WE Astill	run out	3	not out	8
extras		3		19
Total		**124**		**309**

Hambledon Bowling

Newman	15.5	–	1	–	54	–	8	17.3	–	2	–	66	–	5
Llewellyn	12	–	1	–	60	–	2	26	–	3	–	133	–	4
Deer	3	–	0	–	7	–	0	3	–	0	–	11	–	0
Mead	10	–	1	–	38	–	0					
Langridge	14	–	2	–	42	–	1					

Hambledon XII

Mr CB Fry	b Hearne	17	not out	84
Capt EG Wynyard	c Hearne b Dennett	59	not out	9
Mr EM Sprot	c Wilder b Astill	9	c Trott b Jessop	17
CB Llewellyn	c Trott b Astill	0	b Hearne	2
Rev WV Jephson	not out	114	st Butt b Dennett	14
Dr GN Deer	b Roberts	10	did not bat	
P Mead	b Dennett	0	c Trott b Hearne	6
A Stone	c Trott b Killick	6	b Astill	2
Mr E Whalley-Tooker	b Killick	6	did not bat	
Mr W Langridge	b Dennett	2	did not bat	
Mr EMC Ede	b Killick	4	did not bat	
J Newman	c & b Killick	23	c & b Astill	5
extras		27		19
Total		**277**	**158 for 6 wickets**	

England Bowling

Hearne	9	–	0	–	31	–	1	11	–	1	–	32	–	2
Astill	5	–	0	–	23	–	2	9	–	0	–	33	–	2
Leach	3	–	0	–	15	–	0							
Trott	10	–	1	–	45	–	0	2	–	0	–	6	–	0
Killick	10.3	–	2	–	44	–	4	4.3	–	2	–	13	–	0
Jessop	4	–	0	–	9	–	0	13	–	5	–	30	–	1
Dennett	17	–	0	–	74	–	3	9	–	0	–	25	–	1
Roberts	2	–	0	–	9	–	1							

Swallowing his own criticism, and understandably yielding to the curiosity of the occasion, FS Ashley-Cooper turned up to watch and to report the goings-on in his next issue. EV Lucas was there, too. As he was to write much later, ironically in a foreword to Ashley-Cooper's book *The Hambledon Cricket Chronicle*, it was his idea to offer the professionals playing that day a financial inducement based on the number of runs they scored. In the spirit of the times they were celebrating, a reward of two shillings and sixpence (12.5 pence) was offered per run to the professional on either side making the most runs in a single innings during the match. The idea was funded by no less a distinguished visitor than the playwright JM Barrie, author of *Peter Pan*. Albert Trott, as professional a cricketer as ever

The England team and the two umpires gather around the wicket the start of the match against Hambledon, 1908.
(Reproduced by kind permission of Christine Pardoe)

The Hambledon team and the two umpires before the start of the match against England.
(Reproduced by kind permission of Christine Pardoe)

The four men who did so much to stage the Hambledon v England match,
and who also played in it. Left to right: Gilbert Jessop, Edward Whalley-
Tooker, EM Sprot; (seated below) CB Fry.
(Reproduced by kind permission of Christine Pardoe)

stepped onto the field of play and a formidable Test-playing all-rounder, considered the prize as good as won. So he cannot have been best pleased to see the money go to a mere bowler – and a young upstart to boot – at the end of the match, even if he was on the same side. There can be little doubt that George Leach's innings deserved every penny, and a substantial sum it was. Ten pounds bought a great deal in those days, with beer at tuppence a pint.

FS Ashley-Cooper, who devoted a lifetime to researching and writing about cricket, and who took a proprietorial view of the activities on Broadhalfpenny Down at the start of the century.
(Reproduced by kind permission of the MCC)

Ashley-Cooper's scepticism did not entirely desert him immediately after the match. It may have been a success, but it still gave him cause for concern. In *Cricket: A Weekly Record*, he could not bring himself to enthuse about it. Subsequently, he had good reason to be quite severe on a whole clutch of newspaper reports of the game in the national and local press, which he said had contained numerous errors, especially about the old laws of cricket. These reports had clearly been prepared by 'writers unacquainted with the game', he pronounced, casting them into a journalistic outer darkness.

The events of 10 September 1908 left Broadhalfpenny Down with a legal curiosity. The monument itself undoubtedly belongs to the Hambledon Cricket Club. They lay claim to it to this day, and point out that it is not, strictly speaking, part of the present ground's facilities. But the present owners of Broadhalfpenny Down, Winchester College, include the monument as a landlord's fixture, and the lease held by the present occupiers, the Broadhalfpenny Brigands Cricket Club, includes a responsibility to use their 'best endeavours to maintain the monument in good repair'.

Be that as it may, many visitors think that the site for the monument itself was ill-chosen, with the inscription facing the road and partially obstructed by the remaining section of a wooden fence which originally encircled the structure. This opinion has the benefit of hindsight, of course. In 1908, the ground was normally in agricultural use. So the monument was bound to be sited out of the way of the plough. Such a decision was inevitable, and it did nothing to discourage the hundreds of people who arrived over the following weeks to look at it. Nowadays, we wonder how much better it would have been to have the monument positioned in a more focal point on the ground, so that visitors could easily walk around it, photograph it and read the now-fading inscription. Perhaps, one day, it will be moved to a more easily accessible site on Broadhalfpenny Down, still with the Bat and Ball in the background but no longer crammed like an after-thought in a corner. Unfortunately, that is likely to raise yet more legal issues.

Strangely enough, after all the publicity and effort that went into the match in September 1908, it was to prove a frustrating one-off. This glorious flurry of activity was followed by...almost nothing. Writing a short time later under the pseudonym WR Weir, the former publisher of *Cricket: A Weekly Record*, WR Wright, rejoiced in the fact that the glories of the old Hambledon club had been revived. He went on to express the fervent wish that the match between Hambledon and England, during which the monument was unveiled, should become a regular occurrence. He was to be sadly disappointed. There was no serious follow-up, no concerted effort made to resurrect the ground, preserve it, or start cricket again on a regular basis. Ironically, the landowner and the then tenant together made one of the most important and practical contributions towards the future of the ground. They offered to ensure that the area immediately around the pitch used for the 1908 match, which had been so carefully prepared for nearly a year prior to the game, would in future be permanently protected from animals and other uses. This, they hoped, might ensure that the match proposed for the following year against the touring Australian side might take place on an equally good wicket. But it was not to be. The idea was long dead before 1909.

The events leading up to September 1908 turned out to be nothing more than a false dawn. This is doubly difficult to fathom due to the well-earned reputations for making things happen enjoyed by both CB Fry and Edward Whalley-Tooker. In Fry's case, in particular, it seems utterly out of character that he should simply have walked away from the ground and its future well-being, having put so much into the events of September 1908.

All that happened for the few years immediately after the 1908 match, and possibly up to the outbreak of the First World War in 1914, were a few odd games now and then. In 1913, for instance, Hambledon juniors (all aged about thirteen) played a match on

Hambledon Boys XI, 1913. The captain, Hyde Whalley-Tooker (Edward's son, and Christine Pardoe's father) is sitting in the centre of the front row. (Reproduced by kind permission of Christine Pardoe)

Farmland again. Broadhalfpenny Down, probably during the First World War, being grazed by sheep. The 1908 wicket, so lovingly prepared over a whole year beforehand, is long gone. (Reproduced by kind permission of the Hambledon Cricket Club)

Broadhalfpenny Down, but there is no evidence that it was a regular event. The only regular match known to have taken place was an annual commemorative game involving a group of Hambledon members, inevitably led by Edward Whalley-Tooker. It took place each August. This annual affair was not intended to attract huge crowds and cannot have been much more than a game of village cricket. But a few people turned up to watch, and have a glass of beer in the Bat and Ball afterwards. For the rest of the season, though, the now thriving Hambledon village side played at their Brook Lane ground, later called Ridge Meadow. It was their third ground in as many centuries. It was not far from the now fir-covered Windmill Down, which was itself returned to the plough a few years later, and then replanted with trees.

Meanwhile, the parade of disappointed visitors to Broadhalfpenny Down resumed for another twenty years or so. Some time shortly after the 1908 match, a couple visiting Broadhalfpenny Down on something of a cricket pilgrimage paused to see the monument and look over the downland beyond. What they saw can only have left them with mixed feelings. So they went on down to Hambledon village and eventually found themselves hunting tombstones beside the church. When they found it, they were so concerned at the dilapidated state of Tom Sueter's grave that they left money with the verger to pay for its repair and upkeep. Even up to the start of the 1914–18 war, flowers were still to be seen on honest Tom's grave from their generosity.

Many thousands of other pilgrims over the following years encountered the same disappointing views. A grey, glowering, granite column, standing alone on the downs. To the more sensitive souls, it must have appeared to be the very epitome of desolation, especially in winter. The only cheering sight then, as now, was found by turning around and walking across into the Bat and Ball. Almost all of the countless photographs these visitors took of the monument on Broadhalfpenny Down between 1908 and 1925 prove, if such proof were needed, that the land was firmly back in agricultural use, despite the earlier promises that the wicket itself would be protected. Broadhalfpenny Down was now either fenced-off into paddocks or being cropped by grazing sheep. It was almost as though 1908 had never happened.

Stephen Leacock, the political economist turned comic writer – a juxtaposition of talents that requires no further comment – was one of the visitors to the ground during this period. He described the scene at Broadhalfpenny Down in the 1920s as being akin to 'standing in the ruins of Carthage'. The same depressing view met FS Ashley-Cooper when he visited Broadhalfpenny Down during his researches for his book *The Hambledon Cricket Chronicle*, which was published in 1924. It was then a ploughed field again. But now this doyen of cricket writers was to play a crucial part in its long overdue, and lasting revival, with all his doubts of sixteen years before put aside. Once more, a book was to influence events on this famous ground.

The Sleeper Finally Awakes

It was not a dramatic awakening. It was more like a yawn and a stretch, followed by a light doze. Only a little later did the sleeper finally wake up for good. Perhaps, after 130 years or so, that was only to be expected. Expected or not, that is certainly what happened.

Ashley-Cooper's book *The Hambledon Cricket Chronicle* was

The Bat and Ball, circa 1920.
(Reproduced by kind permission of John Barrett/Maureen Wingham)

published in 1924, and it attracted quite a lot of attention. He had been given access to material not previously published, drawn from original records of the Hambledon club held by the local Lubbock family. Some seventy years later, those same papers were to be given to the nation to help the family meet a heavy demand for death duties on the estate of Sir Alan Lubbock, a former chairman of the Hampshire County Council. But when Ashley-Cooper gained access to them they were not public property, and their contents were largely unknown. Much of the detail they record of the vital period in the history of the Hambledon club between 1772 and 1796 is only of passing interest, except to the serious student. There are insights into the manner in which the club was run, minutes of meetings, records of membership and playing staff, financial accounts and some match results. In terms of historical minutiae the book is fascinatingly comprehensive, and it had a considerable impact in 1924 when all this detail was published for the first time. Like Lucas' book of seventeen years before, it focused attention on the place where great events had occurred so long ago. For those with the vision to see, it implicitly reminded readers of the sorry state of Broadhalfpenny Down and its continuing neglect.

Lucas had had his Fry. Ashley-Cooper now had his Altham. There was clearly no time to be lost. That same year, 1924, Harry Altham persuaded Winchester College to take an active interest in the state of this famous ground, and rescue it from oblivion once and for all. He was a powerful advocate. It was his first intervention on behalf of Broadhalfpenny Down, but it was by no means to be his last. He was to play a crucial part in its well-being throughout the rest of his life. Like Fry before him, here was a man of action with powers of persuasion to match.

Harry Altham was a man of many parts – player, coach, schoolmaster, writer, cricket historian, administrator, legislator and Test selector. His total devotion to the game of cricket took him ultimately to the very pinnacle of its organization, when he was elected president of the MCC in 1959. Perhaps more importantly, he was also a much loved man. He was passionate about the game and particularly vigorous in his encouragement of young players. Not surprisingly, he was a man who instinctively inspired friendships which in turn helped to generate support for his many ideas and enterprises. His lifetime in cricket, combined with this natural gift for inspiring others, gave him the pleasure of scores of devoted and enduring friendships all over the world. And after his death in 1965, his reputation and sheer contribution to cricket over so many years rightly earned Harry Altham lasting respect and admiration from those who never knew him, yet now follow in his footsteps.

It was an awesome workload he bore. Having played in the Varsity matches of 1911 and 1912, he briefly joined Surrey before becoming a master at Winchester College. He was to hold that post for thirty years, and bowl in the nets there for over fifty. On his arrival at Winchester, he promptly joined the Hampshire County Cricket Club, and soon found himself on its committee, a position he was to retain for over forty years. From 1946 until his death he was the county's president. In 1941 he was elected to the committee of the MCC, and became treasurer ten years later. In 1954 he was invited to become chairman of the England Test selectors, and had the huge satisfaction of presiding over Len Hutton's side which went to Australia that winter and retained the Ashes – after the breathtaking fast bowling of Frank Tyson and Brian Statham had spearheaded one of the most exciting and dramatic Test series for many years. But all that came later.

Back at the end of the First World War, in which he served with distinction, Harry Altham played a few matches for Hampshire, but quickly found his true niche in the game off the field. In addition to his duties at Winchester and his voluntary work with the county club, he now started work on his history of the game. He became a writer. What he set out to achieve had never been done before: a complete, comprehensive, thorough and well-researched history of the game. But not a text-book, or a reference book; a book that could be read for the sheer pleasure of the writing and its content. His towering manuscript, *A History of Cricket*, was first published in part form in *The Cricketer* and finally published in book form in 1926.

So the state of Broadhalfpenny Down was fresh in his mind when Ashley-Cooper's book came out two years earlier; Altham was already deeply involved in researching the origins and growth of the game. He was acutely aware of the neglected state of the ground. Harry Altham appreciated, perhaps better than anyone else at the time, that unless a permanent solution was found, it was distinctly possible that nobody would ever play cricket on Broadhalfpenny Down again. Furthermore, such a solution was needed sooner rather than later. Broadhalfpenny Down's neglect had gone on far too long.

Winchester College is only fifteen miles from Hambledon, and the College had been a substantial and longstanding landowner in that area of Hampshire for centuries. What could be more logical than that this same landowner should now acquire Broadhalfpenny Down as well? It had the resources, it was an institution of substance with its own origins half-buried in the mists of time, and it could, above all, be relied upon to take ownership of such hallowed turf as a lasting responsibility, shouldered on behalf of the game of cricket itself. Winchester College would be a worthy custodian. And Harry Altham was in the right place to convince the governors to take action.

According to a note written forty years later by the then estates bursar at Winchester College, the decision of the governors in 1924 was strongly influenced by 'the desirability to preserve and protect Broadhalfpenny Down'. From the College's point of view, there were other reasons to make the purchase as well. Broadhalfpenny Down was largely surrounded by Park Farm, which the College had purchased in 1861. Broadhalfpenny Down itself was now owned by Samuel Kittow, of North Farm, Horndean, who had acquired it from the Pease family in 1920. In 1924 the College was still as acquisitive as ever when good-quality farming land came on the market, so there was also a sound commercial reason behind the final decision to put Harry Altham's mind at rest and buy Broadhalfpenny Down. The College finally negotiated the

Harry Altham, author of A History of Cricket
and indefatigable champion of Broadhalfpenny Down.
(Reproduced by kind permission of the MCC)

purchase of fifty-three acres of Mr Kittow's 560-acre farm. The transaction had to be approved by the Minister of Agriculture, who signed a certificate to say that it was 'a fit and proper purchase', and the sale was made on condition that Winchester College 'maintain a suitable stock-proof fence' around the land. The conveyance included 30.8 acres of parcel 42b on the 1905 ordnance survey map (which included the four and a half acres of Broadhalfpenny Down), and another twenty-two acres nearby. The total cost of the 53 acres was £1100 (some £35,000 in today's terms). Some three years later, Winchester College exchanged with neighbouring farmers John and Elizabeth Sykes all but the four and a half acres of Broadhalfpenny Down in a deal which tidied up their respective holdings.

Everybody was now happy, and the cricket world breathed a huge collective sigh of relief. At long last, Broadhalfpenny Down had a benevolent owner whose concern for the ground as a part of cricket history was unquestionable. With some satisfaction, *The Wykehamist* told its distinguished readers at the end of 1924 that 'the College has recently acquired a piece of land of great interest to all lovers of cricket'. The reaction in wider cricketing circles, now that the ground was in safe hands, was equally positive. It was perhaps best summed up by the views of *The Hampshire Chronicle*. Reporting the match staged to celebrate the purchase, it said: 'Broadhalfpenny Down...has been purchased by Winchester College, so that the historic ground will be preserved in perpetuity and is henceforward safe from desecration.'

At the time, the College authorities thought they were buying the monument, too. Neither the land agents nor the solicitors acting for Mr Kittow mentioned that the structure belonged to the Hambledon Cricket Club. No rent for the land it stood on changed hands each year, and there was simply nothing in the documents to indicate that the sale excluded the fixtures and fittings, so to speak. Mr Kittow may have forgotten, or may not have been told of, the exclusion when he made his original purchase of the farm from Mr Pease four years earlier. At the time, it would have been such a minor item in the context of the sale of a 560-acre farm that its omission from their discussions is entirely understandable. It was an omission which extended for seventy years, for the College finally learned the truth during the research for this book.

Of course, buying the hallowed piece of turf on Broadhalfpenny Down was one thing; returning it to a condition fit for cricket was quite another. The remains of the 1908 wicket were long gone. The wickets prepared for the annual matches played by the local Hambledon Cricket Club in the few years following 1908 might have left some semblance of a flat surface somewhere in the middle of the ground. But the depressing truth was that there had never been a prepared cricket square on this ground, and whatever efforts might have been lavished on it in the past were long since either eaten by sheep, swamped by thistles or churned up by the plough. The combination of all these destructive forces over 125 years or so left the first groundsman to contemplate trying to make a good wicket there in 1925 with an almost superhuman task. It was not just the square, of course. The outfield was all rough ground as well. There was no boundary, no pavilion, no water, and no facilities to hand. Everything had to be brought in by truck.

A small group of members of the Hambledon club, led by the indefatigable Edward Whalley-Tooker, undertook to restore the ground, which presently looked more like a ploughed field which had been left for rough grazing. The first game, to celebrate the purchase of Broadhalfpenny Down by Winchester College, was scheduled for July the following year, 1925. In a few short months they had, in effect, to create a cricket ground from scratch. It was a considerable achievement that they were ready in time. The outfield was presentable, and the new wicket behaved remarkably well in the circumstances. It was fiery, but it was playable.

The match took place on Saturday 11 July 1925. It was a twelve-a-side game between the Hambledon Cricket Club and Winchester College. It was billed as a match played on Broadhalfpenny Down 'to celebrate its rescue' from the plough, according to Harry Altham. Of the ground that day, he wrote '...now [1925] it is back in turf again, safe and secure, we may hope for all time, in the pious keeping of Winchester College.'

Hambledon
CRICKET CLUB.
Matches for this Week.

Versus *Winchester College*   Versus

On *Saturday, July 11th 1925*   On

At *Broad Halfpenny. 11.30 a.m.*   At

Hambledon CC

Altham, Major H.S. *H.J. Altham*   *Winchester College.*

Ashton. C.J. *C.J. Ashton*   Awdry, C.E.   4 *C.E. Awdry*

Bonham-Carter, Col. a.f. *Bonham-Carter* Bonham-Carter, a.D. *B.D. Bonham-Carter.*

Cooper. Burton F.J. *Burton F. Cooper*   Bower, m.S.S.   6 *M.B.S. Bower*

Hall. J.C. *Frederick C Hall*   Heming, J.H.

Hall. P.m. *Patrick m Hall*   Fuse. C.A.J.   5 *C.A.J. Fuse*

Knight a.E. *a.E.*   aman. P.J.   10 *P.J. Inman.*

Macdonell, H.C. *H.C. McDonell*   King, E.P.   7 *E.P. King.*

Parwin. G. *Godfrey. Parwin*   Kingsley, P.G.J. 1 *P.G.J. Kingsley.*

Whalley-Tooker. E. *E. Whalley. Tooker* Milligan. P.J.m. 9 *P.J.D. Milligan.*

(Captain)   Scott. H.E.

Wilson. E. Rookley. *E. Rockley Wilson* Scott. R.S.G.

Arnold W.J. *W.J. Arnold*   Snell E.   3 *E. Snell.*

                                         Tew. a.m.   11 *A.m. Tew*

Umpire   Holding, W.W.m. 12 *W. W. Holding*

N. T. Collis   Richardson. a.W. 2 *A. Richardson*

                                         Umpire W. Wainwright

(Signed) *Burton J. Cooper. Hon Sec*

The Hambledon Cricket Club teamsheet for the match on Broadhalfpenny Down, 11 July 1925, to celebrate the transfer of ownership to Winchester College. All the players later signed the sheet.
(Reproduced by kind permission of Hambledon Cricket Club)

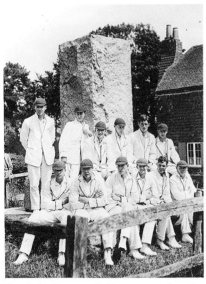

The Winchester College team for the match held 11 July 1925 to celebrate the purchase of Broadhalfpenny Down by the College.
(Reproduced by kind permission of John Barrett/Maureen Wingham)

But he was obliged to observe of the Bat and Ball across the road: 'Time has not dealt kindly with it.' He saw no evidence of the erstwhile romance of earlier times. Nonetheless, this was clearly a moment for celebration, and celebrate they did.

In addition to its own side that day, the College also provided players for the Hambledon XII. Four genuine Hambledon members were supplemented by Wykehamists and others drawn from a team who gloried in the title 'The Gentlemen of Hampshire'. CB Fry was invited to play, a thoughtful touch in view of his efforts in 1908, but he was obliged to decline the invitation. He did, however, turn up to watch. The Hambledon side was captained by the very same Edward Whalley-Tooker who had skippered the club to victory in 1908, and who had put so much effort into making the ground playable once more. And so here he was, this veteran of Hambledon cricket, captaining Hambledon on Broadhalfpenny Down yet again, despite the passage of time. It was a handsome recognition of his unstinting efforts on behalf of the club over so very many years, and a fine gesture on the part of Winchester College and the Hambledon club to invite him to lead the local side. The only concession he made was to put himself in to bat at number eleven. Like Nyren before him, Whalley-Tooker led Hambledon to yet another victory. And what a victory it was. They won a two-innings match in a single day.

Unfortunately, there were a few problems before the match began. That same report in *The Cricketer*, published in July

1925, which referred to the 'many rather amazing blunders' made in 1908 said that they regrettably recurred in 1925. Once again the biggest difficulty for spectators, and players, was the whereabouts of the venue. Where was Hambledon? How do you get there? Once again there were three different answers. Once again the result was chaos. The same smug minority went straight to Broadhalfpenny Down. An embarrassing number applied true Wykehamist logic and went to Winchester, in the erroneous belief that Hambledon must be near Winchester. It is not; fifteen miles separate them. Many others went to the other village of Hambledon near Godalming, Surrey, twenty-five miles away but in the opposite direction. Like their predecessors seventeen years earlier, they also encountered the local narrow lanes. But all was well in the end. One way or another, they all finally arrived at the right Hambledon, and found the famous, if well-hidden, Broadhalfpenny Down.

Nobody was quite sure which team was playing at home. Winchester College were playing on their own ground for the first time; Hambledon were playing on their original ground. It hardly mattered. A crowd of over 4000 turned up to watch the match, which was played in glorious summer weather. They formed their cars around the ground in a huge circle, just as the visitors had done in 1908. Only this time there were charabancs as well, since many spectators had arranged to travel down to the ground in groups. The landlord of the Bat and Ball must have wondered what had hit him. The pub was open all day and generated a torrent of noise during the game, and much singing afterwards. There were famous faces not only on the field but all around the boundary. One distinguished visitor was so taken aback when he was accosted by a sharp-eyed autograph hunter that he confessed afterwards that he had actually spelled his name wrongly when he signed the small boy's book.

The correspondent who reported the match in the next edition of *The Cricketer* wrote: 'For those who saw cricket on Broadhalfpenny Down for the first time, the event must have been a revelation...an experience in a perfect setting, the beauty of the position of the ground, the spirit of the play throughout, and the glorious air.'

The Winchester College v Hambledon match in progress, 11 July 1925. This picture was taken from the first-floor window of the Bat and Ball. (Reproduced by kind permission of John Barrett/Maureen Wingham)

Certainly the match was played in a good spirit. It was a keen, lively contest, played with proper concentration. Early ideas of playing in period costume were rightly abandoned on the grounds that the players wanted to play cricket, not just make light entertainment. After all, they had some fine players on the field, several of whom were county standard; and one had played for England.

He was Rockley Wilson, a former captain of Yorkshire, who went with JWHT Douglas's side to Australia in 1920–21, and played in one Test match. He was now a master at Winchester College, a post he held for forty years. So he was a professional colleague of Harry Altham's as a cricketer and teacher. Even though he was now a slow bowler in his late forties, Wilson was invited to open the bowling for Hambledon with Claude Ashton, a former captain of Cambridge University, whose deliveries were far from slow. On such a lively pitch, they quickly had Winchester College in all sorts of trouble at 26 for 7, Ashton having taken four wickets for seven runs in eight overs.

But this was to be a day of success for the Bonham-Carter family, whose connections with the original Hambledon club went back to the 1700s. Henry Bonham was secretary of the club in 1778. He was also the first man in the recorded history of the game to be dismissed 'stumped'. On 6 October 1778, playing for Hambledon against Surrey at Chertsey, Henry Bonham was given out 'stumped Yalden 9'. Now one of his descendants, a young giant of a man, AD Bonham-Carter, arrived at the wicket, plainly not overawed by the company he was keeping, or the lamentable state of the scoreboard. He was mighty proud of his ancestry, though, and he now set about the bowling that had wrought such havoc as if it were coming from a couple of schoolboys instead of a pair of county players. He took sixes off them both, and had them removed from the attack in no time. According to EV Lucas, having knocked off both bowlers he 'laid bare the pathetic truth that the Hambledon captain hadn't brought any more', for his onslaught had hardly begun. The sixes kept coming. He finished with 85, of which 60 came in boundaries. And when he was finally caught by the wicket-keeper, his cousin Major A Bonham-Carter, the score was 128. The innings closed at 143. It had lasted ninety minutes.

Harry Altham opened the batting for Hambledon, and scored an elegant and stylish 76. His powerful innings included fourteen fours and a six. He was joined in a good stand by the wicket-keeper Major A Bonham-Carter, who scored 56 before being stumped – ironically, and by way of retribution, by his huge cousin, with an elegant sense of family history. The Hambledon first innings closed at 214, a lead of 71. Winchester's second innings was something of a disaster and they were all out for 86, Wilson and Ashton sharing all but one of the wickets to fall. The young hero of the first innings was again top scorer, with 28, six of which came via a smashed car-windscreen, before he was caught when going for yet another big hit. The rest was a formality.

EV Lucas's report also recorded the fact that he had returned home to write it on John Nyren's writing table, given to him by the great man's granddaughters when he was researching his book *The Hambledon Men*, published in 1907. A flurry of other correspondence followed this match, as some of the participants recorded their feelings at having played on Broadhalfpenny Down for the first time. Major Bonham-Carter wrote to Edward Whalley-Tooker, saying, 'I have rarely, if ever, enjoyed a match so much. The enormous trouble you must have taken over that wicket amply repaid you.'

Rockley Wilson told Whalley-Tooker: 'We were all very proud of the opportunity you gave us of playing on the historic ground and I am sure that everyone agreed that they had never spent a happier day. The weather and the view were too beautiful for words and everything was right. High hits, a few old-fashioned shooters, a regular "character" to umpire and everybody friendly and jolly combined to make the day a real success. And Hambledon won!'

Again there is a gap. The ground was now in safe hands, but nothing was done to use it for cricket, at least not on a regular basis. For much of the next ten years or so, it was just left as rough grass. But it was used occasionally to stage an odd assortment of one-off matches. Two years after their first encounter, Winchester College returned to play Hambledon once again, on a day spoilt by rain. That did not prevent some 500 spectators turning up to watch a low-scoring game which Winchester College won by 99 runs. Two years later they met again in a close-fought match which the visitors also won, but this time by a mere 5 runs.

The next game which demands attention occurred on an extraordinary date – 1 January 1929. This must have been the first, and is to date most certainly the last match played on Broadhalfpenny Down on New Year's Day. It was arranged by the tireless Edward Whalley-Tooker and John (later Sir John) Squire 'at the height of the football season, as a modest protest against football encroaching on summer cricket seasons'. According to *The Times*' report, published the next day, it was played in Pickwickian style, without descending into farce. The day was dry, bright and very cold in the January wind. Nobody there that day had any doubts about the accuracy of the Duke of Dorset's observations made 140-odd years earlier. It was indeed a bleak place to play cricket...and they could now add the words 'especially in winter'. To make the match possible at all it was necessary to lay a matting wicket, but the fielders simply had to take their chances on the slippery and wet outfield. With a turn of phrase well worthy of 'The Thunderer', their reporter told *Times* readers that coping with the conditions required 'a high degree of low cunning'.

In addition to an optimistic film-crew, an astonishing 1500

hardy souls turned up to watch the match, or part of it, many of them from their cars or the warmth of the Bat and Ball, the bar parlour of which does not provide the best view of the ground, nor space for that number. It hardly mattered that day. They did, however, contribute to the collection made on behalf of the Royal Hampshire County Hospital and the Hampshire County Cricket Club. They were also entertained by the Hambledon Band, which played a song specially composed for the occasion by Peter Warlock, with words by Bruce Blunt, who played in the match. This song was intended, according to the lyricist, 'to be roared over mugs of beer'. No doubt Tom Sueter and George Leer would have loved it. The words can be found at the end of this volume.

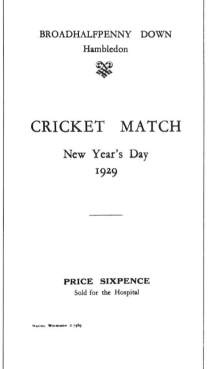

BROADHALFPENNY DOWN

Hambledon

CRICKET MATCH

New Year's Day
1929

PRICE SIXPENCE
Sold for the Hospital

Warren, Winchester D 7569

Programme for the New Year's Day match, 1 January 1929, Hampshire Eskimos v Invalids.
(Reproduced by kind permission of John Barrett/Maureen Wingham)

The two sides, twelve men apiece, called themselves the Invalids and the Hampshire Eskimos. John Squire skippered the Invalids, and Edward Whalley-Tooker captained the Hampshire Eskimos. One foolhardy participant had travelled 600 miles to play and survived a car accident en route. Noah Mann would have understood his motives, even if the rest of his team regarded them with astonishment and disbelief, and even questioned his sanity.

The match was started in grand style by Piccolo Jim, more properly known as ex-Sergeant Major Newland, who – despite the bitter wind – climbed atop the monument in top hat and tails and piped the players onto the field. He was then wise enough to disappear into the pub to get warm again. The match itself was keenly contested. Batting first, the Invalids made 89. AD Peters, who later founded the literary agency that still bears his name, scored 20. They were runs stroked with such aplomb that he might have been batting in July. The first four of the game was credited to BW O'Donnell. And HP Marshall can forever claim the unique distinction of being the first Harlequin captain to hit a six off a lob bowler on Broadhalfpenny Down on New Year's Day. Such is the stuff of cricket records.

In reply, the Eskimos could only manage 78. They lost their first three wickets for nine runs against the fast bowling of RH Lowe, bowling up the hill and into the wind with great energy. His success probably had more to do with trying to keep warm than anything else. By way of counter-attack, H Clark then produced several highly effective if agricultural strokes to get the score up to 75 for 7, but once he had gone, Peters and O'Donnell took the last three wickets for a run apiece.

At this point there was an entirely predictable rush for the bar. The call for rum punch, beer, Scotch and anything else warming and alcoholic which might be immediately to hand was so great that the Bat and Ball was drunk dry in no time. That, too, had not happened these last 140 years. And very embarrassing for landlord Harry Blackman it was too, for the pub had also been eaten out of food by shortly after lunch. In a foolhardy determination to conduct the entire day in the manner of the original times, lunch had been ordered for the players in the form of bread, cheese and beer. Those not satisfied with these arrangements were free to supplement the set menu from their own resources and the pub's supplies. Given the weather conditions, it can have been no surprise to anyone that the pub had quickly run out of food. Now it had run out of drink as well. Trouble was imminent, and it arrived on horseback.

The Hambledon Hounds had set off from the Bat and Ball at the start of the match at 11am that morning. They streamed across the square, bringing the game to a temporary halt, before disappearing into the distance. From time to time

NEW YEAR'S DAY, 1929

on

Broadhalfpenny Down, Hambledon

(Lent by courtesy of the Warden and Fellows of Winchester College)

A CRICKET MATCH

will be played

HAMPSHIRE ESKIMOS	*v.*	INVALIDS
E. WHALLEY-TOOKER (Capt.)		J. C. SQUIRE (Capt.)
G. ALEXANDER		CAPT. R. BERKELEY
E. ANDREWS		J. HOCKIN
G. H. B. BLUNT		R. H. LOWE
R. BUCKSEY		A. G. MACDONELL
H. CLARK		W. H. MAC EWAN
G. COOPER		H. MACKINTOSH
R. GODWIN		H. P. MARSHALL
F. E. MACEY		W. T. MONCKTON
G. PARVIN		B. W. O'DONNELL
A. PYLE		A. D. PETERS
P. SILVESTER		R. STRAUS
		R. H. A. SQUIRE (Reserve)

Umpires : A. BLUNDELL, L. E. WHARTON
Scorers: MRS. J. C. SQUIRE, H. TURNER

The Hambledon Hounds will meet at Broadhalfpenny Hut at 11 o'clock.
The Hambledon Band will be present and will play " The Cricketers of Hambledon,"
specially composed for the occasion by Peter Warlock, with words by Bruce Blunt.
The Evening will be spent at " The George."
There will be a collection for the Royal Hampshire County Hospital and the
Hampshire County Cricket Club.

Teamsheet for the New Year's Day match, 1 January 1929, Hampshire Eskimos v Invalids.
(Reproduced by kind permission of John Barrett/Maureen Wingham)

Well-protected against the elements, two hardy batsmen start out for the wicket,
1 January 1929. Ludo May and Piccolo Jim watch them pass.
(Reproduced by kind permission of John Barrett/Maureen Wingham)

throughout the day, the hunt was seen galloping across the downs in search of the odd fox. But when the huntsmen finally returned to the Bat and Ball towards dusk, there was not a drop of liquor left in the place. They were not pleased. Meanwhile, the cricketers had moved down to the village, largely oblivious to the mayhem they had left behind. They spent the evening enjoying themselves at the George, no doubt singing endless reprises of Bruce Blunt's new song, and possibly considering an attempt to drink the entire village dry as well.

The following year, 1930, two matches took place on Broadhalfpenny Down, both arranged through Edward Whalley-Tooker's connections. As an Old Etonian, he invited the Eton Ramblers to play a match against Hambledon, which finished in an indecisive draw. Then with the aid of his son, Hyde, now a Fellow of Downing College, Cambridge, he initiated what was to prove a short series of annual fixtures between Hambledon and a team of touring undergraduates from the college. Some discussion took place beforehand about the form this particular game should take, and it was eventually agreed that the match should be played under rules which have never been used before or since. The two teams

The hunt stops play, New Year's Day, 1929. Edward Whalley-Tooker is fourth from the left, apparently making a belated appeal, or signalling that he needs a stiff whisky.
(Reproduced by kind permission of Christine Pardoe)

agreed to play under something akin to the laws of 1744, but with a third stump added, despite its chronological inexactitude. The first of these annual two-innings matches ended in an exciting draw, Hambledon just hanging on with their last pair at the wicket and eight runs short of victory.

What mattered was the game itself, not who won, was the students' reassuringly retrospective opinion. But they had vivid recollections of sleeping in one of Whalley-Tooker's barns and driving over to Winchester to clean themselves up on the morning before the game. Camping out in summer in country barns might have seemed quite a lark at the time, and was intended to enable the more impecunious undergraduates to save sufficient money for the more convivial moments of the tour in bars scattered throughout southern England. But if this overnight stop was one way of saving money, it evidently did nothing for personal hygiene.

The following year, Downing College scored a decisive win by eight wickets. The third match, in 1932, produced some mild controversy which may account for the fact that it proved to be the college's last visit. One of the Downing College side, Ronald Taylor, recalls the arrival from London for the match of a certain RC Robertson-Glasgow. He appeared on a 2.25 horse-power motorcycle, which was hardly the ideal mode of transport for a tall man. Robertson-Glasgow's appearance gave Hambledon the advantage of a 'given man', in the parlance of the glory days on Broadhalfpenny Down, and historically speaking was entirely in the spirit of the place. However, this arrangement had not applied in the previous years, and it caught the Downing College side somewhat by surprise.

Raymond Robertson-Glasgow was a first-class player, still turning out occasionally for Somerset to bowl his medium-pace swinging deliveries with a high action. He had played for Oxford in the Varsity matches between 1920 and 1923, and he subsequently represented the Gentlemen against the Players five times. He became best known later as a particularly perceptive cricket correspondent for various daily papers, and he was the author of several highly readable and witty books on cricket. He answered to the nickname 'Crusoe', which he

Piccolo Jim atop the monument,
1 January 1929. (Reproduced by kind
permission of John Barrett/Maureen Wingham)

The kitchen range in the original bar area of the Bat and Ball. This picture was taken about 1929.
(Reproduced by kind permission of Christine Pardoe)

earned from Charlie McGahey, the Essex amateur, after the latter lost his wicket to Robertson-Glasgow in a county match at Taunton. His dismissal happened so fast that Johnny Douglas, the next batsman, did not see what had happened and was still in the dressing-room putting on his gear when McGahey arrived. 'What happened?', he asked breathlessly. The reply was the immortal, if incongruous malapropism: 'I was bowled by an old bugger I thought was dead two thousand years ago – Robinson Crusoe.' Robertson-Glasgow was Crusoe forever after.

But in 1932, on Broadhalfpenny Down, having struggled all the way down from London on his tiny motorcycle, Robertson-Glasgow was not to be trifled with. He bowled his seamers with great effect for Hambledon that day, and quickly knocked back Ronald Taylor's stumps for 9. Now aged eighty-four, Mr Taylor is still mildly upset about it. But he was at least on the winning side of a draw.

A few weeks after the 1931 match against Downing College, another one-off game was staged on Broadhalfpenny Down by the Hambledon Cricket Club. On Saturday 1 August 1931, a match was organized by Captain Philip Goldsmith, an officer in the Royal Navy and then secretary to the Commander-in-Chief, Atlantic Fleet, Admiral Sir Michael Hodges. Philip Goldsmith was a descendant of a Hambledon player during the latter part of the glory days, and his family still lived in Hambledon; it still does today. In April that year, he approached Whalley-Tooker and proposed a match between the local club and a team from HMS *Nelson*, the Admiral's flagship, who would play under the glorious title 'The Ancient Mariners'. The match took place entirely on the initiative of the two men, and their pre-match publicity attracted a huge crowd to watch yet another two-innings match to be played in a single day on Broadhalfpenny Down. Once again, the modest size of the ground and the scale of the hitting sent several car owners home less than happy about the day's proceedings. But the camera crew from British Movietone News got some good footage.

This match, too, was played under a unique set of laws never

Both Hambledon and Downing College teams at the monument, 1931.
(Reproduced by kind permission of Hambledon Cricket Club)

Stumpy Turner and Ludo May, with smock and what he claimed was the original Hambledon team's umbrella, 1 January 1929. The score on the right is unknown.
(Reproduced by kind permission of John Barrett and Maureen Wingham)

used before or since. The idea, this time, was to use a version of the 1744 laws, but with a few new, different and equally eccentric variations. Perhaps the most important was the decision to rule a batsman out if the ball passed through the two-stump wicket, even if the bail was not dislodged. Over-arm bowling was to be allowed and, in the spirit of the period, it was also decided that the crease was only to be scratched on the ground in front of the stumps. Goldsmith consulted FS Ashley-Cooper on numerous aspects of the old laws of the game before the match rules were finalized, and at one stage had to reassure this doyen of cricket correspondents that he and Whalley-Tooker had 'no intention of playing in smock frocks nor, of course, anything so vandalistic as playing with old bats'. Ashley-Cooper's antennae were still in excellent working order, it seems.

After overnight rain, it proved to be a glorious day. The sun shone all through the game. As a spectacle it delighted the crowd, for all the players were in period costume. The Hambledon team turned out in top hats, vest waistcoats, knee breeches, silk stockings and black buckle shoes. The Ancient Mariners were in old tarpaulin naval rig, with pigtails, hard hats, check shirts and striped trousers. The umpires were also attired in period dress. As the players arrived at the ground, having been driven up from the village in a coach and four, they were greeted by ex-Sergeant Major Newland, Piccolo Jim, again standing on top of the monument. He started playing his pipes as they approached the ground, and finally piped them onto the field amid great applause.

The score was kept in the normal way, but the match was also notched by 'old Harry Turner', known locally as 'Stumps'. He had lost a leg in the Great War, but seems to have taken no offence at the nickname. The knife he used that day in 1931 to cut the notches in a stick had been with him all through the retreat from Mons, and he was rightly proud of it. Later in the day, his notched stick was auctioned for £3 5s (£3.25) which was subsequently given to charity. The scoreboard display was kept up by a local gamekeeper, Ludovic May, who told the press that he was wearing a smock which was 150 years old. The reporters made no mention in their reports of the distance they had to put between Mr May and themselves when he imparted this historical gem. He claimed that it had been in use during the glory days. They believed him. He had also brought to the ground an umbrella which he said had been used in 1780 to shelter the Hambledon team of those days when the weather was bad. They believed that too. Not far away, but far enough, John Wisden & Co had on display an old scoring-table used by the Hambledon club, and a bat made in about 1750.

The Hambledon side that day included three men descended from the Hambledon men of the glory days. In addition to Whalley-Tooker and Goldsmith, the third man was Major A Bonham-Carter, who had featured so dramatically in the 1925 game. On this occasion he kept wicket with gloves but no pads, and was described by AER Gilligan, the former England captain, who was there to report the match for the London *News Chronicle*, as 'looking for all the world like an ancient cavalier in the wrong place, rather than a cricketer'. Dick White captained the navy team, and once again Edward Whalley-Tooker led the Hambledon club. He was now sixty-nine years old and had been skippering the club for thirty-seven years. He told Gilligan that he had been captaining cricket teams for fifty-one years in all, starting with his school side when he was eighteen.

The match was attended by over 5000 spectators. Among them were a number of well-known faces from the world of cricket. While England's greatest all-rounder of the time, Wally Hammond, was not there himself, his mother and wife both came up from Southsea for the day. More than 600 cars were parked around the ground and two of them went home with smashed windscreens. Apart from the match itself, which was entertaining enough, the crowds had plenty to keep them amused during the day. Numerous sideshows were set up around the ground, there was food and drink available from several licensed marquees, and the band of HMS *Nelson* played a full programme of music in the intervals throughout the day. Later on that evening, the band of the Royal Marines played dance music on the village green, and there was a bonfire with fireworks to round off the proceedings.

Dick White, as the visiting captain, was invited to select the pitch and take first innings. They scored 102 at their first attempt, which Hambledon bettered on the first innings by 36 notches. But, in their second innings, the Ancient Mariners took the Hambledon bowling apart and scored a rapid 231 before declaring the innings closed with nine wickets down. Needing 195 to win, Hambledon could only manage 132. They

(Reproduced by kind permission of Marion Beagley)

The News Chronicle's *cartoon of Edward Whalley-Tooker bowling lobs in the match between Hambledon and the Ancient Mariners, 1931. (Reproduced by kind permission of Christine Pardoe)*

Hambledon v The Ancient Mariners (HMS Nelson), 1 August 1931. Left to right: Dick White, captain of the Ancient Mariners, Philip Goldsmith, who organized the match and now sets up the stumps, and Edward Whalley-Tooker, captain of Hambledon, who had played in the 1908 match 23 years earlier. (Reproduced by kind permission of Christine Pardoe)

lost by 63 notches. Over 600 runs had been scored in a single day.

During the game, there were several moments of high drama and excitement. Two involved spectacular catches. Hambledon's sixty-nine-year-old captain took a particularly sharp chance close to the wicket to dismiss his opposing captain for 39 in the Ancient Mariners' second innings. It was the sort of half-chance reflex catch nobody expected to stick in the hands of a veteran. But it did. Then, later in that innings, he put Langridge on to bowl and thanks to the athleticism of H Hooker, who was a local gardener and the Hambledon groundsman, E Satterthwaite was dismissed by a truly astonishing catch for 69. Hooker had to run flat-out around the boundary edge even to get close to the ball, and finished by hurling himself full-length through the air at the very last moment to take the catch inches off the ground. The second Duke of Dorset would have been proud of him. In the spirit of the occasion, both skippers bowled underarm lobs during the game. White took five of Hambledon's second-innings wickets with his. And just to prove he could still compete – not that anyone present dared think otherwise – the Hambledon skipper put himself on to bowl even slower lobs and promptly took two wickets.

Most of the other highlights of the day appear to have been closer to moments of amiable farce rather than good cricket. One of the Ancient Mariners, JS Cowie, was bowled by Langridge when his wig fell over his eyes at the crucial moment and blinded him. The laws governing the day did not permit the umpire to call 'dead ball', or even 'no ball', and Cowie was obliged to leave the field to gales of helpless mirth. Later, another player lost hat and wig together, and rearranged them back on his head upside down. Well, he explained afterwards, what was a fellow to do? There were no mirrors out there... Even the umpires got involved in the entertainment. At one point during the afternoon, all eleven fielders asked the same umpire to hold their hats at the same time. He piled them up as precariously as the Leaning Tower of Pisa, and tried to carry on as if this were an everyday occurrence. The huge crowd thought it was all great fun.

For Philip Goldsmith, however, the day had a sad and somewhat sour footnote. At the start of the match, he had received a congratulatory telegram from the MCC, wishing him and the match well. At the end of the day, he found himself confronted with a huge unpaid bill from the caterers. He wrote to *The Hampshire Chronicle* afterwards, appealing to the public for contributions towards meeting the costs of the day. He pointed out that, while 5000 people had been present, only 1200 had bought tickets. Worse than that, 126 people had taken lunch, and eighty-seven had taken tea, and then walked off without paying. With an airy wave, they had claimed to be guests of the organizers and told the caterers that they had not the slightest intention of settling up. Faced with this impasse, Philip Goldsmith asked local residents of Hambledon and the surrounding area for financial help, and said that 'subscriptions may be handed in at the Post Office', presumably the one in Hambledon village. Whether he got the response he needed was never made public. Even Hambledon's offer of the stumps and bails as a commemorative gift after the game hardly compensated him. He suggested the club keep them and put them on display.

Edward Whalley-Tooker reported on the match and the surrounding events to FS Ashley-Cooper afterwards, since the distinguished cricket correspondent had been unable to attend. Whalley-Tooker's letter said that 'we have improved the ground a great deal lately, and I quite hope we have not spoilt it in any way. We want Broadhalfpenny Down to remain as it is.' The message was no doubt received by the self-appointed guardian of Broadhalfpenny Down's integrity with relief.

Then there was another gap, this time of four years. Between 1931 and 1935 the ground was probably not used for cricket at all. If it was, nobody thought the fact worthy of record. The most important events during these years appear to have been one gift and one conversation.

The gift was of the second-oldest cricket bat known, then owned by Miss Ellen Mary Miles of Eastleigh, who in November 1931 bequeathed it to Winchester College. According to the accompanying note, the bat belonged to her 'great-grandfather John Osmond Miles who, according to tradition in the Miles family, used [it] in the first match played on Broad Halfpenny Down by the Hambledon Club'. A cricket ball bequeathed at the same time, and claimed to be from the same period, is much less credible than the bat. Old it is, but it's not that old. The bat, on the other hand, is genuinely a relic of the 1700s. The shape alone tells us that.

The exaggerated and unsupported claim about the ball is unfortunately compounded by Miss Miles when she goes on to refer to her great-grandfather's playing on Broadhalfpenny Down 'soon after 1742'. This statement is supported by no facts or evidence of any kind. Given that her note was written in 1931, she implies a mere four generations spanning almost 200 years. Even allowing for the propensity that cricketers have for long life, this is unlikely. It is much more likely that five or more generations were involved. Were these innocent and trivial mistakes, or do these apparent discrepancies raise more serious doubts? Can we believe her other claims in such circumstances? Perhaps the most that can be said of the bat now held by Winchester College is that it was used on Broadhalfpenny Down at an early stage in the Hambledon club's history, and certainly before the 1770s. But where does that leave the crucial question about the start of cricket on Broadhalfpenny Down and the formation of a cricket team by the Hambledon club? Sadly, it is wide open again. We are left only with the shadowy figure of Squire Land, and the probability – but no more – of cricket on Broadhalfpenny Down some time before 1750.

So much for the gift. The conversation inevitably involved Harry Altham, who found himself bothered by the lack of activity at Broadhalfpenny Down. He must have played a part in what happened next. Common sense, rather than specific evidence, encourages the thought. He was still teaching at Winchester, he was a prominent member of the Hampshire County Cricket Club, and he had long since nailed his colours to the Broadhalfpenny mast.

Did he have a quiet chat with Wilfred Wadham, a keen member of the county club since 1924, one day during the summer of 1935, when they were both enjoying Philip Mead's despatching the ball to all quarters of the county ground? Was it a chance conversation or did someone else introduce them? Or did Altham first meet Wilf Wadham when the county received as a gift a brand new motor car to help move their professional players around the country during the season? It was a singularly generous gift from the local motor trader, and entirely likely that, as a leading member of the club, Altham would have wanted to acknowledge the gift. As he did so, he would quickly have found himself encountering one of the most enthusiastic, knowledgeable and active amateur cricketers ever to walk into the pavilion at Southampton.

Wilf Wadham and his brother John had started a small engineering business at Waterlooville, just a few miles from Broadhalfpenny Down, in 1905. By the mid 1930s they had built up a thriving family business and were well-known in the motor trade. Sponsoring cars for professional cricketers was not the norm at that time, so Wadham's gift to Hampshire CCC was as unusual as it was generous. It also underlines his devotion to cricket in general, and to Hampshire cricket in particular. Not surprisingly, being the cricket fanatic he was, he had started Wadham Bros sports club several years before, and his employees enjoyed the use of a sports ground at Denmead, not far from the company's headquarters. Several of the senior managers played regularly for the firm's side, although Wilf's eyesight had obliged him to give up wicket-keeping some years before talk of a move to Broadhalfpenny Down.

Whatever the circumstances which initiated the discussion between Altham and Wadham about reviving Broadhalfpenny Down as a regular venue for cricket, the die was cast by the end of 1935. Members at the annual dinner of the Wadham Bros sports club in December were told that they would be playing on Broadhalfpenny Down the following summer. The news made banner headlines in the local press that Christmas, even though the formalities were not concluded until early in 1936, when Wilfred Wadham wrote to Winchester College to ask the College to grant his firm a licence to play cricket on Broadhalfpenny Down. The contract was signed on 4 April 1936, just in time for the new season. The first match took place within the month, on what must have been a sporting wicket – but that did not stop Dick Brown scoring 108 for Wadham Bros out of a total of 184. Their opponents Purbrook, honoured with the first fixture of the new era at Broadhalfpenny Down, found the wicket much more difficult and were dismissed for 41. Ivan Angell, who normally performed the functions of company secretary at Wadham Bros, took 4 wickets for 11 runs. He was a tall and – in his younger days, at least – rangy man who fairly thumped the ball into the ground, at great speed and from a considerable height. He was more than useful as a club bowler on any wicket, but he must have relished the thought of bowling regularly on such a wicket as this, now that the contract was literally locked up in his safe. For him, here was the prospect of Christmas every weekend. Over the years ahead he did indeed enjoy great success, and he justifiably became Wadham Bros' leading wicket-taker on Broadhalfpenny Down. Thomas Brett and David Harris would have approved heartily.

Throughout the rest of that summer, the players, with company support, were continuously and enthusiastically improving the ground and its facilities. The four-and-a-half-acre site was fenced off, the whole ground cut and rolled endlessly, and a start made on bringing the square up to a good standard. The little rough-timbered, thatched pavilion, which still stands, was built within the first few weeks, although the one remaining eye-witness of those days is adamant that there was a structure there before 1936, and that they effectively rebuilt it. Sadly, whoever built it put it in the wrong place. It was an understandable mistake for anyone to make if they had not played on Broadhalfpenny Down before. They would quickly enough have discovered their error, as have successive generations of players ever since, as the summer sun sets on the other side of the ground and beams straight into the spectators' eyes all evening.

Wilf Wadham must have been a lucky man. For he was to discover a hidden bonus at the Bat and Ball. As has happened so often already in our story, once again the right man was in the right place at the right time. This time the man was Wilfred Dickens, and he was the landlord of the Bat and Ball. He was equally lucky. He must have seen the arrival of Wilf Wadham and his company's cricket team as manna from heaven. He immediately donned the mantle of Richard Nyren and offered the club his services and support. He would, if Mr Wadham wished, provide teas between innings on match days, the pub's hospitality after the match, and also look after the ground during the week. Even better, Wilfred Dickens knew what he was talking about. He had been on the ground staff at The Oval in 1901, but rapidly come to the conclusion that he was not quite good enough to make a living playing cricket. So he decided to join the navy and see the world. When he retired, he took over the Bat and Ball. Dickens was just what Wilf Wadham needed if he was to make Broadhalfpenny Down the success he, Harry Altham and now Dickens wished. Wadham knew a good thing when he saw one. Done!

Later that year, electricity was brought across the road, but water remained a problem. There was no piped water of any kind available. It still had to be drawn from the 325-foot well in the Bat and Ball. At least there was an electric pump to do the work, something Richard and Frances Nyren never enjoyed. But the water itself still had to be carried by hand across the road, just as it was over 150 years before. The younger members of the side found themselves being volunteered for these duties when the square had to be watered during dry spells, although the water simply drained straight through to the chalk underneath, just as it had always done. These younger players were also expected to help pull the heavy roller over the square before the match and afterwards. On the odd occasion when Wilfred Dickens was unable to prepare a wicket for the following day, they were taken up to the ground to cut and mark a strip. The company simply regarded such activities as special duties after working hours. In 1937, they even took a crop of hay off the outfield before the start of the season in May.

For the next few years, the Wadham Bros cricket team enjoyed the unique distinction of being the first side to play regularly at Broadhalfpenny Down since 1782. Judging by accounts of the matches they played against local and touring sides, they proved themselves worthy custodians of this honour. They were a strong team, certainly by amateur standards, and turned out one side every Saturday throughout the season. Occasionally, they also played evening games. But they never played on Sundays.

Ivan Angell continued to collect wickets by the cart-load, helped by a wicket on which 'a 50 was worth at least 100 anywhere else', according to Bob Murton, who joined Wadham Bros as a boy in 1936 and got the job as a petrol-pump attendant simply because he was known to be a useful young cricketer. Today, having retired as a director of the same firm in 1981, he is now in his eighties, but he remembers those days on Broadhalfpenny Down as if they were yesterday. The wicket was never dangerous, he recalls, but the low, slow bounce of the ball made front-foot play hazardous at the best of times. Often, the ball was simply not there to be hit. (Sixty years later, it still isn't.) Even so, then as now, big scores were made regularly, despite the downland nature of the wicket. Dick Brown followed up his hundred in that first match with plenty more runs over the years. He was the John Small of Wadham Bros, the rock on which the club expected to build its generally healthy totals. His lack of any discernible backlift was evidently quite an advantage. Bob Murton rarely saw him bowled.

But if Dick Brown was the John Small of his day, Bob Murton found himself the Richard Purchase. Within a week of getting the job, he was asked to play cricket for the sports club on the following Saturday afternoon. It was a daunting experience for the fourteen-year-old to find himself rubbing shoulders with the managing director and the company secretary within days of joining the firm. But he was made welcome, and held his place for as long as the company played at Broadhalfpenny Down. In those early days, he was regarded as a young pair of legs to do the running around in the outfield. He quickly made his place safe by excelling in the deep. If he was lucky he batted at nine, and only bowled his medium-pacers when Wadham Bros were in dire trouble. In the fullness of time, he was regularly opening the innings with Dick Brown and he still remembers with pleasure some of the big opening partnerships they shared together. They did his career no harm either.

Two other stalwarts of the Wadham Bros team of those days were George Bush, who shared the new ball with Ivan Angell and could also be relied on for a few runs, and Freddy Perks, whose attitude to cricket echoed that of Gilbert Jessop. The ball was there to be hit, as far and as fast as possible. Sixty years later, there are still a few broken tiles on the roof of the Bat and Ball to prove how effective Freddy Perks was. Another big hitter to visit the ground each season was a giant of a man – a brickyard worker who rejoiced in the curious name 'Farmer' Hill. He played for the nearby village of Harting. Whenever Wadham Bros were playing Harting, the crowds would gather once more, just to see if he could yet again clear the small copse at the top of Broadhalfpenny Down and get the ball into the road beyond. He had done it before. Each year the question was the same – could he do it again? There was a keen sense of disappointment when he failed, worse if he was dismissed before making the attempt. Farmer Hill might have walked straight out of the pages of AG Macdonell's *England, Their England*. He was a true village cricketer, and appears to have achieved something not even Jessop had done. No account of the 1908 match so much as mentions Jessop's hitting the ball out of the ground.

Once it became more widely known that Broadhalfpenny Down was in regular use again, the requests for fixtures started to come from all over England. A few came from abroad as well. Most went to the firm in Waterlooville, but some were addressed simply c/o The Bat and Ball, Hambledon, England. Of course, they got there. In the cricket world, there are few more illustrious addresses than that. Suddenly everybody wanted to play on Broadhalfpenny Down – and who could blame them? The Wadham's management, which meant Wilf Wadham and Ivan Angell, accommodated as many as they could over the years. The Wiltshire Queries, sporting several of their minor counties side, played Wadham Bros while they were on summer tour. Sides raised by local firms, including Thoneycroft at Basingstoke and several of the big insurance companies based in Bournemouth, also got fixtures. So did the Hampshire CCC, who sent a Club and Ground team to play at least one match. One of Wilf Wadham's first decisions, once he had the use of the ground, was to invite the Hambledon Cricket Club to play a match that same summer, despite the short notice. It was intended as a goodwill gesture. The invitation was accepted promptly and gladly, but with slightly mixed feelings. The club's minutes somewhat acidly record a decision of the committee that their team should not travel from the village up to Broadhalfpenny Down 'in a conveyance', as they had done in the past. The first match took place on Saturday 22 August 1936. It became a regular fixture.

One of the most popular, and regular, guest sides to play at Broadhalfpenny Down were Portsmouth Football Club, then one of the country's most successful First Division clubs. What is less well-known is that they also boasted a good cricket team, which included several of their top football professionals.

Wadham Bros' matches against Portsmouth FC inevitably brought good crowds to Broadhalfpenny Down to watch their footballing heroes.

On 17 June 1939, Portsmouth FC and many other regular visitors to Broadhalfpenny Down were invited to a special match arranged to celebrate the completion of major improvements, including a new extension, to the Bat and Ball. Portsmouth had just won the FA Cup and they were not to know that they would keep it longer than any other single winner – the Second World War prevented its being competed for again until 1946. In June 1939, however, few people seriously imagined such a thing could happen, although the storm clouds were now gathering in Europe. In a state of high excitement and unalloyed pride, Portsmouth Football Club brought the FA Cup to Broadhalfpenny Down that day, under the watchful eye of a police constable who had the onerous task of ensuring that this most treasured of all English football trophies was returned safely to Portsmouth by nightfall. One of many photographs taken beside the monument that day now hangs in the Bat and Ball, a poignant reminder to Pompey football fans of things past.

The match itself was between Wadham Bros and Westgate Brewery, the sports club representing Henty and Constable, owners of the Bat and Ball since 1844. Among the notable cricketing personalities to put in an appearance that day were the former England captain 'Plum' (later Sir Pelham) Warner; the then editor of *The Cricketer*, Sir Russell Bencraft, president of Hampshire County Cricket Club; and Colonel Christopher Heseltine, representing the MCC. He had previously represented the MCC on the committee which Henty and Constable had set up a year earlier to oversee the improvements to the Bat and Ball. Mr A Henty, the firm's managing director, had taken the view that the pub was an important and integral part of the history of English cricket, and that while there was no legal obligation on his firm as owners of the Bat and Ball to consult cricket interests about its present facilities or future plans, he did have a moral obligation to do so. His public-spirited approach earned him and his firm a great deal of good publicity. *The Times* told its readers shortly afterwards: 'Henty and Constable deserve praise for preserving the ancient characteristics of the Bat and Ball with their new extension, which has been completed only after prolonged negotiations with the local authority and consultation with the MCC.'

As ever on these occasions, there were some witty speeches made during the celebrations. Plum Warner told his audience that he felt that he should have taken off his shoes and socks when he walked onto Broadhalfpenny Down because he was treading on holy ground. He also claimed for himself a distinction on the cricket field that had escaped even the great Don Bradman. 'I have made a duck in every part of the world,' he said, 'including Spain. Not even the Don has done that.' Sir Russell Bencraft paid tribute to Plum Warner's enormous contribution to cricket over a lifetime in the game, and mused that had Plum Warner been the chairman of selectors during the glory days, when Hambledon were beating England with such monotonous regularity, the results would have been very different. Sir Horace Mann might have found his advice invaluable, and the results a good deal more financially agreeable.

The match itself was yet another triumph for Ivan Angell. In fact, he and his opposite number on the visitors' side appear, between them, to have thoroughly spoiled a good day's sport for everyone else. Wadham Bros scored 136 (Humby 36, Lake 6 for 13), Westgate Brewery 53 (Angell 7 for 16). This was evidently yet another sporting wicket on Broadhalfpenny Down, and Ivan Angell's bowling figures that day remained the best by an amateur on this unique ground for fifty-seven years. Only John Newman, the Hampshire professional, had done better, and that was in 1908.

Six weeks later, on Sunday 20 July 1939, there was another unusual visit. The West Indies touring team, led by RS Grant, asked to see Broadhalfpenny Down. There was even talk beforehand of their playing a one-day game, but the only day free for the visit was a Sunday and Winchester College refused permission for a Sunday game. It was not an unusual decision for those days, but Wilf Wadham, Ivan Angell and Dick Brown were all bitterly disappointed. They dearly wanted the chance to play

The FA Cup, under the watchful eye of the local policeman, is put on display 17 June 1939, surrounded by dignitaries from the Portsmouth Football Club. The club had won it the previous month, and for the worst of reasons held it for seven years.
(Reproduced by kind permission of the Bat and Ball)

against the tourists, a chance that would never come again. Instead, they had to be content with offering the West Indies their hospitality, which was accepted. A splendid tea was laid on at the Bat and Ball, hosted by the Wadham's management and many of the regular players. The talk that afternoon was about the history of the ground but – as is the way with cricketers – the players inevitably discussed the annual match against Hambledon, which Wadham Bros had played the previous day, with even more passion. After tea, the West Indies tourists walked over the road to the hallowed turf. Like Plum Warner a few weeks earlier, the West Indians just managed to keep their shoes on. They wandered over Broadhalfpenny Down for some while, drinking in the atmosphere as thousands had done before, sharing the views Nyren and the others first saw so long before.

So desperately soon after this happy and light-hearted occasion, a dark and terrible gloom fell over all of Europe and much of the rest of the world. The Second World War started on 3 September 1939. The very soul of the free world was threatened, and all minds were now totally focused first on survival and then on victory. Cricket was immediately abandoned. But it was not forgotten over the next five years. It served mainly to provide light relief and relaxation for the troops, wherever they found themselves around the world. And that included those who found themselves stationed within walking distance of Broadhalfpenny Down.

In August 1941, as part of the war effort, the Admiralty requisitioned Leydene House, home of the Peel family who had made their fortune from linoleum in the 1920s. It was now to become the Royal Navy's Signal Training School, and it stood not a mile from Broadhalfpenny Down. Within weeks, the house was full of naval officers on signals training courses. Now and then they needed some means of relaxation, to get away from the pressures for a few hours, and it was not long

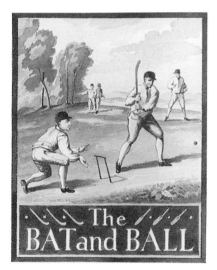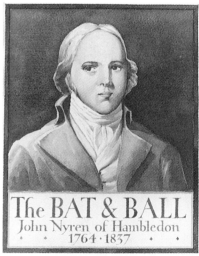

Ralph Ellis's 1939 design for the Bat and Ball pub sign. The side facing Broadhalfpenny Down is a representation of an early 18th century match. The original hangs in the pavilion at Lord's. (Reproduced by kind permission of the MCC)

before some of them realized that Broadhalfpenny Down was just down the road, unused and untended. By the following summer, an informal understanding had been reached with Winchester College that the officers could use the ground for a few matches between themselves, provided that they looked after it for the duration of the war. Once the war was over, the original lease with Wadham Brothers would be respected by all sides. And that is exactly what happened. Various departments of HMS *Mercury* (as the training school was called) played evening games against each other during the summers of 1942, 1943 and 1944. Keith Evans, who played in quite a few of them, also thinks that the odd game was played against a scratch side from Hambledon, but after all this time he cannot be absolutely certain.

Amazingly, also in 1941, Sir Jeremiah Colman found the time and resources to bring out his beautiful book *The Noble Game of Cricket* in a limited edition, which included the now much-discussed original of the supposed scene at Broadhalfpenny Down in 1777. Its very publication must represent one of the coolest examples of *sang-froid* ever demonstrated by the laid-back English gentry.

The *Daily Sketch*, however, had no such aloofness from the titanic struggle going on in Europe and elsewhere. On 11 June 1940, just a few days after the Battle of Dunkirk, it published a photograph of the pub sign at the Bat and Ball, and a few verses intended to cheer its readers. One of them read:

> If only little German boys
> Had gathered round a wicket
> We might have heard much less of guns
> And challenged them at cricket.

It is incidents like this which have, over the years, made the English both the laughing-stock and the despair of other nations. How could Hitler's Germany hope to beat such mind-boggling unconcern? Five years later, it knew the ghastly truth.

And it was time for cricket once again.

Here and Relatively Now

It was never the same again. Victory had come at a terrible price. Once the celebrations were over, reality came rushing back with the harshness of an arctic gale. It was many years before everyday life was anything like normal again, and even then it was different. Denis Compton and Bill Edrich lit up the cricketing firmament in 1947 with a summer of runs and partnerships never seen before or since in a single season. The tourists that golden summer were from South Africa, and Compton and Edrich effectively put them to the sword, just as they did almost every county that came up against all-conquering Middlesex. But for most people, the chief value of that spectacular season was to lighten the otherwise apparently endless gloom. Runs were fine in their place, and it was a joy to read the sports page – there was only one – each morning. But these extraordinary exploits on the cricket field were no substitute for cash, homes, and food in the shops. For the time being, ordinary folk had other priorities.

That did not stop the 1947 South Africans, led by Alan Melville, from taking a day away from their executioners to visit Broadhalfpenny Down, just to see it. But they did not play there, because cricket was still not permitted on a Sunday. There was, however, a sharp irony to their visit. The previous

Wilf Wadham (in a suit) surrounded by the Wadham Bros team and their visitors. This picture was taken to mark the resumption of cricket on Broadhalfpenny Down by Wadham Bros after the war, in July 1945. (Reproduced by kind permission of Peter Wadham)

Wilf Wadham tosses up at the first post-war match on Broadhalfpenny Down, July 1945. Ivan Angell, company secretary and club captain, is on the right. The visiting captain is unknown. (Reproduced by kind permission of Bob Murton)

Test team to visit but not play there had been the 1939 West Indians. Nearly half a century was to pass before the South Africans followed the West Indies onto a cricket field again, a proposition none of them would have believed at that moment.

Back at Wadham Brothers, the pre-war employees had gradually returned to start rebuilding their shattered lives and interrupted careers. Like everyone else, they were changed men. Saturday afternoons playing cricket on Broadhalfpenny Down now had much less appeal. Everyday life presented other, more pressing priorities and there was, in any case, little time and money to spare. The company's sports club gradually resumed activities and some matches were played over the next few years, but with nothing like the regularity or support that the team had enjoyed ten years earlier. Now it was a struggle. Cash was desperately short and, from the company's viewpoint, it became increasingly hard to justify expenditure on anything not directly connected with the immediate well-being of the business. Only a dwindling few employees now used the sports club, and by the end of the 1951 season the harsh decision had been taken to relinquish the lease back to Winchester College.

The Bat and Ball was still in the hands of local brewers Henty and Constable, who, that same year, embarked on a programme of restoration which developed later into a substantial expansion of the original tiny Broadhalfpenny Hutt. These improvements went on, through the subsequent change of ownership to Friary Meux, until the completion of an extensive refurbishment in 1963.

One of the most imaginative and generous decisions Henty and Constable took in those days of austerity so soon after the war was to commission a new pub sign from Ralph Ellis. He had produced a similar new sign in 1939, as part of the refurbishment masterminded by Mr Henty and his committee, and was described at that time as 'one of the country's most distinguished artists' working in the field of inn signs. But his first sign had not survived too well, and now he was commissioned to undertake another. It was to be a copy of the previous one, but his second version, still hanging there forty-

One of the Bat and Ball rugs, made in the Axminster style, but nobody knows by whom, or why. This one hangs in Australia. Others are known to be in the United States.

(Reproduced by kind permission of Bill Dean)

five years later, shows a few minor variations from the original. On one side is a portrait of John Nyren, an odd choice of subject in the circumstances as John, of course, never kept the pub. He lived there as a child but left it in 1771, when he was six years old, when his father Richard took over the George Inn, down in Hambledon village. John brought great fame to himself and to the Bat and Ball, Broadhalfpenny Down and the Hambledon club by writing about them. But it was his father who made it what it was. On the other side of the sign, Ellis created a representation of cricket being played before 1775, when the third stump was added. The original paintings by Ralph Ellis were subsequently put on permanent display in the pavilion at Lord's. They are there still.

Meanwhile, this inn sign has become the source of a mystery which is as yet unsolved. Either after Ellis's original sign had been hung in 1939, or following its replacement after the war, a carpet manufacturer using the Axminster type of weave produced a quantity of rugs measuring 41 inches x 22 inches with the cricket scene from the pub sign woven into the design.

There are rugs of this size and design known to be in the USA and Australia. But nobody now knows which manufacturer produced this rug, although it is known to be one of a set of four, all featuring designs based on pub signs. From time to time, successive landlords of the Bat and Ball have received letters or visitors claiming to have 'the rug', thinking it to be unique – and wanting to know more about it. The truth is a sad disappointment. According to Bill Dean, who lives in Victoria, Australia, they change hands at auctions there, and are classified as antiques.

During the post-war refurbishment programme, successive landlords of the Bat and Ball increasingly put on display whatever cricketing memorabilia from the glory days and afterwards they could find. Much of it can be seen there today. They also acquired various items relating to cricket in general and Hambledon in particular, on permanent loan from the MCC.

Across the road, however, there was now a problem. Just before the beginning of the 1952 season, Wadham Brothers wrote to Winchester College asking to be released from their lease at the end of that September. The letter explained that the costs of maintaining the ground were now out of all proportion to the benefits enjoyed by a dwindling number of employees. The company also offered to remove the pavilion and tool-shed at the same time. The College agreed. Harry Altham was kept abreast of these developments and immediately sprang into action, not for the first time facing the self-appointed task of saving Broadhalfpenny Down from dormancy. Winchester College would continue to own it and ensure its upkeep, so neglect was not a serious risk anymore. But could someone be found who would maintain and use it for cricket?

Altham talked to Hampshire County Cricket Club on an informal basis, but they took the view that additional responsibility for a ground miles away from Southampton and not suitable for first-class cricket was not a prospect that they could contemplate, even for so illustrious a member as their president Harry Altham. There is no firm evidence that he next approached the Hampshire Hogs, but persistent rumour suggests that he did at least talk to them. That led nowhere, too. He then talked to Hambledon Cricket Club, perhaps the most obvious choice. But these were still hard times. Few people had cars to get to Broadhalfpenny Down from the village, the club struggled to turn out one side of a weekend, and in any case it had no need of a second ground, let alone one with no electricity or water, no pavilion worth mentioning, no public transport within miles and which was inclined to be bleak and cold to boot. However attractive the historical idea might be, thank you but no thank you.

Then Harry Altham had an idea. He approached HMS *Mercury*, now firmly established just up the road from Broadhalfpenny Down in Leydene House, from where they had had the informal use of the ground from time to time during the war. The immediate response was positive. More meetings were arranged and it was not long before all the details had been worked out. Among other things, the pavilion and shed should stay. Then, when everything had been agreed, Harry Altham, writing on behalf of Winchester College, put a formal offer to HMS *Mercury* on 30 May 1952, and Captain Dawney equally formally replied in the affirmative ten days later. The deed was done, and most of the 1952 season was still left. Continuity was assured, thanks once more to the energy and influence of Harry Altham. And yet again, the Royal Navy was poised to play an important part in the history of English cricket.

The lease was actually purchased through the Captain's Fund – the personal collective resources of the wardroom officers, whether on the permanent staff or on courses – and not by the navy itself. For the next few years, however, the general upkeep of the ground was taken under the wing of HMS *Mercury*'s groundstaff, with the cricket itself being funded by the ward room.

The gardeners at Leydene House willingly found some spare time to look after this famous addition to their responsibilities. They even devised a system for carting water down to the ground in bowsers to help keep the square in reasonable condition during the dry spells. Later on, the head groundsman at Southampton University, Bob Barratt, was persuaded to come up to Broadhalfpenny Down and advise on its improvement. He prescribed a dosing of Mendip loam to stiffen the surface, and during the years it was applied this appeared to help. It is a prescription which is now in use again. As every groundsman knows, the battle to make and keep downland turf playable is never-ending.

All the talk in 1952 about the future of Broadhalfpenny Down raised a number of other questions, too. Down the road at Brook Lane, some of the older members of Hambledon Cricket Club half-remembered the club's ownership of, and responsibility for, the monument and its fencing. But nobody was quite sure exactly what the legal position was, particularly so far as the fencing was concerned. None of the relevant papers could be found. So in July 1952, the club wrote to the College seeking clarification on ownership of the fence around the monument. 'We think it is our liability,' they offered, and asked the College to confirm whether this was so. The letter then went on to seek permission to repair it. It was, and they did.

It was to be another seven years before the pavilion and toolshed were finally purchased by the new leaseholders. Some time later, HMS *Mercury* told Winchester College that the pavilion had been refurbished 'at considerable expense', a phrase which disguised an expenditure of over £1000, raised by a club appeal to rebuild and re-thatch what had become an embarrassingly decrepit and scarcely useable structure. Nonetheless, the club 'hoped to spend more in future to put and maintain the ground in first-class condition'.

Over the next few years, a number of grand cricket matches were arranged on Broadhalfpenny Down to celebrate special occasions. Wartime food rationing was still in force, of course, and down the road at Hambledon the cricket club there was still having to apply for a licence from the local authority to supply teas to their visiting teams. These licences covered all their home games and were issued at the beginning of each season. One-off special matches each required their own licence to supply food to visitors, whether or not they paid for it.

In 1951, that was just one of the many obstacles facing John Goldsmith, who later wrote the story of Hambledon village and unravelled the mystery of the Madge toast – when the captain of HMS *Mercury* asked him to arrange a cricket match on Broadhalfpenny Down as part of the Festival of Britain. The whole idea behind the Festival was to cheer the nation up, and what could be more appropriate in Hambledon than a period cricket match? The game was to be between Hambledon and a team from HMS *Mercury*. They borrowed the team-name invented in 1931 by John Goldsmith's father for the navy side raised by HMS *Nelson*. This time it was HMS *Mercury* playing as the Ancient Mariners. The match took place in glorious sunshine, with both sides in period costume especially hired for the day and the Ancient Mariners sporting greased pigtails and bare feet. A few less-than-hardy tars cheated, however, and shoes were surreptitiously worn on the outfield. The truly cowardly even wore them to bat.

With great good fortune, John Goldsmith managed to trace Richard Nyren's great-great-great-grandson, who was invited to bowl the first over. Unfortunately, he was not treated with the respect appropriate to the occasion, and the first ball was unceremoniously hooked to leg for two. The next ball was spooned tamely to cover – who was this batting? – until the umpire belatedly thought it best to call 'no ball'. The rest of the over passed without incident.

Like the matches twenty years before, the score was notched on sticks which were sold off afterwards. The whole day was in aid of naval charities, which benefited from a good crowd in generous mood. As usual, the day brought its share of notables to the ground, including this time the granddaughter of the former England captain HDG Leveson Gower. Wren Ana Leveson Gower was based at HMS *Mercury* at the time.

On Saturday 30 May 1953, the ground was the venue for the second period-costume match within two years. Once again a licence to serve food to visitors was required from the local authority, even though this match was to be staged as part of the local celebrations of the coronation of Queen Elizabeth II, which was to take place during the following week. This match

Both teams at the monument for the Festival of Britain match, 30 May 1951. Hambledon are wearing jockey hats, while the Ancient Mariners sport hats of the 1790s. A latter-day Piccolo Jim echoes the picture taken on New Year's Day 1920.
(Reproduced by kind permission of the Bat and Ball)

Foolhardy or brave, a bare-footed Ancient Mariner strikes out during the match.
(Reproduced by kind permission of the Bat and Ball)

Hambledon and the Ancient Mariners gather for the Festival of Britain match, 30 May 1951. Fourth from the left is Ron Barrett, father of Colin. (Reproduced by kind permission of Portsmouth Evening News*)*

on Broadhalfpenny Down was between Hambledon and a side calling themselves the Ancient Firemen.

They were drawn from the fire office of the Commercial Union insurance company, which had a history of providing fire insurance going back to 1696. It was known as the fire office because, in the earliest days of its life, the company found that it was cheaper to employ firemen than to pay claims. William Varney, then manager of the company's Southampton branch, first suggested the idea for the match, and he raised the visiting side from within the company.

Alarm bells of a different kind were ringing at Hambledon long before the event. Minutes of the committee meetings during the months prior to the 1953 game talk of the 1951 match as having been simple and largely resourced by HMS *Mercury*. The 1953 game, on the other hand 'is a very different proposition. We will need help.' Hambledon's confidence that they had matters fully under control was not helped when they learned that Commercial Union were to spend over £100 on costumes for their players. This news rankled somewhat, since

The Ancient Mariners arrive at Broadhalfpenny Down in horse-drawn cart for
the Festival of Britain match against Hambledon, 30 May 1951.
(Reproduced by kind permission of the Bat and Ball)

the Hambledon team were to make do with simple waistcoats, breeches and caps hired from a firm of theatrical costumiers in Brighton. George Beagley, the local tailor, was asked to measure everybody for their kit. When he arrived at the house of umpire Frank Brown, he found Frank flat on his back in bed, suffering from a fever. George explained that he had come to measure him up for his smock. Then he paused, and finally added: 'For your *umpire's* smock.' Frank's initial reaction was horror: 'Good Lord, George, I thought the undertaker had sent you.'

Over the next few weeks, minutes of the club's committee meetings refer with increasing frequency and terseness to the efforts being made throughout the planning of this match to keep the costs and risks under control. Despite risk-management being Mr Varney's stock-in-trade, his hosts were finally in no doubt that he was going too far. 'His schemes are being modified,' says an exasperated note of one committee meeting, leaving the reader in little doubt about the outcome of that particular session.

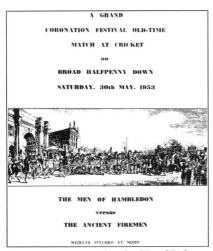

A GRAND
CORONATION FESTIVAL OLD-TIME
MATCH AT CRICKET
on
BROAD HALFPENNY DOWN
SATURDAY, 30th MAY, 1953

THE MEN OF HAMBLEDON
versus
THE ANCIENT FIREMEN
WICKETS PITCHED AT NOON

Programme cover for the Hambledon v The Ancient Firemen match, 30 May 1953.

They were right, too. On the day, a cold wind blew and rain spoiled the whole event. A hardy few people turned up to watch, many of them also dressed in period costume. The teams were driven up to the ground from Hambledon village in horse-drawn carriages, having changed at the New Inn and taken a stirrup cup to fortify themselves against the cold before setting off. The carriages continued to fetch and carry people between the village and the ground all day long, despite the weather.

Six-year-old Graham Barrett was invited to bowl the first ball of the match. He was the Hambledon Cricket Club's mascot at the time, and his family was steeped in the club. His father Ron had played for years and did so that day, his mother Ida scored, and his elder brother Colin was later to become one of Hambledon's greatest captains. Young Graham was not first choice to open the bowling, however. Mr Varney had wanted to get Harry Altham or Sir Pelham Warner, and when neither of them was able to oblige he suggested bringing back Richard Nyren's great-great-great-grandson to perform the honour again. The programme was printed with the announcement that Mr Varney himself would perform the deed. In the event, Graham bowled an over of underarm lobs splendidly, and must be one of the few six-year-olds ever to be the subject of a John Arlott commentary, either on the cricket field or off it. Arlott often used to commentate for charity events at that time, and always brought his own brand of gentle humour and sharp observation to add to the proceedings. His presence behind the microphone on this day at Broadhalfpenny Down gave great pleasure to the crowd, especially when the local hunt streamed across the downs during the game with their red coats flying and their horns calling the hounds to the chase. Not even that nonplussed so accomplished a commentator. John Arlott added another dimension to the match that day, according to those who were there, and he later helped to encourage a generous collection for charity.

The match was, once again, played under 1770 rules, with all the attendant frustrations of no middle stump and no boundaries. Hambledon batted first and made 208 for 7 wickets. The Ancient Firemen replied with 169 for 8 by close of play. It was a draw, and the downpour after tea had finally ruined what was intended to be a rare spectacle. A few days later, the weather was to do the same again and spoil another rare spectacle – the coronation of the new Queen.

During the late 1950s, the Cricket Society hired the ground at Broadhalfpenny Down once a year, for a match of their own. They came down from London in a hired coach, as did their opponents. They called themselves 'The Ablative Absolutes'. Their headquarters and watering-hole was the Warwick Arms public house in Earls Court, London, complete with heavily used shoveha'penny board, from whence they ventured once a year for this particular game of cricket on Broadhalfpenny Down. According to the fixture secretary of the Cricket Society at the time, Tony Robinson, the Ablative Absolutes 'seemed to consist of thespians, schoolmasters and Australian dentists. But they certainly played cricket with their boots on, and were very hard to beat.' The presence in those days of plantain and other weeds growing thoughtfully on a good length appears to have helped the cause of the Cricket Society, since they had bowlers steady enough to take full advantage of such natural, or should it be unnatural, hazards. Michael Watson-Smyth could produce shooters almost to order off such a promising surface, and turned these annual matches more than once. Five for very few seemed par for the course in those days. And the batting side getting past 100 before being all out was achievement indeed. Nothing much had changed, it seems, since the days of Wadham Bros before the war.

The 1956 match produced one of those spectacles for which Broadhalfpenny Down is now famous. The Cricket Society's team that year included the seventy-five-year-old Garfield

Hambly, who was reputed to have played for the Gentlemen of Ireland in 1904. He also understudied Barry Fitzgerald in the Hollywood movie *Going My Way*, which starred Bing Crosby. All of which has little to do with his arrival for this match, despite his advanced years, on a powerful motor bike which he had ridden up from Bristol, some ninety miles away, that morning. With panache that would have done credit to Robinson Crusoe who had arrived in similar fashion a quarter of a century earlier, he promptly put on a pair of highly-polished brown, yes brown, leather pads, marched out to bat and immediately ran out Chris Box-Grainger, doyen of the Cricket Society and a powerful batsman, before he had so much as played himself in. It was a long way to come for such a performance.

Dragging such enthusiasts away from the Bat and Ball after these games was never easy. And one year it was nearly impossible. The fun went on late into the evening. Eventually, only the coach parties were left. The bar was long-since closed and the drinking had gone on longer than it should, not that that was anything new. When, at last, the diehards of the two teams finally strolled out of the doorway of the Bat and Ball and into the mists of a late-evening sunset, what should they see but a scholarly figure coming towards them from the distant boundary. He was clutching a trowel in a manner that displayed elements of a guilt-laden Macbeth, the winner of an egg-and-spoon race, and a cat that had just been at the cream. In the gathering evening mists, they could make out the shape of one John Edwards. He had dug up a piece of Broad-halfpenny Down and was making off with it.

John Edwards, known to his friends as Jack, was an Australian, but not a dentist. He had just played his last game at Broadhalfpenny Down and was going home later that year. Much as Englishmen might disbelieve it, Australians can be sentimental, even about cricket. This parting was too much for Edwards to bear. The idea that he might never see Broadhalfpenny Down again had reduced this fine upstanding man to subterfuge. He had taken a square of turf – thought-fully from the boundary's edge, so as not to inconvenience anyone – and it was going back to Australia with him. Right up to his death, in December 1995 at the age of 85, it was still one of his proudest possessions, although in later years he was somewhat less ready to admit to his innocent mischief that night. He once suggested that it was a ghostly copy of himself who did the dastardly deed. Either way, a piece of Broadhalfpenny Down has been part of a private collection of memorabilia in Victoria, Australia, for over forty years, and will probably become a much sought-after relic now that John Edwards has finished with it. Of course, there is another possible end to this story. Edwards's local cricket club, Oakleigh, recently named its new ground the Jack Edwards Oval. No, no, they couldn't have...

The first recorded match played by the Hambledon club took place in 1756, against Dartford, Kent. Exactly 200 years later, the two clubs planned a repeat of that original match. Again it was to be played at Dartford, but the weather ruined a wonderful celebration. Not a ball was bowled. During a long, wet, depressing day, the two sides decided to attempt a repeat, at Hambledon, the following summer, this time hopefully without the rain. As luck would have it, 1957 was the benefit year of that long-standing and popular Hampshire wicket-keeper/batsman Leo Harrison. What better than a match on Broadhalfpenny Down as part of his benefit programme? Hambledon, the county and Leo Harrison quickly agreed the idea. So when they arrived at Broadhalfpenny Down, somewhat to their surprise Dartford found the Hambledon side that summer was no longer the one which had watched the rain run down

Grand Bi-Centenary Cricket Match

(1757 — 1957)

on Broad Halfpenny Down

Sunday, 14th July, 1957.

HAMBLEDON v. DARTFORD

Programme cover for the bi-centenary (plus one year) Hambledon v Dartford match, 14 July 1957.

their pavilion windows a year previously. Suddenly it had been transformed by the inclusion of county players. Desmond Eagar was to captain a team which now included the West Indian test player Roy Marshall, Colin Ingleby-Mackenzie, Jack Bailey, Tom Pearce and several others from the county circuit.

John Arlott, who lived not far away at Alresford, once again came over for the day and provided commentary in his own inimitable style, making fun of the players and encouraging the collection for Leo Harrison's benefit. Once again the weather was not kind and although play was possible, the crowd was nothing like the size that would have been expected if the sun had shone. The organisers had hoped to collect more than the £70 finally given to Harrison.

On 21 June 1958, for no discernible reason, a repeat of the 1951 match between the Ancient Mariners and Hambledon took place on Broadhalfpenny Down. Of course, by now, the Ancient Mariners, a thin disguise for the HMS *Mercury* side, were playing on their home ground. The laws of 1770 were used for the match, and the players again dressed in period clothing, complete with greased pigtails. The preliminaries were all observed with great thoroughness and respect for the traditions of the 1770s. A bat was used for the toss, the winning captain selected the position of the pitch, and all the bowling was underarm in four-ball overs. The batsmen did not wear any protective pads and used bats curved in the original shape. And as had happened so often in the past on this same ground, the ball frequently passed between the stumps, much to the annoyance of the bowling side.

There were no boundaries, of course, and all the notches were run until the ball was returned to one of the wickets. Modern obstacles like cars and picnic hampers had to be ignored by the fielders, who were left to find their own way through the maze of obstructions around the ground. One hefty blow which went into the road earned seven notches as the fielders struggled to find a way through, over or round the hedge. A stick of notches was cut by Roger Durnford and later sold for charity, although the poor weather on the day kept the crowds down and the takings for naval charities that much less. The match was played, again in keeping with the manner of the day, over four innings. The Ancient Mariners made 88 and 108. Hambledon got 100 and 97 for an unknown number of wickets in scarcely more than an hour, to win with three minutes to spare. Old Everlasting himself, Tom Walker, would have watched this veritable blitz of runs in utter disbelief.

Apart from these few one-off games, most of the 1950s passed with little more than a regular stream of evening games played by the ward room of HMS *Mercury* against local clubs and other organizations capable of turning out a scratch side. The sole purpose of these limited-overs evening games was relaxation and enjoyment, followed by a few beers in the Bat and Ball afterwards. They were great fun and ensured that the ground continued in regular use and was kept...well, 'Bristol fashion'. But the matches themselves need not detain us.

On the other hand, the new and now regular cricket activity on Broadhalfpenny Down was beginning to make an impact on another level. Word spread that there were games to be played on Broadhalfpenny Down. The keenest of the navy's cricketers now sought reasons to spend time at HMS *Mercury*; many local clubs asked for matches; and requests for games started arriving from farther afield.

By 1959, the level of interest and activity had grown to such an extent that it provoked some thoughtful wardroom discussion between Bill Wren, Bob Coomber, Norman Woodcock and Pip Paltridge, keen cricketers all. They knew very well that Broadhalfpenny Down was something special. It was far more than just a playing field conveniently located at the end of the road; more, too, than a place for a few casual evening games and hockey in the winter. This was unique cricket history, and they had it in their hands. If anything was to be done about its future, it was up to them – and it had to be done sooner rather than later. Twice in the recent past Hambledon Cricket Club had approached Winchester College to ask about the possibility of taking over the lease of Broadhalfpenny Down. They were now a stronger and better-resourced club than the one which had so comprehensively turned down Harry Altham's enquiry a few years before, and if

HMS *Mercury* were not going to make any more use of the ground than a few evening matches, they, Hambledon, could and would do so. This news had its effect two miles up the road.

After much discussion, these four men decided to form the Broadhalfpenny Brigands Cricket Club. They had convinced themselves that the right vehicle for the future of the ground was an independent cricket club for which Broadhalfpenny Down would be 'home', and a club which recognized and cared for the historical importance of the ground. As luck would have it, they reached this conclusion at just the right time. Not long afterwards, the number of naval personnel at HMS *Mercury* had risen to a level which allowed the Ministry of Defence, under its own archaic rules, to support the adoption of the Broadhalfpenny Down ground as a second sports-facility for the naval station.

The Ministry of Defence formally took over the lease and responsibility for the ground from HMS *Mercury*, and a new clause was inserted in the lease granted by Winchester College. This permitted the ground to be sub-let to the Broadhalfpenny Brigands Cricket Club. Thus the four founders achieved three important goals. First, the ground now had a cricket club based on it for the first time since 1792. Secondly, they had solved the never-ending problem for the ward room created by the comings and goings of talented and keen cricketers. Sometimes the ward room enjoyed the company of guest players who were playing first-class cricket as and when their naval duties permitted. Mike Ainsworth of Worcestershire and Gerry Tordoff, the Somerset left-hander, both played for HMS *Mercury* from time to time, and their absence or presence inevitably produced extreme fluctuations in the team's strength. It was difficult to manage a fixture list in such circumstances. Continuity of people and standards was only possible with greater flexibility of membership, and that meant disconnecting the club from the navy, at least in part. Now that this had been achieved, the club could invite non-naval personnel to join, which in turn would ensure that its playing strength was more consistent. Thirdly, a structure now existed which meant that those who used the ground would in future contribute to the costs.

One of the earliest issues to arise during the formation of the new club was the question of a name. Broadhalfpenny must form a part. There was no dispute about that. After all, it was one of the most famous words in the cricket lexicon. But how to fit in the naval connection without making it all-embracing? In the end, the irreverence of the word Brigands, with its connotations of piracy, seemed to fit the bill admirably. That was to be it: the Broadhalfpenny Brigands Cricket Club. Why, it even signalled an indication of the club's attitude to playing the game. Two other important decisions were taken at the same time. The president of the club would always be the captain of HMS *Mercury*, at least so long as the naval station existed. Next, the club would always play its matches within striking distance of liquid refreshment. That meant a six-hit. The Bat and Ball just qualified. After all, it depended who was batting...

With a neat sense of history, the then landlord of the Bat and Ball, Leslie Wilson, a passionately keen supporter of the game who took great pride in following Richard Nyren at the pub, offered his services to the new club and was immediately elected treasurer. He also volunteered to supply the teas and other sustenance needed during and after each game. Over the next few years, Leslie and Flora Wilson were to prove themselves more than worthy heirs to Richard and Frances Nyren in that respect. Their catering and hospitality were to become legendary. They also encouraged the cricketing fraternity to visit the pub, and Leslie would often call Patrick Glennie, a long-time Brigands member who lived just down the road in Clanfield, whenever a group of cricket enthusiasts arrived from anywhere in the world to see the ground and have a drink in the Bat and Ball. Patrick Glennie provided instant history lessons on these occasions. Few in his audiences knew much about the place. Most simply knew that it was an important part of the history of the game, and just wanted to know more. Glennie would talk to them for as long as they were willing to listen. Much later, after Leslie Wilson retired, he quietly asked Patrick Glennie to send him a fixture card each year so that he could sit at home in Dorset and visualize the men and the game each Saturday, now that he was unable to be there himself. Like so many others, he too had come to love Broadhalfpenny Down and could hardly bear to leave it. Wilson received a card every year until his death. Patrick Glennie never forgot.

So by 1961, the Broadhalfpenny Brigands Cricket Club was up and away. Within a short time the club had enrolled some twenty-five or so players, several of them civilians and new to Broadhalfpenny Down. It was the start of a process which has never ceased, and thirty-five years later the club now boasts some forty playing members, raising one Sunday team each weekend, with a number of midweek and evening games throughout each season. Of course, the ground has never been particularly suitable for league cricket, and the membership is still focused on playing country house or village cricket in the traditional spirit of the game. That attracts players who can no longer expect to contribute to the pressured environment of a league game, and those who welcome the chance to leave league behind once in a while to play in a more relaxed style.

The drawback of such an approach was acknowledged from the outset. It would be difficult to attract sufficient young members to guarantee continuity and strength. The young should learn their cricket on better wickets than are possible on downland turf. It is a problem that will probably never be fully overcome on Broadhalfpenny Down. But the Brigands' survival for as long as Nyren's team played on the ground, and its vigour nowadays, suggests that the steady inflow of maturer members will continue into the future, more than enough to replace those who have finally decided to hang up their boots.

The founder members also decided to give the Broadhalfpenny Brigands an emblem which reflected their approach to the game. It was to be 'an old time wicket, a bat and bail, a foaming beer tankard on either side, all on a dark green ground'. In the early days of the club, a few brave wives produced some highly individualistic versions of this design on ties for their husbands to wear on the appropriate occasions. But in 1973, the navy once again provided an ingenious answer to the now pressing issue of a standard and widely available club tie. John Roskill, a member who had served at HMS

Mercury, was posted to the island of Mauritius, to command the Royal Navy's Communications Station there. Soon after his arrival in the middle of the Indian Ocean, the secretary of the Broadhalfpenny Brigands, Bryan Burns, received a letter from Roskill saying that there were ladies in Mauritius who were highly-skilled embroiderers and could reproduce any design to order. He had shown them his own version of the Brigands tie and they had convinced him that copying it was no problem. 'Send plain green ties,' he suggested. Bryan Burns bought a box of fifty, and then had a flash of inspiration. He called up the Royal Navy's Fleet Programmer and asked which ship would next be sailing to Mauritius. With ingenuity for which the Royal Navy is famous, Bryan Burns had that box of ties on board when the ship weighed anchor in Portsmouth. Some months later, John Roskill used the same exclusive delivery service to return the ties, all now neatly and uniformly carrying the Brigands design. The cost added to each tie was precisely sixpence.

Around this time, Lord Bessborough invited the Brigands to play at Stansted Park against the staff on his estate. The invitation was accepted with enthusiasm, until one of the founding members landed himself with the unenviable task of reminding his lordship's estate manager that the Brigands had a condition of play in their constitution to the effect that no match could be played beyond a six-hit of liquid refreshment. Grand though the ground at Stansted Park was, and generous though the invitation was, indeed, without wishing to be in any way disrespectful or churlish, well...there was a slight problem. Estate managers are more than equal to such moments of crisis, of course. This was not a problem at all. Come the day, honour was satisfied all round. Carefully set up on tables behind both sightscreens were barrels of ale, and a number of tankards instantly ready for use. Most were beer-stained long before the match was concluded.

Like all local cricket clubs, the Broadhalfpenny Brigands has had its ups and downs over the years. And here is yet another coincidence in this long story of coincidences. Almost exactly 200 years after that crisis of 1769–71 hit Hambledon and

Richard Nyren revived the club at the beginning of its greatest decade, a similar fate befell the present incumbents on Broadhalfpenny Down. The Brigands went through something of a slump in the early 1970s. But once again, self-help and renewed vigour came to the rescue. A small group of members, including that still energetically supportive treasurer and publican, Leslie Wilson; two of the original founders, Bill Wren and Bob Coomber; Ken Bowell who was teaching at Roedean; and Bryan Burns, who was then stationed at HMS *Mercury*, took on the self-appointed task of generating a revival. They effectively started with a clean sheet of paper, and jogged their collective memories for members, addresses and phone numbers with the aid of many a pint at the Bat and Ball. It was a slog, but they turned the club around.

As well as drawing back some old faces, they also took a number of decisions. A renewed effort was needed to develop the club's fixtures, with an eye to the long-term future. In particular, since civilian members were to be vigorously encouraged to join, the club would seek more demanding weekend fixtures to encourage them. After that process had been started, each would feed off the other, or so the thinking went. These stalwarts also set out to make the club more business-like and efficient. Match fees, subscriptions and AGMs were all introduced. To encourage attendance at AGMs, the then chaplain of HMS *Mercury*, Bernard Marshall, combined the harvest festival service each autumn with the Brigands AGM immediately afterwards. Since drinks were to follow, and as he always managed to preach an appropriately brief but relevant cricketing sermon each year, attendance did indeed improve.

Taken together, all these changes had the right effect. Within a couple of seasons, the Brigands had largely achieved the targets they had set themselves. By the mid 1970s, they had a good quality of weekend cricket throughout the season, a larger and stronger playing strength, and the vigorous support of a scrupulous umpire. Don Rock's umpiring helped to raise the playing standards of the club, created a good atmosphere on and off the pitch, and helped achieve the bonus of better relations with nearby clubs, particularly with the Hampshire Hogs and Hambledon.

The first man to join the revived Brigands was Anthony Banes-Walker, who had first played on Broadhalfpenny Down for Romany. He was later to become the first non-navy member to be elected chairman of the club, a post he holds to this day. In essence, the Broadhalfpenny Brigands had grown up. They were now a strong cricket club playing relaxed, competitive amateur cricket in a good atmosphere and in keeping with the best traditions of the game. They played on a unique historical ground and with a world-famous pub literally just across the road. The maturing process had taken twenty years. Not only was the fixture list stronger and more attractive to prospective members, the Brigands could now expect to win a fair share of these new and better matches as well. The one worry remaining was the squeezing-out of a few long-standing but less talented members. The continuation of the evening fixture-list was encouraged to meet their needs.

Both before and after this catharsis in the club's history, the Brigands received a steady stream of enquiries from clubs wanting to arrange a fixture on Broadhalfpenny Down. They came from all over the world, and still do. And while it is entirely understandable why cricketers of all ages and standards would want to play on this ground, the present playing facilities make it impossible, even if the Brigands had the human resources to cope. Sadly, there are always going to be disappointments.

But many teams do play here each season, and others visit just once. Over the years, there have inevitably been some remarkable matches and incidents, but perhaps none more so than the experience of Ray Lindwall, formerly Australia's most feared and fastest opening bowler of the late 1940s and early 1950s. He was then working in England, and turned out for the Lord's Taverners in one of the regular annual matches they played on Broadhalfpenny Down in the 1960s and 1970s. Many of the earlier games were broadcast on ITV, which in those days had little else to fill a Sunday afternoon in summer.

This particular Sunday was 10 September 1961. Ray Lindwall was bowling down the hill in that distinctive, silky approach to the crease of his, with all the whispering menace of an express train. Some of the pace of ten years before had gone, but little of the skill. He was still a formidable opening bowler. Even now, when he delivered it, the ball sped in a low, deceptive arc and seemed to glance off the pitch like a flat pebble over water. At its best, Ray Lindwall's bowling still retained that 'now you see it, now you don't' quality about it, and woe betide any batsman who was not fully prepared at the moment of delivery.

Today, Aussie faced Aussie. At the crease was a certain Wally Rothwell, a born games player, good enough to play first-class cricket, though he never did. He was seconded to HMS *Mercury* from the Royal Australian Navy, and played regularly for the Brigands during the few years he was there. On this particular Sunday, he opened the batting for the Brigands with Mike Ainsworth, the Worcestershire opener. So, Lindwall to Rothwell. The delivery was short and very fast. On the downland turf, it stopped and reared slightly. Rothwell was ready. The bat flashed across his body faster than the eye could follow, and a ferocious hook caught the ball exactly right. It flew high over the outfield, over the boundary, over the pavilion, over the grass beyond, over the hedge, over the road, and finally over the car park of the Bat and Ball. When it finally crashed into the top of the trees bordering the field behind the car park, it was still going up. It scored six. It was worth twelve and, time was, it would have got them on Broadhalfpenny Down. Afterwards, Lindwall said that he had never been hit so hard by any batsman, anywhere, in the whole of his career, even including a well-remembered Hassett hook off the young Lindwall in 1945.

The Taverners games of that era were always big occasions on Broadhalfpenny Down. In addition to the television coverage, which itself brought the crowds in their hundreds, the Taverners fielded sides full of showbiz and sporting fame. A whole host of former England Test players appeared during those years, including bowlers Alf Gover, Jim Laker, John Warr and Jack Flavell, batsmen Jack Robertson, Raman

Subba Row and Ken Barrington, all-rounders Doug Insole and Alan Watkins, and wicket-keeper Arthur McIntyre. And on the ground which can claim to have produced the first and greatest cricket captain of them all, Richard Nyren, another great captain appeared for the first and only time in 1970. Stuart Surridge played on Broadhalfpenny Down that year. He will forever be remembered as the inspirational captain of Surrey who led the county to a unique sequence of five successive county championships in the 1950s, and who proved once again that it is great captains who produce great sides from the talent they encourage, nurture and lead, and not the other way around. Two hundred years might have separated Richard Nyren and Stuart Surridge in time, but nothing separated them on the cricket field. They were kindred spirits.

Meanwhile, the many showbiz stars who played during those years read like the line-up for an evening of light entertainment. Perhaps the top of the bill was the much-loved former Goon, Harry (later Sir Harry) Secombe, who played on Broadhalfpenny Down on three occasions. He had strong support. Also appearing were the comedians and comic actors Brian (later Lord) Rix, Ian Carmichael, Leslie Crowther, Roy Castle, Nicholas Parsons, Bill Pertwee, Bernard Cribbens and a whole host of other actors, writers and presenters, to say nothing of the many former county players who also took part every year. Little wonder, then, that the boys with their autograph books had a field day every year.

But these events were not just about big names, important and welcome though they were. They produced some terrific matches, too. Brigands were reminded at the start of each match that they should finally allow the Taverners to win, but that was never permitted without a good fight. Sometimes defeat was unavoidable anyway, particularly when some of the less extrovert Brigands found themselves walking out to bat, or chasing a high catch, knowing that half of England was watching them on television. It was apt to produce nerves in even the toughest of men. Taverners were used to living their lives in a goldfish bowl. The Brigands were not. The Taverners also knew how to manage a game. Author John Goldsmith,

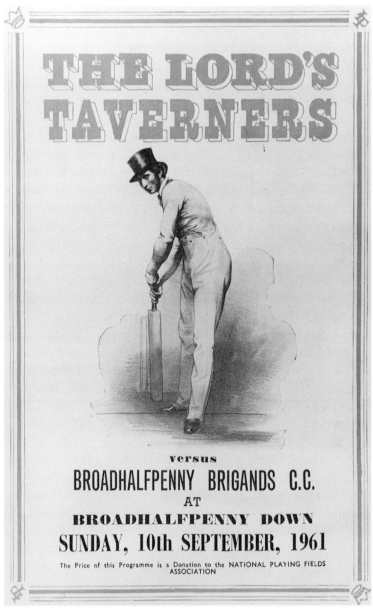

One of the many programmes produced for the matches featuring the Lord's Taverners on Broadhalfpenny Down throughout the 1960s. This was the game in which Lindwall was hooked for the biggest six ever hit off his bowling.

(Reproduced by kind permission of Bryan Burns)

playing for the Brigands in 1962, found himself facing Raman Subba Row's gentle leg-breaks when he arrived at the wicket. He confesses to having not seen the first, but comedian Les Dawson, keeping wicket, was good enough to take it cleanly, and quick enough to 'forget' to take the bails off as Goldsmith floundered outside his crease. The purpose of the day was entertainment, not victory.

Nevertheless, between 1960 and 1972, the Lord's Taverners won nine of the thirteen games they played against the Brigands and lost two, with one match drawn and the last abandoned because of rain. Best of all, of course, were the gates, which produced substantial contributions to the charities supported by the Lord's Taverners. Nobody now knows exactly how much they raised, but it ran into many thousands of pounds over those years. Eventually, however, the Brigands had to face up to the fact that, with the club itself now struggling for survival, the television interest long gone, and the crowds less keen to watch amateurs now that the one-day professional game offered an alternative, these matches must come to an end. It was a decision reached with reluctance, but the wet and abandoned game of 1972 proved to be decisive. It was to be sixteen years before the Lord's Taverners were to play on Broadhalfpenny Down again, when the owners of the Bat and Ball, Friary Meux, invited them for a match.

During the 1960s and early 70s, though, there had been some great moments to enjoy, endless fun on the field, great names to watch, and spectacular incidents like Rothwell's six. One delightful story involved Harry Secombe, when he was bowled first ball. Bill Wren, one of the founders of the Brigands, was umpiring at the bowler's end, and for a split-second his mind was elsewhere. The bails fell, Secombe stood there dumbfounded, and a hideous hush enveloped the ground. This was not supposed to happen. Then, as if galvanized by the awesome silence, Bill Wren suddenly sprang back to life and finally roared a now long-overdue 'no ball'. The crowd roared its approval. Harry Secombe looked mightily relieved, the players on the field howled with laughter and one or two

Brigands walked up to Bill Wren, prodded him carefully and asked him if he was all right. He quickly reassured them that he had merely been day-dreaming. Another time, having confessed in the dressing-room beforehand that nowadays he could scarcely see the ball because his eyesight was so bad, Harry Secombe was dismissed without troubling the scorers. He left the field muttering what was clearly intended as a stage whisper. Long before he had reached the pavilion, the whole crowd had joined in. 'Tennis is my game...tennis is my game...' followed him off the field with affectionate applause.

Yet another of the coincidences which permeate this story occurred in the match played on Sunday 4 September 1966. The Taverners side included David (later Sir David) Frost; Jack Robertson, who, opening for Middlesex during that phenomenal 1947 season, acted as *hors d'oeuvre* to Edrich and Compton, and Charles Fry, grandson of the CB Fry who featured so prominently in the events of 1908. That year, CB Fry had scored 84 not out to set up Hambledon's win. Here, fifty-eight years later almost to the day, his grandson out-scored him with 92. The following year he got another 79.

As with all such charity matches, the professionals enjoyed doing the things they were never allowed to do normally. The batsmen bowled, the bowlers scored the runs, and the wicket-keepers bowled leg-breaks to the despair of those inadequate substitutes now struggling behind the stumps. The Taverners games were no different. Surrey and England batsman Ken Barrington took 5 for 15 in 1965, Jack Robertson took 5 for 39 in 1968, and Ray Lindwall consoled himself with a fifty (68 to be exact) after Wally Rothwell had treated him with such disdain in 1961. That was in a match in which over 600 runs were scored in a day and the Brigands accidentally won by three runs when Vic Ransom caught a sharp chance in the slips off the bowling of Bill Wren, and in the heat of the moment forgot to drop it.

The biggest individual score recorded on Broadhalfpenny Down in modern times, and probably the highest ever made on the ground, occurred in the 1968 Lord's Taverners game. Despite the exceptionally tight bowling of Jack Robertson,

Brian Shattock scored 158 for the Brigands out of their 259, but still finished on the losing side. The Taverners had set a target of 285, of which Dennis Silk, later president of the MCC and subsequently chairman of the Test and County Cricket Board, scored 102.

One of the many other big occasions on Broadhalfpenny Down each summer involves the annual visit of the London New Zealand side. When the fixture was first arranged in the 1960s, it achieved such a high profile among the New Zealand community in London that quite a crowd came down to watch the match. The New Zealand High Commissioner in London was regularly the guest of HMS *Mercury*, and the ward room hosted a lunch for all their guests each year. They were, and still are, one of the strongest visiting sides on the Brigands fixture list, particularly since so many young New Zealanders now play in the English cricket leagues.

Peter Tuke, who has been a Brigand member since 1960, recalls one hysterical conversation he had one year during that decade with a particularly effective and extremely quick fast-bowler who appeared for London New Zealand. It was a piece of repartee which would not have disgraced Monty Python. Someone told Tuke that this young, athletic man was also a ballet dancer – a piece of information which Peter Tuke greeted with utter disbelief. So he decided to test the proposition. He approached the young man, and asked him with as straight a face as he could muster in the circumstances: 'I'm told you're a ballet dancer as well.'

'Yes, I am,' was the reply.

'It's pretty unusual for an opening bowler to be a ballet dancer,' said Tuke, innocently.

'It's pretty unusual for a ballet dancer to be an opening bowler,' came the reply, as quick as a flash. Then the young man added, ruefully, 'It's pretty unusual for a New Zealander to be a ballet dancer, as well.'

There was no answer to that.

Another New Zealand player who appeared a few times in the 1960s and 70s was a young, single businessman who had made a great deal of money in New Zealand and had come to

England to enjoy himself for a few years. He went to the opera, the theatre and an endless round of parties all winter, and played cricket all summer. This was his idea of heaven. One year, he arrived at Broadhalfpenny Down for the annual London New Zealand match having driven straight from an all-night party in London. His lifestyle appeared not to affect his cricket, for he promptly scored 50, took a couple of wickets and then set off to drive straight back to London for another party. He was last rumoured to have bought a four-wheel-drive vehicle and be setting off overland to Singapore, en route for New Zealand. The rumour was further embellished by the news that he was being accompanied by two beautiful young ladies. Not surprisingly, nobody at Broadhalfpenny Down ever heard of him again.

The London New Zealand fixture took something of a knock in 1995 when the match was due to be played on the same day as the Rugby Union World Cup Final. Worse, the kick-off was during the afternoon, since there is no significant time-difference between England and South Africa, where the host nation were playing the All Blacks. All the New Zealanders in the world wanted to watch the match, and those in London were not prepared to travel down to Broadhalfpenny Down that day for a game of cricket. There was a more important match to attend, even if it were only via television. The Bat and Ball offered to set up a television in the bar, the Brigands offered to rearrange the match with a morning innings for one side, and an evening innings for the other, but all to no avail. No New Zealander was going anywhere that day. The match was off, thank you. By way of rough justice, the South Africans won. The result had said it all.

Next year, the Brigands did not remind their guests of the previous year's disaster. Instead, another drama unfolded. It can truly be claimed that Christopher Bazalgette became a legend in his own cricketing lifetime. At the age of fifty-eight he was still bowling over 500 overs and taking over fifty wickets in a season, with a bewildering assortment of slow seamers, and an equally legendary attention to the placement of his field. It was his regular habit to move players a few inches between deliveries, harangue the slip fielders for moving to the wrong place by a matter of millimetres, and generally bamboozle both his own side – especially his captain – and the poor benighted batsman at the other end. If the batsman had not experienced all this mischief-making before, or had not been warned about it, he, poor fellow, might easily convince himself that he was in the presence of a conjuror and get himself out. Now, against some of the strongest opposition faced by the Brigands, Chris Bazalgette took 8 for 79 and broke Ivan Angell's amateur bowling record on Broadhalfpenny Down, which had stood for fifty-seven years.

Several other clubs have played regularly on Broadhalf-penny Down in recent times, and have become a part of what might be called the modern tradition: the Hampshire Hogs and Hambledon, of course, the Cricket Society and the Forty Club, the Grannies and the Rioteers, the Old Stationers and the Stragglers of Asia are just a few. John Tutt brings a touring side for a midweek fixture each year, while some clubs like Teddington and the Optimists owe their fixtures to individuals who are also Brigands members. The Saints have regularly come up from Plymouth, and for years the Brigands made an exception to their rule about always playing at home and went to Plymouth each August for a return match. Next-door neighbours Steep and Hambledon have also enjoyed home-and-away fixtures each year. Like Hambledon, Steep has a number of members who are also Brigands, and nobody underestimates how important this cross-membership is in keeping relations between the clubs in good order. The annual fixture with the boys and common room of Winchester College is another important fixture for much the same reasons, supported by overlapping membership.

One game between the two clubs some years ago involved both teams being skippered by ordained ministers. Bernard Marshall led the Brigands and Paul Bates the Winchester common room. It was a wet and miserable day, but the two captains would have none of it. Their combined prayers having failed, they finally declared with the formality of a papal edict that it was not raining. Then, on the basis that if you believe something fervently enough it will come true, they led their sides out to play the match in a downpour. It was seen through to a finish. The Good Lord was not sympathetic, however. Not only did it not stop raining but, during the game, Marshall was hit on the arm and had to retire hurt. Later, he bowled a couple of overs, only to discover after the match that he had done so with a broken arm.

Over the years, the Brigands have also welcomed many other distinguished clubs. The MCC has played here, as have Incogniti, Romany, the Master Mariners, the Sussex Martlets and scores of other teams. Many, of course, have been touring sides from all over the world. They make quite a catalogue, too. Malgoa Cricket Club arrived from Australia, led by a captain who proudly announced in the Bat and Ball after the game that his house near Sydney, New South Wales, was called 'Hambledon'. Furthermore, he reminded those at the bar, his club was the MCC, and gently suggested that they should not forget it.

The Golden Oldies from New Zealand played a warm-up match on their way to the 1994 international tournament in the Midlands, and batted particularly well for a team who had left winter behind only days before. Their bowling was, however, rusty enough for even this author to take a fifty off them. Auckland, New Zealand, have arrived on more than one occasion and had a good day's cricket on Broadhalfpenny Down. The Brigands have also hosted matches against the St Peter's Collegeans from South Australia and the Sarasota Cricket Club from Florida, USA. This was not a team of Americans, however. They fielded a side largely made up of ex-patriates and players living in the USA but brought up in cricket-playing countries. Before independence, the Rhodesian Ridgebacks paid a visit too.

Many of these visiting teams have met stiffer opposition from the Brigands than they sometimes expected. Every home team has the benefit of local knowledge, of course, but this takes on even more importance than usual on Broadhalfpenny Down, where the downland turf produces an altogether slower and lower bounce. However, this has not prevented the

Brigands from producing a string of high-scoring batsmen since the days of Wally Rothwell. Mike Freeman had a run of big scores through the 1970s but twice got himself out just short of yet another hundred, and in more recent times, Andrew Burns and James Dingemans of the younger generation have both scored hundreds, while Gerry Northwood has got close more than once. Andrew Forsyth completed the 1994 season with an average of over 55, thanks to a series of innings finishing not out. But perhaps the most extraordinary batting feat in modern times on Broadhalfpenny Down belongs to James Dingemans. In July 1996, when playing against the Saints, he scored 100 not out before lunch, which was taken when the Brigands total was 112 for one wicket.

Visitors have also done well with the bat, of course, none better than the 1967 Sydenhurst Ramblers who scored 295 in 105 minutes, David Childs finishing on 114 not out. Two years later, Brian Wilson scored 111 not out for Winchester College and then took 4 for 32 when the Brigands batted. The Cricket Society's visit in 1975 was notable for a pair of hundreds made by a pair of Australians. The Cricket Society declared at 231 for 1, with Kevin Carroll 125 not out and Garry Hansen 101 not out. Patrick Allen, the other opener (and an Englishman), missed out. He got a duck when the score was 5 – all extras. The second-wicket unfinished partnership of 226 was a record for the Cricket Society which still stands. Oddly enough, while the two Australians were at the wicket together no further extras were scored.

But this is fundamentally a bowlers' wicket, despite the spectacular exceptions from time to time, as the Brigands bowling figures testify. Ivan Angell was by no means the only swing bowler to enjoy bowling on Broadhalfpenny Down regularly. Over recent years, Angus Dunlop, Bryan Burns and Barrie Hunter have all produced exceptional performances from time to time, and cumulatively taken countless wickets. A few weeks after Dunlop had taken six against Winchester College in 1985, Hunter took 6 for 32 against Hambledon. He had another six-wicket haul in 1994, this time against the

Twelfth Man Club. Burns took 4 for 6 against the Rioteers in 1990 and 6 for 20 against the Sons of Bacchus in 1996, effectively wrapping up both games in the process. As ever, it was the pitch itself at the centre of events, and these men regularly and successfully exploited it as others had done before them.

Now and again, frustrations with the wicket have become so intense that the scorebook has been used to record the feelings of those involved. In 1986, the scorer commented under the heading Pitch Condition: 'Rough as usual.' Other classics, now buried in the old scorebooks, describe two visiting batsmen in 1976 as having 'retired, too good', while a match against Hambledon in 1985 was said to have been 'serious, competitive and skilful'. In 1991, the outcome of the toss at the start of the annual fixture against London New Zealand was described as 'negotiated', a decision which was subsequently vindicated to the full when London New Zealand declared at 217 for 3, and the Brigands avoided defeat only with the help of the elements.

Finally, the Brigands scorebooks reveal an odd, and somewhat disconcerting connection with their naval origins, and the naval thread that has run all the way through this book. Cricketers are a superstitious lot and, among many other things, dread certain numbers appearing together or in sequence on a scoreboard. To English players in particular, the appearance of 'Nelson', or 111, or any multiple of it, is to be avoided at all costs. The Test umpire and otherwise perfectly rational man, David Shepherd, despite his bulk is famous for jumping to get both feet off the ground, just for a moment, each time that number or a multiple appears when he is officiating. He would have a torrid time on Broadhalfpenny Down. Over the last thirty seasons or so, sides have been dismissed for exactly 111 on fourteen separate occasions, twice batsmen have been stranded not out on the same score, and one player lost his wicket on 111. No other figure comes anywhere close.

Many people who know something about the great win Hambledon had over England in 1777 recall two facts. First, they know Aylward went in at number ten and scored 167. Second, the match took place on Broadhalfpenny Down. Neither is correct, of course. Aylward opened, and the match took place at Sevenoaks Vine. But when did plain facts ever prevent cricketers from finding an excuse for a game? Certainly not on 31 July 1977, when the faintest blurring of these particular 'facts' encouraged Hambledon to arrange a bi-centenary match on Broadhalfpenny Down, ostensibly to celebrate the great win of 1777, against an MCC side masquerading as England. The 'England' side included the Essex bowler Jack Bailey, who later became secretary of the MCC; Mike Griffith, the former Sussex captain; and the Middlesex batsman EA Clark. The side was skippered by the former Kent and England batsman Colin (later Lord) Cowdrey, whose presence served at least two important purposes. First, it kept the county connection with 1777, and more importantly, it brought in the crowds. Over 5000 came to watch on a beautiful summer's day, and sat and stood many rows deep all around the boundary. The match was sponsored by the brewers Ind Coope, owners of the Bat and Ball, who were fully prepared for the event. This time, the cellars were

A huge crowd enjoyed the 1977 match on Broadhalfpenny Down to celebrate the bi-centenary of Hambledon's biggest win over England. Nobody seemed to care that the original game had taken place at Sevenoaks, Kent.
(Reproduced by kind permission of Adrian Magrath)

nearly drunk dry, but not quite.

Hambledon's club captain in 1977 was Colin Barrett, a much loved and devoted member of the club since boyhood. His younger brother Graham had bowled the first ball in 1953, and Colin himself had scored the 1957 Dartford match when he was only thirteen. Now here he was, twenty years later, tossing up on Broadhalfpenny Down with an illustrious England captain. The moment was not lost on him, nor on his many admirers at the club. He had made a lifetime's study of Hambledon and Broadhalfpenny Down, collected an enormous amount of memorabilia, and also had another distinction: he had shown himself to be a born and instinctive captain on the

The Hambledon and England teams gather at the monument for the bi-centenary match, 31 July 1977. Left to right: (top) Roy Newman, Adrian Magrath, Peter Tomkins, Mark Wingham, Greg Murton; (middle) Freddy Millett, Brian Hamblyn, Mike Griffith, Jack Miller, Rob Turner, Steve Horn, Alan Mason, Chris Bazalgette; (ground) Ted Clark, Dudley Owen-Thomas, John Lofting, Michael Mence, Colin Barrett, Charles Fry, Jack Bailey, Colin Cowdrey, Alan Day and umpire Steve Sims.
(Reproduced by kind permission of Adrian Magrath)

Bicentenary Cricket Match

HAMBLEDON C.C.
v.
ENGLAND (MCC)

on Broadhalfpenny Down, Hambledon

SUNDAY, 31st JULY 1977
start 2 pm

ENTRANCE BY PROGRAMME ONLY
ADULTS   Prior to the day   **40p**
          At the gate   **50p**
CHILDREN Prior to the day   **20p**
          At the gate   **30p**

CAR PARK FREE

This match is kindly sponsored by **SKOL LAGER**
'Man of the Match' Award presented by **DOMECQ**

(Reproduced by kind permission of Marion Beagley)

cricket field, a worthy successor to Richard Nyren and Edward Whalley-Tooker. He was one of those rare captains who somehow ensured that everyone playing in the game – friend and foe alike – had an enjoyable day, yet he could winkle a win from the most unlikely of situations and produce performances from his own team that even they marvelled at. They would do anything for him. 'It was both a pleasure and a privilege to play for him,' was the tribute paid to Colin Barrett years later by Peter Tomkins, who played over a thousand games for Hambledon from 1965 to 1994.

Colin Barrett also had an interest in coins. It was typical of the man that, faced with an occasion and an opposing captain of such stature, he should produce a gleaming gold guinea, minted in 1777, with which to toss up at the start of this bicentenary match. He won the toss, and invited the visitors to have first use of the pitch. After the game, Colin gave that coin to his wife Maureen, who has carried it in her purse ever since.

As so often on Broadhalfpenny Down, the wicket was far from first-class and on 31 July 1977 the ball was once again up to its old tricks. First-class players found such antics all very disturbing, whatever their pedigree, and today was no different. At one point, the MCC (sorry, England) were 13 for 1 off ten overs, and it should have been 13 for 2. The crisis came when the first wicket fell at six, and Cowdrey arrived at the wicket to face his first ball. Alan Mason was bowling. Immediately, there was a nasty and worryingly loud snick.

Wicket-keeper Peter Tomkins made no mistake. Or did he? With commendable presence of mind, and despite the temptation, he merely caught the ball and immediately tossed it to slip, without uttering a sound. Neither did anyone else.

This modest piece of indulgent good fortune did Cowdrey little good, however. The pitch continued to play tricks, and one of England's greatest batsmen struggled for forty-five minutes before he was bowled by Robert Turner for 13. Few club bowlers, if any, have dismissed an England captain twice in one afternoon, but Alan Mason and Robert Turner did that day. Eventually, the 'England' side scrambled to 154 before declaring with eight wickets down. They then had the slight indignity of watching the Hambledon openers treat both the vagaries of the pitch and their bowling – including Cowdrey's leg-spinners – with disdain, as Turner and Adrian Magrath put 62 on the board, without loss, at slightly better than a run-a-minute. Finally, with the professionals facing possible defeat, Jack Bailey took a belated and determined hand in the match. Hambledon buckled somewhat under the pressure, but held on to finish with 124 for 8. Skipper Colin Barrett was undefeated on 40. It was an innings Richard Nyren would have applauded to the echo – just what his side needed from their captain at that moment. It had earned them a draw in the face of a serious effort by the professionals to force a win.

The man of the match award, sponsored by Domecq's Double Century Sherry (what else could it possibly be on this particular occasion?), was rightly won by Robert Turner. During the day, he had taken two wickets, bowled the England captain, taken a catch and put together the day's top score of 45 in an opening stand of 62. No-one else came close. He received a dozen bottles of Domecq Sherry, one of which will forever remain unopened.

In recent years, a succession of one-off matches have been staged on Broadhalfpenny Down. In fact, they have become so frequent that the description of them as special scarcely applies any longer. That is not to suggest that they are anything less than special to the participants. Players and spectators alike come from all over the world just to see

Broadhalfpenny Down, let alone play on it. For every cricketer with a feeling for the game and its history, that moment when he first walks out to the centre of the ground to start a match or an innings will live with him for ever. Now that its availability for cricket is as permanently secure as its place in cricket history, the succession of players who experience that sensation as they walk out on Broadhalfpenny Down for the first time is set to continue indefinitely.

Many of these matches are played for charity purposes, of course, just as the Lord's Taverners matches were. The location attracts high-profile players, and they attract the crowds. In 1979, for instance, the Army played Hambledon in a charity match in aid of the Army Benevolent Fund. No less a distinguished military general than Sir Edwin (later Lord) Bramall, chief of the general staff and the most senior officer in the British army at the time, opened the batting for the Army, in a side captained by a junior officer in the Light Infantry, better known as the international athlete Alan Lerwill. Not quite an echo of Lord John Sackville and his gardener, but almost.

Sparks (Sportsmen Pledged to Aid Research into Crippling) raised a side to play Hambledon in September 1981, in aid of their charity and the Church of England Children's Society. Nearly a thousand came to watch and contributed several hundred pounds to the two charities. The Sparks side included a familiar mix of sportsmen and showbiz personalities, including the Kent batsman Arthur Phebey and the Middlesex and England fast bowler John Price, actor Robert Powell, England rugby international Roger Uttley and comic actor Bill Pertwee. The substantial figure of Patrick Moore, astronomer to the people, turned up and was due to play. But he finally thought better of it, and watched instead – something he was well-used to doing. Although it never became dark enough to see the stars, he stayed to the end.

Sparks were unable to stop Colin Barrett once more leading Hambledon to victory, this time by 32 runs. Robert Turner and Adrian Magrath were at it again, putting on over 100 for the first wicket. The day had its diversions off the field, not the least being Bill Frindall's commentary on the match. This had more in common with music-hall than *Test Match Special*, and his imitations of Fred Trueman and Brian Johnston, among others, were so good that they brought the match to a temporary halt at times.

Similar disorder occurred during a match staged on Broadhalfpenny Down on 22 June 1985, to celebrate the bicentenary of *The Times*. The publishers Collins had just released a book edited by Marcus Williams, *Double Century: 200 Years of Cricket in The Times*, and the match was arranged by way of celebration. David Frith, editor of *Wisden Cricket Monthly*, led the Collins XI, which included the Warwickshire and England fast bowler Bob Willis, while *The Times* XI had the shrewdest England captain of modern times, Mike Brearley, at the helm. Rain spoiled the day and there was never a chance of a result. Willis showed no enthusiasm whatever for bowling with a wet ball on a slippery surface in the pouring rain. Nor was he much amused when Patrick Glennie, keeping score from the relative warmth and comfort of the pavilion, allowed his irrepressible sense of mischief to get the better of him and called out 'bowler's name?' when the massive figure of Bob Willis was asked to perform after lunch.

When Mike Brearley arrived at the wicket, Frith set a wildly exaggerated 'bodyline' field for him, with an arc of fielders from backward short-leg round to silly mid-on. All nine fielders were involved. The rest of the field was deserted. Unblinkingly (Frith's description) Brearley tapped the first ball towards the vast open spaces in the covers and helped himself to an easy single. The fact that the ball had been propelled down a line outside his leg-stump had nothing whatever to do with it. Neither did he question why that distinguished cricket correspondent John Woodcock, umpiring for the day just to remind himself what it was like to make all those difficult decisions on the spur of the moment, failed to call 'no ball'. However, having negotiated this piece of gentle farce, Brearley went on to make an elegant 50 which included eight 4s. It was one of the highlights of the day.

The presence of Mike Brearley on Broadhalfpenny Down brings the number of truly outstanding cricket captains known to have played on the ground to five. In poker parlance, we have a full house: three first-class players – Richard Nyren, Stuart Surridge and now Mike Brearley; and a pair of amateurs – Edward Whalley-Tooker and Colin Barrett. Or, cut another way, three Hambledon captains and a pair of visitors.

While Brearley's elegant batting was enchanting the few hardy spectators not tempted by the warmth across the road, inside the Bat and Ball John Arlott had been fortifying himself against the elements with his beloved red wine since mid-morning. After lunch he was called upon to make a speech. It was magnificent. It lasted twenty minutes, and the whole company wanted him to go on all afternoon. It was word perfect, measured, amusing, elegant, interesting, appropriate and fun; absolutely brilliant. Later, now back at the bar, he was heard reciting Nyren's words from memory and bewitching all within earshot. Even if the sun had been shining it would still have represented better entertainment than that on offer across the road.

The House of Lords staged their annual match against the House of Commons on Broadhalfpenny Down during the late 1980s, but no record of it appeared in *Hansard* and the teams and scores are now lost. Politicians are rarely lost so quickly. About the same time, a one-day game was staged between a touring Australian Colts XI and an England Colts XI, but again the details are gone.

The bicentenary of the birth of John Nyren was celebrated in some style on 15 December 1964 by more than 100 members and guests of the Hambledon Cricket Club at a splendid dinner held in the village hall. All the men so closely associated with Broadhalfpenny Down over the preceding years were there, as were a great many well-known figures from cricket in general and Hampshire cricket in particular. Sir Pelham Warner, happily no longer barefoot, introduced the president of Hampshire County Cricket Club and the one man who had done more to rescue Broadhalfpenny Down than anyone else in modern times, Harry Altham, whom he described as a veritable Churchill of Cricket – writer, historian and activist.

At the end of a finely-crafted speech, delivered with style and affection, Altham himself awarded John Nyren the eternal presidency of the cricket writers' guild, since he had been without doubt the first and best of all cricket correspondents.

Strangely enough, important though this event was in the context of cricket history and its literature, to say nothing of its local importance, the dinner itself gained surprisingly little notice at the time. Yet the media feature regularly at Broadhalfpenny Down, and have done for decades. The ground is a magnet every time cricket history, or the origins of the game, gets into the news again, something which occurs surprisingly often. Just as often, it is selected as a venue for an event entirely of the media's making. And for some extraordinary reason, the newspaper reporters and TV and radio broadcasters always seem to want to make their programmes about this most sunny of summer games out of season, in conditions more like the middle of winter. It is a perversity only they could explain.

Even in the middle of June, 1980, when an old-fashioned match was staged between Hambledon and the Broadhalf-penny Brigands just for the cameras of Southern Television, the producers managed to pick a miserable day. Historical inaccuracies littered the shoot. The rules were pre-1777, but the assortment of clothing worn for the day was mostly early-Georgian. Some of it failed to last the day out, despite some frantic needlework on the boundary from time to time. The Brigands wicket-keeper had a particularly torrid and revealing time, and was reduced to stooping rather than crouching in an effort to keep himself decent. The bats were specially made for the match by Wisden's of Brighton, but they were up against modern balls. They coped, just. Nobody bothered much about the scores, and neither side was sure of the exact result in the end. Hambledon were thought to have scored 117 and the Brigands 104. What mattered was the film in the can.

Slightly more stylish, and certainly more serious, batting appeared in David Frith's 1982 video *Benson and Hedges Golden Greats: Batsmen*. It opened on Broadhalfpenny Down with a heavily-clothed John Arlott extemporizing to some extent to camera on a bitter spring day, while he tried to enthuse about batsmanship as though the sun were beating down on his back. Even he was obliged to start with the words: 'You must wonder that cricket began in England at all when you get an arctic wind like this on a match day. But this bald Hampshire down...became the source of the history of cricket.' Afterwards, in the warmth of the pub, Arlott was more relaxed and produced yet another of his masterly performances from a script carefully crafted for him by David Frith, read through, memorized, and then delivered with instant improvement in only a couple of takes.

A similarly bitter day greeted Harry Secombe and Brian Johnston, that other much-loved radio and television commentator whose career coincided with John Arlott's for so

The match staged for Southern Television, 12 June 1980. Colin Barrett is keeping wicket in the original manner, without gloves.
(Reproduced by kind permission of John Barrett/Maureen Wingham)

long, to the delight of millions of listeners all over the world. Different as chalk and cheese, Arlott capable of producing magical descriptions from the most ordinary of situations, his mind prompted by acute observation and a feel for words; and Johnners, as he was universally known, all boyish enthusiasm and an irrepressible sense of fun. Both men shared much more than commentary boxes; they shared a passion for the game, a profound understanding of its subtleties, and an unending disbelief that they were actually paid to do something they would probably have done for nothing.

Now it was Johnners's turn to freeze on Broadhalfpenny Down. It was April 1989 and Yorkshire Television were recording another of Harry Secombe's *Highway* programmes. These were transmitted each Sunday evening and this one was scheduled to go out at the height of the summer. The programme was based on Hambledon, and the producer decided to invite Johnners to talk to Harry Secombe about the history of the game and the ground. They dressed in white flannels and blazers and sat in deckchairs thoughtfully provided to give the scene a summer feel. The two men chatted while the cameras rolled. At one point the conditions got the better of the shivering Secombe, who could not resist a question to the owner of the most famous proboscis in cricket and broadcasting: 'Well, if this is summer, why's your nose turned so blue?' Laughter. Cut – and it stayed cut. Perhaps it later found its way into one of those hugely popular programmes of out-takes and gaffes. The line was certainly worthy of it.

Two other cricketing enthusiasts from the world of showbiz were roped in for this programme. Both the lyricist Tim (later Sir Tim) Rice, who went on to win Hollywood Oscars and become president of the Lord's Taverners – and Johnners' great friend, the entertainer and lyricist Richard Stilgoe, took part in the programme. When the director came to shoot Stilgoe's spot, he managed to create an even more ludicrous sight than freezing 'spectators' in deckchairs, if that were possible. Richard Stilgoe found himself sat at a white piano set up in the middle of Broadhalfpenny Down, in a biting wind and his fingers numb with cold, trying to look as though this was

Brian Johnston and Colin Barrett recording Down Your Way, 1982.
(Reproduced by kind permission of John Barrett/Maureen Wingham)

nothing unusual at all. He then recorded one of the cleverest and funniest songs even he has ever written. When the programme was finally broadcast two months later on a warm summer's evening, he had achieved the impossible. Nobody watching, who had not been on the ground that day, would ever have known that he was chilled to the marrow, playing and singing in what felt like sub-zero temperatures. The suggestion for a new song for the programme had come from the producer, but Richard Stilgoe came up with the dinosaur theme. The lyrics are at the end of this book. It turned out to be one of his most popular pieces. Few songs have ever been heard for the first time in such circumstances, and Stilgoe hopes – for his part – that they never are again, at least not with him at the piano.

Later, they all went down to Hambledon village, where Ida Barrett, long-time scorer for the Hambledon Cricket Club and mother of the then club captain, warmed them all up with cups of tea and the inevitable chocolate cake. Brian Johnston's need for chocolate cake was legendary, and Ida Barrett did not fail him. A short time later, after Harry Secombe had used the loo, Ida told him she would put up a plaque to tell the world of this unique event. This was too much for Johnners. He insisted that he would use it too, so that his name might be included as well.

This was not the first time Brian Johnston had met Ida and Colin Barrett. He had used her house as a base during his recording of an edition of *Down Your Way* in 1982, when he started the programme with an interview with Colin about the history of the village and the cricket club. At the time, Colin Barrett was also the club's secretary and he already had a vast knowledge of its history and a huge collection of memorabilia. The two men went up to the ground at Broadhalfpenny Down, sat on the base of the monument and recorded a few minutes of material with what was obviously mutual pleasure. They talked about Nyren and Small, Sueter and Leer, Harris and Lumpy. They talked about the laws and the equipment of the glory days. They could have gone on for ever. The listener could sense that only the demands of the programme's timing brought the chat to what was for them a premature end. But not before Colin Barrett had told Brian Johnston of the 'tremendous honour' he felt at being appointed captain of the most famous of all cricket clubs.

Colin Barrett's choice of music was no surprise to anyone who knew him – it was the theme music from BBC TV's cricket highlights programme which follows each day of a home Test match. It is called 'Soul Limbo'. After they had finished recording the interview, Johnners and Colin Barrett went off to the New Inn in Hambledon, where they spent the next three hours talking about cricket, and seriously endangering the production schedule for the rest of the programme. But they were not to be diverted. This was a meeting of like minds.

Colin Barrett died tragically young and at the height of his powers as a cricket captain, in 1991. He was only forty-six. Hambledon church was packed for the service of thanksgiving which was held a short time later. The tributes were handsome and honoured this true lover of the game. Everyone knew the music he would have wished to include in the service, and it was. Perhaps for the first time ever 'Soul Limbo' was played on the organ that day. It was a rendering that drained the emotions and brought tears to the eye. Quite apart from the effect it had on the congregation, the performance itself represented an achievement for the organist, David Burgess. Sheet music was unobtainable, so he had listened to Ida Barrett's recording of the *Down Your Way* programme of nine years before, and transcribed it from ear to paper, scoring it for the organ as he wrote.

Brian Johnston stayed in touch with Ida Barrett right up to his own death three years later. She got a Christmas card from him every year without fail. He was devoted to Broadhalfpenny Down and Hambledon, and its well-being mattered deeply to him. Sadly, in the end, it mattered almost too much.

At the end of the 1992 season, the Ministry of Defence formally relinquished the lease on Broadhalfpenny Down and the question of its future was yet again thrown open. The decision of the MoD was taken as part of the expenditure review of the armed forces. HMS *Mercury* was to close down, and there was no way that the MoD could continue to act as tenant of a piece of land of no interest whatsoever to it or the navy. The tea-leaves had been read some time beforehand by Brigands members with close naval connections, and a review of the club's position and prospects had already been completed two years earlier under the leadership of David Farquharson, who had first raised the issue. He had a team of three to help his deliberations – solicitor Philip Yetman, a member for some years, to advise on any legal aspects which might arise, the club's chairman Anthony Banes-Walker and Peter Tuke, one of the club's elder statesmen. As a result of their discussions over many months, the Brigands developed a plan. It was simple, far-sighted and would benefit all the parties involved. But could they convince Winchester College?

In essence, they proposed setting up an independent trust to secure the long-term future of Broadhalfpenny Down as a cricket ground, to fund improved facilities, particularly for special matches, and to encourage young cricketers. The trustees would include representatives of the MCC, Hampshire County Cricket Club, the Cricket Society, Hambledon Cricket Club, and, of course, Winchester College as owners and the Broadhalfpenny Brigands as tenants of the ground. Simultaneously, Hambledon's third XI would be granted sufficient games on Broadhalfpenny Down to complete the home legs of their Saturday league programme, and the ground would be made available on an ad hoc basis for special matches from time to time, as future circumstances might demand and permit.

Once it was known that the MoD was giving up the existing lease, Hambledon Cricket Club also decided to make an application to take over the tenancy of Broadhalfpenny Down. It was their historical home, after all; the monument was erected and paid for by the club, they needed Broadhalfpenny Down for their third XI, and they had the resources to maintain the ground to the standard expected. Chris de Mellow presented a powerful and persuasive case for Hambledon to resume playing here.

Winchester College had the unenviable task of making a choice between these two strong applications, both with different but convincing arguments in their favour, and both expected to co-operate after the decision, whichever way it went. The irony would not have been lost on Harry Altham, who had twice struggled years earlier to find anyone remotely interested in preserving the ground as a unique piece of cricket history, maintaining it properly, and keeping it in regular use. Now, here were two equally persuasive candidates. It was a judgement that would have taxed Solomon.

Hubert Doggart drew the short straw. He was asked to advise the College authorities. He was the ideal man to express an informed opinion. He was a Wykehamist and had taught at the College before becoming headmaster of King's School, Bruton. He was also a former pupil of Harry Altham. Perhaps even more to the point, he was a former president of the MCC and a cricketer of distinction. He had played for Sussex and England. He had, incidentally, made the highest number of runs ever scored by an English player in his first first-class innings – 215 not out for Cambridge University against Lancashire in May 1948. It was a score he was to exceed the following year, when he took 219 not out off Essex and shared a stand of 429 with John Dewes. In more recent times, he had played cricket at Broadhalfpenny Down.

It was the trust that swung it. It would provide a permanence if anything were to happen to the tenant, whomever that might be. It would provide a vehicle to 'warn, advise and encourage'. It would also provide a vehicle to fund improvements and safeguard the interests of cricket in general, as well as those of Winchester College in particular. These considerable benefits, plus the inescapable fact that the Brigands had already looked after the ground well (and for longer than the original Hambledon team had used it), finally helped to push the decision their way. The College authorities were also mindful that Broadhalfpenny Down was the Brigands' only ground and was used by the club throughout the season for first XI matches. In September 1992, the Warden and Fellows of Winchester College decided to grant a lease on the ground for fourteen years from the start of the 1993 season to the Broadhalfpenny Brigands Cricket Club. Two conditions applied. First, that Hambledon play their third XI home matches there, and secondly, that the Brigands initiate the formation of the trust.

Today, Hambledon do indeed play their Saturday league fixtures on Broadhalfpenny Down, special matches do take place there regularly, and the trust is in being thanks in large measure to the efforts of Peter Tuke, who brought to reality what the review team first visualized. In purely practical terms, the trust's short-term purpose is to raise capital to provide a fund for maintenance of the ground if this were ever to be needed, and to raise project finance for permanent improvements to the ground. That is what it is now doing, although it has – for purely legal reasons – subsequently changed itself into an association.

Curiously, no mention of ownership of the monument seems to have arisen during the negotiations of 1992. Hambledon did not mention it in their submission, and the Brigands had assumed it was a part of the lease. Indeed, responsibility for the upkeep of the monument *is* included in the lease. So, in effect, Winchester College have charged responsibilities on a structure they don't own, to a tenant who has no legitimate interest, on behalf of the owner who was not consulted. No doubt it will all be sorted out one day, and in the meantime no harm is done. The monument is there, and there it will stay.

The ownership of the pavilion, on the other hand, is in no doubt. It was bought by HMS *Mercury*, and handed over to the club years ago for the quixotically bureaucratic reason that, under MoD regulations, HMS *Mercury* was entitled to one pavilion only, and that was on another ground. So the pavilion became Brigands property, at least until the 1992 negotiations, when ownership passed to Winchester College. But it remains the Brigands' responsibility. Of course, it will never be an adequate substitute for the original lodge. It is also on the wrong side of the ground.

It has long been a part of the Brigands tradition to play limited-overs evening games each season. Indeed, that was the club's original purpose, back in the 1950s. They are still an important part of the annual fixture-list. Usually these games are against comparatively local sides. Some are played on a home-and-away basis over alternate seasons. Starting at 6pm, lasting twenty overs per side, and with limits on the number of overs to be bowled and runs scored before retirement by each player, these matches are played as much for midweek fun and relaxation as for the result. They are keenly fought, for all that.

Such games inevitably have a light touch to them, of course, and sometimes these evening matches have produced some hysterical moments of outrageous comedy. The original source of amusement is usually the mish-mash of players involved. Evening games inevitably oblige teams to include some players who either cannot, or do not wish to, play at weekends. Then there are the occasional cricketers, people living near the ground, men who enjoy playing from their memory-bank, so to speak, in circumstances which they hope will not embarrass or disadvantage their younger and fitter team-mates too much. Opponents' sides often consist of the same curious combination of age, experience and stiffness on the one hand, teenage enthusiasm on the other, and an assortment in between. The skipper's aim on such an evening is the achievement of the magic number 'eleven' rather than anything which might without extravagance be described as 'a balanced side'.

Such ill-assorted teams are almost bound to produce moments of high drama, especially since these matches are always played at a frenetic pace. Short-term tactics have a huge impact – as do single incidents of success or failure – in such a microcosm of a game. When these moments occur, they can involve anything from stunning achievement and ingenuity to pure farce. They can raise the game to its heights, or generate comedy and mayhem in an instant.

One example says it all. The Brigands' opponents were chasing a modest total, their openers were well set and ahead of the run-rate. They were likely to win at a canter. Then a wicket fell and – generously – the opposition's skipper sent in to bat at number three a short, round, weatherbeaten yokel of a man who clearly had only the dimmest memory of how to hit the ball.

It later transpired that he was normally the team's umpire, but had wanted to play in this particular evening game. Indeed his place at number three in the batting order was entirely in keeping with the spirit of these matches. Until, that is, the Brigands saw him attempt to play the first ball he received. They instantly realized that here was their best route to an unlikely win. Who better to have at the wicket than a man who could not hit the ball? Not only could he not hit it to score runs, he could not hit a catch to a fielder either. It was the perfect strategy. The same unspoken thought went simultaneously through every Brigand head: 'We mustn't get him out.' Suddenly, the batsman at the other end found himself being given an easy single whenever he was on strike. It took him a while to figure out why.

The biggest problem for the bowlers was to avoid bowling our tame batsman out. Mostly, this was achieved with aplomb by bowling just outside his off-stump – until one ghastly moment when the ball popped off a length, brushed his arm, and the wicket-keeper was so taken by surprise that he forgot to drop it. A foolish young man in the outfield appealed for the catch and the umpire (one of the now-frustrated batting side), evidently with great relief, put his finger up to give the batsman out. At which point the honour of the umpires' union came to the Brigands' rescue. This batsman, remember, was their regular first-team umpire. He knew a thing or two about the laws, and this was, for him, a moment of crisis.

'No, no,' he said. 'It hit me here,' and indicated his left arm. 'That's not out.' 'Yes, yes,' chorused the Brigands in support. 'Of course it's not out. Please, you must stay.' And stay he did. For five more overs. It took several minutes before the fielders finally suppressed their mirth at this fortuitous turn of events, though what the adjudicating umpire made of it all he never said. He must have felt somewhat crushed, and frustrated, at the continuing presence at the crease of their non-scoring batsman while the overs ticked away, and with them their chance of victory.

Then fate took a hand again. Yet another ball bowled well outside the off-stump, but this one turned prodigiously, cut across the crease and knocked off the leg-bail. On the instant, a shout from the Brigand standing at short square-leg: 'It bounced back off the keeper's pads.' It was the verdict of a man who, for most of the working week, would normally be described as 'an eminent QC'.

'Yes, yes, it came off the keeper.' This reinforcement came from the colonel fielding just backward of square-leg. Mayhem followed. The Brigands – taking their cue from such distinguished and trustworthy fellows – chorused noisily about the true path of the ball immediately prior to the bails being dislodged. The batsman clearly did not know what had happened. So he stood his ground, confused, awaiting the umpire's decision. The umpire probably didn't know the truth either, since the batsman's pads must have obscured his view. But he had had enough. 'Out,' he roared, finger aloft. He knew a good thing when he saw it.

And while the number-three bat slowly retired to the pavilion, having held up an end for ten overs of a twenty-over innings, scoring three runs in the process, the enduring sight of an eminent QC and a retired colonel supporting each other in paroxysms of laughter, tears pouring down their cheeks, will live in the memory as the epitome of evening cricket.

Oh, the result? The scores finished level, a tie. So there was no great harm done.

The colonel was the regular source of other entertainment during evening games at that time. He was a mimic. He was also a very good one. He broadcast on local radio from time to time, commentating on sporting events in the area. So he understood the techniques of commentary, and the importance of verbal colour in the description of facts.

Sometimes he would practise during a game. If you had the misfortune to be standing at slip when he was in the gully, you were in danger of being assailed by a remarkable impression of the soft, dark-brown Hampshire burr of John Arlott wafting gently from that quarter, muttering observations about the actions of bowlers, batsmen and fielders as they struggled to imitate the actions of their first-class heroes.

'...and he stumbles across from mid-off, stoops awkwardly...clutches at a ball long gone towards the boundary...trips...and falls like an oversized sack of potatoes on the edge of the square. The planet shudders...'

You could almost hear the original John Arlott, the colonel was so good. He produced gems like that on many an evening, and cared not a fig if it made concentration difficult for the rest of us. Nor should he have done. He belonged to the 'cricket is fun' school of thought.

In January 1994, the Ind Coope management of the Bat and Ball announced that they were converting it to a family-style restaurant to be called 'Natterjacks'. It was news that stunned the cricketing world. Quite apart from the fact that a natterjack is a rather ugly type of toad, this was a decision of the most extraordinary kind whichever way the rest of the world looked at it.

As later events were to prove, it was unsound commercially, since the pub stood literally miles from any community. Clanfield is the nearest village, and even that is one and a half miles away – just a fraction nearer than Hambledon itself. The road junction outside the pub is the mere meeting of local lanes, and in the winter it is a bleak place indeed. In spite of its location, or perhaps because of it, the Bat and Ball has never depended on passing traffic. There is little of it. Few people would have reason to go there, were it not for the pub's unique place in cricket history. Cricket is its primary source of revenue and always will be.

The astonishing and utterly unexpected announcement from the brewery was made without planning permission from the local authority for a change of use, and the retrospective application for permission met with stiff opposition both locally and from the cricketing world. But the management was adamant. Both the interior and exterior were changed. The bar area was cut down to a bar-reception, snacks were removed from the bar, and much of the cricketing memorabilia was moved out of the building and stored in a nearby garage, or shifted to less prominent positions on the walls. The fact that much of it was on permanent loan from the MCC appeared to count for nothing. The locals, if residents of Hambledon village some two miles away can be called locals, boycotted the pub almost to a man. And they stayed away, too. Even when these extreme changes were later modified, the locals were slow to return.

The brewery's decision generated a storm of protest, even if it did nothing for the business. They were accused of acting with arrogance, with ignorance, and in a way which was both socially and historically irresponsible. What they had done was widely regarded as utter folly and totally against the interests of the one community which had supported it for generations – the cricketers who came from all parts of the world to see the ground and the pub, hopefully to enjoy its hospitality.

Worse, some critics quickly pointed out that the brewery had passed up an opportunity to exploit a world-famous sporting icon, one of the very few places anywhere in the world forever linked to a great sporting event – and in this case, one going back over 200 years. The need to generate trade was accepted – but the best way to do it had been ignored, and the one existing source of income discarded. It was an expensive, mistaken and predictable failure. Commercial reality quickly proved the point.

Within two years, a change of attitude and management at the brewery, and a change of management at the pub itself, had resulted in a decisive move back towards the *status quo*. The name Natterjacks was quietly allowed to fade into the background, the bar was opened up again, snacks went on sale to drinkers again, and the restaurant was still there for those who wished to use it. But not before a small group of cricket enthusiasts had made more than one offer to buy either the pub or the business from the brewery, and had left a permanent offer to talk if the brewery ever wanted to sell. Other independent pub-management companies were also known to have expressed interest. These enquiries got nowhere.

On the day of the original announcement, however, the shocked cricket world was up in arms. Brian Johnston, not only the most distinguished of cricket commentators but a man who found it quite impossible to disguise his feelings whether on air or in private, went on the BBC's *Today* programme, broadcast at breakfast time, to protest at this appalling decision, which flew in the face of all logic. It was clear to millions of listeners that he was deeply upset. He promised never to drink Ind Coope's beers again, and for the most dreadful of reasons he never did. Shortly afterwards he suffered the heart attack from which he died a few days later.

Meanwhile, Hampshire and England's most elegant of left-handed batsmen, David Gower, went on television to complain bitterly about 'this terrible decision'. The national and local press carried hundreds of column-inches of highly critical comment, and so the barrage went on. Letters arrived by every post from leading cricketers and many of the professional game's top administrators, pointing out – among other things – that Tetley, sponsors of the England team at that time, were part of the same company (Allied Lyons was the parent company of both Ind Coope and the Tetley Brewery). Later, the news got abroad and that produced a second wave of criticism from cricketers in Australia and elsewhere. The new management team at the Bat and Ball must have thought the whole world had just fallen in on them. The distinction many of their angry correspondents tried to make that they were not against the Bat and Ball, nor the brewery, but only against this foolish decision, was probably lost on the management at that time.

On 25 March 1996, barely two years later and after a total change of heart and management at Allied Domecq (as the parent company was now called) and at the Bat and Ball, the world learned that all was now well again. Natterjacks was dead. Common sense, and cricket, had won. Even the then Prime Minister, John Major, found time in the midst of yet another crisis over Europe to write, 'I am sure that this decision will be welcomed by cricket-lovers the world over.' Now, of course, having been through this quite unnecessary hoop, it is clear that the Bat and Ball is safe for the foreseeable future. Public opinion, the cricket community worldwide and planning restrictions would make any future attempt at such a fundamental change impossible to contemplate. Whatever its precarious past, the furore over Natterjacks and an even more recent change of ownership has probably had the effect of securing the future of the Bat and Ball for the cricket world.

The decision came too late for Bill Galbraith, who had been the popular landlord of the Bat and Ball in the years leading up to the Natterjacks fiasco. His job went to a new manager under the new regime. Now the Bat and Ball had its third manager in as many years, and this time it was a young lady. Louise Hodgkins had been appointed towards the end of 1995. She immediately realized that cricket, and the pub's relation-ship with the Broadhalfpenny Brigands – and with the Bat and Ball Cricket Club which Bill Galbraith had formed in 1992 – was the key to the long-term success of the pub. The changes she initiated that summer, which have been built on vigorously ever since, immediately boosted the business and brought the cricket community flocking back.

Bill Galbraith was an unusual man. He was a Scot, and he had a passion for cricket. Standing in the long line of successors to Richard Nyren as landlord of the Bat and Ball was something that pleased him mightily. When he first took over the pub, he found himself unable to answer all the questions which customers asked him about it and the ground opposite. So he revived the practice started by Leslie Wilson several years before of asking Patrick Glennie to drive up from Clanfield and talk about the history of Broadhalfpenny Down, whenever the pressure for information became too intense.

Galbraith's love for the place also caused him concern. He had an eerie premonition of what was to follow barely a year later. Originally, his worries were expressed in terms of what might happen to the Bat and Ball if it fell into the hands of someone not interested in cricket. Over the previous two centuries, such a calamity had happened more than once. He cast around for some way of keeping the Bat and Ball associated with cricket, but which was independent of the publican running it. With the help of Chris Bazalgette, advertising manager of *The Cricketer*, who just happened to be a member of the Broadhalfpenny Brigands, the Hambledon Cricket Club, the Hampshire Hogs and a dozen other clubs farther afield, he came up with the idea of the Bat and Ball

Cricket Club. Its objective was to create a lasting and practical link between the pub and cricket, and to provide an opportunity for cricket-lovers to support such a notion by becoming members.

The club was launched in February 1993 with the help of a substantial donation from Ind Coope, and three years later over 200 cricket enthusiasts from all over the world had become members. The club's plan was to play a few one-off fixtures each season, arrange social occasions and provide a focus for other aspects of the game associated with cricket in Hampshire. Some of the earliest fixtures were against touring sides from abroad, including the Australian Crusaders in 1993, the South African Warthogs and the British Columbia XI from Canada, both in 1994. Two years later, a game was arranged with the Royal Household, Windsor XI, and played on Broadhalfpenny Down, with a return game the following season at Windsor Castle.

Twice the Bat and Ball Cricket Club has staged matches on Broadhalfpenny Down against the county side. The first was the club's inaugural game in 1993, and the second took place on 20 June 1995, in aid of the county's centenary appeal fund. On a glorious summer's day, several thousand spectators watched the Bat and Ball Invitation XI play Hampshire. The Invitation XI included England Test players Derek Underwood and Bob Taylor, West Indies fast bowler Malcolm Marshall (captain for the day), batsmen Alvin Kallicharran and Phil Simmons, and all-rounder Roger Harper. The county side was led by their popular captain, Mark Nicholas, in his last season with the club. Marshall, of course, had been on the Hampshire staff for many years, and the spectacle of the Hampshire side grovelling at his feet as he walked out to bat against them brought tears of mirth to the face of many a county supporter.

Hampshire were invited to bat first and were quickly reduced to 43 for 5, largely through the deadly bowling of Derek Underwood whose recall to the England side looked increasingly imminent as he took 3 for 22 off eight overs. Marshall had mercy and then took him off. Ian Hunter, who normally plays for Burridge in the Hampshire league, found himself playing for the Invitation XI after a last-minute withdrawal. Suddenly, here he was being given the ball by Malcolm Marshall and asked to bowl at the county batsmen. He seized the chance with both hands and finished with 2 for 40, including the dismissal of Mark Nicholas, caught and bowled for 36. The star with the bat was Shaun Udal, normally better known for his flighted off-breaks. That day, however, he enjoyed a big innings and hit a vigorous 95 before Ian Hunter deprived him of his century.

The Bat and Ball Invitation XI got close, but not close enough. At the end of their forty overs they had made 193 for 9. The two West Indian Test batsmen had both got into the twenties, and then got themselves out. John Hardy, who at various times had played for Hampshire, Somerset and Gloucestershire, made 41. But it was not quite enough. The match was a draw, with the honours divided. Both sides might have snatched victory at the last, but neither did so.

Barely two months after their announcement that Natterjacks was dead, the owners, Allied Domecq, unexpectedly sold the Bat and Ball to a local brewery, George Gale and Co Ltd. Based at nearby Horndean, the new owners immediately let it be known that the Bat and Ball was to become one of its flagship pubs, and reassuringly added that no dramatic changes were planned. It was to remain a high-quality traditional English pub, proud of its unique connection with cricket and managed with that in mind. At the beginning of 1997, the brewery appointed a new licensee, Dick Orders, to develop the business and its links with the cricketing world. He came with a good pedigree, having previously played for the Army and for Gloucestershire Colts.

Later in the year that Brian Johnston died, 1994, his wife Pauline, with members of his family and several friends prominent in broadcasting and cricket, set up a trust fund in his memory. Its aim was to raise funds which would provide investment income to be distributed to good causes, particularly those in which Brian Johnston took an interest. One of the beneficiaries was the Down's Syndrome Trust, a charity with which his whole family became involved after the birth of their daughter Joanna, who was a sufferer.

That summer, a cricket match was arranged on Broadhalfpenny Down in aid of this particular charity. The Brian Johnston Memorial XI played a scratch Brigands mid-week side. Initially the cricket was conducted in a light-hearted manner, with little attention given to the business of winning. Participation was more important, as was entertainment of the sadly small number of spectators who were asked to dig into their pockets in support of the Trust. The following year, the Trust provided a trophy, a Brian Johnston Champagne Moment award, to be competed for annually. Brian Johnston had been instrumental in the creation of the Champagne Moment award at Test matches, decided by a majority vote taken among all the BBC commentators present on *Test Match Special*. This was to be a Broadhalfpenny Down echo of the same award.

The first winner was Chris Bazalgette. On this particular occasion, however, it was not Chris's bowling that won him the Champagne Moment award. It was a catch. And what a catch it was. Standing at deep mid-off, some forty yards from the bat, he suddenly found himself facing a ball travelling at head height and at a velocity which must have been well in excess of 100 miles an hour. This was a colossal blow, right off the meat of the bat, and it was going straight for Chris Bazalgette's head. It was a desperate moment. Even in those few split-seconds, his knees buckled slightly and the colour drained from his features. Then it happened. Both hands went up...the ball struck them a mighty smack...and stuck fast. A great whoop of joy and relief – the ball was hurled skywards – and the back-slapping congratulations from the rest of his team must have left his shoulders even more sore than his hands.

The more discerning of them later suggested that the true Champagne Moment had occurred just a fraction of a second before the catch, when they saw that squall of disbelief, horror and anticipated-pain pass across his face as he fully realized the enormity of the crisis that was hurtling towards him.

This midweek incident happened during one of the most

exhausting sequences of events ever to befall a fielding side. It occurred at Broadhalfpenny Down over the period between 13 August and 3 September 1995. Between 6.49pm on 13 August and 2.57pm on 3 September, no visitor's wicket fell on Broadhalfpenny Down during a normal Brigands' weekend fixture. Meanwhile, 407 runs were scored by Brigands' opponents. The circumstances were these.

On 13 August, playing the Twelfth Man Cricket Club, the Brigands took their last opponent's wicket at 6.49pm, after which they scored another six runs for victory by three wickets. The following weekend, there were no matches at the ground because the Brigands were on tour in the West Country. The next weekend, their visitors were the Hampshire Hogs, the distinguished and rightly famous amateur county team with a history which goes back to 1887. At Broadhalfpenny Down on 27 August 1995, a new first-wicket record was set for the Hogs by an enormous partnership of 263 for no wicket, declared. Nic Wolstenholme, a nineteen-year-old county prospect who had already played for the Hampshire under-17 and under-19 XIs, scored 154 not out, and Jonathan Grant, the Hogs' fixture secretary, got 100 not out. Wolstenholme's 154 was a mere four runs short of equalling the highest score ever recorded on Broadhalfpenny Down. If his captain John Bristow had known Nic Wolstenholme was so close, the declaration would probably have been delayed by another over or so. But this crucial fact did not come to light until the following year, during the research for this book.

The next Sunday, 3 September, the Brigands played the Forty Club, which was captained on the day by Roger Vernier, an exuberant club cricketer who came from that other cradle of early cricket, Farnham, Surrey, and whose half-French ancestry did nothing to diminish his enthusiasm for the game. The visitors batted first and their opening partnership was finally broken at 2.57pm when the score had reached 138. Mike Jones bowled John Bristow for 60. This was the very same John Bristow who had captained the Hampshire Hogs the previous weekend and had sat in the pavilion for the entire afternoon with his pads on, waiting to bat. He had finally got to the wicket a week later. After Bristow's dismissal, the Brigands could have been forgiven for wondering if it had been worth it. Bob Shergold was the next man in and he tore their bowling apart, bludgeoning a tumultuous 132.

Outside the first-class game, and only then in the context of five-day Test matches, there can be few instances of over 400 runs being scored between wickets falling. As for three weeks passing between dismissals on a ground in regular use, this event may even be unique. The fielders and bowlers involved hoped it stayed that way. Of course, as they reminded themselves afterwards, there was a period of over 100 years when no wicket fell at Broadhalfpenny Down; but nobody then scored 400 runs either.

The Duke of Dorset tried to organize the very first overseas tour of a cricket team, in 1789, but it only got as far as the Kent coast. The first which managed to get on a boat and play cricket at the other end of its journey didn't go to Australia, as most people assume. It went to North America. It left England in September 1859 and played five matches on the East Coast of the United States and Canada.

Almost exactly to the day, 136 years later, an American team played on Broadhalfpenny Down. It was not the first team from America to tour England. There had been many sides before. Most notably, the Gentlemen of Philadelphia toured regularly in the latter part of the nineteenth century. They came at least five times between 1884 and 1908, and distinguished themselves sufficiently against good opposition for some of their games to be recorded in *Wisden*.

Of course, many other American clubs have toured England over the years, but most of them were not playing to a standard which interested *Wisden*. They had fun, though, even if it sometimes went too far. On one occasion, in 1870, the members of the Staten Island Cricket Club, New York, persuaded their hosts at The Oval to play poker after the game. During the course of the evening, Staten Island CC is reputed to have won the sheep-grazing rights to the ground. Perhaps the inebriated members of Surrey County Cricket

Club knew a thing or two about transporting sheep across the Atlantic and felt this gamble was affordable. On the other hand, both parties at the poker table might have been beyond caring about the consequences of the bet. Fortunately for Test cricket in England, there has never been an attempt made by the Staten Island club to enforce its rights to graze sheep, even so much as on the outfield, let alone on the hallowed square.

In 1997, Staten Island CC tried but failed to arrange a match on Broadhalfpenny Down. Might they have gambled for the grazing rights, which would have been far more valuable than those at The Oval? Hampshire downland is serious sheep country, nothing like a manicured London lawn. Be that as it may, neither Staten Island, nor any other touring side made up of Americans, is thought to have played at Broadhalfpenny Down until 1995. The only side from the USA known to have played there previously consisted of ex-patriates and players born and brought up in cricket-playing countries who just happened to be living in Florida.

So the match between Hambledon and the Los Angeles Krickets on Broadhalfpenny Down on Friday 22 September 1995 was almost certainly the first involving a side of Americans. How and why they came is as remarkable as any of the events that preceded their arrival. The LA Krickets had played cricket for about three months before coming to England. They had been introduced to the game as part of a rehabilitation programme for the long-term homeless of Los Angeles. Ted Hayes, an Afro-American with a clear vision of the needs of the poor and a can-do approach to finding the people and resources needed to deal with this growing problem, had been involved in providing shelter and support to the homeless of Los Angeles for over ten years.

David Sentance was an Englishman working in Los Angeles with the British-American Chamber of Commerce. He introduced Ted Hayes to the game of cricket in December 1994, and over the next few months they met members of the forty or so teams playing in the Los Angeles cricket leagues. Several, including Stephen Speak, formerly of Lancashire's second XI, and Leo Magnus, ex-Gloucestershire second XI, joined in a project to bring cricket into Ted Hayes's Dome Village community.

Their collective purpose was to exploit the sheer novelty of the game, which was virtually unknown to almost all the residents, give them the chance to play it and then discover how to play it better. The might hopefully gain some self-confidence from their new skills and the fact that they were doing something few others in the USA – especially the indigenous population – were able to do.

As David Sentance put it: 'For many of these players, the opportunity to take part in a multi-racial, peaceful competition is something entirely new. It's teaching them to handle conflict in a non-violent way, and it's a perfect way to learn about the mental discipline we all need to cope with life.'

There are many reasons for playing cricket, and most people in those parts of the world where it has been played for generations know them all very well. But how many times

The Los Angeles Krickets on tour, September 1995.
(Reproduced by kind permission of David Sentance)

before has a reason as powerful as David Sentance's come to light? It might sound a little too much like the words of a sociology professor to some ears, but there was no mistaking the excitement and the pleasure the LA Krickets experienced at Broadhalfpenny Down that September day.

Before arriving, the sum of their cricketing knowledge was three months' experience on an asphalt strip, set in a public park. Yet between September 14 and 25, they played six matches in England, including one against Scotland Yard at South Hampstead's ground in North London. Bearing in mind the horrifically deprived, crime-infested backgrounds of some of these players, this match might well have been their first non-confrontational experience of 'cops and robbers'.

The tour had been organized at great speed, while there must still have been doubt in some minds about the team's ability to perform adequately on the field. But they need have had no concern. The LA Krickets fielded at times with an athleticism which would have done credit to a county side. Against Hambledon, for instance, Tom Fitzpatrick took two particularly good catches, despite being without his beloved baseball glove. The throwing was breathtaking; but what else should be expected from young people who watch and play American football, basketball and baseball at home?

The bowling was surprisingly consistent. The ball was not always delivered exactly on the spot, but it was there far more often than not, and proved to be anything but the pushover the Hambledon batsmen were expecting. In their forty overs, Hambledon scored 193 for 6. The honour of being the first American to take a wicket on Broadhalfpenny Down went to Theo Hayes III,

The Los Angeles Krickets at the monument, September 1995.
(Reproduced by kind permission of Giles Lyon)

the eldest son of the man who had done so much to get them all there in the first place. He bowled Simon James for 13 when the score was 43.

The Krickets' batting showed clear signs of the baseball influence, which was hardly surprising in the circumstances, and there was a good deal of bottom hand in many of the shots. But they hit the ball hard enough. Keith Hartog's 13 against Hambledon's league bowlers was a remarkable achievement for a man who had picked up a bat for the first time less than three months earlier. The Krickets finished with 165 off thirty-nine overs and lost the match by a mere 28 runs. But nobody worried too much about the result. This was a day when the match itself was everything, and the importance of the venue was lost on none of the visitors, who were hungry for every scrap of history they could gather during the day.

As Terry Wood, chairman of the Hambledon club, wrote in the match programme: 'We are no strangers to hosting touring sides from throughout the world, including Australia, New Zealand, Germany and Holland. But it would be fair to say that this match is a little bit different – and all the more special for that.' Indeed it was. For a start, Mr Wood was away on

The Los Angeles Krickets take the field, September 1995, the first all-American side ever to walk onto Broadhalfpenny Down.
(Reproduced by kind permission of Giles Lyon)

honeymoon, and apologized in the programme for his absence on the grounds that he did not want his wife to be a cricket widow, at least, he added, 'so soon into our marriage'.

This match was also special for the media attention it received. There must have been as many reporters and camera crews as players at times during the day, and the start of the match was delayed for over half-an-hour because so many players were being interviewed. Later in the afternoon, four TV crews lined the top of the ground like evenly-placed boundary markers; BBC-South, Meridian, Sky Sports, and NBC from New York. The subsequent coverage back in the USA surprised even the organizers. ABC News in Los Angeles carried match reports of the whole tour, CNN broadcast a piece in its weekly sports profiles series, and Dan Rather, the David Frost of American TV, reported the Broadhalfpenny Down match on CBS nationwide.

So, yet another first for Broadhalfpenny Down. Coverage of a club game on prime-time television in the United States of America. What would Richard Nyren have made of that? Or the Duke of Dorset?

There is a poignant footnote to this story. When the team got back to Los Angeles airport, Roger Simon was immediately re-arrested for violation of his probation. He did not have permission to leave the country, following his involvement in the civil riots of a year or so earlier, and subsequent conviction. His letters from jail to Ted Hayes after his re-arrest were not those of a hardened criminal. They expressed the feelings of a man who had seen beyond the grief-stricken environment in which he grew up, and now knew that there were better things out there. That tour changed his view of life. One day it may change his way of life too.

Meanwhile, the local police department asked David Sentance and Ted Hayes to introduce cricket as part of their gang abatement programme, and plans were made to build a cricket stadium in downtown Los Angeles. Broadhalfpenny Down might yet supply a square of turf for that one, too.

What a perfect summer's day it was. A gentle heat haze lifted from the Meon Valley below us. A scorching sun blazed down from a cloudless sky. It was as hot as an English summer can be. Not even a breeze cooled the face. Corn in the fields beyond the boundary stood stock still, disturbed only by the mice and birds hunting for insects. The butterflies just spread their wings in the sunshine. Even they could not find the energy to fly. The buzz of those insects, and the distinctive call of Shelley's skylarks high above, added to a sense of wonder at the beauty, peace and pleasure of it all. It was a joy to be alive. There was nowhere else on earth to be at that moment.

From the pavilion came the occasional flutter of applause when action at the wicket stirred the spectators sufficiently. Mostly they just sat in the sun, eyes half closed behind their sunglasses, dreaming, watching contentedly, some waiting their turn to bat. For them, the idea of coming out to bat would have prompted mixed feelings; the notion of running about in the heat, tangled up with the wish to score a few runs, on a perfect summer's day, on a pitch as famous as this one. In any case, weren't the two batsmen at the crease doing well enough already...why wish their downfall...it's best just sitting,

Three pairs of father and son on the same side in a match on Broadhalfpenny Down. The Broadhalfpenny Brigands team against Whitchurch on 2 August 1995 included (left to right): Barnaby and Ashley Mote, Andrew and Bryan Burns, Richard and Harry Bates.

watching, at least for the moment.

Bat hit ball, runs accumulated, wickets fell from time to time. In the field we conserved energy, except when saving runs depended on it. The bowlers paced themselves through long spells of maximum effort, knowing that a rest would follow. The noon-day sun came and went. This was an all-day game against an opposition we knew well and whose company we thoroughly enjoyed. We all played hard, we all wanted to win. But – cliché though it may be – this was one of those days when the winner was the game of cricket itself. We were all here because of our love for the game, on a perfect day and on a unique ground.

That day, as usual, I was fielding at slip. Bernard Marshall, veteran of cricket in Cornwall, playing member of the MCC, ex-Royal Navy chaplain, liver of life to the full and something of a one-off amongst churchmen, stood at gully. Like all close fielders, we chatted between balls and between overs.

'Bernard,' I said. 'Bernard, is heaven like this?'

For a moment there was no reply. He gave the suggestion quite a lot of thought. It had not been intended as a loaded question, but to a churchman it might have seemed so. Eventually came his answer: 'It doesn't come much better,' he said. Diplomatic, certainly. I like to think it's true as well.

About the time of that little exchange, I found my mind thinking back those 200 years, and wondering what Richard Nyren, John Small, Tom Sueter and all the others made of days such as this. They would have experienced everything we experienced that day, except for a few minor changes to the handful of buildings visible from Broadhalfpenny Down. Even the Bat and Ball across the road is still much the same today. They would have known such blissful summer days as this, heard those same skylarks. It was as though time had truly stood still. Perhaps they too wanted such days to go on for ever.

And then it struck me. In a way, they have. As I looked around at my fellow Brigands that blistering summer's day in 1994 on Broadhalfpenny Down, I couldn't help wondering if we hadn't all been here before, on this same spot, playing cricket. The sense of *déjà vu* was irresistible. It was a spontaneous thought, no effort was required. The heat of the day had got to me, I confess. And yet...the idea would not go away. There were the same characters, the players of long ago, still playing. The names and clothing were different, but little else.

These idle daydreams had reminded me of a simple truth – the fact is, nothing has changed. The passing pageant of players is endless. It is the game that endures. After all, as the Duke of Dorset asked all those years ago, 'What is human life but a game of cricket?'

Into the Crystal Bat and Ball

So far, we have been looking behind. Now, at last, we can turn around and look the other way.

Broadhalfpenny Down and the Bat and Ball together present the world of cricket with a problem and an opportunity. It is a problem to the extent that a number of different interests are involved, each with their own agenda and objectives. They do not necessarily conflict, and more often than not – especially in recent times – they have happily coincided and been mutually supportive. But the fact that they are different, and disconnected, leaves a continuing potential for problems in the future. The voluntary goodwill which is taken for granted today cannot be guaranteed indefinitely without changes in the underlying structures and relationships.

Added to which, the location is and always will be something of a problem. The only way to Broadhalfpenny Down is by car, via winding lanes running through sleepy Hampshire villages, most of whose inhabitants are there precisely because they are quiet and largely undisturbed. The location of Broadhalfpenny Down is – in itself – an argument for doing very little to it in the future.

As for the ground itself, Broadhalfpenny Down will never be

a site for first-class matches. It has none of the essential ingredients. In any case, Hampshire have big plans for a new ground near Southampton and they already have locations for first-class games in Portsmouth and Basingstoke, both of which would like more county matches staged on their grounds. There is no place for Broadhalfpenny Down in all that. If Hampshire were to look around for other places at which to play their matches, Bournemouth and Winchester would be at the top of the list. Worse, Broadhalfpenny Down has a soil structure totally unsuited to the first-class game. It is not even good enough for top-grade league cricket. A huge investment would be required to change that, and for no discernible purpose in the foreseeable future.

Yet Broadhalfpenny Down is now perceived as the spiritual home of the game, regardless of the facts. No amount of clarification of what actually happened here – as opposed to what so many people *think* happened here – will change that belief, nor diminish the interest it generates. For most people, the subtle distinction between 'being where cricket started' and 'being where cricket grew up' is trivial. It matters only to the aficionados. In any case, this century has seen an ever-increasing acceptance of the unique place Broadhalfpenny Down and the Bat and Ball have in the collective mind of the cricketing world, and much has already been done to protect and preserve it. The real issue, today, is how best to plan for the future, and how best to structure our response to the protective efforts we have inherited from previous generations.

The formation of a trust, proposed by the Brigands in their bid to retain the lease on the ground in 1992 and subsequently put into effect by the club at the invitation of Winchester College, is clearly a vital step in the right direction. Its somewhat optimistic pursuit of charitable status proved a lengthy detour, but the underlying concept must be right. The association, as it now is, offers the cricketing world an ideal vehicle on which to build a solid and successful future for this historic site.

After all, membership of the cricket community is free, and the Bat and Ball is cricket's clubhouse and pavilion. It once

The Bat and Ball today.

served the players and members of the Hambledon club. Now it serves the Broadhalfpenny Brigands. But in truth, it is the clubhouse and pavilion to the whole cricketing world. Every cricketer knows he belongs here and every past owner and tenant has learned that for themselves, sometimes with pleasure and sometimes, sadly and surprisingly, against their will. For the thousands of people who arrive here every year, it is enough just to have made the journey, seen Broadhalfpenny Down and enjoyed a drink and a few reminiscences in the bar. For the visiting players who take a drink here and enjoy good company after a match, it is a very special experience. For a lucky handful, it is home, and that is something else again.

But what of its future? The time has come to stand back from the past and the present, and look at Broadhalfpenny Down from a new perspective. What might it become in the decades ahead? If we were standing here in a hundred years' time, what would we hope to see? The picture is not difficult to visualize, given what we know of past history and present needs. What do we see in the crystal ball?

Broadhalfpenny Down and the Bat and Ball are now owned and run by a single organization, a trust consisting of all the parties interested in its well-being. As a totality, it is a well-equipped and fully resourced focus for the history of the game. In the south-west corner of the ground, looking from the outside exactly like the original of the 1770s, stands a fine period building – an exact replica of the lodge. Water and electricity was brought to the ground long since, and a few additional acres adjoining the south-west corner were purchased from the neighbouring farmer to make room for the new facilities. The transaction did no more than bring parcel 11 of over a century before back to its original shape. These improvements all started when the Lottery Fund was encouraged to support a massive ground restoration and enhancement programme on Broadhalfpenny Down back in the late 1990s.

But when you walk inside the Broadhalfpenny Lodge (as it's now known), what you see is quite different from its original counterpart. As you wander around, you quickly encounter two fine modern dressing-rooms for the players, complete with all the latest facilities, a players' dining-room for big match days, and a restaurant and bar for spectators. Outside, the original casual seating area for members can be recreated on match days, with flags and bunting flying from the superstructure, and a little white picket-fence finishing off a perfect environment from which to watch a match. Even the new electronic scoreboard has been carefully incorporated into the design of the building to provide all the information spectators now expect, but without spoiling the overall appearance of the lodge.

At the back, unobtrusively hidden from the view of the spectators on the other side of the ground, you walk into an adjoining building to find squash courts and a pair of indoor cricket-nets, which provide an ideal all-the-year-round facility for members and for the club's youth cricket programme. These facilities help all players to improve standards, fitness and performances and are open to visiting teams and local clubs as well.

Off to the side of the open reception area in the lodge is an attractive and brightly-lit shop which offers visitors a huge range of cricket memorabilia, books and magazines, clothing and modern equipment. A little coffee shop nearby provides somewhere for visitors to sit and chat, and browse through their latest purchases. But the highlight of any visit to the lodge is a tour of the cricket museum. Here is Nyren's manuscript, and the writing table he used which was later given by his granddaughters to EV Lucas. Wisden's have loaned the old scoring-table used by the Hambledon club during the glory days. Here is Tom Walker's bat, on permanent loan from Lord's, as are the original drawings for Ralph Ellis's pub sign. The minutes of the Hambledon club meeting on 25 September 1771, when the width of the bat was decided, and the miniature bat given to Richard Nyren twenty years later both have places of honour, as do the now well-washed and carefully preserved smock worn by Ludovic May in 1931, and his umbrella from the glory days. Here is Bernard Cancellor's first beautiful design for the monument in 1908, the one that was never built, now projected by three-dimensional laser to display it in all the glory he first imagined but never saw. Here is the 1908 silver half-crown hidden under the plinth by Thomas Beck when the monument was first erected. Benignly looking down on it all are portraits of the men who wrote the three great books about the glory days – John Nyren, EV Lucas and FS Ashley-Cooper – to which someone has thoughtfully added a sketch of Arthur Haygarth in honour of the man who did so much to capture Hambledon's early match records before it was too late. All these treasures, and scores of others, are here for every cricket enthusiast who wants to see them. Back where they belong, and now displayed in ideal conditions.

Around the ground, raked seating and the framework of small grandstands remind the visitor of the scene on big match days, when overseas touring teams and representative sides visit and play against each other and the home teams. The original monument has been moved to a prominent place beside the lodge, not just to make way for parking and the new drive across the top of the ground, but also to display it properly in a place of honour. No longer is it an afterthought stuck in a corner by the hedge.

Across the road from the car park area, the Bat and Ball remains the focus of attention during and after matches, the bar area restored to its original shape and character but enlarged in the same style to allow more people to enjoy its special atmosphere. It too offers a restaurant service, staffed by the same catering team which manages the kitchens in the lodge. But the menus vary and offer spectators greater choice.

The key to commercial success long ago proved to be the creation of sustained interest in the lodge all the year round. The summers largely take care of themselves, with a hectic summer programme from mid-April to mid-September. The winters take somewhat more effort, to keep the place busy. But there is plenty going on for all that. The steady stream of visitors which has always arrived on the off-chance at Broadhalfpenny Down and the Bat and Ball still keeps the place healthily ticking over. But nowadays there are many more organized events to bring people out during the winter months.

Matches played on the other side of the world can be watched ball-by-ball on a huge three-dimensional television

Visualization of the 'new' lodge on the original site in the south-west corner of the ground.
(Reproduced by kind permission of Chris Turner and David Hoare)

screen set up in the reception area, and scores of spectators come to view for the day, effectively transported for a few hours each night to the other side of the globe. Warmth from the sunlamps and cool beer from the bar reproduce the grandstand atmosphere with incredible realism, and the whole place takes on a carnival atmosphere for the entire match.

At other times, club dinners, meetings, lectures, social events and video-shows of past cricket tours from around the world fill many an evening. The meeting and dining facilities are hired out to other clubs who want to hold their annual dinners here, too, when the shop and museum are opened especially for them. Today, the Broadhalfpenny Down complex is a thriving, successful, fully funded enterprise, attracting large numbers of devotees from all over the world, meeting their cricketing needs and interests in today's world, and

paying handsome tribute to the glory days of the game and the incredible men who played here so long ago.

While such fanciful speculation on what might exist on Broadhalfpenny Down in a hundred years' time may not appeal to all tastes, and seem a huge change from what we see here today, the truth is less dramatic. In outward appearance, the rebuilt lodge would fit into the landscape as it once did. It would be bigger and have a greater depth, but to the casual eye it would look the same. The views around the ground would still be the same. That wonderful ambience on a hot summer's day would still be here, and so would the bleak winter wind. The location would be unchanged, and the atmosphere on a match day would be as exciting as ever.

If anything, my flight of imagination does no more than build on the concept of the trust and at the same time put the scene at Broadhalfpenny Down during the glory days into a future context. In that sense it is we, today, who have missed out. We never saw it as it was, and we will not see it as it might one day be again.

But future generations might thank us for making a start. They surely deserve no less.

For the Record

The following record-performances on Broadhalfpenny Down have come to light during research for *The Glory Days of Cricket*. Because many of the early match details are lost, the following cannot be confirmed as the best performances ever. They *may* be the best; they are *certainly among* the best.

HIGHEST INDIVIDUAL SCORE
Brian Shattock, 158
Broadhalfpenny Brigands v Lord's Taverners, 1968

BEST BOWLING ANALYSIS
John Newman, 8 for 54
Hambledon v England, 1908 (This was the match staged to celebrate the unveiling of the monument. John Newman was a Hampshire professional.)
(The best performances by amateurs are Chris Bazalgette's 8 for 79 for the Broadhalfpenny Brigands v London New Zealand, 1996, and Ivan Angell's 7 for 16 for Wadham Bros v Westgate Brewery, 1939.)

HIGHEST TOTAL
357 (John Small senior 136 not out,
Richard Nyren 98, Thomas Brett 68)
Hambledon v Surrey, 1775
(A single-innings total of 403, with James Aylward scoring 167, was recorded by the Hambledon club against England in 1777, during the match which also resulted in Hambledon's biggest win – by an innings and 168 runs. But the game was played at Sevenoaks Vine.)

HIGHEST PARTNERSHIP
263 (for 0 dec)
Nic Wolstenholme 154 not out,
Jonathan Grant 100 not out
Hampshire Hogs v Broadhalfpenny Brigands, 1995

CRICKET ON BROADHALFPENNY DOWN
c1742 – 1792 Hambledon club
1792 – 1908 Out of use
1908 – 1936 Few matches organized by Hambledon Cricket Club, Winchester College and others
1936 – 1951 Wadham Brothers Ltd
1952 – 1959 HMS *Mercury*
1959 – Broadhalfpenny Brigands Cricket Club

Postscript

John Nyren's Manuscript

I had hoped that my researches for this book might reveal one or two items of memorabilia. The most I hoped for was the discovery of Richard Nyren's miniature bat, presented to him in September 1791 on a poignant occasion which marked the end of the glory days as definitively as no other single event could have done. Despite my best efforts, including scores of conversations, phone calls and letters, it has still not come to light.

But something else has, something truly astonishing – unique, and previously unknown. It is a handwritten manuscript of John Nyren's masterpiece, *The Cricketers of my Time*. As in the original published version, it is preceded by *The Young Cricketer's Tutor* and followed by at least part of his *Memoranda*. It appears to be a first fair-copy prior to submission to the printers. Most of the changes between it and the first edition are either additions to, or minor improvements in the text.

Of course, John Nyren's *The Cricketers of my Time* was published in part-form a year before the first edition of his book. Not only does the original include several vivid passages which – for now unfathomable reasons – Nyren removed from the book version, they also throw – for us – new light on the period in general and the glory days in particular.

The serialized version, together with an analysis of the newly-discovered manuscript, is being published as a companion volume to *The Glory Days of Cricket* early in 1998. It will provide the first opportunity to read John Nyren's original version of *The Cricketers of my Time* since 1832.

Appendix

The Poetry of Broadhalfpenny Down

Broadhalfpenny Down has provoked a good deal of verse over the last 200 years or so, for reasons which this book has hopefully made clear. It has not always been poetry for the aficionado, but it is none the worse for that. For the cricket romantic, there is still merit in these diverse attempts to capture something of the doings of the Hambledon club and the atmosphere of Broadhalfpenny Down during the glory days and beyond.

The Rev. Reynell Cotton, pillar of the original club, was the first to be inspired to verse by the exploits of the men of Hambledon. He wrote the following to celebrate the club's astonishing achievements and the place it had gained in the world of cricket in those days. His words were published by order of the Hambledon club minutes of 5 June 1781. Describing the pleasure he got from listening to the singing of this and many other songs in the Bat and Ball after their matches, John Nyren quoted a couplet of the poet Isaac Watts (1674-1748):

> I have been there, and still would go;
> 'Twas like a little heaven below!

These are the Rev. Cotton's verses, which gave Nyren so much delight:

ASSIST, all ye Muses, and join to rehearse
An old English Sport, never praised yet in Verse;
'Tis CRICKET I sing, of illustrious Fame,
No Nation e'er boasted so noble a Game.
Derry down, down, down, derry down.

Great Pindar has bragg'd of his Heroes of old,
Some were swift in the Race, some in Battle were bold,
The Brows of the Victor with Olive were crown'd.
Hark, they shout, and Olympia returns the glad Sound.
    Derry down...

What boasting of Castor and Pollux his Brother,
The one fam'd for riding, for bruising the other?
Compar'd with our Heroes, they'll not shine at all;
What were Castor and Pollux to NYREN and SMALL?
    Derry down...

Here's guarding and catching, and throwing and tossing,
And bowling and striking, and running and crossing;
Each Mate must excel in some principal Part:
The Pentathlon of Greece could not show so much Art.
    Derry down...

The Parties are met, and array'd all in white;
Fam'd Elis ne'er boasted so pleasing a Sight;
Each Nymph looks askew at her favourite Swain,
And views him half stripp'd both with Pleasure and Pain.
    Derry down...

The Wickets are pitch'd now, & measur'd the Ground,
Then they form a large Ring, and stand gazing around.
Since Ajax fought Hector, in Sight of all Troy,
No Contest was seen with such Fear and such Joy.
    Derry down...

Ye Bowlers take heed, to my Precepts attend:
On you the whole Fate of the Game must depend;

Spare your Vigour at first, nor exert all your Strength,
But measure each Step, and be sure pitch a Length.
    Derry down...

Ye Fieldsmen look sharp, lest your pains ye beguile;
Move close like an Army, in Rank and in File;
When the Ball is return'd, back it sure, for I trow
Whole States have been ruin'd by one overthrow.
    Derry down...

Ye Strikers observe, when the Foe shall draw nigh,
Mark the Bowler advancing – with vigilant Eye;
Your skill all depends upon Distance and Sight:
Stand firm to your Scratch, let your Bat be upright.
    Derry down...

And now the game's o'er, lo Victory sings,
Echo doubles her Chorus, and Fame spreads her Wings;
Let's now hail our Champions, all steady and true,
Such as Homer ne'er sung of, nor Pindar e'er knew.
    Derry down...

BUCK, CURRY, and HOGSFLESH, and BARBER and BRETT,
Whose Swiftness in bowling was ne'er equall'd yet;
I had almost forgot, they deserve a large Bumper,
Little GEORGE, the long Stop, and TOM SUETER, the
Stumper.
    Derry down...

Then why should we fear either SACKVILLE or MANN,
Or repine at the Loss of both BAYTON and LAND?
With such Troops as those we'll be Lords of the Game,
Spite of MINSHULL and MILLER, and LUMPY and FRAME.
    Derry down...

Then fill up your Glass, he's the best that drinks most.
Here's the HAMBLEDON CLUB, who refuses the Toast!
Let's join in the Praise of the Bat and the Wicket,
And sing in full Chorus the PATRONS of CRICKET.
    Derry down...

And when the Game's o'er, and our Fate shall draw nigh,

(For the Heroes of Cricket like others must die),
Our Bats we'll resign, neither troubled nor vex'd,
    And give up our Wickets to those who come next.
        Derry down...

Andrew Lang's verses were probably written just after the turn of the last century. They reflect the increasing interest in the fate of Broadhalfpenny Down. His lines include two curious references, however, one of which is a simple typing error, and the other a complete mystery. In line two, Barber is mistakenly spelled Barker in the original version, but has been corrected here. In verse three, following the mention of Tom Sueter, Lang mentions 'Brown'. Who was he? No Brown appears in any of the great matches, and there is no obvious near-misspelling of any of the other players to explain it. Not even that high priest of cricket exactitude, FS Ashley-Cooper, lists a Brown either as a player or as a member of the Hambledon club. Did Andrew Lang know something none of the rest of us know?

In the Envoy, 'Prince' is a reference to Prince Ranjitsinhji, and 'Hirst' is George Hirst, the Yorkshire and England all-rounder. With CB Fry, all three would have been cricketing heroes of Andrew Lang, as they were for all followers of cricket at that time. There are some suggestions that this poem was first published in 1884, in which case the Envoy must have been added some twenty years later. In 1884, Ranji, Hirst and Fry were still toddlers.

BALLADE OF DEAD CRICKETERS
Ah, where be Beldham now, and Brett,
Barber, and Hogsflesh, where be they?
Brett, of all the bowlers fleetest yet
That drove the bails in disarray?
And Small that would, like Orpheus, play
Till wild bulls followed his minstrelsy?
Booker, Quiddington, and May?
Beneath the daises, there they lie!

Cricket Song
for the Hambledon Club

The first two pages of music for the Rev. Reynell Cotton's song of praise in Hambledon and its cricketers.

2. Great Pin-dar has bragg'd of his her-oes of old, Some were

swift in the race, some in bat-tle were bold; The brows of the vic-tors with

ol-ives were crown'd; Hark! they shout, and Ol-ym-pia re-turns the glad sound. Der-ry

down, down, down, derry down.

Dal Segno. 𝄊

And where is Lambert, that would get
The stumps with balls that broke astray?
And Mann, whose balls would ricochet
In almost an unholy way
(So do baseballers 'pitch' today);
George Leer, that seldom let a bye,
And Richard Nyren, grave and gray?
Beneath the daises, there they lie!

Tom Sueter, too, the ladies' pet,
Brown that would bravest hearts affray;
Walker, invincible when set,
(Tom, of the spider limbs and splay);
Think ye that we could match them, pray,
These heroes of Broad-halfpenny,
With Buck to hit, and Small to stay?
Beneath the daises, there they lie!

Envoy

Prince, canst thou moralize the lay?
How all things change below the sky?
Of Fry and Hirst shall mortals say,
'Beneath the daises, there they lie!'

Three poems written in the early part of the twentieth century
are all linked to Windmill Down, although they have as much
– if not more – relevance to Broadhalfpenny Down. They are
included here for that reason.

The first was written by Alfred Cochrane, poet and essayist,
in about 1900. But who told him that Harris bowled slows?

ENGLAND, PAST AND PRESENT

But for an hour to watch them play,
Those heroes dead and gone,
And pit our batsmen of today
With those of Hambledon!

Our Graces, Nyrens, Studds, and Wards
In weeks of sunny weather,
Somewhere upon Elysian swards,
To see them matched together!
Could we but see how Small withstands
The three-foot break of Steel.
If Silver Billy's 'wondrous hands'
Survive with Briggs or Peel!
If Mann, with all his pluck of yore,
Can keep the leather rolling,
And, at a crisis, notch a score,
When Woods and Hearne are bowling!

No doubt the Doctor could bewitch
His quaint top-hatted foes,
Though, on a deftly-chosen pitch,
Old Harris bowled his slows;
And Aylward, if the asphodel
Had made the wicket bumpy,
Would force the game with Attewell,
And Stoddart collar 'Lumpy'.

When time of all our flannelled hosts
Leaves only the renown,
Our cracks, perhaps, may join the ghosts
That roam on Windmill Down,
Where shadowy crowds will watch the strife,
And cheer the deeds of wonder
Achieved by giants whom in life
A century kept asunder.

The author Eric Parker published his book *Between The Wickets* in 1926. It included the following poem, the last verse of which was quoted by Harry Altham at the dinner held in Hambledon village hall on 15 December 1964 to celebrate the bicentenary of the birth of John Nyren.

This is the place: here is the story told
Of those first players in that far-off June
That shines still on these Hampshire downs. Behold
The very turf, the pitch where some high noon
'Lumpy' would choose his sloping wicket, soon
To rouse deep-throated chorus from the ring,
Vying with Beldham, Walker, Brett to bring
Fame to the tales that Nyren's readers con,
Names for undreamt of rhymers yet to sing,
When primroses are out at Hambledon.

Gone are the days, yet hither, as of old
Come players for the game; moon follows moon,
Still the same happy echoes fill the wold,
Still the down's deep wood the pigeons croon,
About the old inn parlour village shoon
(Ale-fragrant still the air) go clattering,
And gardeners bowl and blacksmiths catches fling,
And bat from ball cracks music, and upon
Green turf the high sun dies to evening,
When primroses are out in Hambledon.

And so where wickets stand or grass is rolled,
From Windmill Down to Sydney, the same boon,
Born of the game, continues. Caught or bowled
The players pass – one law for lord or loon.
The piper changes: who should change the tune
Le roi est mort! E'en so: God save the King!
For Lockwood's, we shall watch Macaulay's swing,
Hobbs follows Grace, Holmes Hirst, Tate Richardson,
Carr can still show us Jessop's larruping,
When primroses are out in Hambledon.

Friend, tis the end begins. The play's the thing.
We win or lose again, remembering
We shall find sunlit swards by Acheron,
And toss bright obols, each returning spring
When primroses are out in Hambledon.

The poet William Kerr wrote the next piece some time during the 1920s. Mynn and Pilch are players from the early 1800s. The others belong to cricket's golden age.

PAST AND PRESENT

Daisies are over Nyren, and Hambledon
Hardly remembers any summer gone:
And never again the Kentish elms shall see
Mynn, or Fuller Pilch, or Colin Blythe.
– Nor shall I see them, unless perhaps a ghost
Watching the elder ghosts beyond the moon.
But here in common sunshine I have seen
George Hirst, not yet a ghost, substantial,
His off-drives mellow as brown ale, and crisp
Merry late cuts, and brave Chauserian pulls;
Waddington's fury and the patience of Dipper;
And twenty easy artful overs of Rhodes,
So many stanzas of the Faerie Queen.

Bruce Blunt wrote the following lyrics to commemorate the match played on Broadhalfpenny Down on 1 January 1929. It was intended 'to be roared over mugs of beer', in the best traditions of the past. It was splendidly set to music by Peter Warlock, the talented young English composer who had already built quite a reputation for both bleak and rumbustious compositions. This was certainly one of the latter. Sadly, Warlock's promising musical career was cut short barely a year later.

I'll make a song of Hambledon and sing it at The George
Of balls that flew from Beldham's bat like sparks from
Fennex's forge,
The centuries of Aylward and a thousand-guinea bet,
And Sueter keeping wicket to the thunderbolts of Brett.

Chorus:
Then up with every glass and we'll sing a toast in chorus;
The cricketers of Hambledon who played the game before us,

Peter Warlock's music for Bruce Blunt's lyrics, written and first performed for the game on New Year's Day, 1929.
(Reproduced by kind permission of Stainer and Bell Ltd)

The stalwarts of the olden time who rolled a lonely down
And made the king of games for men, with Hambledon the
crown.

Altho' they sang the nights away, their afternoons were spent
In beating men of Hertfordshire, and flogging men of Kent.
And when the flower of England fell to Taylor and his peers
The fame of Hambledonians went ringing down the years.

The sun has left Broadhalfpenny, and the moon rides over-
head,
So pass the bottle round again for drinking to the dead;
To Small and his companions who gathered, lose or win
To take their fill of Nyren's best, when Nyren kept the inn.

Francis Brett Young wrote much of his poetry during the 1930s.
The following lines were first published, however, in 1944.

ON WINDMILL DOWN, 1789

...Then there was Beldham,
William Beldham – Silver Billy us always called 'en,
For his hair was so white as a wheatfield, come October.
Harry Hall, the ginger-bread maker, learnt 'en the game:
Hall were no great player himself, but he made young Beldham
Keep his left elbow up and hold his bat plumb-straight
In the line of the ball when he swung. 'Twere a gallant sight
To see Silver Billy smack 'em all over the field,
And never lift one. That lad, he danced on his toes
Like Jack Broughton, the boxer. And run! He could lance like
a deer,
To pick up the ball full-pelt, as neat as a swallow
Nips gnats in the air! You'd ought to a' see'd 'en cut
Off the point of the bat, with a crack like a pistol-shot,
The ball shaving daisies all the way to the boundary,
And shepherds a'lepping like lambs of an April evenin'
To save their old shins – not one of 'em could a'stopped it
Howsomever he tried. But I 'low the best of all

Was when him and Lord Frederick Beauclerk was in together:
Lord Frederick had royal blood in 'en, so 'twere said,
For his grammer were Nelly Gwynn, King Charles' fancy,
But when Billy and him walked out to the pitch, side by side,
You couldn't tell which were the farmer and which the
  gentleman,
The pair on 'em looked that majestic. And when they got set
You'ld a'thought they was brothers born, the way they gloried
In basting the bowling between 'em. There wasn't a ball,
Long or short, high or low, but Lord Frederick went into it
Wrist and shoulder. And Billy the same. They looked
  something grander
Than human mortals, them two – so light on their feet
As hobby-hawks skimmin' a hedge, or pewits a 'runnun'
Afore they do light on the down. I can see them now:
Billy Beldham's silvery head and his lordship's white hat
Thridding to and fro like shuttles: the crowd on their feet
Hollerin' out: 'Go hard...go hard! Tich and turn, tich and turn!
Try another! One more!' – and the fielders runnin' like hares
On every side of the wicket. Ay, that was music!
Afore now I've a'see'd Silver Billy notch ten runs
Off one snick past slip and an overthrow. Them was the days!

When that much-loved broadcaster and cricket commentator
Brian Johnston appeared in Harry Secombe's ITV programme
Highway, which was recorded in and around Hambledon, his
old friend and lyricist Richard Stilgoe wrote a song especially
for the occasion. Richard Stilgoe performed it sitting at a white
piano perched incongruously on Broadhalfpenny Down on a
bitter early-spring day.

  It is one of two of his poems presented by the author to the
Broadhalfpenny Brigands in 1994, to hang in the pavilion on
Broadhalfpenny Down in lasting memory of Brian Johnston,
who loved the place so much. (The other was the verses read
at Brian Johnston's service of thanksgiving in Westminster
Abbey, London, in May 1994.)

IT ALL BEGAN AT HAMBLEDON

At Hambledon, upon this spot, high up on Hampshire's chalk,
A million trillion years ago, the dinosaurs did walk.
The great Gattingosauruses – short-legged, with thick necks.
That fearsome great carnivore, Bothamosaurus Rex.
Across this very turf they strode – one short and fat, one tall –
And came across an ancient pub they call the Bat and Ball.
Declared Gattingosaurus – 'There's a field and a pub,
It's the ice-age, and it's raining – we should start a cricket
    club!'
So it all began at Hambledon, a billion years ago –
Brian Johnston saw it, and Brian ought to know.

Bothamosaurus Rex then found a Pterodactyl's egg,
And rubbed it on his salty tail, so it would swing to leg.
He went and pulled three trees up from a nearby Hampshire
    thicket –
And cried, 'Look, Gatt – the wheel!' Gatt said, 'Rubbish –
    that's a wicket.'
And then Gattingosaurus found a club of slate so vast,
So long and wide from side to side that no ball could get past.
Bothamosaurus Rex then took the obvious revenge,
And made the wickets bigger – which is how we got
    Stonehenge.

Yes it all took place at Hambledon, as the world began to wake,
And Brian Johnston watched while eating prehistoric cake.

They batted through the Stone Age, the scores became colossal
Boycottodon was in so long he turned into a fossil.
They said, 'If only we had Hickthyosaurus in the side –
But he hasn't been here long enough, and isn't qualified.'
Eventually the dinosaurs of Hambledon got sent
A letter postmarked London (which was forwarded from
    Kent).
'The Mammouth Cricket Club (that is the M.C.C. to you)
Is happy to inform you that your membership's come through.'
And so the dinosaurs marched off to London in their hordes –

They're not extinct at all – they're all alive and well at Lord's.
They sleep in the pavilion, dreaming neolithic dreams
And ev'ry now and then wake up, and pick the England teams –

But it all began at Hambledon – it did – I do declare –
Brian Johnston told me, and he knows, 'cos he was there.

*

The final word belongs to the little-known poet Dorothy
Spring, whose evocative words about the last match of the
season seem to offer an echo of the end of the glory days.

LAST MATCH

High festival today –
The village team against the County men;
And after that, no more.

They start correctly, then
Suddenly filled with merriment, they play
Time-honoured jokes: a ball
That drops to pieces when it hits the bat;
An ear-splitting 'How's that?"
Just as the batsman hits a hefty four.
And now a few leaves fall,
And down the village street the church clock chimes,
The sadness of last times.

Ninety for nine the village have, and then
Improbably, the last two make a stand,
Conjuring strange and most unnatural runs
Like rabbits from a hat. It starts to rain.
The pessimistic ones
Go home. We have our tea. It stops again.
And soon the County men
Are hitting sixes up and down the land.

Seventy-nine for four; the sun comes out.
A sheepdog potters thoughtfully about
At deep mid-on, and starts to dig a hole.

Someone says let it bowl.
At ten to six they pass the village score.

And we, the lookers-on,
Turned homeward, as our fellows dead and gone
Turned homeward from the downs by Hambledon;
And – as did they –
Hoard squirrel-like the pleasures of the day:
Broad-spoken pleasantries; the curving flight
Of sixes; the perennial delight
Of stolen runs; the lovely panther-leap
Of one fantastic catch.

All these are ours, to keep
And talk of on some bleak December night.

This was the year's last match.

Cricket Bibliography

PRINCIPAL SOURCES

Cricket 1742–1751, FS Ashley-Cooper, private printing, 1900

Cricket: A Collection of all the Grand Matches 1771–1791, W Epps (Troy-Town Rochester, 1799)

Cricket, A Weekly Record of the Game, various issues, 1882–1914

The Cricketers of my Time, John Nyren (Effingham Wilson, 1833)
   – and handwritten draft mss

The Cricket Field, The Rev. James Pycroft, BA (Longman, 1851)

Cricket Highways and Byways, FS Ashley-Cooper (George Allen and Unwin, 1927)

Cricket Scores 1719–1829, collected by FS Ashley-Cooper, unpublished mss

Cricket Scores 1730–1773, HT Waghorn (Blackwood, 1899)

Cricket Scores and Biographies, vol 1, Arthur Haygarth (Lillywhite, 1862)

The Dawn of Cricket, HT Waghorn (Electric Press, 1906)

The Field is Full of Shades, GD Martineau (Sporting Handbooks, 1946)

Fresh Light on 18th Century Cricket, GB Buckley (Cotterell, 1935)

Fresh Light on Pre-Victorian Cricket, GB Buckley (Cotterell, 1937)

The Hambledon Cricket Chronicle 1772–1796, FS Ashley-Cooper (Herbert Jenkins, 1924)

The Hambledon Men, edited by EV Lucas (Henry Frowde, 1907)

The Laws of Cricket, RS Rait-Kerr (Longmans Green, 1950)

Matches 1786–1822, Henry Bentley (MCC, 1823)

Old English Cricket, six booklets by H P-T (PF Thomas) (Richards, 1923–9)

A Peep into the Past, WR Weir (WR Wright) (Ayres, 1902)

Review of *The Young Cricketer's Tutor*, The Rev. John Mitford, in *The Gentleman's Magazine*, July and September 1833

Wisden Cricket Almanack, various years, from 1864

Scrapbooks and collected papers, the property of John Barrett, collected by his father Colin Barrett.

Unpublished minutes, correspondence, scorebooks and other papers, the property of the Broadhalfpenny Brigands Cricket Club.

Unpublished minutes, correspondence, accounts, and other papers, the property of Hambledon Cricket Club.

Family scrapbook, the property of the late Mike Nyren.

Unpublished correspondence, scrapbooks and the draft mss of John Nyren's *The Cricketers of my Time*, the property of Christine Pardoe, collected by her grandfather Edward Whalley-Tooker.

Family scrapbook, the property of Peter Wadham.

Unpublished minutes, correspondence and documents, the property of Winchester College.

OTHER PUBLICATIONS AND REFERENCES

Annals of Lord's and History of the MCC, Alfred Taylor (JW Arrowsmith, 1903)

Barclays World of Cricket, general editor EW Swanton (Collins Willow in association with Barclays Bank, third edition 1966)

Bibliography of Cricket, compiled by EW Padwick (The Library Association, second edition 1984, and volume two 1991)

Book of Cricket Verse, edited Gerald Brodribb (Rupert Hart-Davis, 1953)

Bibliography of Works by FS Ashley-Cooper, Neville Weston, private printing, 1933

The Cradle of Cricket, WR Weir (WR Wright), private printing, 1909

Cricket, edited by Horace Hutchinson (Country Life, 1903)

Cricket in North Hants, John May (Warren & Son, 1906)

Cricket Notes, William Bolland (Trelawney Saunders, 1851)

Cricket Notices 1744–1845, GB Buckley, unpublished ms, 1940

Cricket – Way of Life, Christopher Martin-Jenkins (Century, 1984)

The Cricketer, various issues, from 1921

Curiosities of Cricket, Jonathan Rice (Pavilion Books, 1993)

Early Books on Cricket, David Rayvern Allen (Europa Publications, 1987)

Echoes From Old Cricket Fields, Frederick Gale (David Nutt, 1871, revised 1896)

Encyclopaedia of Cricket, Maurice Golesworthy (Robert Hale, 1962)

English Cricket, Christopher Brookes (Weidenfeld and Nicolson, 1978)

English Cricket, Neville Cardus (Collins, 1945)

The English Game of Cricket, Charles Box (The Field, 1877)

46 Not Out, RC Robertson-Glasgow (Hollis & Carter, 1948)

The Game of Cricket, Frederick Gale (Swan Sonnenschein Lowrey, 1887)

From Hambledon to Lord's, edited by John Arlott (Barry Shurlock, 1948)

Hambledon, John Goldsmith (Phillimore, 1994)

Hambledon Cricket and The Bat and Ball Inn, Diana Rait-Kerr (Friary Meux, 1951)

Hambledon's Cricket Glory, series of booklets, RD Knight, private printing, from 1975

Hampshire County Cricket, Harry Altham, John Arlott, Desmond Eagar and Roy Webber (Phoenix, 1957)

Hambledon, Hants, Past and Present, Dora Goldsmith (T Martin & Sons, 1908)

The Heart of Cricket, anthology edited by Hubert Doggart (The Cricketer/Hutchinson, 1967)

A History of Cricket, HS Altham (George Allen and Unwin, 1926)

A History of Cricket, Benny Green (Barrie and Jenkins, 1988)

A History of Cricket in Hampshire, 1760–1914, John Simons (Hampshire County Council, 1993)

Kings of Cricket, Richard Daft (Arrowsmith, 1893)

A Life Worth Living, CB Fry (Eyre & Spottiswoode, 1939)

The MCC 1787–1937, various contributors (*The Times*, 1937)

My Cricket Collection, Neville Weston, private printings, 1929-1974

The Noble Cricketers, anonymous, private printing, 1778

The Noble Game of Cricket, Sir Jeremiah Colman (Batsford, 1941)

Nyren – A Short Biography, Neville Weston, private printing, 1933

The Nyrens of Eartham and Hambledon, Edmund Esdaile, private printing, 1967

Through the Covers, anthology edited by Christopher Lee (Oxford University Press, 1996)

Quilt Winders and Pod Shavers, Hugh Barty-King (Macdonald & Jane's, 1979)

The Spirit of Cricket, anthology edited by Christopher Martin-Jenkins (Faber and Faber, 1994)

Winchester College Cricket, EB Noel (Williams & Norgate, 1926)

Index